Business Essentials

Supporting HNC/HND and Foundation degrees

Business Decision Making

Course Book

In this July 2010 edition:

- Full and comprehensive coverage of the key topics within the subject
- Activities, examples and quizzes
- Practical illustrations and case studies
- Index
- Fully up to date as at July 2010
- Coverage mapped to the Edexcel Guidelines for the HNC/HND in Business Mandatory Unit 6

Second edition 2010
First edition 2007

Published ISBN 9780 7517 6832 9
(previous edition 9780 7517 4478 1)
e-ISBN 9780 7517 7669 0

British Library Cataloguing-in-Publication Data
A catalogue record for this book is available from the British Library

Published by
BPP Learning Media Ltd
BPP House, Aldine Place
London W12 8AA

www.bpp.com/learningmedia

Printed in the United Kingdom

Your learning materials, published by BPP Learning Media Ltd, are printed on paper sourced from sustainable, managed forests.

We are grateful to Edexcel for permission to reproduce the Guidelines for the BTEC Higher Nationals in Business.

A note about copyright

Dear Customer

What does the little © mean and why does it matter?

Your market-leading BPP books, course materials and e-learning materials do not write and update themselves. People write them: on their own behalf or as employees of an organisation that invests in this activity. Copyright law protects their livelihoods. It does so by creating rights over the use of the content.

Breach of copyright is a form of theft – as well as being a criminal offence in some jurisdictions, it is potentially a serious breach of professional ethics.

With current technology, things might seem a bit hazy but, basically, without the express permission of BPP Learning Media:

- Photocopying our materials is a breach of copyright
- Scanning, ripcasting or conversion of our digital materials into different file formats, uploading them to facebook or e-mailing them to your friends is a breach of copyright

You can, of course, sell your books, in the form in which you have bought them – once you have finished with them. (Is this fair to your fellow students? We update for a reason.) But the e-products are sold on a single user licence basis: we do not supply 'unlock' codes to people who have bought them second-hand.

And what about outside the UK? BPP Learning Media strives to make our materials available at prices students can afford by local printing arrangements, pricing policies and partnerships which are clearly listed on our website. A tiny minority ignore this and indulge in criminal activity by illegally photocopying our material or supporting organisations that do. If they act illegally and unethically in one area, can you really trust them?

Contents

Introduction

BPP Learning Media's **Business Essentials** range is the ideal learning solution for all students studying for business-related qualifications and degrees. The range provides concise and comprehensive coverage of the key areas that are essential to the business student.

Qualifications in business are traditionally very demanding. Students therefore need learning resources which go straight to the core of the topics involved, and which build upon students' pre-existing knowledge and experience. The BPP Learning Media Business Essentials range has been designed to meet exactly that need.

Features include:

- In-depth coverage of essential topics within business-related subjects
- Plenty of activities, quizzes and topics for discussion to help retain the interest of students and ensure progress
- Up-to-date practical illustrations and case studies that really bring the material to life
- A glossary of terms and full index

In addition, the contents of the chapters are comprehensively mapped to the **Edexcel Guidelines**, providing full coverage of all topics specified in the HND/HNC qualifications in Business.

Each chapter contains:

- An introduction and a list of specific study objectives
- Summary diagrams and signposts to guide you through the chapter
- A chapter roundup, quick quiz with answers and answers to activities

Other titles in this series:

Generic titles

Economics

Accounts

Business Maths

Mandatory units for the Edexcel HND/HNC in Business qualification

Unit 1	Business Environment
Unit 2	Managing Finance
Unit 3	Organisations and Behaviour
Unit 4	Marketing Principles
Unit 5	Business Law
Unit 6	Business Decision Making
Unit 7	Business Strategy
Unit 8	Research Project

Pathways for the Edexcel HND/HNC in Business qualification

Units 9 and 10	Finance: Management Accounting and Financial Reporting
Units 11 and 12	Finance: Auditing and Financial Systems and Taxation
Units 13 and 14	Management: Leading People and Professional Development
Units 15 and 16	Management: Communications and Achieving Results
Units 17 and 18	Marketing and Promotion
Units 19 and 20	Marketing and Sales Strategy
Units 21 and 22	Human Resource Management
Units 23 and 24	Human Resource Development and Employee Relations
Units 25-28	Company and Commercial Law

For more information, or to place an order, please call 0845 0751 100 (for orders within the UK) or +44(0)20 8740 2211 (from overseas), e-mail learningmedia@bpp.com, or visit our website at www.bpp.com/learningmedia.

If you would like to send in your comments on this Course Book, please turn to the review form at the back of this book.

Study Guide

This Course Book includes features designed specifically to make learning effective and efficient.

- Each chapter begins with a summary diagram which maps out the areas covered by the chapter. There are detailed summary diagrams at the start of each main section of the chapter. You can use the diagrams during revision as a basis for your notes.
- After the main summary diagram there is an introduction, which sets the chapter in context. This is followed by learning objectives, which show you what you will learn as you work through the chapter.
- Throughout the Course Book, there are special aids to learning. These are indicated by symbols in the margin:

Signposts guide you through the book, showing how each section connects with the next.

Definitions give the meanings of key terms. The *glossary* at the end of the book summarises these.

Activities help you to test how much you have learned. An indication of the time you should take on each is given. Answers are given at the end of each chapter.

Topics for discussion are for use in seminars. They give you a chance to share your views with your fellow students. They allow you to highlight holes in your knowledge and to see how others understand concepts. If you have time, try 'teaching' someone the concepts you have learned in a session. This helps you to remember key points and answering their questions will consolidate your knowledge.

Examples relate what you have learned to the outside world. Try to think up your own examples as you work through the Course Book.

Chapter roundups present the key information from the chapter in a concise format. Useful for revision.

- The wide **margin** on each page is for your notes. You will get the best out of this book if you interact with it. Write down your thoughts and ideas. Record examples, question theories, add references to other pages in the Course Book and rephrase key points in your own words.

- At the end of each chapter, there is a **chapter roundup** and a **quick quiz** with answers. Use these to revise and consolidate your knowledge. The chapter roundup summarises the chapter. The quick quiz tests what you have learned (the answers often refer you back to the chapter so you can look over subjects again).

- At the end of the Course Book, there is a glossary of definitions and an index.

Part A

Sources for the Collection of Data

Chapter 1 :

THE COLLECTION AND STORAGE OF DATA

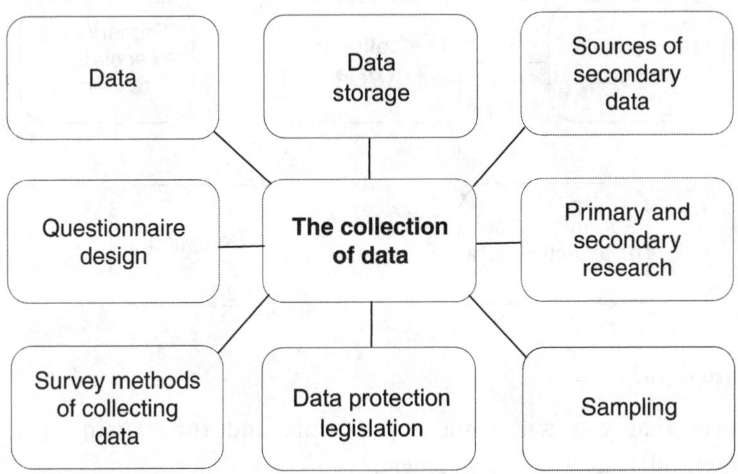

Introduction

Organisational data is a collection of raw facts relating to the enterprise and its environment. It can be classified in a number of ways eg, quantitative / qualitative, discrete / continuous, internal /external, formal/ informal, primary / secondary.

Much of a manager's work will involve the use of data and information, collected and stored internally or externally. Decisions regarding the future plans and operations of the organisation will incorporate information about past performance, future market potential, industry and company statistics etc, all of which will need to be gathered, processed and analysed.

In this chapter we will be looking at data collection. In Chapter 2 we will consider how it should be analysed once it has been collected.

Your objectives

After completing this chapter you should:

(a) Be aware of the various types of data

(b) Know about the sources of secondary data

(c) Know the appropriate sampling method to use in particular circumstances

(d) Be aware of the advantages and disadvantages of interviews and postal questionnaires

(e) Be able to design questionnaires

1 DATA

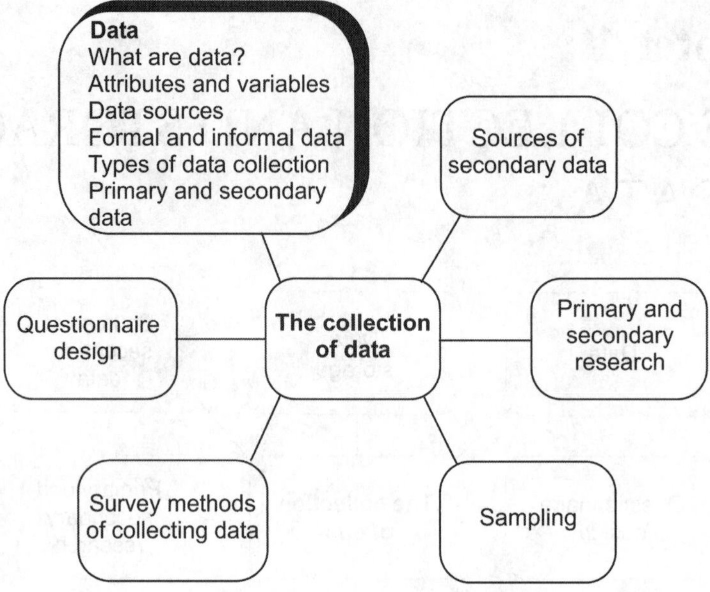

1.1 What are data?

'Data' is a term that you will come across time and time again in your study of quantitative methods, but what does it mean?

Definition

Data is simply a 'scientific' term for facts, figures, information and measurements.

Data therefore include the number of people with red hair who pass their driving test each year, the number of goals scored by each football team in the second division in the current season to date, and the profit after tax for the past ten years of the four biggest supermarket chains.

1.2 Attributes and variables

Data may be of several types. The first distinction to make is between attributes and variables.

Definition

An **attribute** is something an object either has or doesn't have.

An attribute cannot be measured. For example, an individual is either male or female. There is no measure of *how* male or *how* female somebody is: the sex of a person is an attribute. This type of data is qualitative.

NOTES

Definition

> A **variable** is something which can be measured.

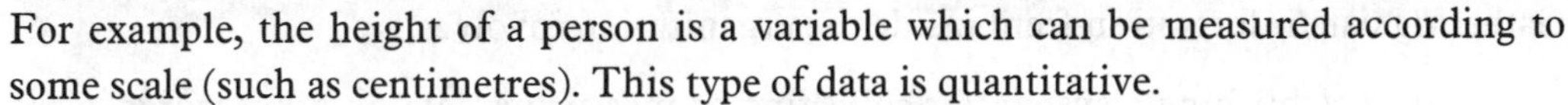

For example, the height of a person is a variable which can be measured according to some scale (such as centimetres). This type of data is quantitative.

Discrete and continuous variables

Variables can be further classified as discrete or continuous.

(a) Discrete variables can only take a finite or countable number of values within a given range. Examples of such variables include 'goals scored by Chachont United against Willford City', 'shoe size' and 'number of people entering SupaSave SupaMarket in Rutminster between 9.05 am and 9.10 am on a particular day'. If we arbitrarily chose a range of 0 – 10, 2 goals could be scored but not $2\frac{1}{2}$, a (British) shoe size could be $5\frac{1}{2}$ but not 5.193 and 9 people could enter the supermarket but not 9.999.

(b) Continuous variables may take on any value. They are measured rather than counted. For example, it may be considered sufficient to measure the heights of a number of people to the nearest centimetre but there is no reason why the measurements should not be made to the nearest 1/100 cm. Two people who are found to have the same height to the nearest centimetre could almost certainly be distinguished if more precise measurements were taken.

Activity 1 **(20 minutes)**

Look through the following list of surveys and decide whether each is collecting data on attributes, discrete variables or continuous variables.

(a) A survey of statistics textbooks, to determine how many diagrams they contain.

(b) A survey of cans in a shop, to determine whether or not each has a price sticker.

(c) A survey of athletes to find out how long they take to run a mile.

(d) A survey of the heights of telegraph poles in England.

1.3 Data sources

Data collected by an organisation may be internal (from the organisation itself) or external (from outside the organisation).

Internal data

These relate to activities or transactions performed within the organisation, eg administrative tasks such as correspondence or payroll calculations, the production of

products and services, or the sale of those products. Often these activities generate costs and revenues, so much of the internal data collected will be quantitative.

Internal sources of data can be classified according to the department of the organisation to which it relates: eg, Purchasing, Production, Sales, and Marketing among others.

Gathering data/information from inside the organisation involves:

(a) Establishing a system for collecting or measuring data, in other words, what data is collected, how frequently, by whom and by what method – and how it is processed, filed (or stored) and communicated;

(b) Relying to some extent on the informal communication lines between managers and staff eg, word of mouth, conversations at meetings, email and so on.

External data

Organisations need to collect data relating to the outside world or the 'environment' of the organisation.

Data relating to the environment of an organisation might be classified under the following headings:

(a) Political (such as government policy)
(b) Economic (such as inflation or exchange rates)
(c) Social (such as buying-patterns or fashion)
(d) Technological (such as materials and production methods)
(e) Competitive (such as the behaviour of customers, suppliers and rivals)

1.4 Formal and informal data

Data from outside the organisation may be formal or informal. Informal gathering of data from outside sources goes on all the time, consciously or unconsciously, because we all learn what is going on in the world from newspapers, television or radio.

For some types of data, the formal collection from outside sources needs to be the responsibility of particular individuals within the organisation. For example:

- A tax specialist within the organisation will be expected to gather facts about changes in tax law and determine whether it will affect the organisation
- Companies registering under the Data Protection Act should appoint a data registration officer with the responsibility for finding out the procedure for keeping personal details
- Research and development work needs someone to co-ordinate data on similar work being done by other companies
- Market research is undertaken by specialists to find out about the opinions and buying attitudes of potential customers

1.5 Types of data collection

There are three main types of data collection: census, sample survey, and administrative by-product. Each has advantages and disadvantages over the other. The method chosen will depend on a number of factors.

Census – this refers to data collection about *everyone* or *everything* in a group or population. So, if you collected data about the weight of *everyone* in your department it would be regarded as a department census. Because everyone in the group has had data collected about them, this method gives a high degree of accuracy and allows further detailed information about small subgroups to be made. The disadvantages are the costs and time involved. Conducting a census can be expensive for large populations and the time taken to do a census can be long compared to a survey.

Sample survey – in this type of data collection only *part of the total population* is approached for data. So, if you collected data about the weight of ten people in a department of 50, it would be a sample survey of the department rather than a census. The advantages of choosing this method are that a survey costs less than a census and results are obtained far more quickly. Of course, depending on sample size, results have a degree of inaccuracy, and information on small population sub-groups or small area geography is not usually obtainable, unlike a census.

Administrative by-product data is collected as a by-product of an organisation's day-to-day operations. Examples include data on: births, deaths, marriages, divorces, airport arrivals, and motor vehicle registrations. For example, prior to a marriage license being issued, a couple must provide the registrar with information about their age, sex, birthplace, whether previously married, and where they live. The main advantage is that data is collected about everyone who uses that organisation's service, resulting in a high degree of accuracy. Data is also collected on an on-going basis, allowing trend analysis. The disadvantages includes its lack of flexibility – data items may be limited to essential administrative information, unlike a survey, and the agency which controls the data may restrict access to outsiders or charge for access.

1.6 Primary and secondary data

The data used in a statistical survey, whether variables or attributes, can be either primary data or secondary data.

Definitions

Primary data are collected especially for the purpose of whatever survey is being conducted.

Raw data are primary data which have not been processed at all, but are still just (for example) a list of numbers.

Secondary data are data which have already been collected elsewhere, for some other purpose, but which can be used or adapted for the survey being conducted.

There are several methods of obtaining sample data.

(a) **Observation** can be used as a means of obtaining sample data where quantitative data is required. For example, if data is needed about the volume of traffic passing along a road at a certain time of day, observers (either people or recording equipment) can be placed so as to count the traffic as it passes by. Observation can also be used to study consumer behaviour, although this is usually within a controlled experiment.

(b) **Experimentation** – a range of techniques are used in experimentation. Customer preferences may be determined by 'blind' testing. At a higher level, different marketing strategies may be test-marketed.

(c) The use of **questionnaires** provides a quick, cheap method of conducting a survey but it suffers from several defects, which may lead to biased results.

  (i) The people completing the forms (respondents) may be unaware of the requirements and place different interpretations on the questions. This problem will be aggravated if the questions are badly phrased.

  (ii) Large numbers of forms may not be returned or only returned partly completed. This may well lead to biased results as the respondents who reply are likely to be those most interested in the survey.

  (iii) Respondents may give false or misleading information, if, for example, they have forgotten material facts, desire to give a favourable impression of their circumstances, or simply out of a sense of mischief.

  Questionnaires can be used in a variety of ways as follows.

  (i) Telephone interviews

  (ii) Personal interviews conducted by market researchers in the interviewee's home

  (iii) Postal surveys

  (iv) For self-completion, perhaps at the place of purchase

(d) **Qualitative techniques** – a relatively expensive method, but one which may yield more valid results, is to conduct unstructured individual or group interviews. The lack of structure may make analysis difficult but the results may be more valid in that they are not the result of the prompting of the structured interview.

(e) **Consumer panels (test panels)** – some research firms have created consumer panels consisting of a representative cross-section of consumers who have agreed to give regular information about their attitudes or buying habits through personal visits or mail questionnaires. Consumer panels with personal visits are called home audit panels and panels which send data by post are called diary panels. For example, a panel of households might keep a purchase diary of the goods they have bought, and submit this diary regularly to the market research company. Panels might be established for a long-term or short-term period.

(f) **Trade audits or retail audits** – trade audits are carried out among panels of wholesalers and retailers, and the term 'retail audits' refers to panels of retailers only. A research firm sends auditors to selected outlets at regular intervals to count stock and deliveries, thus enabling an estimate of throughput to be made.

  Retail audits, because they provide continuous monitoring of retail activity, may be of value to a manufacturing firm for the following reasons.

  (i) Changes in retail sales provide an early warning of problems the manufacturer may soon have to expect in ex-factory sales.

(ii) They indicate long-term trends in the market place, thus providing helpful information for strategic marketing planning.

(iii) In the shorter term, they may indicate the need for changes in pricing policy, sales promotion or advertising, distribution policy, package design or product design.

An advantage of using primary data is that the investigator knows where the data came from, the circumstances under which they were collected, and any limitations or inadequacies in the data.

In contrast, note the following inadequacies of secondary data.

(a) Any limitations in the data might not be known to the investigator, because he or she did not collect them.

(b) The data might not be entirely suitable for the purpose they are being used for.

Secondary data are sometimes used despite their inadequacies, simply because they are available cheaply whereas the extra cost of collecting primary data would far outweigh their extra value.

Activity 2 **(5 minutes)**

In the Human Resources management system, what data would be included in the standing details about an employee?

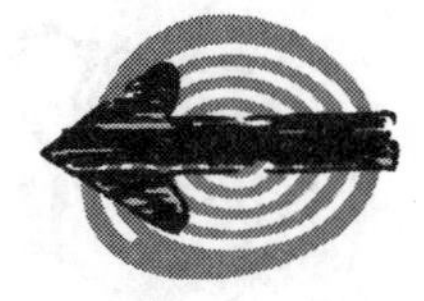

Now that we have some idea of the different types of data, we can address ourselves to the problem of getting hold of them

2 SOURCES OF SECONDARY DATA

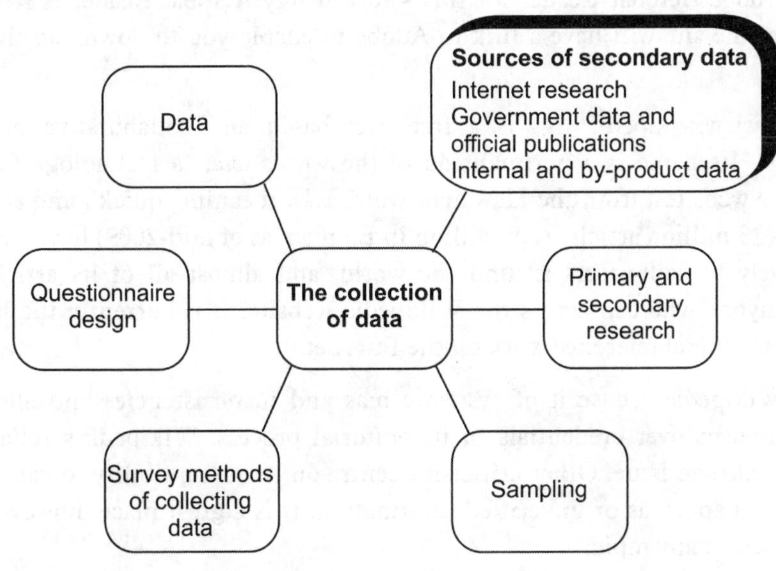

2.1 Internet research

The Internet is a global interconnection of networks. Using browsers such as Microsoft's Internet Explorer or Netscape's Navigator, it is possible to access businesses, academic institutions, trade associations, government agencies, medical facilities, scientific establishments and private individuals through the Net.

Accessing the Internet requires the user to have a computer with a modem and a subscription to a service provider such as America On Line (AOL), Demon or BT Internet. Websites are recognised by the prefix www. Companies operating in the UK typically have sites with citations such as www.companyname.co.uk while those aiming at an international audience are more likely to be referenced as www.companyname.com. A non-profit-making organisation would have the suffix .org after its name as in www.charity.org and a university or academic institution would be completed by the initials '.ac', as in www.university.ac.

Researchers sometimes need company data for competitor benchmarking, sourcing suppliers or building profiles of customers and potential customers. Only a few years ago company literature was the basis of such searches. Today company websites are brimming with useful information. They contain pictures of products, maps of distributors, data sheets, company histories, press releases, and sometimes financial background. The information is nearly always more extensive and current than printed brochures and it is available in an instant.

Search engines such as Lycos, Google, AltaVista, or Yahoo! are useful tools for finding what you need in the millions of pages of publicly accessible information. By typing in the keyword or phrase, a search can be made on the Web.

Some websites will allow you to download articles free eg, www.ft.com and others such as the Economist Intelligence Unit provide information only for their subscribers to download. The Encyclopedia Britannica is also online (www.britannica.com) and can be accessed using a word search or by browsing alphabetically.

Many of these articles will be in PDF (portable document file) format. You will need to download Adobe Acrobat Reader for this – fortunately Acrobat Reader is free and it is possible that the site will have a link to Adobe to enable you to download the software yourself.

Wikipedia (www.wikipedia.org) is a free, web-based and collaborative multilingual encyclopedia. Its name is a portmanteau of the words *wiki* (a technology for creating collaborative websites, from the Hawaiian word *wiki*, meaning 'quick') and *encyclopedia.* Wikipedia's 13 million articles (2.9 million in English, as of mid-2009) have been written collaboratively by volunteers around the world, and almost all of its articles can be edited by anyone who can access the Wikipedia website. It is currently the largest and most popular general reference work on the Internet.

Critics of Wikipedia accuse it of systemic bias and inconsistencies and allege that it favours consensus over credentials in its editorial process. Wikipedia's reliability and accuracy are also an issue. Other criticisms centre on its susceptibility to vandalism and the addition of spurious or unverified information. It is a great place, however, to get a quick overview of any topic.

There are over 10,000 user groups (also called news groups or discussion groups) on the Internet covering almost every subject. They are roughly organised by topic, ranging

from hobbies and recreation (prefixed by rec) through to computers (comp), science (sci), culture, religion, as well as 'alternative' subjects (alt).

Directories are useful sources of data for research. They provide details of companies that either supply or consume goods and they are the usual source for preparing sample frames (list of companies or people to be interviewed). The directories may also provide a profile of a company, detailing its size by giving the number of employees, or whether it is an agent or producer. *Yellow Pages* (www.yell.co.uk) is one of the most comprehensive general directories since every company in the UK with a telephone number is given a free entry. Other countries also have Yellow Pages on the Internet. Within the Yell Group, The Business Database supplies data on around 1.5 million UK businesses sourced from the free-line entries in the Yellow Pages printed directories. From its web site it is possible to run counts and download lists for sample frames.

Online databases and market data

An online database such as Dun and Bradstreet (www.dnb.com), provides information on businesses by sector, number of employees and turnover. Profound from Dialog (www.dialog.com) provides access to a range of business and economic information, including news archive from over 5,000 publications, financial reports from over 4.5 million companies, market research reports, country data, economic data and broker reports. A good source of market research data, offering full or part reports is www.marketresearch.com – this allows access to a collection of over 40,000 publications from over 350 research firms.

There are an increasing number of websites that offer archive material to researchers without having to sign up, though there usually is a fee for the report or part of it. The table of contents is available free and there are many synopses of reports, which may be sufficient for those requiring just an overview.

Other external sources include banks, stockbrokers, trade and professional associations, media owners, local authorities and government sponsored organisations.

2.2 Government data and official publications

In the UK, the *Annual Abstract of Statistics* is an easy way into the major series of statistics and is available in hard copy from Her Majesty's Stationery Office – HMSO. This and many other government publications can be purchased online from www.tso-online.co.uk.

Government departments' websites are an excellent source of information and data. A gateway to all government sites is www.ukonline.gov.uk. A lot of government statistics previously only available in print, such as Social Trends, Economic Trends and Regional Trends, are now available free online in PDF format at www.statistics.gov.uk – the website of the Office of National Statistics (ONS). The site allows searching by themes such as agriculture/fishing/forestry, commerce, energy, industry, education, crime and justice, the labour market, the population and so on.

Retail prices are very important to a wide variety of users.

(a) For the government, the Retail Prices Index (RPI) indicates the degree of success there has been in fighting inflation.

(b) For employees, the RPI may give an indication of how much wages need to rise to keep pace with inflation.

(c) For consumers, the RPI indicates the increases to be expected in the prices of goods in shops.

(d) For businesses, the RPI may give a broad indication of how much costs should have been expected to rise over recent years and months.

(e) For pensioners and social security recipients, the movement in the RPI is used to update benefit levels.

One of the cornerstones of the government's statistical service and a massive source of data is the decennial Census of Population. Researchers use census output for segmentation by demographics and survey planning (eg setting quota samples).

The Department for Business, Innovation and Skills' (formerly the Department for Business, Enterprise and Regulatory Reform) website www.bis.gov.uk outlines the DBIS's work programme and links to the government funded business links site – www.businesslink.org – a national network of advice agencies for business. They provide training and support with a variety of business issues including start-up, business planning, marketing and finance. The UK employment law site www.emplaw.co.uk gives access to up-to-date information on the law and also lists solicitors who are specialised in this field.

Another government source of data about companies is Companies House (www.companieshouse.gov.uk) giving access to financial and other data on UK registered companies. Searching for a company can be carried out using its name or its unique company registration number.

In addition to the free basic company details, certain company documents and reports can be purchased for very modest sums by credit card and delivered electronically. These include scanned image documents of the latest company accounts, annual returns, current appointments and outstanding mortgages.

There are many other official publications that can be accessed – some more examples follow.

(a) The Bank of England issues a quarterly publication, which includes data on banks in the UK, the money supply and government borrowing and financial transactions.

(b) The individual Economic Development Councils of the National Economic Development Office publish many data about their industries.

(c) Other bodies such as the World Bureau of Metal Statistics can provide data on an international basis.

(d) International bodies include: the United Nations' Yearbook of International Statistics (details of trade by commodity); the Organisation for Economic Co-operation and Development collects data on the foreign trade of member countries (the OECD Monthly Statistics of Foreign Trade) and produces macroeconomic forecasts for member countries (the OECD Economic Outlook); and the IMF 's International Financial Statistics show the balance of payments and related items.

Activity 3 **(5 minutes)**

What sort of daily information on financial matters would you find in the *Financial Times*?

2.3 Internal and by-product data

Your employer probably has large amounts of information, not designed for your research, but may be useful to you, and this will be held on a departmental basis.

(a) **The accounts department** will have financial data, a procedures manual with accounting policies, tax details, management accounts and balance sheets.

(b) **The sales and marketing department** will keep sales reports by region, details of sales by customer and by product, competitor intelligence, customer complaints, marketing research and prospects reports, brand strategy and values and details of distribution chains.

(c) **Production and operations** will have operations data, process flow charts, input prices and product costings, transport costs and details on efficiency and capacity.

(d) **The human resources department** will have data on the number of employees, recruitment procedures, training programmes, staff turnover details and details of pay.

Definition

A **data warehouse** consists of a database, containing data from various operational systems and reporting and query tools.

A data warehouse contains data from a range of sources eg, sales order processing system, nominal ledger entries, credit card transactions, demographic data and purchase data from checkout counter scanners at supermarkets and retail stores. The result should be a coherent set of data available to be used across the organisation for management analysis and decision-making as well as for research purposes. It is all by-product data in that it has not been collected in the database for a specific reason, but is secondary data that is still considered useful.

Definition

Data mining is the analysis of large pools of data to unearth unsuspected or unknown relationships, patterns and associations that can be used to guide decision-making and predict future behaviour.

In simple terms the data warehouse is a large database (either functional or corporate) used to store historic data and the term data mining relates to the ability to access data using sophisticated software and interfaces. Data mining results include the following.

(a) **Associations** – or when one event can be correlated to another event eg, disposable nappy purchasers buy baby wipes a certain percentage of the time.

(b) **Sequences** – or one event leading to another later event eg, a pay rise followed by an increase in productivity.

(c) **Classification** – or the recognition of patterns and a resulting new organisation of data eg, profiles of customers who make purchases.

(d) **Clustering** – or finding and visualising groups of facts not previously known. A data mining tool will discover different groupings within data.

(e) **Forecasting** – or simply discovering patterns in the data that can lead to predictions about the future.

Data mining can also be used to locate individual customers with specific interests or determine the interests of a specific group of customers.

3 PRIMARY AND SECONDARY RESEARCH

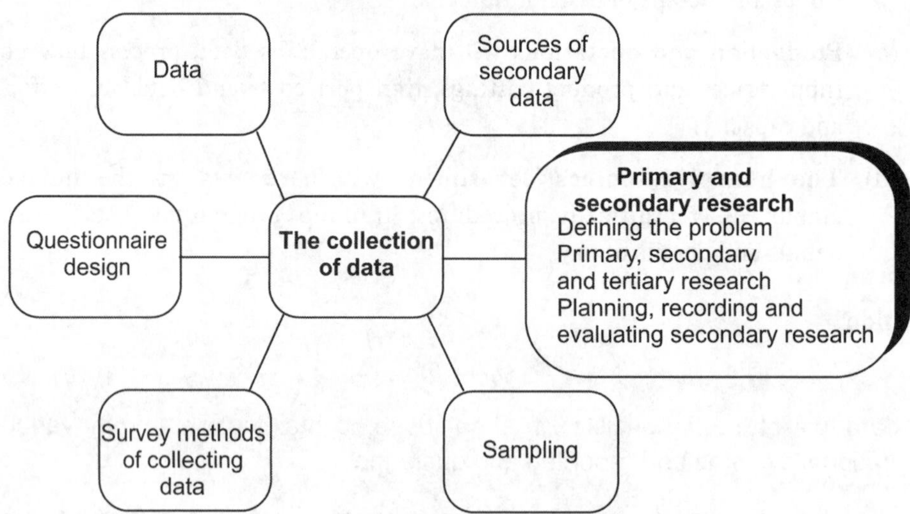

3.1 Defining the problem

When carrying out research it is essential to define the problem very carefully. As you prepare to do the research ask yourself the following questions:

- What do I already know about this topic area?
- What do I need to find out?
- What are the main problems/issues involved?
- Are there different viewpoints about this topic?
- What different parts or areas are there to this topic?
- Who will I use as respondents?

These questions and the answers to them will help guide you in your research and will help familiarise you with the topic.

To generate the data/information requirements you need to define – and report – the following.

- Scope
- Focus
- Contexts

Scope of your enquiries

Scope means the boundaries of what you are doing.

(a) Time period for the collection of your data. This may require consideration of:

   (i) Frequency (eg, review of financial statements – annually)

   (ii) Start and end dates of the event you are describing (eg, when it was decided to buy a new information system)

   (iii) Sensible time period for the subject in question (eg, the costs and benefits of a new information system need a reasonably long time horizon – two or three years, not just one month – to be assessed).

(b) Geography – global, international, regional, local businesses, industries or environment

(c) Type of industry or business sector.

(d) Size of a transaction – for example, auditors look at 'material' and/or representative items, not everything.

You may need to justify your scope when you report on the problem – for example, if you have chosen an unusual time period, there may be a good reason (eg, before and after adoption of some new legislation).

Focus of analysis

The focus means what you are collecting data about.

Here are some examples:

(a) Individuals (eg, with a problem dealing with motivation issues).

(b) Groups of people (eg, a department, such as 'the sales force', suppliers).

(c) Procedures and processes within an organisation (eg, how investment decisions are made).

(d) Events, actions or decisions (eg, the adoption of a new piece of legislation, or the decision to buy a subsidiary).

(e) Inputs (eg, material, informational) or outputs.

(f) An organisation as a whole.

You may, of course, collect data about a number of the above.

Contexts

By context we mean factors in the immediate environment of the problem area, such as the unique characteristics of the company, which will affect:

(a) The data collection methods employed; and
(b) The content of what you need to define.

For example, motivational issues for managers in a company that has just been taken over and has seen a round of redundancies, may be quite different from a successful firm that is taking people on and needs to integrate them into the organisation.

EXAMPLE

Let us assume that your organisation has asked you to analyse the impact of existing or impending legislation, which relates to the relationships businesses have with their suppliers. One aspect of this is a proposal by the government to make it much easier for suppliers to sue for interest on bills that are paid late. Here are some research tasks.

1 Exploring ideas – are the people in the purchasing department aware? Do they care or know about the small print? What about the sales ledger department? Does the firm want to charge its own customers for late payment?

2 Analysis – review creditors and debtors ledger for payment periods. What is the maximum potential loss if this change is implemented? If the firm paid early, would it run up bank overdraft fees? If creditors are a source of finance, how expensive are they?

3 Describing facts – if the firm has a large sales force, you may – if allowed – send a questionnaire to a sample (which can include all of them!) asking them if they know about the change and the terms and conditions they currently offer. The same could be sent to a buying department.

3.2 Primary, secondary and tertiary research

Primary research – can also be referred to as fieldwork. It is information that does not exist until you carry out your own investigations. This may be in the form of surveys, in-depth interviews and postal or face-to-face questionnaires. For market research it can include:

(a) Test marketing – where one of your products is placed in a selected store in order to determine the demand; and

(b) Competitor scans – where you visit outlets that sell a similar product or service to the one that you wish to provide; collecting any promotional/point of sale material from such outlets can prove particularly useful.

Survey (primary) research is a cost effective way of finding out what people think, want, need or do. There are two main types of survey research.

(a) **Quantitative research** is concerned with numbers and statistical analysis, typically of large-scale surveys. It provides numerical data as a result of each respondent being asked the same series of questions. This method works because, by talking to a relatively small number of people, you can find out about a far larger number but it only does this if the people interviewed (the sample) are a representative subgroup of the total group of interest (the universe) and it only works if the 'right' questions are asked.

(b) **Qualitative research** is another process that aims to collect primary data. Its main methods are the open-ended interview, whether this is a depth

NOTES

interview (one-to-one) or a group discussion (focus group), and projective techniques. The form of the data collected is narrative rather than isolated statements reduced to numbers. Its main purpose is to understand people's behaviour and perceptions rather than to measure them. The key to qualitative research is to allow the respondents to say what they feel and think in response to flexible, 'prompting' questioning, rather than to give their responses to set questions and often set answers in a questionnaire.

Activity 4 **(5 minutes)**

You have been asked to join a group to discuss a new type of breakfast cereal that is being developed. The manufacturers need to find out your perception of the product. What type of research would this be?

	Quantitative research	Qualitative research
Objective/ purpose	To quantify data and generalise results from a sample to the population of interest To measure the incidence of various views and opinions in a chosen sample Sometimes followed by qualitative research which is used to explore some findings further	To gain an understanding of underlying reasons and motivations To provide insights into the setting of a problem, generating ideas and/or hypotheses for later quantitative research To uncover prevalent trends in thought and opinion
Sample	Usually a large number of cases representing the population of interest Randomly selected respondents	Usually a small number of non-representative cases Respondents selected to fulfil a given quota
Data collection	Structured techniques such as on-street or telephone interviews	Unstructured or semi-structured techniques eg individual depth interviews or group discussions
Data analysis	Statistical data is usually in the form of tabulations Findings are conclusive and usually descriptive in nature.	Non-statistical
Outcome	Used to recommend a final course of action	Exploratory and/or investigative Findings are not conclusive and cannot be used to make generalisations about the population of interest Develop an initial understanding and sound base for further decision making

NOTES

We will be looking at each type of survey, and their respective advantages and disadvantages, in later sections.

Although surveys offer a quick, efficient and cost-effective way of obtaining the required data, they are not straightforward. Without skill, tact and expertise the results may easily become contaminated with bias and error and the conclusions subsequently drawn will be useless.

A famous example of this occurred years ago in the United States, when somebody was asked to conduct an opinion poll (which is a form of survey) on whether the next president was likely to be Democrat or Republican. The survey was carried out, but in an inappropriate way. The survey officer *telephoned* people, and in those days far more Republican than Democrat voters had telephones. The survey was useless, because it had not been planned properly.

The reason why the opinion poll turned out so badly was that the population for the survey had not been defined properly. In data collection, the word 'population' refers to the entire collection of items being considered. The opinion poll should have used the population 'all Americans of voting age', whereas it actually used the population 'all Americans with a telephone'.

There are three main types of error that can appear in survey methods of collecting data.

(a) **Sampling error** arises when the sample of the population surveyed (if the entire population is not being investigated) is not representative of the population from which it is drawn. For example, if a sample of the population of a city were composed entirely of babies less than three months old, the sample would obviously not be representative of the population of the city.

(b) **Response error** can occur even when all members of the population are surveyed and arises because respondents are either unable (through ignorance, forgetfulness or inarticulateness) or unwilling (due to time pressure, desire for privacy, guessing and so on) to respond.

(c) **Non-response error** can occur either if respondents refuse to take part in the survey or are 'not at home'.

We will be focusing on sampling in the next section.

Secondary research – is where you use information that other people have gathered through primary research. Before carrying out any primary research it may be more advisable to look at secondary research first since the data already exists, is readily available, can be gathered at much lower costs, and is very useful in orienting oneself to the problem and developing hypotheses. Other benefits include the following.

(a) Providing a background to primary research. Even if it does not fulfil the exact requirements of the research brief, it may help to determine key variables that any subsequent primary research will need to investigate and it may help to identify key trends.

(b) Acting as a substitute for field research. Published data may fully meet all the current research objectives, avoiding the need for expensive primary research. Even if it does not answer all the questions, the scope and potential cost of the primary research may be substantially reduced.

(c) Gaining information on other companies without alerting them to the fact that research is being undertaken. For example, if an organisation wishes to acquire another (target) company it could gather information that would be inconspicuous compared with a primary research study, which might alert the target to the situation.

Nevertheless, before using secondary data you need to check on:

- Whether the secondary data is relevant
- The cost of acquiring it
- Its availability
- The extent to which the data might be biased
- The accuracy of the data
- Whether the data is sufficient to meet the research objectives

Tertiary research – is where you use others' secondary research. It is generally a good idea to avoid tertiary research.

What sort of research should you do?

Below is an example from an unpublished undergraduate dissertation. See if you can identify areas of primary and secondary research.

EXAMPLE: PRIMARY AND SECONDARY RESEARCH

The aim was to find out what environmental information companies make available to external parties and how useful this is. I decided that the best method to gather this information was to become an external party myself and write to them asking for their annual reports and any published environmental information. This way, my research would not be subject to individual company bias concerning what they publish, as a survey or interview may be.

Comparisons were only made on the information that I received. This may have had its limitations in that more information could exist, but this was a representative sample of what an average external reader would receive – the objective in question.

I selected seven companies to request such information from; this small number would allow a more detailed focus on issues. Five companies were selected from those mentioned in an article (in an accounting journal) on environmental reporting together with two randomly selected companies of my own.

The dimensions of performance that I concentrated my analysis on would enable me to discover if what writers believed was actually being communicated matched what I found was disclosed in reality.

The annual reports were requested, to see what environmental disclosure they contained and also to discover if any financial environmental information was present in anticipation of the future environmental accounting chapter in the same journal.

One weakness of the survey was the narrow range of companies considered. A study of companies not recommended by the journal and operating in several differing industries, may provide more issues. Although this may prove difficult if not enough environmental data is disclosed to make comparisons. To question the companies via

telephone rather than an 'official' letter may result in a more relaxed attitude reaping more open responses.

Environmental questionnaire

Next, I wanted to discover how the internal background of the firms can affect the external environmental communication they may or may not produce.

I thought a questionnaire was appropriate to reach the large amount of companies that I wanted to involve. I chose thirty companies from the catalogue of annual reports at Wheatley library (see appendix twelve), consciously trying to include a range of industries. Measures were implemented to increase the chances of companies replying.

- I obtained contact names by telephoning the companies beforehand.
- A stamped addressed envelope was enclosed for replies.
- Anonymity was ensured.
- The questions took a closed category format, meaning all respondents had to do was tick relevant boxes.
- Only fourteen questions were asked.

I also structured the questions to start general before getting more specific to ease respondents into the correct way of thinking. The questionnaire can be seen in appendix eleven.

My approach was successful, indicated by the 73% response rate of which 18% were unwilling to take part. This left me with eighteen completed questionnaires, split equally over service and manufacturing industries.

To conduct my analysis I first identified the main categories of environmental disclosure methods and issues that the majority of the companies portrayed. I then formed questions from these.

Comment

Both the journal that was used in the initial investigation into the problem/project and the companies published financial statements are **secondary research**.

A survey **you** conduct with a questionnaire you have designed, with regard to a sample, is **primary research**. You aim to get a statistically significant result.

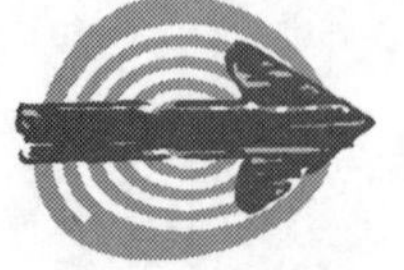

We will come back to this project when discussing questionnaire design.

3.3 Planning, recording and evaluating secondary research

A written plan is a help to secondary research if the search for published data is to be efficient. Before visiting a library or logging-on, the information sought should be specified in some detail, although flexibility and some ingenuity are also needed (eg looking for relevant data under wider or narrower classifications and creatively making connections). In the case of online database searching, a planned approach is particularly vital if log-on costs are to be kept to a minimum; the search strategy should be planned off-line.

The secondary research plan should also include a timetable. How long should be spent on the secondary research? This will depend on the breadth of the information sought, the type of data and the resources to be used. It is difficult to generalise. However, what can be said is that diminishing returns apply and after quite a short time, the extra information gained falls in proportion to the time spent searching.

Once found, data needs recording in the form of notes or photocopies. In the case of on-line searches the equivalent is downloading into files. The sources of any data should always be recorded as they may need to be attributed, their accuracy evaluated and, if necessary, retraced.

All secondary data accessed through secondary research was originally generated through primary research. Thorough validation requires going back to the source and understanding the methodology used: was it based on some sort of census, on a sample survey, on some crude formula using a ratio or merely on anecdotal evidence?

3.4 Data manipulation

After editing, data may be manipulated by computer to produce the desired output. The software used to manipulate data will depend on the form of output required. Software applications such as word processing, desktop publishing, graphics (including graphing and drawing), databases and spreadsheets are commonly used.

Following are some ways that software can manipulate data.

(a) **Spreadsheets** are used to create formulas that automatically add columns or rows of figures calculate means and perform statistical analyses. They can be used to create financial worksheets such as budgets or expenditure forecasts, balance accounts and analyse costs.

(b) **Databases** are electronic filing cabinets. They are used to systematically store data for easy access to produce summaries, stocktakes or reports. A database program should be able to store, retrieve, sort, and analyse data.

(c) **Charts** can be created from a table of numbers and displayed in a number of ways, to show the significance of a selection of data. Bar, line, pie and other types of charts can be generated and manipulated to advantage.

Processing data provides useful information called *output.* Computer output may be used in a variety of ways. It may be saved in *storage* for later *retrieval* and use. It may be printed on paper as tables or charts, put on a transparent slide for overhead projector use, saved on floppy disk for portable use in other computers, or sent as an electronic file via the Internet to others. The types of output are limited by the available output devices and their format is determined by the need to communicate information to someone.

Applications software can also be divided into two classes:

(a) Personal productivity tools; and
(b) Other computer applications.

Personal productivity tools are commercial products designed to handle standard computing tasks such as word processing, numerical analysis, data manipulation and storage, and data presentation. Typical products are:

(a) **Word processing** – this software is designed for the creation of documents: letters, reports, newspaper articles and books. MS Word and OpenOffice Writer are typical word processing products.

(b) **Spreadsheets** – these packages are an electronic development of accounts used by bookkeepers to organise business information, and are very useful for handling tabular data. Addition, subtraction, division, multiplication and totalling can be done very quickly, and all results can be automatically recalculated later if new data is inserted. Formatting and graphing facilities are used to aid analysis and presentation. Hundreds of functions are included to enable typical statistical, engineering, economics and business calculations to be performed automatically. Examples are functions for the calculation of compound interest and standard deviation. Typical Spreadsheets packages include MS Excel, MS Works and Lotus 123.

(iii) **Databases** – these packages are a convenient way of organising and storing data in a uniform fashion. Data can be quickly and systematically searched, sorted and presented. They can be used by people with no special training to create mailing lists or record store inventories, but they can also be used by professional programmers to produce complex applications to assist with running a business. MS Access, MS Works and Lotus Approach are typical database packages.

(iv) **Presentation** – these packages are used to illustrate talks and lectures and have almost replaced hand-drawn or typed overhead projector slides. In many presentations and lectures given in industry today, the presenter plugs a Notebook computer directly into a projector to show slides on a screen. MS PowerPoint and Lotus Freelance are typical presentation packages.

(v) **Graphics** – this software enables any user to create drawings, paint pictures and enhance or manipulate scanned pictures. MS Paint is a typical graphics package.

(vi) **Desktop publishing** – these packages are intended to enhance the final appearance or layout of text and graphics to make them suitable for publishing. Graphics can come from a library of clip art, be created by drawing or paint package, or be a scanned image such as a photo. MS Publisher is a typical desktop publishing package.

4 SAMPLING

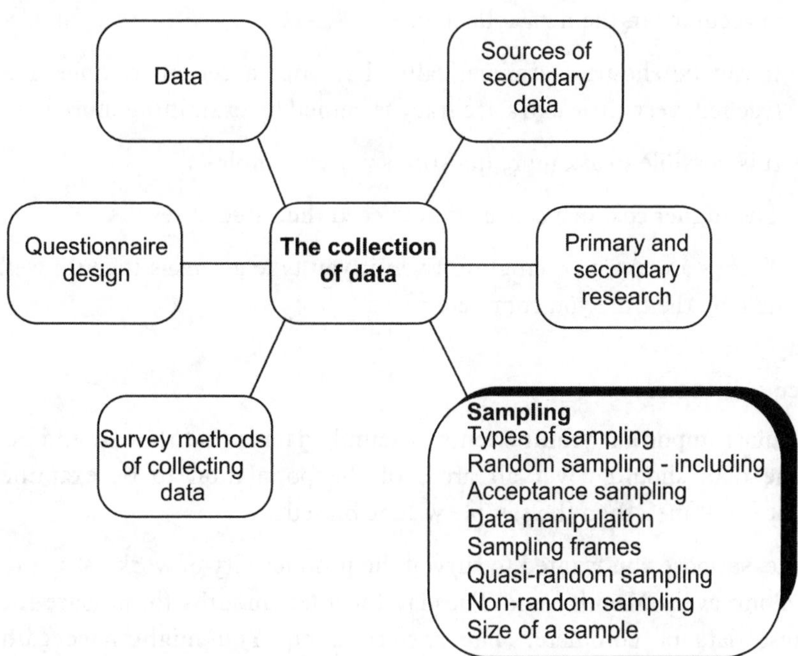

4.1 Types of sampling

Definition

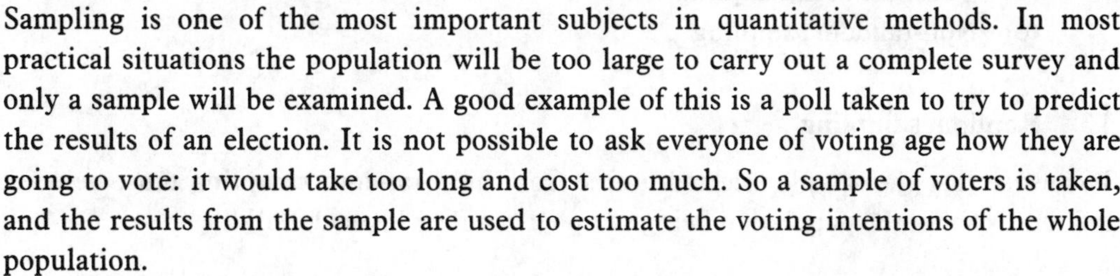

Sampling involves selecting a sample of items from a population.

Sampling is one of the most important subjects in quantitative methods. In most practical situations the population will be too large to carry out a complete survey and only a sample will be examined. A good example of this is a poll taken to try to predict the results of an election. It is not possible to ask everyone of voting age how they are going to vote: it would take too long and cost too much. So a sample of voters is taken, and the results from the sample are used to estimate the voting intentions of the whole population.

Occasionally a population is small enough that all of it can be examined: for example, the examination results of one class of students. This type of survey is quite rare, however, and usually the investigator has to choose some sort of sample.

Definition

When all of the population is examined, the survey is called a **census**.

You may think that using a sample is very much a compromise, but you should consider the following points.

(a) In practice, a 100% survey (a census) never achieves the completeness required.

(b) A census may require the use of semi-skilled investigators, resulting in a loss of accuracy in the data collected.

(c) It can be shown mathematically that once a certain sample size has been reached, very little extra accuracy is gained by examining more items.

(d) It is possible to ask more questions with a sample.

(e) The higher cost of a census may exceed the value of results.

(f) Things are always changing. Even if you take a census it could well be out of date by the time you complete it.

The choice of a sample

One of the most important requirements of sample data is that they should be complete. That is, the data should cover all areas of the population to be examined. If this requirement is not met, then the sample will be biased.

For example, suppose you wanted to survey the productivity of workers in a factory, and you went along every Monday and Tuesday for a few months to measure their output. Would these data be complete? The answer is no. You might have gathered very thorough data on what happens on Mondays and Tuesdays, but you would have missed out the rest of the week. It could be that the workers, keen and fresh after the weekend, work better at the start of the week than at the end. If this is the case, then your data will give you a misleadingly high productivity figure. Careful attention must therefore be given to the sampling method employed to produce a sample.

Sampling methods fall into three main groups.

(a) Random sampling
(b) Quasi-random sampling
(c) Non-random sampling

4.2 Random sampling

To ensure that the sample selected is free from bias, **random sampling** must be used. Inferences about the population being sampled can then be made validly.

Definition

> A simple **random sample** is a sample selected in such a way that every item in the population has an equal chance of being included.

For example, if you wanted to take a random sample of library books, it would not be good enough to pick them off the shelves, even if you picked them at random. This is because the books which were out on loan would stand no chance of being chosen. You would either have to make sure that all the books were on the shelves before taking your sample, or find some other way of sampling (for example, using the library index records).

A random sample is not necessarily a perfect sample. For example, you might pick what you believe to be a completely random selection of library books, and find that every one of them is a detective thriller. It is a remote possibility, but it could happen. The only way to eliminate the possibility altogether is to take 100% survey (a census) of the books, which, unless it is a tiny library, is impractical.

Acceptance sampling

Manufacturers are interested in the quality of the product that they produce and consumers are interested in the quality of the product that they buy. Quality often means different things to different people but can generally be regarded as meaning that the product meets certain targets. For a battery, quality might mean that it works when we buy it, whilst for a packet of crisps quality might mean that we have over a certain minimum amount of crisps in the packet.

Complete, or 100%, inspection involves inspecting *each* item that is produced to see if it meets the desired quality level. This might seem to be the best procedure to meet quality targets but in fact it has a number of drawbacks.

- If there are a lot of items to inspect then it can become an expensive option and take a long time
- If testing quality results in the destruction of the item (eg weapons) then 100% inspection is clearly not a viable alternative
- Even operating 100% inspection, defective items may still slip through unless the inspection is itself 100% effective. For example, if the probability that a quality inspector misses a defective item is 1 in 100 then the probability of the inspector detecting 100 defective items (ie missing none of them) is only 0.37 (each defective item has a chance of 0.99 of detection – so the total probability is $(0.99)^{100} = 0.37$ to detect them all).

Generally 100% inspection is operated for items where the consequences of letting a defective item through could be quite severe eg avionic systems.

If we decide not to operate 100% inspection, for whatever reason, then the alternative is to take a sample of a certain size from a *batch* (sometimes called *lot*) of items and operate 100% inspection on the sample. From the results of the sample we decide whether to:

- *Accept* the entire batch – ie pass it as suitable for our customers; or
- *Reject* the entire batch – ie refuse to pass it as suitable for our customers.

Typically, if the proportion of defective items in the sample is below a certain level then we accept the batch – otherwise we reject it. This type of scheme is known as *acceptance sampling*.

Definition

Acceptance sampling is 'the middle of the road' approach between no inspection and 100% inspection.

A point to remember is that the main purpose of acceptance sampling is to decide whether or not the lot is likely to be acceptable, not to estimate the quality of the lot.

The scheme by which representative samples will be selected from a population and tested to determine whether the lot is acceptable or not is known as an **acceptance plan**

or **sampling plan**. There are two major classifications of acceptance plans: some based on **attributes** and others based on *variables*.

Sampling plans can be **single, double** or **sequential**.

(a) **Single sampling** – in this scheme we take a single sample (of size to be determined) from a batch and accept the batch provided the number of defectives found in the sample falls below a certain number (the *acceptance number*).

(b) **Double sampling** – this is an obvious extension of the single sample scheme where two samples are drawn and the first sample inspected. The batch can then be accepted or rejected upon the results of this inspection, or the second sample to be inspected and the decision made upon the combined result.

(c) **Sequential sampling** – with this scheme we keep testing items from the batch and after **each** item is inspected we make a decision to either accept or reject the batch, or to continue sampling. The distinction from multiple sampling lies in the fact that in multiple sampling we pre-specify the maximum number of samples we will take. With sequential sampling we (potentially) could end up conducting 100% inspection on the entire batch. Contrast this with double sampling above where we could, at most, take two samples – typically both samples comprising less than the entire batch.

    Sequential acceptance sampling minimises the number of items tested when the early results show that the batch clearly meets, or fails to meet, the required standards. The procedure has the advantage of requiring fewer observations, on average, than fixed sample size tests for a similar degree of accuracy. Examples of fields in which the technique may be used include clinical trials with new drugs or treatments and inspection sampling of manufactured goods;

The procedure for a single sampling plan operates as follows: select n items at random from the lot. If the number of defectives in the sample set is less than c, the lot is accepted. Otherwise, the lot is rejected.

In order to measure the performance of an acceptance or sampling plan, the Operating Characteristic (OC) curve is used – see below. This curve plots the probability of accepting the lot (Y-axis) versus the lot fraction or percent defectives.

NOTES

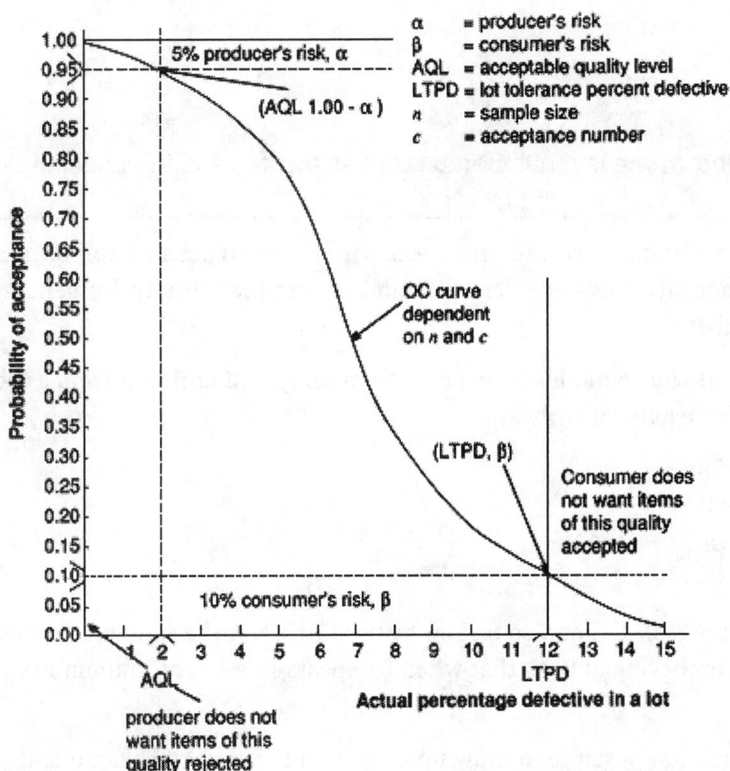

Figure 1.1: Operating Curve

The Operating Characteristic's (OC) curve shown above begins with a probability of acceptance of 1.0 (since material with no defectives will at all times be accepted); and it terminates with a probability of zero (since a lot of 100% defectives will always be rejected). It is a graph displaying standards at which the batch would be accepted and is defined by the following elements.

(a) **Acceptable Quality Level (AQL)** – the smallest percentage of defectives that will make the lot definitely acceptable; a level that the customer prefers. This means lots at or better than the AQL are accepted at least 95% of the time and rejected at most 5% of the time.

(b) **Lot Tolerance Percent Defective (LTPD)** – the largest percentage of defectives that will make the lot definitely unacceptable. Customers cannot tolerate more defectives than this percentage. This means that lots at or worse than the LTPD are rejected at least 90% of the time and accepted at most 10% of the time.

(c) **Producer's risk** (described by the Alpha symbol α) – the probability of lots that meet the AQL will not be accepted. This is the Type I error, the error committed when rejecting a good lot, and is frequently set at 5%.

(d) **Consumers' risk** (described by the Beta symbol ß) – the probability of lots that exceed the LTPD will be accepted. This is the Type II error, the error committed when accepting a bad lot, and is frequently set at 10%.

(e) **n** – sample size taken for your sampling plan

(f) **c** – where rejections would occur when defects exceeded this percent.

4.3 Sampling frames

Definition

A **sampling frame** is a numbered list of all the items in the population.

If random sampling is used then it is necessary to construct a sampling frame. Once this has been made, it is easy to select a random sample, simply by generating a list of random numbers.

For instance, if you wanted to select a random sample of children from a school, it would be useful to have a list of names:

0 J Absolam
1 R Brown
2 S Brown
...

Now the numbers 0, 1, 2 and so on can be used to select the random sample. It is normal to start the numbering at 0, so that when 0 appears in a list of random numbers it can be used.

Sometimes it is not possible to draw up a sampling frame. For example, if you wanted to take a random sample of Americans, it would take too long to list all Americans.

A sampling frame should have the following characteristics.

(a) **Completeness**. Are all members of the population included on the list?

(b) **Accuracy**. Is the information correct?

(c) **Adequacy**. Does it cover the entire population?

(d) **Up-to-dateness**. Is the list up-to-date?

(e) **Convenience**. Is the sampling frame readily accessible?

(f) **Non-duplication**. Does each member of the population appear on the list only once?

Two readily available sampling frames for the human population of Great Britain are the council tax register (list of dwellings) and the electoral register (list of individuals).

Activity 5 **(5 minutes)**

From the researcher's point of view, what might be the weakness of the Electoral Register as a sampling frame?

Random number tables

Assuming that a sampling frame can be drawn up, then a random sample can be picked from it by one of the following methods.

(a) The lottery method, which amounts to picking numbered pieces of paper out of a box

(b) The use of random number tables

Set out below is part of a typical random number table.

93716	16894	98953	73231
32886	59780	09958	18065
92052	06831	19640	99413
39510	35905	85244	35159
27699	06494	03152	19121
92962	61773	22109	78508
10274	12202	94205	50380
75867	20717	82037	10268
85783	47619	87481	37220

You should note the following points.

(a) The sample is found by selecting groups of random numbers with the number of digits depending on the total population size, as follows.

Total population size	*Number of random digits*
1 – 9	1
1 – 99	2
1 – 999	3

The items selected for the sample are those corresponding to the random numbers selected.

(b) The starting point on the table should be selected at random. After that, however, numbers must be selected in a consistent manner. In other words, you should use the table row by row or column by column. By jumping around the table from place to place, personal bias may be introduced.

(c) In many practical situations it is more convenient to use a computer to generate a list of random numbers, especially when a large sample is required.

EXAMPLE: RANDOM NUMBER TABLES

An investigator wishes to select a random sample from a population of 800 people, who have been numbered 000, 001, ..., 799. As there are three digits in 799 the random numbers will be selected in groups of three. Working along the first line of the table given earlier, the first few groups are as follows.

937 161 689 498 953 732

Numbers over 799 are discarded. The first four people in the sample will therefore be those numbered 161, 689, 498 and 732.

Drawbacks of random sampling

(a) The selected items are subject to the full range of variation inherent in the population.

(b) An unrepresentative sample may result.

(c) The members of the population selected may be scattered over a wide area, adding to the cost and difficulty of obtaining the data.

(d) An adequate sampling frame might not exist.

(e) The numbering of the population might be laborious.

Quasi– and non-random sampling

In many situations it might be too expensive to obtain a random sample, in which case quasi-random sampling is necessary, or else it may not be possible to draw up a sampling frame. In such cases, non-random sampling has to be used.

4.4 Quasi-random sampling

Quasi-random sampling, which provides a good approximation to random sampling, necessitates the existence of a sampling frame.

The main methods of quasi-random sampling are as follows.

(a) Systematic sampling
(b) Stratified sampling
(c) Multistage sampling

Systematic sampling

Systematic sampling may provide a good approximation to random sampling. It works by selecting every nth item after a random start. For example, if it was decided to select a sample of 20 from a population of 800, then every 40th (800 ÷ 20) item after a random start in the first 40 should be selected. The starting point could be found using the lottery method or random number tables. If (say) 23 was chosen, then the sample would include the 23rd, 63rd, 103rd, 143rd, ..., 783rd items.

The gap of 40 is known as the sampling interval.

The investigator must ensure that there is no regular pattern to the population which, if it coincided with the sampling interval, might lead to a biased sample. In practice, this problem is often overcome by choosing multiple starting points and using varying sampling intervals whose size is selected at random.

If the sampling frame is in random order (such as an alphabetical list of students) a systematic sample is essentially the same as a simple random sample.

A systematic sample does not fully meet the criterion of randomness since some samples of the given size have zero probability of being chosen. However, the method is easy and cheap, and hence is widely used.

Stratified sampling

This is the best method of choosing a sample in many situations. The population must be divided into strata or categories.

If we took a random sample of all cost and management accountants in the country, it is conceivable that the entire sample might consist of members of the Chartered Institute of Management Accountants working in public companies. Stratified sampling removes this possibility as random samples could be taken from each type of employment, the number in each sample being proportional to the total number of cost and management accountants in each type (for example, those in partnerships, those in public companies and those in private companies).

EXAMPLE: STRATIFIED SAMPLING

The number of accountants in each type of work in a particular country are as follows.

Partnerships	500
Public companies	500
Private companies	700
Public practice	800
	2,500

If a sample of twenty were required, the sample would be made up as follows.

		Sample
Partnerships	$\frac{500}{2,500} \times 20$	4
Public companies	$\frac{500}{2,500} \times 20$	4
Private companies	$\frac{700}{2,500} \times 20$	6
Public practice	$\frac{800}{2,500} \times 20$	6
		20

The strata frequently involve multiple classifications. In social surveys, for example, there is usually stratification by age, sex and social class. This implies that the sampling frame must contain information on these three variables before the threefold stratification of the population can be made.

Advantages of stratification are as follows.

(a) It ensures a representative sample since it guarantees that every important category will have elements in the final sample.

(b) The structure of the sample will reflect that of the population if the same proportion of individuals is chosen from each stratum.

(c) Each stratum is represented by a randomly chosen sample and therefore inferences can be made about each stratum.

(d) Precision is increased. Sampling takes place within strata and, because the range of variation is less in each stratum than in the population as a whole and variation between strata does not enter as a chance effect, higher precision is obtainable. (For this to occur, the items in each stratum must be as similar as possible and the difference between the individual strata must be as great as possible.)

NOTES

Note, however, that stratification requires prior knowledge of each item in the population. Sampling frames do not always contain this information. Stratification from the electoral register as to age structure would not be possible because the electoral register does not contain information about age.

Multistage sampling

This method is normally used to cut down the number of investigators and the costs of obtaining a sample. An example will show how the method works.

EXAMPLE: MULTISTAGE SAMPLING

A survey of spending habits is being planned to cover the whole of Britain. It is obviously impractical to draw up a sampling frame, so random sampling is not possible and multistage sampling is to be used instead.

The country is divided into a number of areas and a small sample of these is selected at random. Each of the areas selected is subdivided into smaller units and again a smaller number of these is selected at random. This process is repeated as many times as necessary and, finally, a random sample of the relevant people living in each of the smallest units is taken. A fair approximation to a random sample can be obtained.

Thus, we might choose a random sample of eight areas, and from each of these areas, select a random sample of five towns. From each town, a random sample of 200 people might be selected so that the total sample size is $8 \times 5 \times 200 = 8{,}000$ people.

The main **advantage** of this method is one of **cost saving** but there are a number of **disadvantages**.

(a) There is the possibility of bias if, for example, only a small number of regions are selected.

(b) The method is not truly random as once the final sampling areas have been selected the rest of the population cannot be in the sample.

(c) If the population is heterogeneous, the areas chosen should reflect the full range of the diversity. Otherwise, choosing some areas and excluding others (even if it is done randomly) will result in a biased sample.

The sampling methods looked at so far have necessitated the existence of a sampling frame (or in multistage sampling, sampling frames of areas, sub-areas and items within selected sub-areas). It is often impossible to identify a satisfactory sampling frame and, in such instances, other sampling methods have to be employed.

4.5 Non-random sampling

There are two main methods of non-random sampling, used when a sampling frame cannot be established.

(a) Quota sampling
(b) Cluster sampling

Quota sampling

In quota sampling, randomness is forfeited in the interests of cheapness and administrative simplicity. Investigators are told to interview all the people they meet up to a certain quota. A large degree of bias could be introduced accidentally. For example, an interviewer in a shopping centre may fill her quota by meeting only people who can go shopping during the week. In practice, this problem can be partly overcome by subdividing the quota into different types of people, for example on the basis of age, sex and income, to ensure that the sample mirrors the structure or stratification of the population. The interviewer is then told to interview, for example, 30 males between the ages of 30 and 40 from social class C1. The actual choice of the individuals to be interviewed, within the limits of the **quota controls**, is left to the field worker.

Advantages of quota sampling

(a) It is cheap and administratively easy.

(b) A much larger sample can be studied, and hence more information can be gained at a faster speed for a given outlay than when compared with a fully randomised sampling method.

(c) Although a fairly detailed knowledge of the characteristics of a population is required, no sampling frame is necessary because the interviewer questions every person she meets up to the quota.

(d) Quota sampling may be the only possible approach in certain situations, such as television audience research.

(e) Given suitable, trained and properly briefed field workers, quota sampling yields enough accurate information for many forms of commercial market research.

Disadvantages of quota sampling

(a) The method can result in certain biases (although these can often be allowed for or may be unimportant for the purpose of the research).

(b) The non-random nature of the method rules out any valid estimate of the sampling error in estimates derived from the sample.

Conclusion

Quota sampling cannot be regarded as ultimately satisfactory in research where it is important that theoretically valid results should be obtained. It can be argued, however, that when other large sources of error exist, such as non-response, it is pointless to worry too much about sampling error.

EXAMPLE: QUOTA SAMPLING

Consider the figures in the stratified sampling example above, but with the following additional information relating to the sex of the accountants.

NOTES

	Male	*Female*
Partnerships	300	200
Public companies	400	100
Private companies	300	400
Public practice	300	500

An investigator's quotas might be as follows.

	Male	*Female*	*Total*
Partnerships	30	20	50
Public companies	40	10	50
Private companies	30	40	70
Public practice	30	50	80
			250

Using quota sampling, the investigator would interview the first 30 male cost and management accountants in partnerships that he met, the first 20 female cost and management accountants in partnerships that he met and so on.

Cluster sampling

Cluster sampling involves selecting one definable subsection of the population as the sample, that subsection taken to be representative of the population in question. The pupils of one school might be taken as a cluster sample of all children at school in one county.

Cluster sampling benefits from low costs in the same way as multistage sampling.

The advantages of cluster sampling are that it is a good alternative to multistage sampling if a satisfactory sampling frame does not exist and it is inexpensive to operate because little organisation or structure is involved. There is, however, the potential for considerable bias.

Activity 6 **(25 minutes)**

Describe four methods a brewery could employ to test the market for a new canned beer. Discuss the relative advantages and disadvantages of each method chosen.

4.6 The size of a sample

As well as deciding on the appropriateness of a particular sampling method for a given situation, the size of the sample actually selected must also be given consideration.

Although, in certain circumstances, statistical processes can be used to calculate sample sizes, there is no universal law for determining the size of the sample. Two general considerations should, however, be borne in mind.

(a) The larger the size of the sample, the more accurate the results.

(b) There reaches a point after which there is little to be gained from increasing the size of the sample.

Despite these principles other, mainly administrative factors, play a role in determining sample size.

(a) **Money and time available.**

(b) **Degree of precision required.** A survey may have the aim of discovering residents' reaction to a road widening scheme and hence a fairly small sample, producing imprecise results, would be acceptable. An enquiry into the safety of a new drug would, on the other hand, require an extremely large sample so that the information gained was as precise as possible.

(c) **Number of subsamples required.** If a complicated sampling method such as stratified sampling is to be used, the overall sample size will need to be large so as to ensure adequate representation of each subgroup (in this case, each stratum).

5 SURVEY METHODS OF COLLECTING DATA

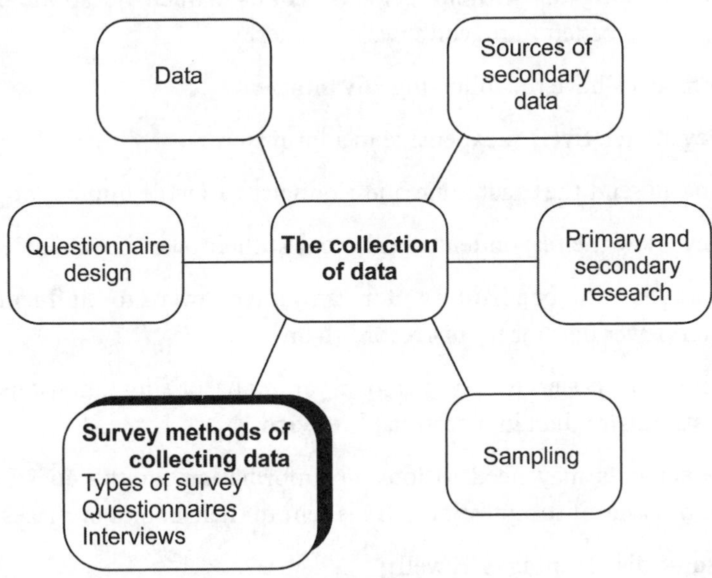

5.1 Types of survey

Surveys can be divided into two broad categories:

(a) The questionnaire
(b) The interview

Questionnaires are usually paper-and-pencil instruments that the respondent completes. Interviews are completed by the interviewer based on what the respondent says. Sometimes, it is hard to tell the difference between a questionnaire and an interview. For instance, some people think that questionnaires always ask short closed-ended questions while interviews always ask broad open-ended ones. But you will see questionnaires with open-ended questions (although they do tend to be shorter than in interviews) and there will often be a series of closed-ended questions asked in an interview.

Survey research has changed dramatically. There are now automated telephone surveys that use random dialling methods. Increasingly, survey research is tightly integrated with the delivery of service. Your hotel room may have a survey on the desk. Your waiter

may present a short customer satisfaction survey with your bill. You may be asked to complete a short survey when you visit a web site. E-surveying is a new way of asking people's opinions on issues that matter to you. E-surveyors use the Internet to conduct surveys: they sent respondents an e-mail containing a questionnaire, they place a pop-up survey on a web page or they publish a survey on a secured web page where only respondents with a valid keyword can answer.

If you are conducting an e-mail survey at work, you can **attach** a document or spreadsheet to the email, asking the respondent to open the document or spreadsheet, complete it, save it and return. You may be able to ask your questions in the e-mail itself, asking the respondent to reply and return the e-mail.

5.2 Questionnaires

When most people think of questionnaires, they think of postal surveys. This type of survey covers all methods in which the questionnaire is given to the respondent and returned to the investigator without personal contact. Such questionnaires could be posted but might also be left in pigeonholes or on desks.

Postal questionnaires have the following **advantages.**

(a) They are relatively inexpensive to administer.

(b) You can send the exact same questionnaire to a wide number of people.

(c) They allow the respondent to fill it out at their own convenience.

(d) There is no opportunity for an interviewer to influence responses (interviewer bias) or to mis-record them.

(e) It may be easier to ask personal or embarrassing questions in a postal questionnaire than in a personal interview.

(f) Respondents may need to look up information for the questionnaire. This will be easier if the questionnaire is sent to their homes or places of work.

But there are some **disadvantages** as well:

(a) Response rates from postal surveys are often very low.
(b) They are not the best vehicles for asking for detailed written responses.

A second type is the **group administered questionnaire**. A sample of respondents is brought together and asked to respond to a structured sequence of questions. Traditionally, questionnaires were administered in group settings for convenience. The researcher could give the questionnaire to those who are present and be fairly sure that there would be a high response rate. If the respondents are unclear about the meaning of a question they could ask for clarification. And, there are often organisational settings where it is relatively easy to assemble the group (in a company or business, for instance).

What is the difference between a group administered questionnaire and a group interview or focus group? In the group administered questionnaire, each respondent is handed a questionnaire and asked to complete it while in the room. Each respondent completes one. In the group interview or focus group, the interviewer facilitates the session. People work as a group, listening to each other's comments and answering the questions. Someone takes notes for the entire group – people do not complete an interview individually.

A less familiar type of questionnaire is the **household drop-off** survey. In this approach, a researcher goes to the respondent's home or business and hands the respondent the questionnaire. In some cases, the respondent is asked to post it back or the interviewer returns to pick it up. This approach attempts to blend the advantages of the postal survey and the group administered questionnaire. Like the postal survey, the respondent can work on the questionnaire in private and when it is convenient. Like the group administered questionnaire, the interviewer makes personal contact with the respondent who can then ask questions about the study and get clarification on what is to be done. Generally, this would be expected to increase the percentage of people who are willing to respond.

5.3 Interviews

Interviews may be **qualitative** or **quantitative**. Qualitative data can often provide greater insight than quantitative data and does not lend itself to the simple application of standard statistical methods. Qualitative work is carefully planned. The interviewer will have an inconspicuous checklist of topics but the procedure will be as unstructured as possible. Neither interviewer nor respondent is bound by the structure of a questionnaire in an unstructured interview. Interviewers are free to word such questions as they wish. The order in which questions are covered may also be varied. This will allow the respondent to control the data flow and for the interviewer to explore more thoroughly particular views of the respondent and why they are held.

In a quantitative study the procedure is structured, data collection proceeds at a quick pace and it is possible to process the data electronically.

Quantitative research

There are basically two types of interview that can be used for quantitative research– the **personal (face to face) interview** and the **telephone interview**.

Personal interview

With this type of interview the interviewer works directly with the respondent. Unlike with mail surveys, the interviewer has the opportunity to probe or ask follow-up questions, and interviews are generally easier for the respondent, especially if opinions or impressions are sought. Interviews can be very time-consuming and they are resource intensive. The interviewer is considered a part of the measurement instrument and interviewers have to be well-trained in how to respond to any contingency.

Advantages of personal interviews

(a) The interviewer is able to reduce respondent anxiety and allay potential embarrassment, thereby increasing the response rate and decreasing the potential for error.

(b) The routing ('if yes go to question 7, if no go to question 10') of questions is made easier due to the experience of the interviewer.

(c) Interviewers can ask, within narrow limits, for a respondent's answer to be clarified.

(d) The questions can be given in a fixed order with a fixed wording and the answers can be recorded in a standard manner. If there is more than one interviewer involved in the survey this will reduce variability.

(e) Standardised questions and ways of recording the responses mean that less-skilled interviewers may be used, thereby reducing the cost of the survey.

(f) Pictures, signs and objects can be used.

Disadvantages of personal interviews

(a) They can be time consuming.

(b) They can be costly to complete.

(c) Questionnaires can be difficult to design.

(d) Questions must normally be kept relatively simple, thus restricting the depth of data collected.

(e) Questions must normally be closed because of the difficulties of recording answers to open questions.

(f) Interviewers cannot probe vague or ambiguous replies.

Telephone interviews

Like personal interviews, they allow for some personal contact between the interviewer and the respondent. And, they allow the interviewer to ask follow-up questions. Telephone interviews are a relatively fast and low-cost means of gathering data compared to personal interviews. They are most useful when only a small amount of information is required and also benefit the respondent in terms of the short amount of time taken up by the interview.

CATI (computer-assisted telephone interviewing) has been used successfully by insurance services and banks as well as consumer research organisations. The telephone interviewer calls up a questionnaire on screen and reads questions to the respondent. Answers are then recorded instantly on computer. Complex questions with questionnaire routing may be handled in this way.

Advantages of telephone interviews

(a) The response is rapid.

(b) A wide geographical area can be covered fairly cheaply from a central location. There is no need for the interviewer to travel between respondents.

(c) It may be easier to ask sensitive or embarrassing questions.

Disadvantages of telephone interviews

(a) A biased sample may result from the fact that a proportion of people do not have land-line telephones and many of those who do are ex-directory. For those people with mobile 'phones there is no directory enquiry service or book to find out their telephone number.

(b) It is not possible to use 'show cards' or pictures.

(c) The refusal rate is much higher than with face-to-face interviews.

(d) It is not possible to see the interviewee's expression or to develop the rapport that is possible with personal interviews.

(e) The interview must be short.

(f) Respondents may be unwilling to participate for fear of being sold something.

Qualitative research

Depth interviews and group discussions are the two most commonly used qualitative research methods

Depth interviews

Motivational research often uses the psychoanalytic method of depth interviews. The pattern of questioning should assist the respondent to explore deeper levels of thought. Motives and explanations of behaviour often lie well below the surface. It is a time-consuming and expensive process. In a depth interview the key line of communication is between the interviewer and the respondent. They have an open-ended conversation, not constrained by a formal questionnaire, and the qualitative data are captured as narrative by means of an audio or videotape. Depth interviews may have fewer than ten respondents.

Focus groups

Usually consist of eight to ten respondents and an interviewer taking the role of group moderator. The group moderator introduces topics for discussion and intervenes as necessary to encourage respondents or to direct discussions if they threaten to wander too far off the point. The moderator will also need to control any powerful personalities and prevent them from dominating the group.

Advantages of focus groups

(a) The group environment with 'everybody in the same boat' can be less intimidating than other techniques of research, which rely on one-to-one contact (such as depth interviews).

(b) What respondents say in a group often sparks off experiences or ideas on the part of others.

(c) Differences between consumers are highlighted, making it possible to understand a range of attitudes in a short space of time.

(d) It is easier to observe groups and there is more to observe simply because of the intricate behaviour patterns within a collection of people.

(e) Social and cultural influences are highlighted.

(f) Groups provide a social context that is a 'hot-house' reflection of the real world.

(g) Groups are cheaper and faster than depth interviews.

Disadvantages of focus groups

(a) Group processes may inhibit some people from making a full contribution and may encourage others to become exhibitionistic.

(b) Group processes may stall to the point where the moderator cannot retrieve them.

(c) Some groups may take on a life of their own, so that what is said has validity only in the short-lived context of the group.

(d) It is not usually possible to identify which group members said what, unless the proceedings have been video recorded.

(e) It is not easy to find a common time when all can participate.

6 QUESTIONNAIRE DESIGN

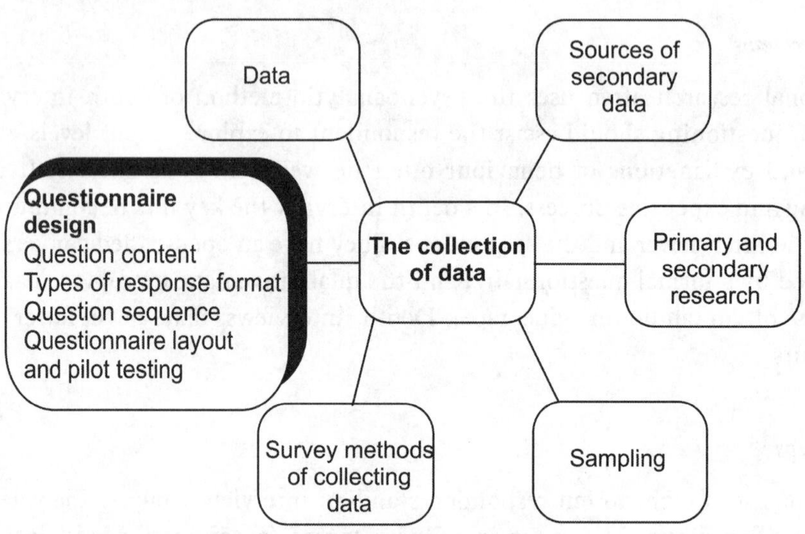

6.1 Introduction

Questionnaires are typically used for survey research to determine the current status or 'situation,' or to estimate the distribution of characteristics in a population. Writing a questionnaire is one of the most critical stages in the survey development process. Much of it is common sense, but there are intricacies that you should be familiar with. It is common sense to require that the concepts be clearly defined and questions unambiguously phrased; otherwise, the resulting data are apt to be seriously misleading.

Here are some ground rules to keep in mind before writing the first word.

(a) Each question should relate directly to your survey objectives.

(b) Every respondent should be able to answer every question (unless instructed otherwise).

(c) Each question should be phrased so that all respondents interpret it the same way.

(d) Each question should provide answers to what you need to know, not what would be nice to know.

6.2 Question content

When deciding on question content it is vital to think about the following.

(a) Is the question necessary?

(b) Will the respondent understand the question?

The language used should be that of the respondent group. Think about the different language used by managing directors and teenagers.

(c) Will the question elicit the required data?

A survey often fails to generate the required data because of badly phrased questions or questions that are too ambiguous to elicit specific information. Double-barrelled questions ('Do you often go to pubs and restaurants?') should be split, and words describing frequency ('often', 'slightly', 'somewhat') should be avoided as they have a wide range of interpretation.

Activity 7 **(5 minutes)**

What might be a better way of asking 'Do you often go to the cinema?'

(d) Does the respondent have the necessary data to be able to answer the question?

The ability of the respondent to answer will depend on three factors.

(i) If respondents do not know the answer to a question they may try to bluff their way out of what they see as an embarrassing situation by guessing. Such answers lead to errors in the conclusions drawn from the data collected. Questions should therefore be phrased so that it does not appear that the interviewer is suggesting that the respondent should know the answer.

(ii) Questions relating to unimportant/ infrequent events or to events some time in the past are likely to tempt respondents to guess. This may introduce error and so it is better to 'jog' respondents' memories in some way.

(iii) Even the most articulate of respondents may find it difficult to be verbally adept about their feelings, beliefs, opinions and motivations.

(e) Is the respondent willing and able to answer the questions?

A respondent may refuse to answer one or more questions on a questionnaire (non-response) or many 'refuse' by providing a wrong or distorted answer. Certain techniques can be employed to eliminate distorted, wrong or inaccurate answers.

(i) Assess whether the question is really necessary (especially if it will cause embarrassment or a loss of prestige).

(ii) Reassure respondents of the importance of the question and of the value of their response.

(iii) Begin a 'difficult' question with a statement which implies the topic of the question is common or quite usual.

(iv) Imply that the behaviour in which you are interested is an attribute of a third party (someone other than the respondent).

(v) Provide respondents with a card listing possible responses, identified by a letter or a number, to potentially embarrassing questions. Respondents need only provide the appropriate letter or number as their answer.

(vi) When analysing the data, replies to questions related to image or prestige should be upgraded or downgraded as necessary.

Activity 8 **(5 minutes)**

How might the question be rephrased?

'Do you visit the pub to get drunk?'

Question phrasing

Given below is a checklist of factors to consider when translating data requirements into words.

(a) Use a style of language appropriate to the target population.

(b) Avoid long questions.

(c) Avoid vague and ambiguous words.

(d) Avoid biased words and leading questions.

(e) Do not use double-barrelled questions.

(f) Avoid negative questions.

(g) Do not encourage respondents to guess.

(h) Avoid questions which assume respondents possess all the relevant information pertaining to the question.

6.3 Types of response format

Use scales that provide the information needed and are appropriate for respondents. Some choices are:

(a) **Fixed response** (quantitative)

- Yes-No
- Multiple choice
- Rating scale/Continuum
- Rank ordering

(b) **Narrative response** (qualitative) – this allows respondents greater freedom of expression. There is no bias due to limited response ranges and the respondents can qualify their answers. On the other hand, these responses are time consuming to code and the researcher may misinterpret (and therefore misclassify) a response.

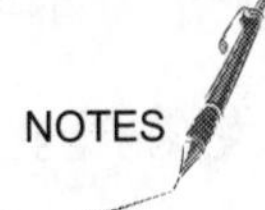

Questions can be open or closed. Open questions are difficult to analyse. An open question might be worded like this:

'How did you travel to work today?'

The responses may be so numerous that analysis becomes onerous and time consuming. The designer of the questionnaire should instead try to offer a full range of possible responses to the question, perhaps like this.

'Please indicate how you travelled to work today.'

By bus ☐

By train ☐

By private car ☐

On foot ☐

By bicycle/motorcycle ☐

I did not go to work today (illness, holidays etc) ☐

I work at home ☐

I do not work ☐

Other (please give details) ....'

The responses from this closed question will be much easier to analyse. It is important, however, to avoid putting such lists of responses in order of supposed popularity.

Activity 9

What types of problem can you envisage arising from the use of multiple-choice questions? How can such problems be overcome?

6.4 Question sequence

(a) Start with quota control questions to determine right away whether the interviewee is the right type of person. Quota control questions might identify whether the interviewee is employed or unemployed, under 40 over 40 and so on. Such questions enable you to terminate worthless interviews as early as possible.

(b) Move on to questions which will engage interest, reassure and give a foretaste of what is to follow.

(c) Questions should be in logical order as far as possible, but if difficult questions are necessary it may be more appropriate to put them at the end.

(d) Avoid questions which suggest the answers to later questions. This will cause bias.

6.5 Questionnaire layout and pilot testing

(a) Use good quality paper.

(b) The questionnaire should be as short as possible. Questionnaires that are too long may discourage the respondent from even starting.

(c) If respondents have to complete the questionnaire themselves, it must be as approachable as possible. Consider the use of lines, boxes, different typefaces or print sizes and small pictures. Use plenty of space.

(d) Make sure that the instructions which guide the respondent through the questionnaire are as user friendly as possible and are kept to a minimum.

(e) Explain the purpose of the survey at the beginning of the questionnaire and, where possible, guarantee confidentiality. Emphasise the date by which it must be returned.

(f) At the end of the questionnaire, thank the respondent and make it clear what they should do with the completed questionnaire.

EXAMPLE: QUESTIONNAIRE

We come back to the example that we looked at earlier in this chapter from an unpublished undergraduate dissertation about how firms report on the environment.

Environmental questionnaire

Please answer as many questions as applicable ticking the relevant boxes.

All answers will be treated as anonymous.

No.	Question	Answer
Q1	Is your company predominantly operating in a service or manufacturing industry? Service... Manufacturing....................................	 ....
Q2	What is your company's average annual turnover?	
Q3 (a)	Does your company have a separate environmental department or manager? Environmental department.......................... Environmental manager............................. Neither..	 ....
Q3 (b)	If you do have an environmental department or manager how long has this been operational?	....
Q4	Does your company have separate environmental policy? Yes.. No... If Yes, are all employees made aware of this? Yes.. Some are, some are not............................	 ....

No.	Question	Answer
Q5	Does your company utilise any of the following environmental initiatives? (Please tick all that are applicable.)	
	Energy conservation	....
	Control of emissions...	....
	Recycling...	....
	Reusing...	....
	Buying from environmentally friendly suppliers	....
	Monitoring and controlling waste...	....
	Using recycled stationery...	....
	Tree planting...	....
	Other...	....
	Please state...	....
Q6	Is your company aware of any environmental impacts it may have?	
	Yes – and we are controlling them...	....
	Yes – and we are investigating them...	....
	Yes – but other organisational matters are our priority at the moment...	....
	No – we do not affect our environment...	....
	No – don't know...	....
Q7	Does your company publish any environmental information?	
	Yes..........................	....
	No (if no go to question 12)	....
Q8	If environmental information is published, what was the motivation behind it?	....
	Shareholder pressure	....
	Government legislation...	....
	Competitive advantage	....
	Concern for the environment...	....
	Other	
	Please state...	
Q9	Who is your intended audience for published environmental information?	
	• Shareholders...	....
	• Government...	....
	• Employees...	....
	• Competitors...	....
	• Suppliers...	....
	• General public...	....
	• Other	....
	Please state	

No.	Question	Answer
Q10	Is this published information: • Included in your Annual Report? .... • Distributed at a time other than that when annual report is published?	 ....
Q11	What form does this published information take? • Narrative disclosure .... • Statistical indicators.. • Mixture of narrative and statistical.. • Financial data.. • Environmental achievements.. • Environmental targets..	 ....
Q12	Does your company have separate environmental information that it uses for internal management decisions? • Yes.. • No – we use the published environmental data................................. • No – we do not incorporate environmental data in management decisions..	 ....
Q13	If you do have environmental information, is this part of an environmental management system? • Yes.. • No.. If no, are there any plans to introduce such a system? • Yes.. • No..	 ....
Q14	Does your company believe environmental impacts are going to be an increasing business issue? • Yes.. • No..	 ....
	Thank you very much for your time and help. **Please return completed questionnaires in the stamped addressed envelope provided.**	

Pretesting the questionnaire will uncover faults in its design before it is too late and should therefore ensure that the final version of the questionnaire gathers the required data.

Activity 10 **(40 minutes)**

The following questionnaire has been designed to find out some information about the users of Redwood's Public Library. There are some errors in this questionnaire. Read through and see how many you can find.

Name: Telephone:	
1	How often do you use the services offered by the library?
2	How many books or publications have you borrowed from the library? 0 1-5 5-10 10-15 20-50 50-100
3	The last time you used the library, what was the purpose of your visit? Search for a book Search for a periodical Get information from a librarian Study peacefully
4	Were your needs satisfied? Yes/No
5	How satisfied are you with the quality of service provided by the library and the attitude of the library staff? 1 2 3 4 5
6	What do you dislike about the library?
7	Are there any improvements that could be made to the library in order to provide a better service? Yes/No
8	Do you approve or disapprove of the recent proposals made by the Library Management Review Committee, such as the proposal to double fines for overdue books? Approve/Disapprove (Go to Question 11)
9	Are you aware of these proposals? Yes/No

10	Why do you disapprove of these proposals?
11	Are you against not having longer opening hours? Against/Not against
12	Level of education
	THANK YOU FOR YOUR HELP

7 DATA STORAGE

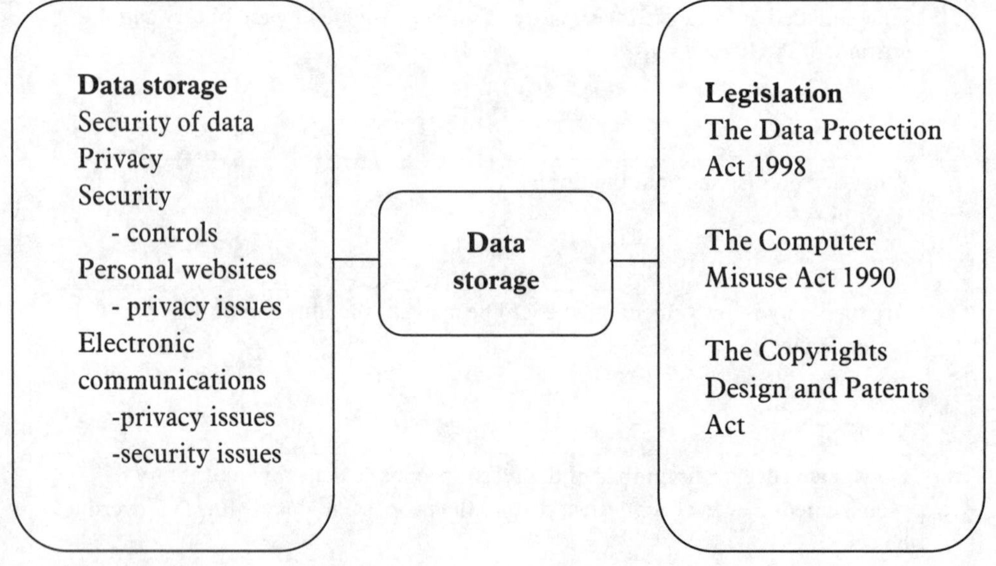

7.1 Security of data

Privacy and **security** issues are of key importance to individual organisations. Threats to them can be caused by the use of **personal** (social networking) **websites** and **electronic messaging services**

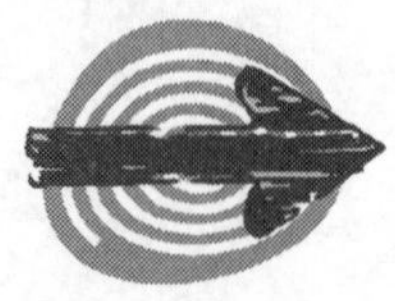

We have covered controls needed to protect specific data and information which are held within an organisation's system, so we now turn to other wider privacy and security issues.

NOTES

7.2 Privacy

Definition

> **Privacy** is the right of the individual to control the use of information about him or her, including information on financial status, health and lifestyle.

The right of an individual to have their **privacy** respected has become an increasingly important issue for business organisations. This is because many store and collect data about, for example, their employees and customers.

Many developed nations have enacted privacy laws and the UK is no exception. The Data Protection Act 1998 replaced the earlier Act of 1984 and gives rights to the individual about how their data is collected, stored and used.

The Act sets out various rules which organisations must follow concerning the **collection, use**, and **disclosure of information** about an **individual**. It also provides guidance **on data quality, security, access** and the **correction** of such **data**.

Businesses must only collect **necessary information**, and what they do collect must be **collected fairly** and **openly**. The **purpose** that the information will be used for must be disclosed and the **individual's consent** must be obtained if it is used for a different purpose.

Data must be of **sufficient quality**, this means it should be **accurate, complete** and **up to date**. It must be kept **secure** through the use of passwords or physical controls such as locked cabinets. Once it is no longer needed it must be **destroyed securely**.

Individuals generally have a right to **inspect** the data held about them and organisations must take steps to **correct incorrect information** or to inform the individual why the information cannot be amended.

7.3 Security

Definition

> **Security** can be defined as 'The protection of data from accidental or deliberate threats which might cause unauthorised modification, disclosure or destruction of data, and the protection of the information system from the degradation or non availability of services'. (*Lane: Security of computer based information systems*)

Information systems with links to other systems such as the **Internet** are exposed to security risks. Some of the main risks are explained below.

Security risks associated with information systems	
Risk	**Explanation**
Hackers and eaves-droppers	Hackers attempt to gain unauthorised access to information systems. They may attempt to damage a system or steal information. Hackers use tools like electronic number generators and software which enables rapid password attempts. Data that is transmitted across telecommunications links is exposed to the risk of being intercepted or examined during transmission (eavesdropping).
Viruses	A virus is a small piece of software which performs unauthorised actions and which replicates itself. Viruses may cause damage to files or attempt to destroy files and damage hard disks. When transmitted over a network, such as the Internet, into a 'clean' system, the virus reproduces, therefore infecting that system. Types of virus include: • E-mail viruses spread using e-mail messages and replicate by mailing themselves to addresses held in the user's contacts book. • Worms copy themselves from machine to machine on a network. • Trojans or Trojan horses are hidden inside a 'valid' program but perform an unexpected act. Trojans therefore act like a virus, but they aren't classified as a virus as they don't replicate themselves. • Trap doors are undocumented access points to a system allowing controls to be bypassed • Logic bombs are triggered by the occurrence of a certain event. • Time bombs are triggered by a certain date.
Hoaxes	An associated problem is that of hoax virus warnings. There are a vast number of common hoaxes, most of which circulate via e-mail. Many are a variation of one of the most 'popular' early hoaxes – the Good Times hoax. This hoax takes the form of a warning about viruses contained in an e-mail. People pass along the warning because they are trying to be helpful, but they are in fact wasting the time of all concerned.
Denial of service attack	A fairly new threat, relating to Internet websites is the 'denial of service attack'. This involves an organised campaign to bombard an Internet site with excessive volumes of traffic at a given time, with the aim of overloading the site.

7.4 Security controls

The **risks** identified above can be **minimised** through a variety of controls that provide network and communications security.

(a) **Anti-virus software**

The main protection against viruses is anti-virus software. Anti-virus software, such as McAfee or Norton searches systems for viruses and removes them. Such programs also include an auto-update feature that downloads profiles of new

viruses, enabling the software to check for all known or existing viruses. Very new viruses may go undetected by anti-virus software – until the anti-virus software vendor updates their package and the organisation installs the update.

(b) **A firewall**
External e-mail links can be protected by way of a **firewall** that may be configured to virus check all messages, and may also prevent files of a certain type being sent via e-mail (eg .exe files, as these are the most common means of transporting a virus). Firewalls can be implemented in both **hardware** and **software**, or a **combination of both**. A firewall disables part of the telecoms technology to prevent unauthorised intrusions. However, a determined hacker may well be able to bypass this.

(c) **Encryption**
Data that is transmitted across telecommunications links is exposed to the risk of being intercepted or read during transmission (known as 'eavesdropping'). **Encryption** is used to reduce this risk. Encryption involves **scrambling the data** at one end of the line, **transmitting** the scrambled data, and **unscrambling it** at the receiver's end of the line. A person intercepting the scrambled data is unable to make sense of it.

(d) **Electronic signatures**
Encryption often makes use of electronic signatures in the data scrambling process by using public key (or asymmetric) cryptography signatures. Public key cryptography uses two keys – public and private. The private key is only known to its owner, and is used to scramble the data contained in a file. The 'scrambled' data is the electronic signature, and can be checked against the original file using the public key of the person who signed it. This confirms that it could only have been signed by someone with access to the private key. If a third party altered the message, the fact that they had done so would be easily detectable.

An alternative is the use of encryption products which support key recovery, also known as key encapsulation. Such commercial encryption products can incorporate the public key of an agent known as a Key Recovery Agent (KRA). This allows the user to recover their (stored or communicated) data by approaching the KRA with an encrypted portion of the message. In both cases the KRA neither holds the user's private keys, nor has access to the plain text of their data.

(e) **Authentication**
Authentication is a technique of making sure that a message has come from an authorised sender. Authentication involves adding extra data in a form previously agreed between sender and recipient.

(f) **Dial back security**
Dial-back security operates by requiring the person wanting system access to dial into the network and identify themselves first. The system then dials the person back on their authorised number before allowing access.

We shall now look at privacy and security issues in two specific areas – personal websites and electronic communications.

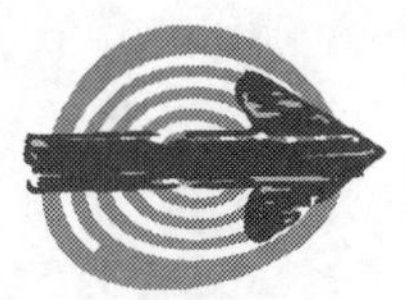

7.5 Personal websites

The success of **social networking** sites such as **Twitter**, **Facebook** and **Myspace** has resulted in many individuals having their own web pages where they can **share information** about themselves with friends, family and others.

Although all different, social networks share a number of common features which include the following.

(a) User profiles which hold personal information about the user such as their date of birth, interests and family relations.

(b) Media such as photos and video which are uploaded by the user and held within their user profile for viewing by other users.

(c) Messaging services that allow users within the network to communicate with each other.

(d) Apps and widgets (small software programs) such as games or quizzes that users can share, some of which can be used to collect information about the user.

The true power of these sites is the ability of users to create large networks, or groups, consisting of themselves and others. Users can search the site for their real life friends using personal information such as their date of birth and town where they live and 'add them' as virtual friends on the network. The site itself may suggest others individuals which a user may wish to add as friends based on virtual friends that they have in common. Once connected, the two friends can view each other's personal information and media stored on the system.

7.6 Privacy issues – personal websites

Privacy issues concerning personal websites relate to who can access information about an individual. Clearly, a person with a Facebook account who has completed their user profile and has uploaded photos of themselves clearly expects somebody to see them – a privacy issue occurs when someone whom the individual does not want to see the information gains access to it.

Such unauthorised bodies could include ex-partners, advertisers or bullies from school, but increasingly organisations are searching social networks as part of the recruitment process when hiring an employee, or while an employee is absent on sick leave. There have been instances where embarrassing party photos have resulted in an offer of employment being withdrawn, and employees have been sacked for being spotted online avoiding work.

Organisations therefore face ethical decisions over whether to spy on their employees' private lives and whether what an employee does in their private life should affect their career prospects. However, like their employees, organisations also have a right to protect their own privacy which may be affected by comments posted online by their employees.

In response to privacy concerns and public outcries, many social networks have taken steps to improve the privacy of their users. There has been a mixed response, and users are able to protect their privacy to some degree, but they need to spend time configuring the range of privacy settings available to them – something not all users will do.

EXAMPLES

In the UK in 2009, a 16-year-old female was sacked as an administrator for making disrespectful comments about her job on Facebook and inviting other members of staff to read them. Her employer stated that the same result would have occurred if the employee had posted the comments on a staff noticeboard and that her comments undermined their relationship and made her job untenable.

In July 2009, Australian cricketer Philip Hughes stated on Twitter that he had been dropped from the latest Ashes squad before the team was announced. This breached the Australian cricket team's right to privacy and may have handed the opponents, England, an advantage in the forthcoming match.

7.7 Security issues – personal websites

For organisations and employees, security issues can be potentially more harmful than breaches of privacy. Some potential security issues include:

(a) Loss of confidential information. Employees may be privy to confidential or sensitive information which if made public could cause their employer to lose competitive advantage, for example trade secrets about a new product or plans to acquire a competitor. Such information would spread very quickly across a social network if released accidentally or deliberately.

(b) System damage. Social network applications could be a cover for viruses or other malicious software which may be downloaded into the employee's or organisation's system through use of the social network.

(c) Identity theft. Much of the information posted on social networks, such as dates of birth, location, addresses and phone numbers, is of use to identity thieves who pose as their victims in order to obtain money or goods. Individuals should ideally not post such information online, or if they do, ensure only those they trust can see it.

(d) Damage to reputation. Organisations and users must protect their social network accounts from hackers or unauthorised individuals who may attempt to gain access to their profile in order to ruin their reputation, for example, by making obscene comments about others.

EXAMPLES

In March 2010, a military operation by the Israeli Defence Force had to be cancelled after one of the soldiers due to take part posted the day and location that the attack was due to occur on Facebook.

Vodafone UK was forced to issue a public apology when an employee posted a homophobic tweet on the company's twitter account which was sent to its 8,500 followers. The employee gained access to the account through an unattended keyboard.

7.8 Electronic communications

Since the dawn of the Internet, email has grown to be the most popular method of electronic communication. It allows near instantaneous communication between users around the world with the added benefit that documents which relate to the message can be attached to it.

Email revolutionised how organisations do business by speeding up the flow of information, allowing the paperless storage of information and for people to communicate without needing to be in the same room or at the end of a phone line.

After the world got the taste for instantaneous communication, electronic messaging services such as those provided by MSN and Yahoo! began to be developed. These run on similar principles to email but are designed to be more informal. Once logged onto the system, users can send and receive messages instantaneously from others who are also on-line. The systems are so quick that users can chat in real time.

Recent developments in electronic messaging include the ability to send a video feed from a webcam while chatting and to share files over the system.

7.9 Privacy issues – electronic communications

Privacy issues concerning electronic communications differ to those relating to personal websites. Information held in user accounts of social networks can be amended or deleted at anytime so the user has control over what others see. However electronic messages, once sent, are a permanent record which the recipient can control, including the facility to send them onto others without the original sender's permission. Therefore, it is important for users to be careful about what information they include in emails and electronic messages.

Emails and messages sent through an organisation's system can be stored and analysed at any time by employers so it is very important that employees do not send anything which is inappropriate.

7.10 Security issues – electronic communications

Emails and electronic messages in themselves are a low security risk, however they can be used as a vehicle to breach a system's security. Examples of security risks include:

(a) Viruses and malicious software. These can be hidden in email attachments or Internet links sent through an electronic messaging service. Once opened they may infect the user's computer or network unless anti-virus software is in place.

(b) Phishing attacks. These are where innocent or official looking emails or messages are sent which entice the user to provide sensitive or confidential information. They are commonly in the form of emails which appear to be from a user's bank which require the entry of account information that enables the phisher to access and empty their victim's account.

(c) Leaking. Confidential emails between employees or between employees and third parties are at risk of being leaked to the public by those with high-level access to an organisation's email system or by the recipient themselves.

(d) Unintended distribution. A common fault with email systems is that messages can be sent to a person with the same or similar name as the intended recipient by

accident. Another problem is where a user 'replies to all' rather than just replying to the sender of an email.

(e) Impersonation. Instant messaging services offer users no guarantee that the person they are chatting with are actually who they say they are. It is especially important to be wary about providing any personal information over such systems.

EXAMPLES

In 2010 thousands of fake emails were sent by scammers purporting to be from Her Majesty's Revenue and Customs (HMRC). Recipients were told that they were due a tax refund and to provide the sender with their bank or credit card details to facilitate the transfer. The tax authority issued a warning about these phishing attacks and stated that it only informed customers about tax refunds by post.

---

8 DATA PROTECTION LEGISLATION

Definition

The **Data Protection Act 1998** aims to protect the rights of **individuals** in relation to information organisations hold about them.

8.1 Why is privacy an important issue?

In recent years, there has been a growing popular fear that information about individuals which was stored on computer files and processed by computer could be misused. In the UK the current legislation is the Data Protection Act 1998. This Act replaced the earlier Data Protection Act 1984.

Definition

Privacy is the right of a person to be free of unwanted intrusion by others into their lives or activities.

8.2 The Data Protection Act 1998

The Data Protection Act 1998 is an attempt to protect the individual. The Act covers manual and computer systems.

8.3 Definitions of terms used in the Act

In order to understand the Act it is necessary to know some of the technical terms used in it.

(a) Personal data is information about a living individual, including expressions of opinion about him or her. The 'living individual' could come from within the organisation or from outside e.g. job applicant, person who works for a supplier, person who works for a customer etc.

(b) Data users are organisations or individuals who control personal data and the use of personal data.

(c) A data subject is an individual who is the subject of personal data.

8.4 The Data Protection Principles

There are certain Data Protection Principles which data users must comply with.

DATA PROTECTION PRINCIPLES

1 Personal data shall be processed fairly and lawfully and, in particular, shall not be processed unless:

   (a) At least one of the conditions in Schedule 2 of the Act is met. The Schedule 2 conditions are shown below (only one of these need be met):

      (i) With the consent of the subject. Consent cannot be implied: it must be by freely given, specific and informed agreement.

      (ii) As a result of a contractual arrangement.

      (iii) Because of a legal obligation.

      (iv) To protect the vital interests of the subject.

      (v) Where processing is in the public interest.

   (b) In the case of sensitive personal data, the processing of 'sensitive data' is not allowed, unless express consent has been obtained or there are conflicting obligations under employment law. Sensitive data includes data relating to race, political opinions, religious beliefs, physical and mental health, sexual orientation and trade union membership.

2 Personal data shall be obtained only for one or more specified and lawful purposes, and shall not be further processed in any manner incompatible with that purpose or those purposes.

3 Personal data shall be adequate, relevant and not excessive in relation to the purpose or purposes for which they are processed.

4 Personal data shall be accurate and, where necessary, kept up to date.

5	Personal data processed for any purpose or purposes shall not be kept for longer than is necessary for that purpose or those purposes.
6	Personal data shall be processed in accordance with the rights of data subjects under this Act.
7	Appropriate technical and organisational measures shall be taken against unauthorised or unlawful processing of personal data and against accidental loss or destruction of, or damage to, personal data.
8	Personal data shall not be transferred to a country or territory outside the European Economic Area unless that country or territory ensures an adequate level of protection for the rights and freedoms of data subjects in relation to the processing of personal data.

8.5 Registration under the Act

The Data Protection Registrar keeps a Register of all data users. Unless a data user has an entry in the Register they may not hold personal data. Even if the data user is registered, they must only hold data and use data for the **purposes** which are registered.

8.6 The rights of data subjects

The Act includes the following rights for data subjects.

(a) A data subject may seek compensation through the courts for damage and any associated distress caused by the loss, destruction or unauthorised disclosure of data about himself or herself or by inaccurate data about himself or herself.

(b) A data subject may apply to the courts for inaccurate data to be put right or even wiped off the data user's files altogether. Such applications may also be made to the Registrar.

(c) A data subject may obtain access to personal data of which he is the subject. (This is known as the 'subject access' provision.) In other words, a data subject can ask to see his or her personal data that the data user is holding.

(d) A data subject can sue a data user for any damage or distress caused to him by personal data about him which is incorrect or misleading as to matter of fact (rather than opinion).

8.7 Other relevant Acts

The **Computer Misuse Act 1990** makes it a criminal offence to attempt to access, use or change any computer system to which you do not have authorised access rights.

In the UK most law relating to copyright is contained within the **Copyright Designs and Patents Act 1988**. Computer software is covered by copyright legislation. A breach of **software licence** conditions usually means the owners' copyright has been infringed.

In this section we take a brief look at two other Acts relevant to computer systems. We look at Acts from the UK - many other countries have similar legislation. The two Acts we will look at are The Computer Misuse Act 1990 (relating to hacking) and The Copyright Designs and Patents Act 1998 (covering copying of software).

8.8 The Computer Misuse Act 1990

The Computer Misuse Act 1990 makes it a criminal offence to attempt to access, use or change any computer system to which you do not have authorised access rights. Therefore, it is a criminal offence to attempt to by-pass security controls such as passwords. Hacking falls under the terms of the Act, which also makes it an offence to deliberately introduce a virus to a system.

8.9 The Copyright, Designs and Patents Act 1998

In the UK most law relating to copyright is contained within the Copyright, Designs and Patents Act 1988. The Copyright (Computer Software) Amendment Act 1985 had already granted computer programs the status of a literary work and therefore entitled to copyright protection granted under copyright legislation.

When a user purchases software they are merely buying the rights to use the software in line with the terms and conditions within the licence agreement. The licence will be issued with the software, on paper or in electronic form. It contains the terms and conditions of use, as set out by the software publisher or owner of the copyright. A breach of the licence conditions usually means the owners' copyright has been infringed.

8.10 Software piracy

The unauthorised copying of software is referred to as software piracy. If an organisation is using illegal copies of software, the organisation may face a civil suit, and corporate officers and individual employees may have criminal liability.

The most common type of software piracy in a business setting is referred to as Corporate Over-Use. This is the installation of software packages on more machines than there are licences for. For example, if a company purchases five single-user licences of a software program but installs the software on ten machines, then they will be using five infringing copies. In the UK, the Copyright, Designs and Patents Act 1998 specifically allows the making of back-up copies of software, but only providing it is for lawful use.

Chapter roundup

- This chapter has concentrated on the practical problems of collecting data.
- An attribute is something an object has either got or not got. It cannot be measured. A variable is something which can be measured.
- Variables can be discrete (may take specific values) or continuous (may take any value).
- Data may be primary (collected specifically for the current purpose) or secondary (collected already).
- Examples of secondary data include published statistics and historical records.
- Primary data can be collected using surveys. There are two main types of survey: interviews and postal questionnaires. Interviews can be face to face or performed over the telephone.
- Questionnaire design involves considering question content, question phrasing, types of response format, questions required and layout. Questionnaires should be pretested.
- Data are often collected from a sample rather than from a population. A sample can be selected using random sampling (using random number tables or the lottery method), quasi-random sampling (systematic, stratified and multistage sampling) or non-random sampling (quota and cluster sampling). Ensure that you know the characteristics, advantages and disadvantages of each sampling method.
- Once data have been collected they need to be presented and analysed. It is important to remember that if the data have not been collected properly, no amount of careful presentation or interpretation can remedy the defect.
- Privacy and security issues are of key importance to individuals and organisations. Threats to them can be caused by the use of personal (social networking) websites and electronic messaging services.
- The **Data Protection Act 1998** aims to protect the rights of **individuals** in relation to information organisations hold about them.
- The **Computer Misuse Act 1990** makes it a criminal offence to attempt to access, use or change any computer system to which you do not have authorised access rights.
- In the UK most law relating to copyright is contained within the **Copyright, Designs and Patents Act 1988**. Computer software is covered by copyright legislation. A breach of **software licence** conditions usually means the owners' copyright has been infringed.

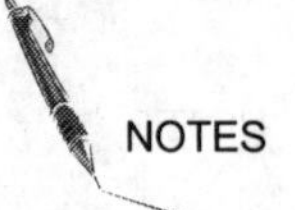

Quick quiz

1. What is a discrete variable?
2. What are secondary data?
3. List some of the UK sources of published statistics.
4. What types of error can appear in survey methods of collecting data?
5. What factors relating to question sequence should be considered when designing a questionnaire?
6. What are the advantages and disadvantages of personal interviews?
7. List the arguments in favour of using a sample.
8. What is a simple random sample?
9. What is stratified sampling?
10. List three administrative factors which may affect the size of a sample.
11. Name three pieces of important data legislation in the UK.

Answers to quick quiz

1. A discrete variable is a variable (something which can be measured) which can only take a finite or countable number of values within a given range.
2. Secondary data are data which have already been collected elsewhere, for some other purpose, but which can be used or adapted for the survey being conducted.
3. *The Office for National Statistics* publishes:
   - *Monthly Digest of Statistics*
   - *Annual Abstract of Statistics*
   - *Economic Trends*
   - *Financial Statistics*

   Other sources:
   - *The Department of Employment Gazette*
   - *The Bank of England Quarterly Bulletin*
   - *Population Trends*
   - *The Blue Book on National Income and Expenditure*
   - *Annual Abstract of Statistics*
   - *Monthly Digest of Statistics*
   - *Financial Times*
4. - Sampling error
   - Response error
   - Non-response error
5. (a) Start with quota control questions to determine right away whether the interviewee is the right type of person.

   (b) Move to questions which will engage interest, reassure and give a foretaste of what is to follow.

(c) Questions should be in a logical order as far as possible, but if difficult questions are necessary, it may be more appropriate to put them at the end.

(d) Avoid questions which suggest the answers to later questions; this will cause bias.

6 *Advantages of personal interviews*

(a) The interviewer is able to reduce respondent anxiety and allay potential embarrassment, thereby increasing the response rate and decreasing the potential for error.

(b) The interviewer's experience makes the routing of questions easier (for example, 'if yes go to question 7, if no go to question 10').

(c) Interviewers can ask, within narrow limits, for a respondent's answer to be clarified.

(d) The questions can be given in a fixed order with a fixed wording and the answers can be recorded in a standard manner. This will reduce variability if there is more than one interviewer involved in the survey.

(e) Standardised questions and ways of recording the responses mean that less skilled interviewers may be used, thereby reducing the cost of the survey.

(f) Pictures, signs and objects can be used.

Disadvantages of personal interviews

(a) They can be time-consuming.

(b) The cost per completed interview can be higher than with other survey methods.

(c) Questionnaires can be difficult to design.

(d) Fully-structured interviews have particular disadvantages.

(i) Questions must be kept relatively simple, thus restricting the depth of data collected.

(ii) Questions must normally be closed because of the difficulties of recording answers to open questions.

(iii) Interviewers cannot probe vague or ambiguous replies.

7 (a) In practice, a 100% survey (census) number achieves the completeness required.

(b) A census may require the use of semi-skilled investigators, resulting in a loss of accuracy in the data collected.

(c) It can be shown mathematically that once a certain sample size has been reached, very little extra accuracy is gained by examining more items.

(d) It is possible to ask more questions with a sample.

(e) The higher cost of a census may exceed the value of results.

(f) Things are always changing. A census could well be out of date by the time you had completed it.

8 A simple random sample is a sample selected in such a way that every item in the population has an equal chance of being included.

9 Stratified sampling is a method which involves dividing the population into strata or categories and a randomly chosen sample is chosen from each strata which directly reflects the structure of the population.

10
- Money and time available
- Degree of precision required
- Number of subsamples required

Answers to activities

1 (a) The number of diagrams in a textbook is a discrete variable, because it can only be counted in whole number steps. You cannot, for example, have 26¼ diagrams or 47.32 diagrams in a book.

(b) Whether or not a can possesses a sticker is an attribute. It is not something which can be measured. A can either possesses the attribute or it does not.

(c) How long an athlete takes to run a mile is a continuous variable, because the time recorded can, in theory, take any value, for example 4 minutes 2.0643 seconds.

(d) The height of a telegraph pole is a continuous variable.

2 The standing details of each employee would include their name, address, date of birth, position, pay, national insurance number, holiday entitlement and date of commencement of employment.

3 The *FT* will have details on the FTSE 100 Index, foreign exchange rates, interest rates, gilts and other stock prices

4 This type of group discussion would be qualitative research.

5 The weakness of the Electoral Register as a sampling frame is the fact that it excludes young adults and immigrants.

6 (a) The brewery could try to supply the beer to a random sample of beer drinkers, and then ask for their views. Such samples are taken in such a way that every member of the population (in this case, all beer drinkers and perhaps all potential beer drinkers) has an equal chance of being selected for the sample. The main advantage of random sampling is that it allows mathematical analysis of the data to be carried out. The main disadvantage is that a random sample can be difficult and expensive to collect. The brewery may well find that it is impossible to compile a list of all beer drinkers from which to select a sample.

(b) Stratified sampling may well be appropriate. The population would first be divided into groups, perhaps by age or by weekly beer consumption, and then samples would be selected from each group (reflecting the proportion of the population in the group). The main advantage of stratified sampling is that it ensures that each group is represented in the sample. The main disadvantage is that preliminary work is needed to determine which groupings are likely to be useful and the proportion of the population in each group.

(c) Cluster sampling may well be a practical alternative, giving some of the benefits of both random sampling and stratified sampling. The population could be divided geographically into beer drinkers at public houses in different regions of the country and beer purchasers at off-licences within these regions. A sample of regions could be selected, and a sample of public houses and off-licences in each selected region could be chosen. All consumers at the chosen public houses and off-licences would then form the sample. The main advantage of cluster sampling is its relative cheapness. The main disadvantage is that the sample obtained will not be truly random, so some forms of statistical analysis will not be possible.

(d) Quota sampling has the advantage of being even cheaper than cluster sampling, but the disadvantage of producing a sample which is even further from being random. Researchers would simply visit a selection of public houses and off-licences and interview the first beer drinkers they met until they had fulfilled some quota (say, ten men and ten women).

7 'Do you go to the cinema (a) once a week, (b) once a month, (c) twice a year?'

8 'Do you think that people go to the pub simply to get drunk?'

9 Here are some ideas. You may have thought of others.

(a) Capturing a full range of possible responses to a question such as 'In which store do you buy the majority of your clothes?' can be impractical.

This problem can be overcome by listing the most popular stores and using an 'other (please specify)' option

(b) The position of the alternative responses may introduce bias.

This problem can be overcome (but not entirely) by producing different versions of the questionnaire.

(c) An unbalanced set of alternative responses could be provided such as the following.

Q: What do you think of TV programme 'XXX'?

A: 1	2	3
Too boring	Very dull	Indifferent

Obviously such response sets should not be used.

10 Outlined below are just some of the possible problems with the Redwood Public Library questionnaire. You may have found other problems with this questionnaire.

Introduction: – there is no introduction telling the respondent what the purpose of the survey is and what will be done with the results. In this type of survey, it is important to receive accurate results in order to 'screen out' those respondents who are not library users.

If you were looking for open and honest results, name and telephone number would not be asked. People like to know that the information they provide is confidential and will be kept that way.

NOTES

Question	
1	This question is open and may be better worded as a closed question in order to be able to compare the responses of the people questioned. Also, this question does not address over what period of time (ie, in the last twelve months, the last month, the last week, etc.) the library was visited.
2	The question asks about borrowing books or publications. What if you borrowed both? What response would you select if you had borrowed five books and publications? Would you select 1–5 or 5–10? The range after 15 and before 20 is missing. The other issue with this question is the reference period. Has the borrowing taken place over the last year, the last ten years or the last month?
3	As a closed question, respondents are only given the option of four answers to choose from. However, there may be other reasons for going to the library. An 'Other' category with a 'please specify' space, or a longer list to choose from, such as social activity or book signing could also be added. As well, it might prove useful to add an instruction to this question that states 'mark all that apply'. This way the respondent can choose several options instead of one.
4	The question as asked is fine, but does not go far enough in getting the details. The library likely needs to know why the respondent's needs were not satisfied. This question should include a second part that asks the respondent to describe why his or her needs were not satisfied.
5	This is a double-barrelled question. The first problem is that you are asking the respondent two different things in one question. The second problem consists of the response categories provided. There are no instructions as to how to grade the responses. Do respondents rank the response? If so, what does 1 represent? Does 5 stand for poor or excellent?
6	This is an open question, which makes the various possible responses difficult to code and tabulate. If a list of answers (including a final 'Other' choice with a space to specify the response) were provided, it would be a lot easier for respondents to answer and data analysers to tabulate the results.
7	This question asks for a 'Yes' or 'No' response, however, the respondent may not know, or may have no opinion regarding any improvements to the library.

Question	
8	This question should come after question 9 because the respondents are asked whether they approve or disapprove of the entire set of proposals. What if the respondent was not aware of the proposals? What if the respondent agreed with some of the proposals and disagreed with others? The available responses may not give you a true measure of the proposals. The wording of Question 8 should be changed in order to avoid bias in the response. The 'Go to' part of Question 8 also contains a problem. It sends the respondent to Question 11; therefore respondents who answered 'disapprove' to Question 8 would not be given the opportunity to respond to Questions 9 or 10. The instruction should read '(Go to Question 10)'.
9	This question ('Are you aware of these proposals?') should come before Question 8 ('Do you approve of disapprove of the recent proposals...?') since Question 9 is only relevant to Question 8 if the answer is 'Yes'. Also, Question 9 could be improved by instructing respondents to select the appropriate 'Yes' or 'No' category.
10	Unfortunately, this question is very open.
11	This question is worded in a way that presents the reader with a double negative. Because it is not entirely clear what the question is asking, some respondents could interpret it in different ways. A simple solution would be to reword it to say: 'Are you in favour of the library extending the hours of operation?' Include a list of responses such as '__Yes __No __ Don't care'.
12	This particular question is a sensitive one and one which respondent's may not feel inclined to answer or answer truthfully. It may be best to delete this question. If, however, the level of education were relevant to the information being collected and needs to be asked, then a closed question would allow for better quantitative analysis.

Part B

Techniques to Analyse Data

Chapter 2 :
DATA PRESENTATION

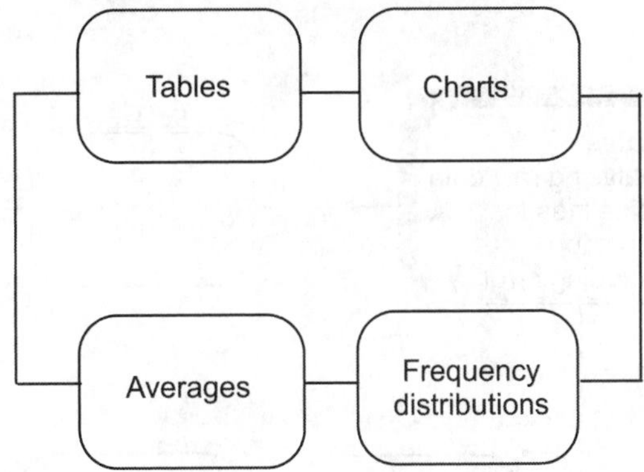

Introduction

You now know how to collect data. So what do you do with them next? You have to analyse and present the data you have collected so that they can be of use. This chapter begins by looking at how data can be presented in tables and charts. Such methods are helpful in presenting key data in a concise and easy to understand way. They are, however, purely descriptive and offer little opportunity for further detailed numerical analysis of a situation.

Data that are a mass of numbers can usefully be summarised into a frequency distribution (effectively a table which details the frequency with which a particular value occurs). Histograms and ogives are the pictorial representation of grouped and cumulative frequency distributions and provide the link between the purely descriptive approach to data analysis and the numerical approach.

There are two initial measures that we can take from a set of data to help in such a situation: a measure of centrality (an average) and a measure of dispersion (or spread). In this chapter we will be looking at averages – their calculation, advantages and disadvantages and in the next chapter we will look at measures of dispersion.

An average is a representative figure that is used to give some impression of the size of all the items in the population. You may have thought that an average is simply 'an average' but there are in fact three main types of average: the mean, the mode, and the median.

Your objectives

After completing this chapter you should:

(a) Be able to present data using tables, pie charts and bar charts

(b) Be able to construct frequency distributions

(c) Be able to prepare histograms

(d) Be able to draw ogives

BPP LEARNING MEDIA

(e) Know the circumstances in which each data presentation format should be used

(f) Understand the difference between the arithmetic mean, mode and median of a set of data and be aware of their advantages and disadvantages

(g) Be able to calculate the arithmetic mean, mode and median of both ungrouped and grouped data

1 TABLES

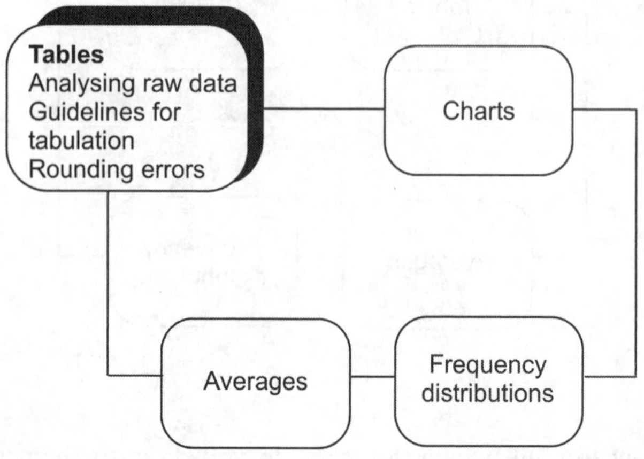

1.1 Analysing raw data

Definition

A **table** is a matrix of data in rows and columns, with the rows and columns having titles

Raw data (the list of results from a survey) needs to be summarised and analysed to give them meaning. This chapter starts with one of the basic ways – the preparation of a table.

Tabulation means putting data into tables. Since a table is two-dimensional, it can only show two variables. For example, the resources required to produce items in a factory could be tabulated, with one dimension (rows or columns) representing the items produced and the other dimension representing the resources.

Resources for production: all figures in pounds

	Product items				
	A	*B*	*C*	*D*	*Total*
Resources					
Direct material A	X	X	X	X	X
Direct material B	X	X	X	X	X
Direct labour grade 1	X	X	X	X	X
Direct labour grade 2	X	X	X	X	X
Supervision	X	X	X	X	X
Machine time	X	X	X	X	X
Total	X	X	X	X	X

To tabulate data, you need to recognise what the two dimensions should represent, prepare rows and columns accordingly with suitable titles, and then insert the data into the appropriate places in the table.

1.2 Guidelines for tabulation

The table shown above illustrates certain guidelines which you should apply when presenting data in tabular form. These are as follows.

(a) The table should be given a clear title.

(b) All columns should be clearly labelled.

(c) Where appropriate, there should be clear sub-totals.

(d) A total column may be presented; this is usually the right-hand column.

(e) A total figure is often advisable at the bottom of each column of figures.

(f) Tables should not be packed with so much data that reading the information is difficult.

(g) Eliminate non-essential information, rounding large numbers to two or three significant figures.

(h) Do not hide important figures in the middle of the table. Consider ordering columns or rows by order of importance or magnitude.

EXAMPLE: TABLES

The total number of employees in a certain trading company is 1,000. They are employed in three departments: production, administration and sales. There are 600 people employed in the production department and 300 in administration. There are 110 male juveniles in employment, 110 female juveniles, and 290 adult females. The remaining employees are adult males.

In the production department there are 350 adult males, 150 adult females and 50 male juveniles, whilst in the administration department there are 100 adult males, 110 adult females and 50 juvenile males.

Required

Draw up a table to show all the details of employment in the company and its departments and provide suitable secondary statistics to describe the distribution of people in departments.

SOLUTION

The basic table required has the following two dimensions.

(a) Departments
(b) Age/sex analysis

Secondary statistics (not the same thing as secondary data) are supporting figures that are supplementary to the main items of data, and which clarify or amplify the main data.

A major example of secondary statistics is percentages. In this example, we could show one of the following.

(a) The percentage of the total work force in each department belonging to each age/sex group

(b) The percentage of the total of each age/sex group employed in each department

In this example, (a) has been selected but you might consider that (b) would be more suitable. Either could be suitable, depending of course on what purposes the data are being collected and presented for.

Analysis of employees

	Department							
	Production		*Administration*		*Sales*		*Total*	
	No	%	No	%	No	%	No	%
Adult males	350	58.4	100	33.3	**40	40	*490	49
Adult females	150	25.0	110	36.7	**30	30	290	29
Male juveniles	50	8.3	50	16.7	**10	10	110	11
Female juveniles	*50	8.3	*40	13.3	**20	20	110	11
Total	600	100.0	300	100.0	100	100	1,000	100

* Balancing figure to make up the column total

** Balancing figure then needed to make up the row total

1.3 Rounding errors

Rounding errors may become apparent when, for example, a percentages column does not add up to 100%. Any rounding should therefore be to the nearest unit and the potential size of errors should be kept to a tolerable level by rounding to a small enough unit (for example, to the nearest £10, rather than to the nearest £1,000).

2 CHARTS

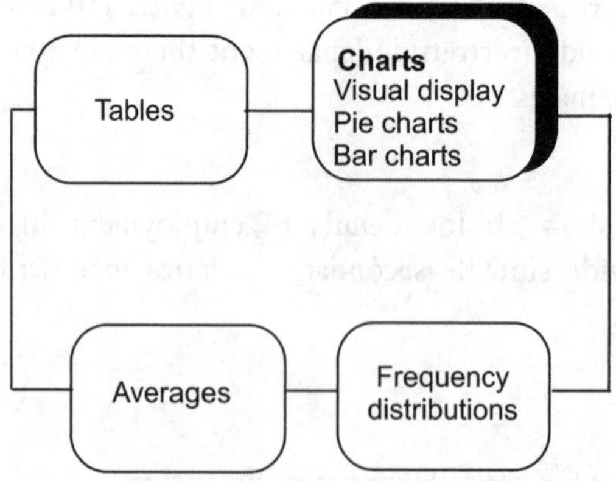

2.1 Visual display

Instead of presenting data in a table, it might be preferable to give a visual display in the form of a chart.

The purpose of a chart is to convey the data in a way that will demonstrate its meaning or significance more clearly than a table of data would. Charts are not always more

appropriate than tables, and the most suitable way of presenting data will depend on the following.

(a) What the data are intended to show. Visual displays usually make one or two points quite forcefully, whereas tables usually give more detailed information.

(b) Who is going to use the data. Some individuals might understand visual displays more readily than tabulated data.

We will be looking at the creation and interpretation of graphs and charts using spreadsheets in Chapter 6.

2.2 Pie charts

Definition

A **pie chart** is used to show pictorially the relative sizes of component elements of a total.

Such charts are called pie charts because they are circular, and so have the shape of a pie in a round pie dish and because the 'pie' is then cut into slices. Each slice represents a part of the total.

Pie charts have sectors of varying sizes, and you need to be able to draw sectors fairly accurately. To do this, you need a protractor. Working out sector sizes involves converting parts of the total into equivalent degrees of a circle.

EXAMPLE: PIE CHARTS

The costs of production at Factory A and Factory B during March 20X2 were as follows.

	Factory A		*Factory B*	
	£'000	%	£'000	%
Direct materials	70	35	50	20
Direct labour	30	15	125	50
Production overhead	90	45	50	20
Office costs	10	5	25	10
	200	100	250	100

Task

Show the costs for the factories in pie charts.

SOLUTION

To convert the components into degrees of a circle, we can use either the percentage figures or the actual cost figures.

(a) Using the percentage figures, the total percentage is 100%, and the total number of degrees in a circle is 360°. To convert from one to the other, we multiply each percentage value by 360/100 = 3.6.

	Factory A		*Factory B*	
	%	Degrees	%	Degrees
Direct materials	35	126	20	72
Direct labour	15	54	50	180
Production overhead	45	162	20	72
Office costs	5	18	10	36
	100	360	100	360

(b) Using the actual cost figures, we would multiply each cost by

	Factory A	*Factory B*
$\frac{\text{Number of degrees}}{\text{Total cost}}$	$\frac{360}{200} = 1.8$	$\frac{360}{250} = 1.44$

	Factory A		*Factory B*	
	£'000	Degrees	£'000	Degrees
Direct materials	70	126	50	72
Direct labour	30	54	125	180
Production overhead	90	162	50	72
Office costs	10	18	25	36
	200	360	250	360

A pie chart could be drawn for each factory, as follows. A protractor is used to measure the degrees accurately to obtain the correct sector sizes, although most people use a spreadsheet program to do it.

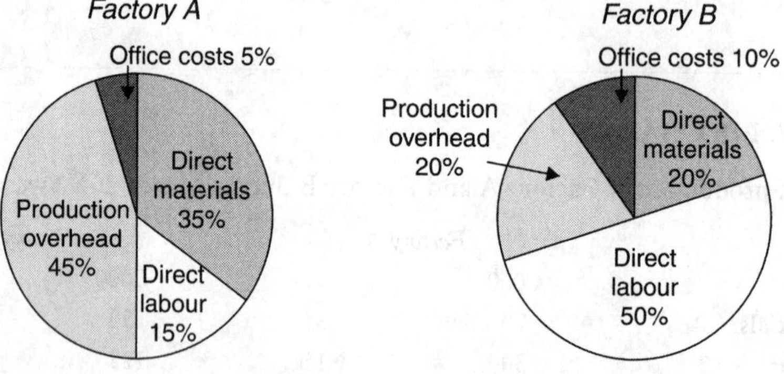

The advantages of pie charts are as follows.

(a) They give a simple pictorial display of the relative sizes of elements of a total.

(b) They show clearly when one element is much bigger than others.

(c) They can sometimes clearly show differences in the elements of two different totals. In the example above, the pie charts for factories A and B show how factory A's costs mostly consist of production overhead and direct materials, whereas at factory B, direct labour is the largest cost element.

The disadvantages of pie charts are as follows.

(a) They show only the relative sizes of elements. In the example of the two factories, for instance, the pie charts do not show that costs at Factory B were £50,000 higher in total than at Factory A.

(b) They involve calculating degrees of a circle and drawing sectors accurately, and this can be time consuming.

(c) It is sometimes difficult to compare sector sizes accurately by eye.

2.3 Bar charts

Definition

A **bar chart** is a chart in which quantities are shown in the form of bars.

The bar chart is one of the most common methods of presenting data in a visual form.

There are three main types of bar chart.

(a) Simple bar charts
(b) Component bar charts, including percentage component bar charts
(c) Multiple (or compound) bar charts

Simple bar charts

A simple bar chart is a chart consisting of one or more bars, in which the length of each bar indicates the magnitude of the corresponding data item.

EXAMPLE: A SIMPLE BAR CHART

A company's total sales for the years from 20X1 to 20X6 are as follows.

Year	*Sales* £'000
20X1	800
20X2	1,200
20X3	1,100
20X4	1,400
20X5	1,600
20X6	1,700

The data could be shown on a simple bar chart as follows.

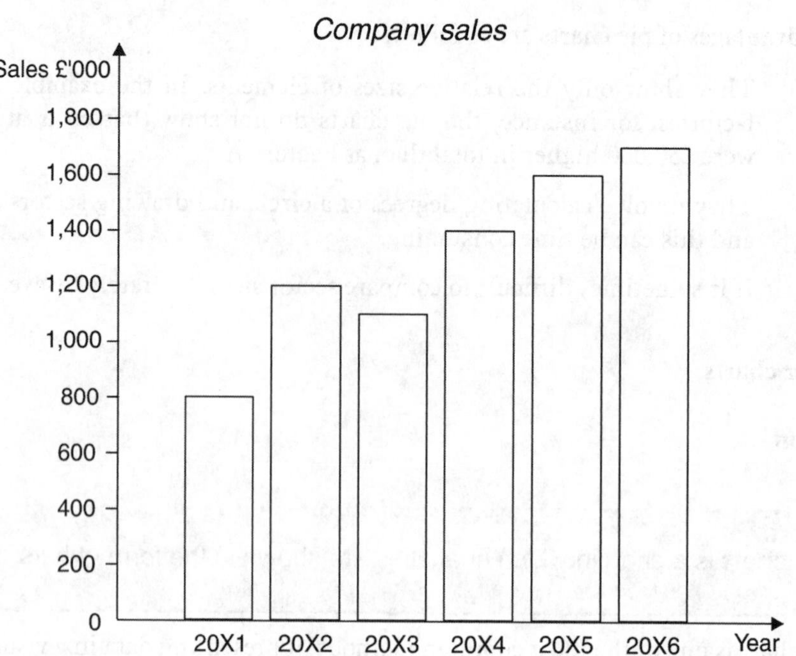

Figure 2.1: Simple bar chart

Each axis of the chart must be clearly labelled, and there must be a scale to indicate the magnitude of the data. Here, the y axis includes a scale for the amount of sales, and so readers of the bar chart can see not only that sales have been rising year by year (with 20X3 being an exception) but also what the actual sales have been each year.

Simple bar charts serve two purposes.

(a) They show the actual magnitude of each item.

(b) They enable one to compare magnitudes, by comparing the lengths of bars on the chart.

Component bar charts

A component bar chart is a bar chart that gives a breakdown of each total into its components.

EXAMPLE: A COMPONENT BAR CHART

Charbart plc's sales for the years from 20X7 to 20X9 are as follows.

	20X7	*20X8*	*20X9*
	£'000	£'000	£'000
Product A	1,000	1,200	1,700
Product B	900	1,000	1,000
Product C	500	600	700
Total	2,400	2,800	3,400

A component bar chart would show the following.

(a) How total sales have changed from year to year
(b) The components of each year's total

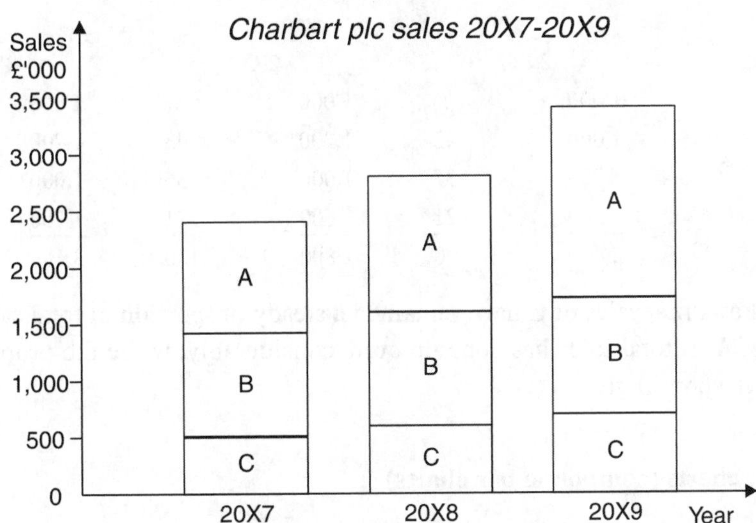

In this diagram the growth in sales is illustrated and the significance of growth in product A sales as the reason for the total sales growth is also fairly clear. The growth in product A sales would have been even clearer if product A had been drawn as the bottom element in each bar instead of the top one.

Percentage component bar charts

The difference between a component bar chart and a percentage component bar chart is that with a component bar chart, the total length of each bar (and the length of each component in it) indicates magnitude. A bigger amount is shown by a longer bar. With a percentage component bar chart, total magnitudes are not shown. If two or more bars are drawn on the chart, the total length of each bar is the same. The only varying lengths in a percentage component bar chart are the lengths of the sections of a bar, which vary according to the relative sizes of the components.

EXAMPLE: A PERCENTAGE COMPONENT BAR CHART

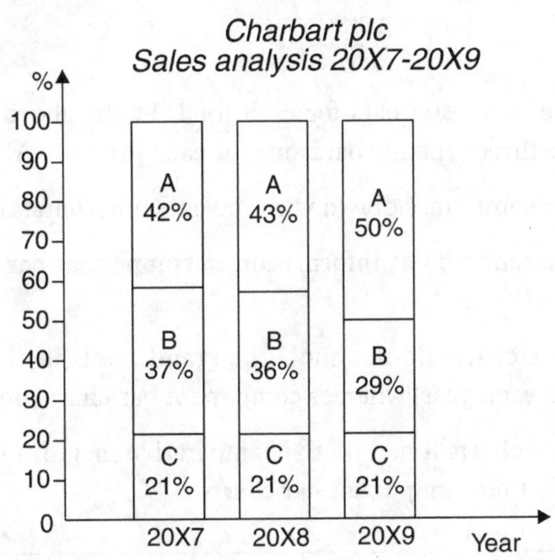

The information in the previous example of sales of Charbart plc could have been shown in a percentage component bar chart as follows.

Working

	20X7		*20X8*		*20X9*	
	£'000	%	£'000	%	£'000	%
Product A	1,000	42	1,200	43	1,700	50
Product B	900	37	1,000	36	1,000	29
Product C	500	21	600	21	700	21
Total	2,400	100	2,800	100	3,400	100

This chart shows that sales of C have remained a steady proportion of total sales, but the proportion of A in total sales has gone up quite considerably, while the proportion of B has fallen correspondingly.

Multiple bar charts (compound bar charts)

A multiple bar chart (or compound bar chart) is a bar chart in which two or more separate bars are used to present sub-divisions of data.

EXAMPLE: A MULTIPLE BAR CHART

The data on Charbart plc's sales could be shown in a multiple bar chart as follows.

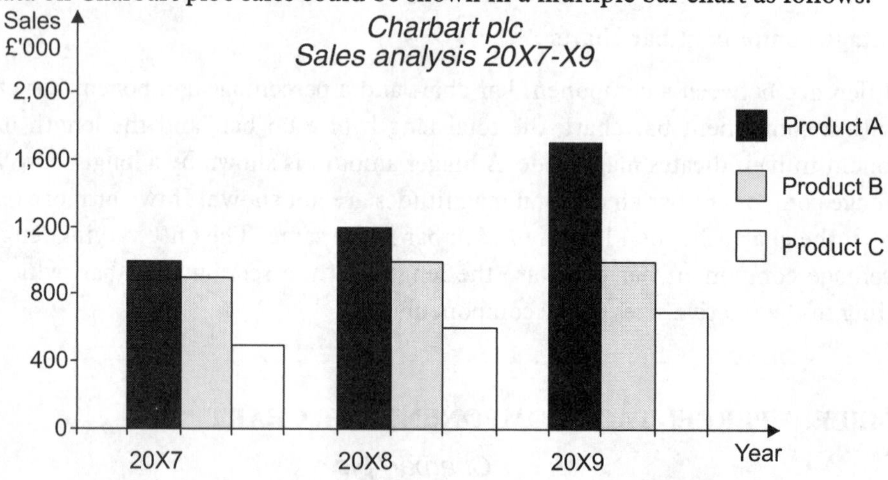

A multiple bar chart uses several bars for each total. In the above example, the sales in each year are shown as three separate bars, one for each product, A, B and C.

Multiple bar charts are sometimes drawn with the bars horizontal instead of vertical.

Multiple bar charts present similar information to component bar charts, except for the following.

(a) Multiple bar charts do not show the grand total (in the above example, the total output each year) whereas component bar charts do.

(b) Multiple bar charts illustrate the comparative magnitudes of the components more clearly than component bar charts.

Activity 1 **(40 minutes)**

Income for Lemmi Bank in 20X0, 20X1 and 20X2 is made up as follows.

	20X0	*20X1*	*20X2*
	£'000	£'000	£'000
Interest income	3,579	2,961	2,192
Commission income	857	893	917
Other income	62	59	70

Required

Using the above data, draw the following.

(a) A simple bar chart
(b) A component bar chart
(c) A percentage component bar chart
(d) A compound bar chart

3 FREQUENCY DISTRIBUTIONS

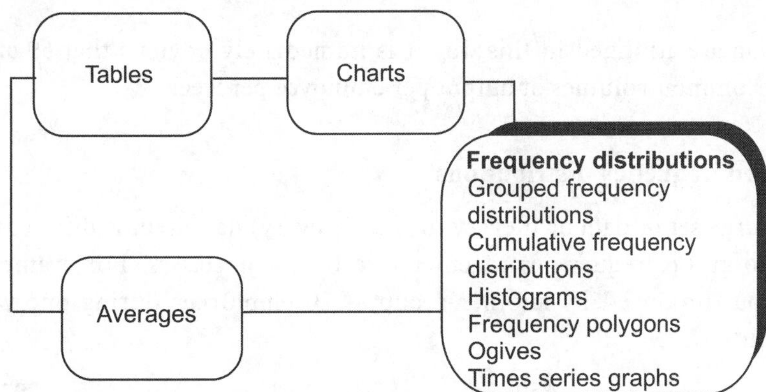

3.1 Introduction

Frequently the data collected from a statistical survey or investigation are simply a mass of numbers.

65	69	70	71	70	68	69	67	70	68
72	71	69	74	70	73	71	67	69	70

The raw data above yield little information as they stand; imagine how much more difficult it would be if there were hundreds or even thousands of data items. The data could, of course, be arranged in order size (an array) and the lowest and highest data items, as well as typical items, could be identified.

Definition

A **frequency distribution** (or *frequency table*) records the number of times each value occurs (the *frequency*).

Many sets of data, however, contain a limited number of data values, even though there may be many occurrences of each value. It can therefore be useful to organise the data into a frequency distribution recording the number of times each value occurs. A frequency distribution for the data shown above (the output in units of 20 employees during one week) is as follows.

Output of employees in one week in units

Output	*Number of employees (frequency)*
Units	
65	1
66	0
67	2
68	2
69	4
70	5
71	3
72	1
73	1
74	1
	20

When the data are arranged in this way it is immediately obvious that 69 and 70 units are the most common volumes of output per employee per week.

3.2 Grouped frequency distributions

If there is a large set of data or if every (or nearly every) data item is different, it is often convenient to group frequencies together into bands or classes. For example, suppose that the output produced by another group of 20 employees during one week was as follows, in units.

1,087	850	1,084	792
924	1,226	1,012	1,205
1,265	1,028	1,230	1,182
1,086	1,130	989	1,155
1,134	1,166	1,129	1,160

The range of output from the lowest to the highest producer is 792 to 1,265, a range of 473 units. This range could be divided into classes of say, 100 units (the class width or class interval), and the number of employees producing output within each class could then be grouped into a single frequency, as follows.

Output	*Number of employees (frequency)*
Units	
700 – 799	1
800 – 899	1
900 – 999	2
1,000 – 1,099	5
1,100 – 1,199	7
1,200 – 1,299	4
	20

Note, however, that once items have been 'grouped' in this way their individual values are lost.

Grouped frequency distributions of continuous variables

As well as being used for discrete variables (as above), grouped frequency distributions (or grouped frequency tables) can be used to present data for continuous variables.

EXAMPLE: A GROUPED FREQUENCY DISTRIBUTION FOR A CONTINUOUS VARIABLE

Suppose we wish to record the heights of 50 different individuals. The information might be presented as a grouped frequency distribution, as follows.

Height (cm)	*Number of individuals (frequency)*
Up to and including 154	1
Over 154, up to and including 163	3
Over 163, up to and including 172	8
Over 172, up to and including 181	16
Over 181, up to and including 190	18
Over 190	4
	50

Note the following points.

(a) It would be wrong to show the ranges as 0–154, 154–163, 163–172 and so on, because 154 cm and 163 cm would then be values in two classes, which is not permissible. Although each value should only be in one class, we have to make sure that each possible value can be included. Classes such as 154–162, 163–172 would not be suitable since a height of 162.5 cm would not belong in either class. Such classes could be used for discrete variables, however.

(b) There is an *open-ended* class at each end of the range. This is because heights up to 154 cm and over 190 cm are thought to be uncommon, so that a single 'open-ended' class is used to group all the frequencies together.

Preparing grouped frequency distributions

To prepare a grouped frequency distribution, a decision must be made about how wide each class should be. You should, however, generally observe the following guidelines.

(a) The size of each class should be appropriate to the nature of the data being recorded, and the most appropriate class interval varied according to circumstances.

(b) The upper and lower limits of each class interval should be suitable 'round' numbers for class intervals which are in multiples of 5, 10, 100, 1,000 and so on. For example, if the class interval is 10, and data items range in value from 23 to 62 (discrete values), the class intervals should be 20–29, 30–39, 40–49, 50–59 and 60–69, rather than 23–32, 33–42, 43–52 and 53–62.

(c) With continuous variables, either:

   (i) the upper limit of a class should be 'up to and including ...' and the lower limit of the next class should be 'over ...'; or

(ii) the upper limit of a class should be 'less than...', and the lower limit of the next class should be 'at least ...'.

Activity 2

The commission earnings for May 20X3 of the assistants in a department store were as follows (in pounds).

60	35	53	47	25	44	55	58	47	71
63	67	57	44	61	48	50	56	61	42
43	38	41	39	61	51	27	56	57	50
55	68	55	50	25	48	44	43	49	73
53	35	36	41	45	71	56	40	69	52
36	47	66	52	32	46	44	32	52	58
49	41	45	45	48	36	46	42	52	33
31	36	40	66	53	58	60	52	66	51
51	44	59	53	51	57	35	45	46	54
46	54	51	39	64	43	54	47	60	45

Required

Prepare a grouped frequency distribution classifying the commission earnings into categories of £5 commencing with '£25 and under £30'.

You should be able to interpret a grouped frequency distribution and express an interpretation in writing. In the previous example on heights, an interpretation of the data is fairly straightforward.

(a) Most heights fell between 154 cm and 190 cm.

(b) Most heights were in the middle of this range, with few people having heights in the lower and upper ends of the range.

3.3 Cumulative frequency distributions

Definition

A **cumulative distribution** (or cumulative frequency table) can be used to show the total number of times that a value above or below a certain amount occurs

Here is a grouped frequency distribution that we looked at earlier:

Output Units	Number of employees (frequency)
700 – 799	1
800 – 899	1
900 –999	2
1,000 – 1,099	5
1,100 – 1,199	7
1,200 – 1,299	4
	20

There are two possible cumulative frequency distributions for this.

1.	Cumulative frequency
≥ 700	20
≥ 800	19
≥ 900	18
≥1,000	16
≥1,100	11
≥1,200	4

2.	Cumulative frequency
< 800	1
< 900	2
<1,000	4
<1,100	9
<1,200	16
<1,300	20

Notes

(a) The symbol > means 'greater than' and ≥ means 'greater than or equal to'. The symbol < means 'less than' and ≤ means 'less than or equal to'. These symbols provide a convenient method of stating classes.

(b) The first cumulative frequency distribution shows that of the total of 20 employees, 19 produced 800 units or more, 18 produced 900 units or more, 16 produced 1,000 units or more and so on.

(c) The second cumulative frequency distribution shows that, of the total of 20 employees, one produced under 800 units, two produced under 900 units, four produced under 1,000 units and so on.

3.4 Histograms

Definition

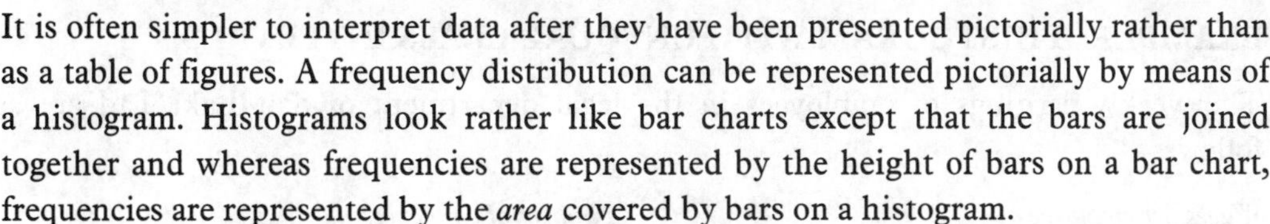

A **histogram** is the pictorial representation of a frequency distribution.

It is often simpler to interpret data after they have been presented pictorially rather than as a table of figures. A frequency distribution can be represented pictorially by means of a histogram. Histograms look rather like bar charts except that the bars are joined together and whereas frequencies are represented by the height of bars on a bar chart, frequencies are represented by the *area* covered by bars on a histogram.

Histograms of frequency distributions with equal class intervals

If all the class intervals are the same, as shown below, the bars of the histogram all have the same width and the heights will be proportional to the frequencies.

Output Units	Number of employees (frequency)
700 – 799	1
800 – 899	1
900 –999	2
1,000 – 1,099	5
1,100 – 1,199	7
1,200 – 1,299	4
	20

The histogram looks almost identical to the bar chart except that the bars are joined together.

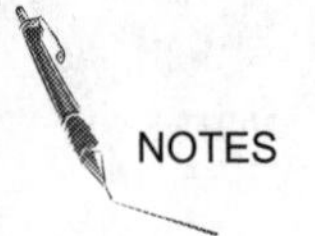

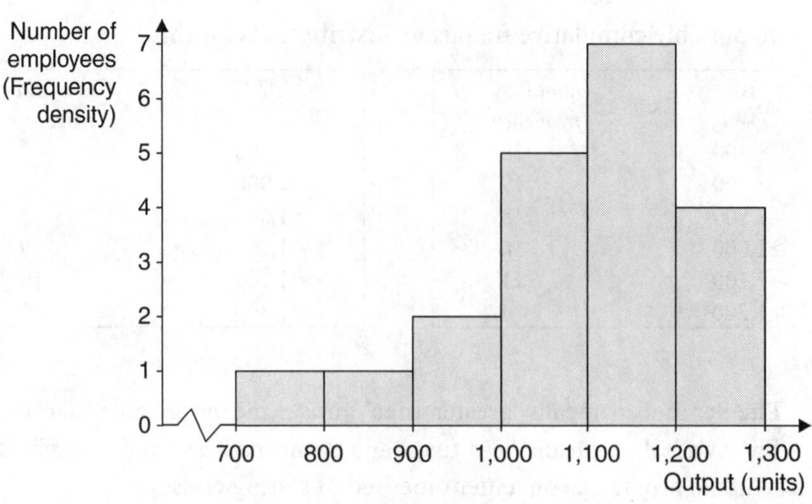

Figure 2.2: Histogram

Note that the discrete data have been treated as continuous, the intervals being changed to >700 but ≤ 800, >800 but ≤ 900 and so on.

Because the bars are joined together, when presenting discrete data the data must be treated as continuous so that there are no gaps between class intervals. For example, for a cricketer's scores in various games the classes would have to be ≥0 but <10, ≥10 but <20 and so on, instead of 0–9, 10–19 and so on.

Histograms of frequency distributions with unequal class intervals

If a distribution has unequal class intervals, the heights of the bars have to be adjusted for the fact that the bars do not have the same width.

EXAMPLE: A HISTOGRAM WITH UNEQUAL CLASS INTERVALS

The weekly earnings of employees in the legal department of Salt Lake Ltd are as follows.

Wages per employee	*Number of employees*
Up to and including £600	4
>£600 ≤ £800	6
>£800 ≤ £900	6
>£900 ≤ £1,200	6
>£1,200	3

The class intervals for wages per employee are not all the same, and range from £100 to £300.

A histogram is drawn as follows.

(a) The width of each bar on the chart must be proportionate to the corresponding class interval. In other words, the bar representing wages of >£600 ≤ £800, a range of £200, will be twice as wide as the bar representing wages of >£800 ≤ £900, a range of only £100.

(b) A standard width of bar must be selected. This should be the size of class interval which occurs most frequently. In our example, class intervals £100, £200 and £300 each occur once. An interval of £200 will be selected as the standard width.

(c) Open-ended classes must be closed off. It is usual for the width of such classes to be the same as that of the adjoining class. In this example, the class 'up to and including £600' will become > £400 ≤ £600 and the class 'more than £1,200' will become>£1,200 ≤ £1,500.

(d) Each frequency is then multiplied by (standard class width ÷ actual class width) to obtain the height of the bar in the histogram.

(e) The height of bars no longer corresponds to *frequency* but rather to *frequency density* and hence the vertical axis should be labelled frequency density.

(f)

Class interval	*Size of interval*	*Frequency*	*Adjustment*	*Height of bar*
>£400 ≤ £600	200	4	× 200/200	4
>£600 ≤ £800	20	6	× 200/200	6
>£800 ≤ £900	10	6	× 200/200	12
>£900 ≤ £1,200	30	6	× 200/300	4
>£1,200 ≤ £1,500	30	3	× 200/300	2

(i) The first two bars will be of normal height.

(ii) The third bar will be twice as high as the class frequency (6) would suggest, to compensate for the fact that the class interval, £100, is only half the standard size.

(iii) The fourth and fifth bars will be two thirds as high as the class frequencies (6 and 3) would suggest, to compensate for the fact that the class interval, £300, is 150% of the standard size.

Histogram of weekly earnings in the legal department: Salt Lake Ltd

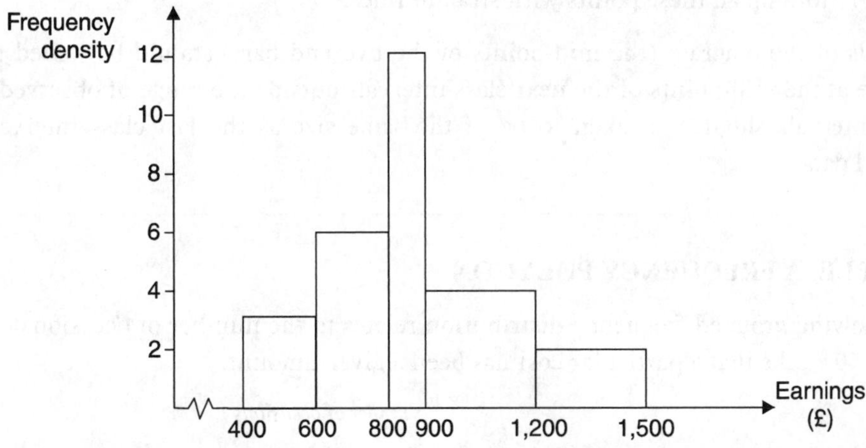

Note that the data is considered to be continuous since the gap between, for example, £799.99 and £800.00 is so small.

Activity 3 **(10 minutes)**

The sales force of a company have just completed a successful sales campaign. The performances of individual sales staff have been analysed as follows, into a grouped frequency distribution.

Sales	*Number of sales staff*
Up to £10,000	1
>£10,000 ≤ £12,000	10
>£12,000 ≤ £14,000	12
>£14,000 ≤ £18,000	8
>£18,000 ≤ £22,000	4
>£22,000	1

Required

Draw a histogram from this information.

3.5 Frequency polygons

A histogram is not a particularly accurate method of presenting a frequency distribution because, in grouping frequencies together in a class interval, it is assumed that these frequencies occur evenly throughout the class interval, which is unlikely. To overcome this criticism, we can convert a histogram into a frequency polygon, which is drawn on the assumption that, within each class interval, the frequency of occurrence of data items is not evenly spread. There will be more values at the end of each class interval nearer the histogram's peak (if any), and so the flat top on a histogram bar should be converted into a rising or falling line.

A frequency polygon is drawn from a histogram, in the following way.

(a) Mark the mid-point of the top of each bar in the histogram.
(b) Join up all these points with straight lines.

The ends of the diagram (the mid-points of the two end bars) should be joined to the base line at the mid-points of the next class intervals outside the range of observed data. These intervals should be taken to be of the same size as the last class intervals for observed data.

EXAMPLE: A FREQUENCY POLYGON

The following grouped frequency distribution relates to the number of occasions during the past 40 weeks that a particular cost has been a given amount.

Cost £	*Number of occasions*
> 800 ≤ 1,000	4
>1,000 ≤ 1,200	10
>1,200 ≤ 1,400	12
>1,400 ≤ 1,600	10
>1,600 ≤ 1,800	4
	40

Task

Prepare a frequency polygon.

SOLUTION

A histogram is first drawn, in the way described earlier. All classes are of the same width.

The mid-points of the class intervals outside the range of observed data are 700 and 1,900.

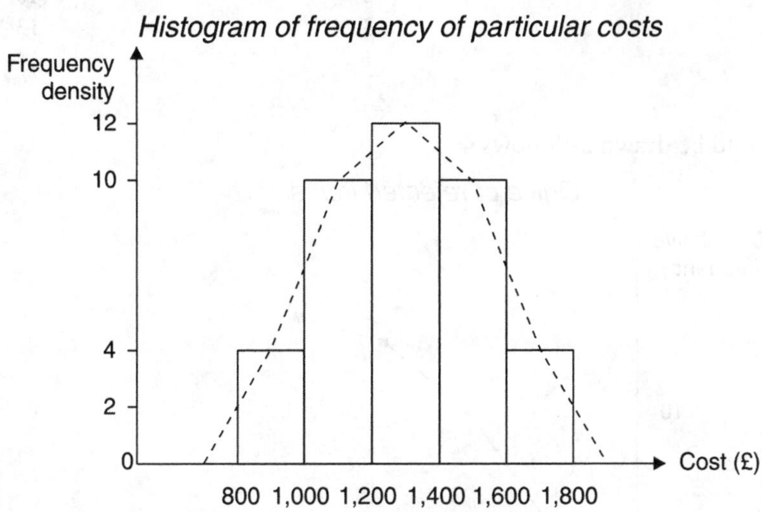

Frequency curves

Because a frequency polygon has straight lines between points, it too can be seen as an inaccurate way of presenting data. One method of obtaining greater accuracy would be to make the class intervals smaller. If the class intervals of a distribution were made small enough the frequency polygon would become very smooth. It would become a curve.

3.6 Ogives

Definition

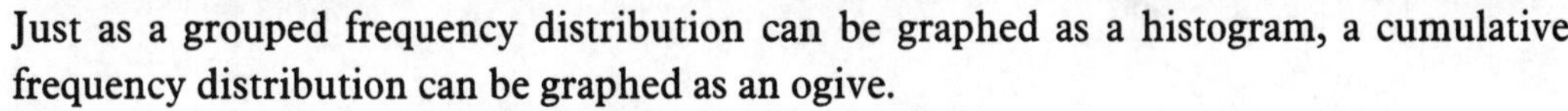

An **ogive** shows the cumulative number of items with a value less than or equal to, or alternatively greater than or equal to, a certain amount.

Just as a grouped frequency distribution can be graphed as a histogram, a cumulative frequency distribution can be graphed as an ogive.

EXAMPLE: OGIVES

Consider the following frequency distribution.

Number of faulty units rejected on inspection	*Frequency*	*Cumulative frequency*
$>0 \leq 1$	5	5
$>1 \leq 2$	5	10
$>2 \leq 3$	3	13
$>3 \leq 4$	1	14
	14	

An ogive would be drawn as follows.

Ogive of rejected items

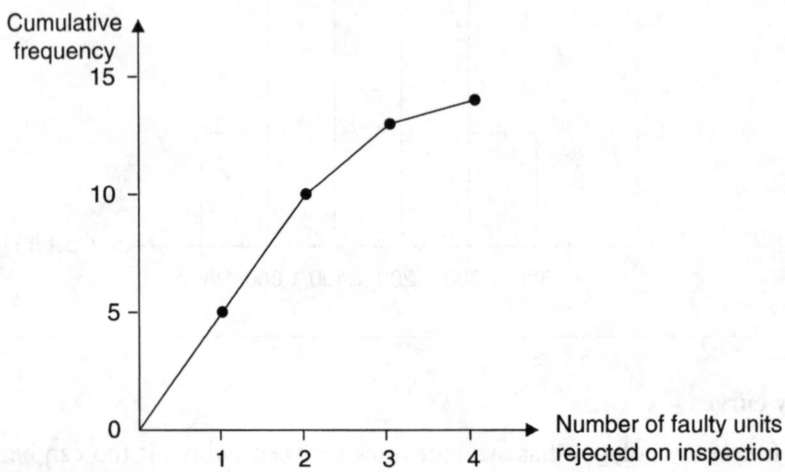

The ogive is drawn by plotting the cumulative frequencies on the graph, and joining them with straight lines. Although many ogives are more accurately curved lines, you can use straight lines in drawing an ogive in an examination. An ogive drawn with straight lines may be referred to as a cumulative frequency *polygon* (or cumulative frequency *diagram*) whereas one drawn as a curve may be referred to as a cumulative frequency *curve*.

For grouped frequency distributions, where we work up through values of the variable, the cumulative frequencies are plotted against the *upper* limits of the classes. For example, for the class 'over 2, up to and including 3', the cumulative frequency should be plotted against 3.

Activity 4 **(10 minutes)**

A grouped frequency distribution for the volume of output produced at a factory over a period of 40 weeks is as follows.

Output (units)	*Number of times output achieved*
>0 ≤ 200	4
>200 ≤ 400	8
>400 ≤ 600	12
>600 ≤ 800	10
>800 ≤ 1,000	6
	40

Task

Draw an appropriate ogive, and estimate the number of weeks in which output was 550 units or less.

We can also draw ogives to show the cumulative number of items with values greater than or equal to some given value.

EXAMPLE: DOWNWARD-SLOPING OGIVES

Output at a factory over a period of 80 weeks is shown by the following frequency distribution.

Output per week Units	*Number of times output achieved*
> 0 ≤ 100	10
>100 ≤ 200	20
>200 ≤ 300	25
>300 ≤ 400	15
>400 ≤ 500	10
	80

If we want to draw an ogive to show the number of weeks in which output exceeded a certain value, the cumulative total should begin at 80 and drop to 0. In drawing an ogive when we work down through values of the variable, the descending cumulative frequency should be plotted against the lower limit of each class interval.

Lower limit of interval	*Frequency*	*Cumulative ('more than') frequency*
0	10	80
100	20	70
200	25	50
300	15	25
400	10	10
500	0	0

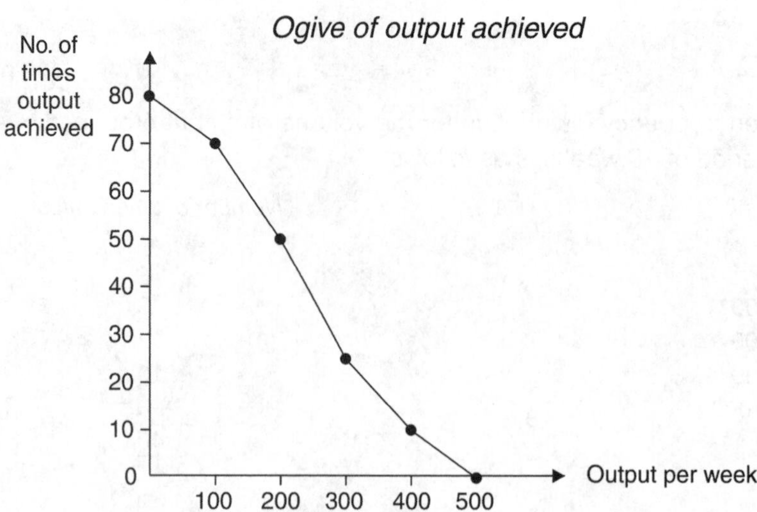

Make sure that you understand what this curve shows.

For example, 350 on the x axis corresponds with about 18 on the y axis. This means that output of 350 units or more was achieved 18 times out of the 80 weeks.

Activity 5 **(5 minutes)**

If you wanted to produce an ogive showing the cumulative number of students in a class with an exam mark of 55% or more, would you need an upward-sloping or a downward-sloping ogive?

3.7 Time series graphs

Definitions

A **time series** consists of numerical data collected, observed or recorded at regular intervals of time each hour, day, month, quarter or year. More specifically, it is any set of data in which observations are arranged in chronological order. A graph of a time series is called a **historigram** (note the 'ri'; this is not the same as a histogram).

Examples of time series are the weekly prices of coffee in Brazil, the monthly consumption of electricity in a certain town, the monthly total of passengers carried by rail, the quarterly sales of a certain car, the annual rainfall in London over a number of years, the enrolment of students in a college or university over a number of years and so forth.

A time series graph measures time on the x-axis and the variable or variables in which we are interested on the y-axis. They also reveal trends. A trend is a general tendency for a variable to rise or fall.

A component time series is data in which various classifications (for example, sales in the four branches of a retail organisation each month) can be thought of as the components of a meaningful total (the total monthly sales of the retail organisation). A multiple time series, on the other hand, is data which have classifications for each time period that cannot be added to form meaningful totals. An example would be prices of selected food items, such as tea (per packet), bread (per loaf) and caviar (per jar).

We will be returning to this topic in Chapter 5.

EXAMPLE: TIME SERIES

The following data show the sales of a product in the period 20X6–X8.

Year	*Quarter 1*	*Quarter 2*	*Quarter 3*	*Quarter 4*
	'000	'000	'000	'000
20X6	86	42	57	112
20X7	81	39	55	107
20X8	77	35	52	99

Required

Plot a time series of the above data.

SOLUTION

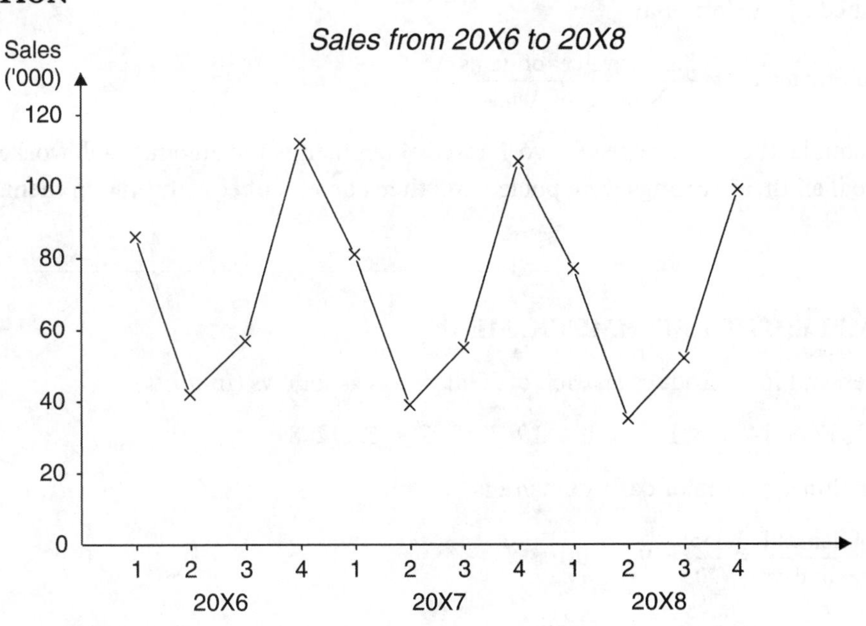

4 AVERAGES

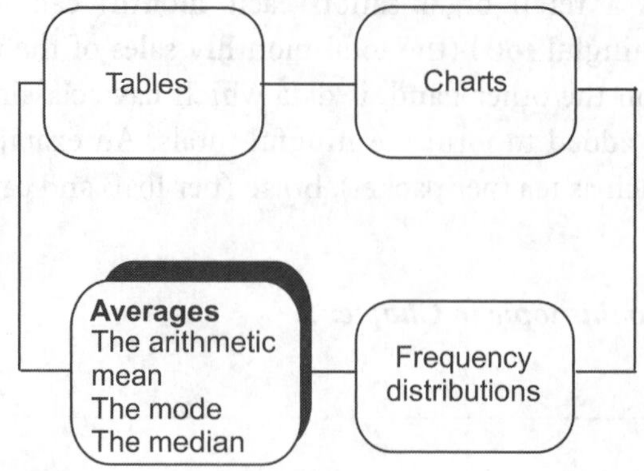

4.1 The arithmetic mean

Definition

The **arithmetic mean** is calculated from the sum of values of items divided by the number of items. The arithmetic mean of a variable x is shown as $\bar{x}$ ('x bar').

The arithmetic mean is the best known type of average. For ungrouped data, it is calculated by the formula

$$\text{Arithmetic mean} = \frac{\text{Sum of values of items}}{\text{Number of items}}$$

For example, the mean wage of a work force of ten men is the amount each worker would receive if all their earnings were pooled and then shared out equally among them.

EXAMPLE: THE ARITHMETIC MEAN

The demand for a product on each of 20 days was as follows (in units).

3 12 7 17 3 14 9 6 11 10 1 4 19 7 15 6 9 12 12 8

The arithmetic mean of daily demand is

$$\frac{\text{Sum of demand}}{\text{Number of days}} = \frac{185}{20} = 9.25 \text{ units}$$

The arithmetic mean of a variable x is shown as $\bar{x}$ ('x bar').

Thus in the above example $\bar{x}$ = 9.25 units.

In the above example, demand on any one day is never actually 9.25 units. The arithmetic mean is merely an average representation of demand on each of the 20 days.

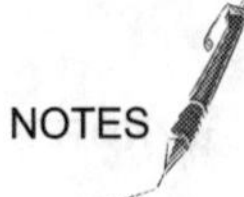

Finding the arithmetic mean of data in a frequency distribution

When analysing data it is more likely that you will be asked to calculate the arithmetic mean of a frequency distribution. In our previous example, the frequency distribution would be shown as follows.

Daily demand	*Frequency*	*Demand × frequency*
x	*f*	*fx*
1	1	1
3	2	6
4	1	4
6	2	12
7	2	14
8	1	8
9	2	18
10	1	10
11	1	11
12	3	36
14	1	14
15	1	15
17	1	17
19	1	19
	20	185

$$\bar{x} = \frac{185}{20} = 9.25$$

The summation sign, sigma(Σ)

The statistical notation for the arithmetic mean of a set of data uses the symbol Σ (sigma). Σ means 'the sum of' and is used as shorthand to mean 'the sum of a set of values'.

Thus, in the previous example:

(a) Σf would mean the sum of all the frequencies, which is 20;

(b) Σfx would mean the sum of all the values of 'frequency multiplied by daily demand', that is, all 14 values of fx, so Σfx = 185.

The symbolic formula for the arithmetic mean of a frequency distribution

Using the Σ sign, the formula for the arithmetic mean of a frequency distribution is

$$\bar{x} = \frac{\Sigma fx}{n} \text{ or } \frac{\Sigma fx}{\Sigma f}$$

where n is the number of values recorded, or the number of items measured.

Finding the arithmetic mean of grouped data in class intervals

You might also be asked to calculate (or at least approximate) the arithmetic mean of a frequency distribution, where the frequencies are shown in class intervals.

Using the previous example, the frequency distribution might have been shown as follows.

NOTES

Daily demand	*Frequency*
$> 0 \leq 5$	4
$> 5 \leq 10$	8
$>10 \leq 15$	6
$>15 \leq 20$	2
	20

There is, of course, an extra difficulty with finding the average now; as the data have been collected into classes, a certain amount of detail has been lost and the values of the variables to be used in the calculation of the mean are not clearly specified.

To calculate the arithmetic mean of grouped data we therefore need to decide on a value which best represents all of the values in a particular class interval.

The mid-point of each class interval is conventionally taken, on the assumption that the frequencies occur evenly over the class interval range. In the example above, the variable is discrete, so the first class includes 1, 2, 3, 4 and 5, giving a mid-point of 3. With a continuous variable (such as quantities of fuel consumed in litres), the mid-points would have been 2.5, 7.5 and so on. Once the value of x has been decided, the mean is calculated in exactly the same way as in Paragraph 4.1

EXAMPLE: THE ARITHMETIC MEAN OF GROUPED DATA

Daily demand	*Mid point*	*Frequency*	
	x	*f*	*fx*
$>0 \leq 5$	3	4	12
$>5 \leq 10$	8	8	64
$>10 \leq 15$	13	6	78
$>15 \leq 20$	18	2	36
		$\Sigma f = 20$	$\Sigma fx = 190$

$$\text{Arithmetic mean } \bar{x} = \frac{\Sigma fx}{\Sigma f} = \frac{190}{20} = 9.5 \text{ units}$$

Because the assumption that frequencies occur evenly within each class interval is not quite correct in this example, our approximate mean of 9.5 is not exactly correct, and is in error by 0.25.

As the frequencies become larger, the size of this approximating error should become smaller.

Finding the arithmetic mean of combined data

Suppose that the mean age of a group of five people is 27 and the mean age of another group of eight people is 32. How would we find the mean age of the whole group of thirteen people?

Remember that the arithmetic mean is calculated as

$$\frac{\text{Sum of values of items}}{\text{Number of items}}$$

The sum of the ages in the first group is 5 × 27 = 135
The sum of the ages in the second group is 8 × 32 = 256
The sum of all 13 ages is 135 + 256 = 391

The mean age is therefore $\frac{391}{13}$ = 30.07 years.

Activity 6 **(5 minutes)**

The mean weight of 10 units at 5 kg, 10 units at 7 kg and 20 units at X kg is 8 kg. What is the value of X?

The advantages and disadvantages of the arithmetic mean

The **advantages** of the arithmetic mean are as follows.

(a) It is easy to calculate.

(b) It is widely understood.

(c) The value of every item is included in the computation of the mean and so it can be determined with arithmetical precision and is representative of the whole set of data.

(d) It is supported by mathematical theory and is suited to further statistical analysis.

The **disadvantages** of the arithmetic mean are as follows.

(a) Its value may not correspond to any actual value. For example, the 'average' family might have 2.3 children, but no family can have exactly 2.3 children.

(b) An arithmetic mean might be distorted by extremely high or low values. For example, the mean of 3, 4, 4 and 6 is 4.25, but the mean of 3, 4, 4, 6 and 15 is 6.4. The high value, 15, distorts the average and in some circumstances the mean would be a misleading and inappropriate figure. (Note that extreme values are not uncommon in economic data.)

Activity 7 **(10 minutes)**

For the week ended 15 November, the wages earned by the 69 operators employed in the machine shop of Mermaid Ltd were as follows.

Wages	*Number of Operatives*
≤ £300	3
>£300 ≤ £350	11
>£350 ≤ £400	16
>£400 ≤ £450	15
>£450 ≤ £500	10
>£500 ≤ £550	8
>£550	6
	69

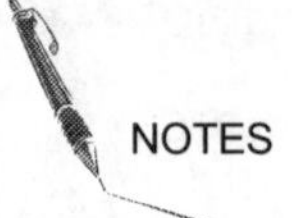

Required

Calculate the arithmetic mean wage of the machine operators of Mermaid Ltd for the week ended 15 November.

4.2 The mode

The second type of average is the mode or modal value.

Definition

The **mode** is an average which indicates the most frequently occurring value.

EXAMPLE: THE MODE

The daily demand for stock in a ten-day period is as follows.

Demand	*Number of days*
Units	
6	3
7	6
8	1
	10

The mode is 7 units, because it is the value which occurs most frequently.

Finding the mode of a grouped frequency distribution

The mode of a grouped frequency distribution can be calculated from a histogram.

EXAMPLE: FINDING THE MODE FROM A HISTOGRAM

Consider the following grouped frequency distribution.

Value		*Frequency*
At least	*Less than*	
0	10	0
10	20	50
20	30	150
30	40	100

The modal class (the one with the highest frequency) is 'at least 20, less than 30'. But how can we find a single value to represent the mode?

What we need to do is draw a histogram of the frequency distribution.

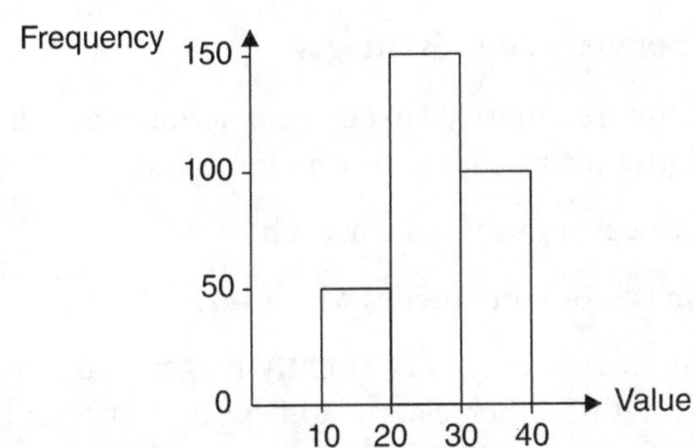

The modal class is always the class with the tallest bar, which may not be the class with the highest frequency if the classes do not all have the same width.

We can estimate the mode graphically as follows.

(a) Join with a straight line the top left-hand corner of the bar for the modal class and the top left-hand corner of the next bar to the right.

(b) Join with a straight line the top right-hand corner of the bar for the modal class and the top right-hand corner of the next bar to the left.

Where these two lines intersect, we find the estimated modal value. In this example it is approximately 27.

Histogram showing mode

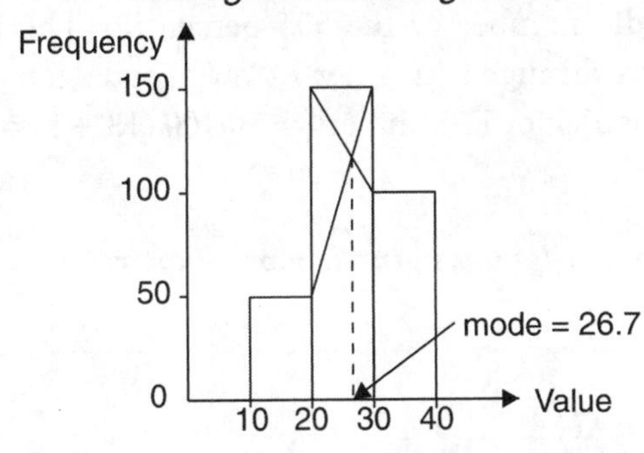

We are assuming that the frequencies occur evenly within each class interval but this may not always be correct. It is unlikely that the 150 values in the modal class occur evenly. Hence the mode in a grouped frequency distribution is only an estimate.

The advantages and disadvantages of the mode

The mode is a more appropriate average to use than the mean in situations where it is useful to know the most common value. For example, if a manufacturer wishes to start production in a new industry, it might be helpful to him to know what sort of product made by that industry is most in demand with customers.

The **advantages** of the mode are as follows.

(a) It is easy to find.

(b) It is not influenced by a few extreme values.

(c) It can be used for data which are not even numerical (unlike the mean and median).

(d) It can be the value of an actual item in the distribution.

The mode does have a number of **disadvantages**.

(a) It may be unrepresentative; it takes no account of a high proportion of the data, only representing the most common value.

(b) It does not take every value into account

(c) There can be two or more modes within a set of data.

(d) If the modal class is only very slightly bigger than another class, just a few more items in this other class could mean a substantially different result, suggesting some instability in the measure.

4.3 The median

The third type of average is the median.

Definition

> The **median** is the value of the middle member of a distribution once all of the items have been arranged in order of magnitude.

The median is the middle number or the 50th percentile. The position of a particular percentile (P) in n items arranged in order of magnitude can be calculated by P/100 (n+1). Calculating the median of 13 numbers = 50/100 (13 +1) = 7th number.

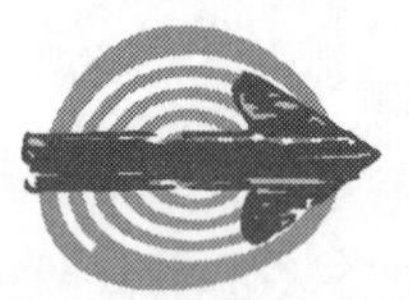

We will be looking at percentiles again in the next chapter.

EXAMPLE: THE MEDIAN

The median of the following nine values:

8 6 9 12 15 6 3 20 11

is found by taking the middle item (the fifth one) in the array:

3 6 6 8 9 11 12 15 20

The median is 9.

The middle item of an odd number of items is calculated as the $\frac{(n+1)^{th}}{2}$ item.

Consider the following array.

1 2 2 2 3 5 6 7 8 11

The median is 4 because, with an even number of items, we have to take the arithmetic mean of the two middle ones (in this example, (3 + 5)/2 = 4). When there are many items, however, it is not worth doing this.

Activity 8 **(10 minutes)**

The following times taken to produce a batch of 100 units of Product X have been noted.

21 min	17 min	24 min	11 min	37 min	27 min
20 min	15 min	17 min	23 min	29 min	30 min
24 min	18 min	17 min	21 min	24 min	20 min

What is the median time?

Finding the median of an ungrouped frequency distribution

The median of an ungrouped frequency distribution is found in a similar way. Consider the following distribution.

Value x	*Frequency* f	*Cumulative frequency*
8	3	3
12	7	10
16	12	22
17	8	30
19	5	35
	35	

The median would be the (35 + 1)/2 = 18th item. The 18th item has a value of 16, as we can see from the cumulative frequencies in the right hand column of the above table.

Finding the median of a grouped frequency distribution

We can establish the median of a grouped frequency distribution from an ogive.

EXAMPLE: THE MEDIAN FROM AN OGIVE

Construct an ogive of the following frequency distribution and hence establish the median.

Class	*Frequency*	*Cumulative frequency*
£		
≥ 340 < 370	17	17
≥ 370 < 400	9	26
≥ 400 < 430	9	35
≥ 430 < 460	3	38
≥ 460 < 490	2	40
	40	

SOLUTION

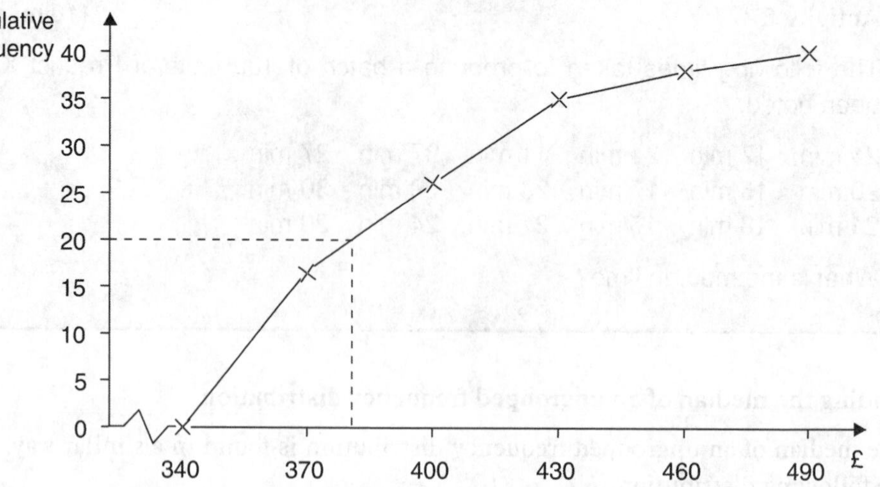

The median is at the $\frac{1}{2} \times (40 + 1)$ = between the 20th and 21st item. Reading off from the horizontal axis on the ogive, the value of the median is approximately £380.

Note that because we are assuming that the values are spread evenly within each class, the median calculated is only approximate.

The advantages and disadvantages of the median

The median is only of interest where there is a range of values and the middle item is of some significance. Perhaps the most suitable application of the median is in comparing changes in a 'middle of the road' value over time.

The median is easy to understand and (like the mode) is unaffected by extremely high or low values. It can be the value of an actual item in the distribution. On the other hand, it fails to reflect the full range of values, it is unsuitable for further statistical analysis and arranging the data in order of size can be tedious.

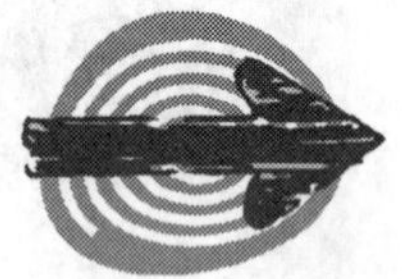

In the next chapter we will go on to look at measures of dispersion. These are used to describe the amount of scatter around the centre of the distribution. They include range, mean deviation, variance, standard deviation, and coefficient of variation.

Chapter roundup

- This chapter has considered a number of ways of presenting data and looked at the three main types of average.
- Tables are a simple way of presenting information about two variables.
- Charts often convey the meaning or significance of data more clearly than would a table.
- There are three main types of bar chart: simple, component (including percentage component) and multiple (or compound).
- Frequency distributions are used if values of particular variables occur more than once. Make sure that you know the difference between grouped frequency and cumulative frequency distributions.
- A frequency distribution can be represented pictorially by means of a histogram. The number of observations in a class is represented by the area covered by the bar, rather than by its height. Frequency polygons and frequency curves are perhaps more accurate methods of data presentation than the standard histogram.
- An ogive shows the cumulative number of items with a value less than or equal to, or alternatively greater than or equal to, a certain amount.
- The arithmetic mean is the best known type of average and is widely understood. It is used for further statistical analysis.
- The mode is the most frequently occurring value.
- The median is the value of the middle member of an array.
- The arithmetic mean, mode and median of a grouped frequency distributions can only be estimated approximately.
- You should now be able to calculate any of the three averages for a basic set of values, an ungrouped frequency distribution and a grouped frequency distribution.

Quick quiz

1 What are the main guidelines for tabulation?

2 What are the disadvantages of pie charts?

3 Name the three main types of bar chart.

4 How would you prepare a grouped frequency distribution?

5 What is a cumulative frequency distribution?

6 What are the computations needed to draw a histogram?

7 How would you draw a frequency polygon from a histogram?

8 How would you draw an ogive?

9 State a formula for the arithmetic mean of a frequency distribution.

10 Define the mode.

11 Explain how to estimate the mode from a histogram of a distribution.

12 Define the median.

13 How is the median of a grouped frequency distribution estimated?

Answers to quick quiz

1 (a) The table should be given a clear title.
  (b) All columns should be clearly labelled.
  (c) Where appropriate, there should be clear sub-totals.
  (d) A total column may be presented; this is usually the right hand column.
  (e) A total figure is often advisable at the bottom of each column of figures.
  (f) Tables should not be packed with too much data.
  (g) Round large numbers to two or three significant figures.
  (h) Order columns/rows by order of importance or magnitude.

2 (a) They only show the relative sizes of elements.
  (b) They involve calculating degrees of a circle and drawing sectors accurately (this can be time consuming).
  (c) It is sometimes difficult to compare sector sizes accurately by eye.

3
- Simple bar chart
- Component bar chart
- Compound bar chart

4 To prepare a grouped frequency distribution a decision must be made about how wide each class should be.
  (a) The size of each class should be appropriate to the nature of the data being recorded, and the most appropriate class interval varied according to circumstances.
  (b) The upper and lower limits of each class interval should be suitable 'round' numbers for class intervals which are in multiples of 5, 10, 100, 1000 and so on.
  (c) With continuous variables, either:
    (i) The upper limit of a class should be 'up to and including...' and the lower limit of the next class should be 'over...' or
    (ii) The upper limit of a class should be 'less than...', and the lower limit of the next class should be 'at least...'.

5 A cumulative frequency distribution (or cumulative frequency table) can be used to show the total number of times that a value above or below a certain amount occurs.

6 (a) The width of each bar on the chart must be appropriate to the corresponding class interval.
  (b) A standard width of each bar on the chart must be proportionate to the corresponding class interval which occurs most frequently.
  (c) Open-ended classes must be closed off. It is usual for the width of such classes to be the same as that of the adjoining class.

(d) Each frequency is then multiplied by (standard class width ÷ actual class width) to obtain the height of the bar in the histogram.

(e) The height of the bars no longer correspond to a frequency but rather to a frequency density and hence the vertical axis should be labelled frequency density.

7 A frequency polygon is drawn from a histogram in the following way.

(a) Mark the mid-point of the top of each bar in the histogram.

(b) Join up all these points with straight lines.

(c) The ends of the diagram (the mid-points of the two end bars) should be joined to the base line at the mid-points of the next class intervals outside the range of the obscured data. These intervals should be taken to be of the same size as the last class intervals for observed data.

8 An ogive shows the cumulative number of items with a value less than or equal to, or alternatively greater than or equal to a certain amount. It is drawn by plotting the cumulative frequencies of different class intervals.

9 Arithmetic mean, $\bar{x} = \frac{\Sigma fx}{n}$ or $\frac{\Sigma fx}{\Sigma f}$

10 The mode is an average which indicates the most frequently occurring value.

11 The mode can be estimated as follows.

(a) Join the left-hand corner of the bar for the modal class and the top left-hand corner of the next bar to the right with a straight line.

(b) Join the top right-hand corner of the bar for the modal class and the top right-hand corner of the next bar to the left with a straight line.

(c) The estimated modal value can be found where these two line ((a) and (b)) intersect.

12 The median is the value of the middle member of a distribution once all of the items have been arranged in order of magnitude.

13 The median of a grouped frequency distribution can be estimated from an ogive. The median will be the point where the present $\frac{n+1}{2}$ item (found on the vertical axis) corresponds to a value on the horizontal axis.

Answers to activities

1 (a)

20X0	*20X1*	*20X2*
£'000	£'000	£'000
3,579	2,961	2,192
857	893	917
62	59	70
4,498	3,913	3,179

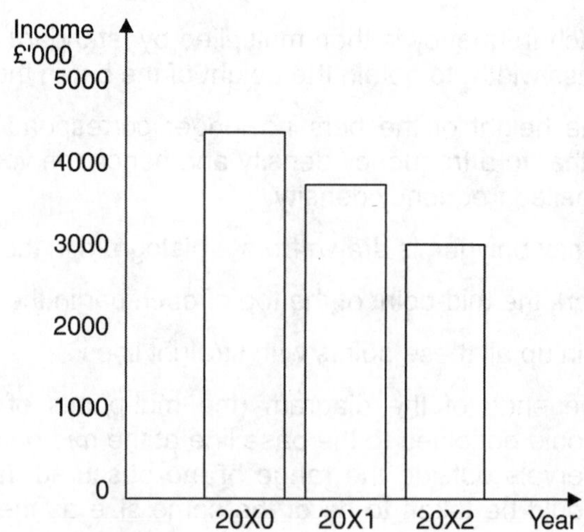

(b)

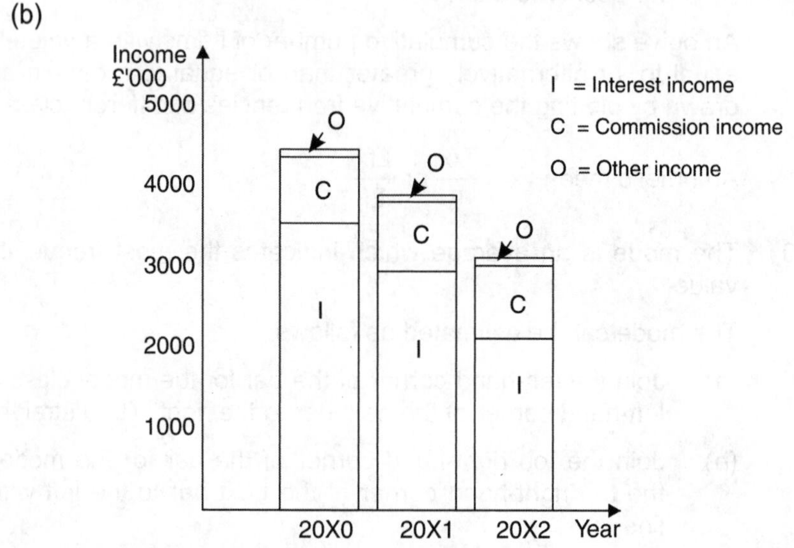

(c)

20X0		20X1		20X2	
£'000	%	£'000	%	£'000	%
3,579	80	2,961	76	2,192	69
857	19	893	23	917	29
62	1	59	1	70	2
4,498	100	3,913	100	3,179	100

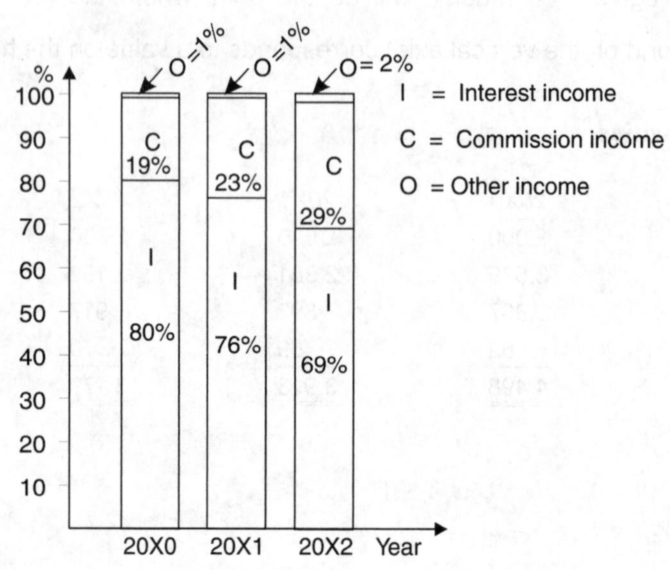

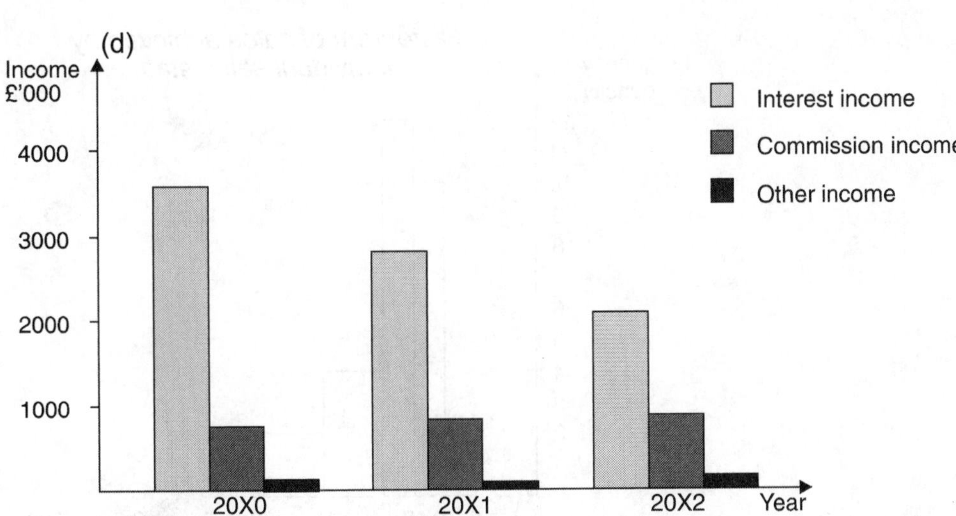

2 We are told what classes to use, so the first step is to identify the lowest and highest values in the data. The lowest value is £25 (in the first row) and the highest value is £73 (in the fourth row). This means that the class intervals must go up to '£70 and under £75'.

We can now set out the classes in a column, and then count the number of items in each class using tally marks.

Class interval	*Tally marks*	*Total*
£25 and less than £30	///	3
£30 and less than £35	////	4
£35 and less than £40	~~////~~ ~~////~~	10
£40 and less than £45	~~////~~ ~~////~~ ~~////~~	15
£45 and less than £50	~~////~~ ~~////~~ ~~////~~ ///	18
£50 and less than £55	~~////~~ ~~////~~ ~~////~~ ~~////~~	20
£55 and less than £60	~~////~~ ~~////~~ ///	13
£60 and less than £65	~~////~~ ///	8
£65 and less than £70	~~////~~ /	6
£70 and less than £75	///	3
	Total	100

3 Before drawing the histogram, we must decide on the following.

(a) A standard class width: £2,000 will be chosen.

(b) An open-ended class width. In this example, the open-ended class width will therefore be £2,000 for class '≤ £10,000' and £4,000 for the class '>£22,000'.

Class interval	*Size of width* £	*Frequency*	*Adjustment*	*Height of block*
≤ £10,000	2,000	1	× 2/2	1
>£10,000 ≤ £12,000	2,000	10	× 2/2	10
>£12,000 ≤ £14,000	2,000	12	× 2/2	12
>£14,000 ≤ £18,000	4,000	8	× 2/4	4
>£18,000 ≤ £22,000	4,000	4	× 2/4	2
>£22,000	4,000	1	× 2/4	1/2

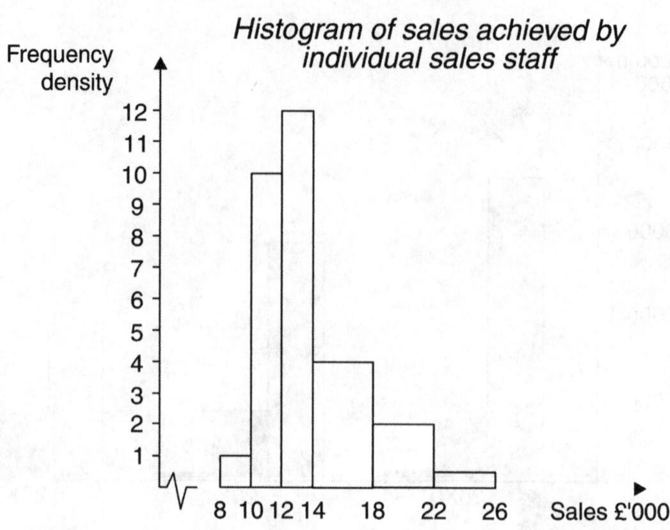

4

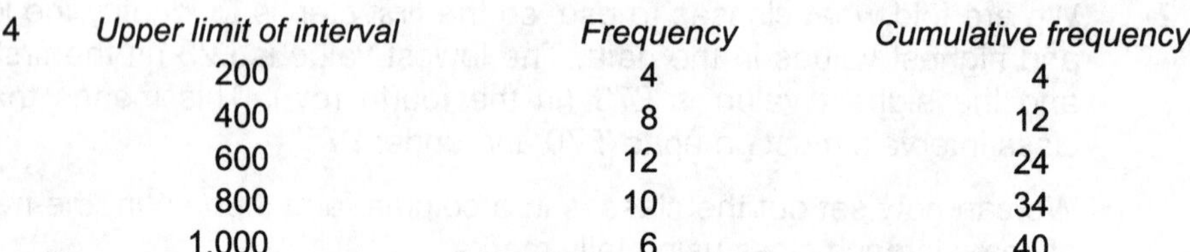

Upper limit of interval	Frequency	Cumulative frequency
200	4	4
400	8	12
600	12	24
800	10	34
1,000	6	40

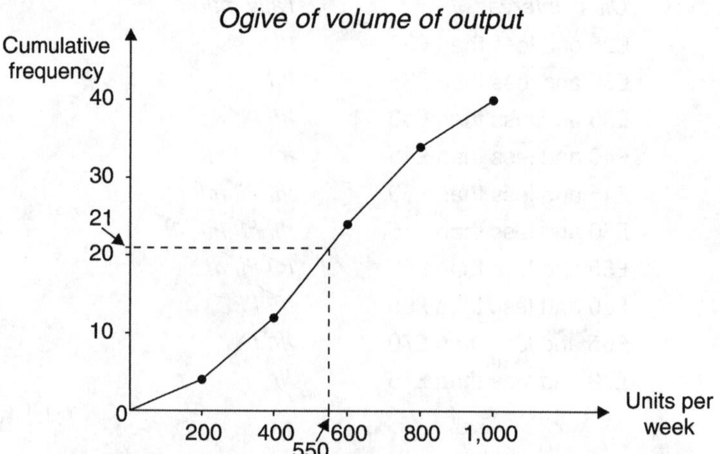

The dotted lines indicate that output of up to 550 units was achieved in 21 out of the 40 weeks.

5 A downward-sloping ogive

6 $\text{Mean} = \frac{\text{Sum of values of items}}{\text{Number of items}}$

Sum of first 10 units = $5 \times 10 = 50$ kg

Sum of second 10 units = $7 \times 10 = 70$ kg

Sum of third 20 units = $20 \times X = 20X$

Sum of all 40 units = $50 + 70 + 20X = 120 + 20X$

$\therefore$ Arithmetic mean = $8 = \frac{120 + 20X}{40}$

$$\therefore \quad 8 \times 40 = 120 + 20X$$
$$320 - 120 = 20X$$
$$10 = X$$

7 The mid-point of the range 'under £300' is assumed to be £275 and that of the range over £550 to be £575, since all other class intervals are £10. This is obviously an approximation which might result in a loss of accuracy; nevertheless, there is no better alternative assumption to use. Because wages can vary in steps of only 1p, they are virtually a continuous variable and hence the mid-points of the classes are halfway between their end points.

Mid-point of class	*Frequency*	
x	*f*	*fx*
£		
275	3	825
325	11	3,575
375	16	6,000
425	15	6,375
475	10	4,750
525	8	4,200
575	6	3,450
	69	29,175

Arithmetic mean = $\frac{£29,175}{69}$ = £422.83

8 The times can be arranged as follows.

11	15	17	17	17	18	20	20	21
21	23	24	24	24	27	29	30	37

The median = 21 mins. (We could have found the average of the 9th and 10th items if we had wanted to.)

NOTES

Chapter 3 :
DISPERSION AND SKEWNESS

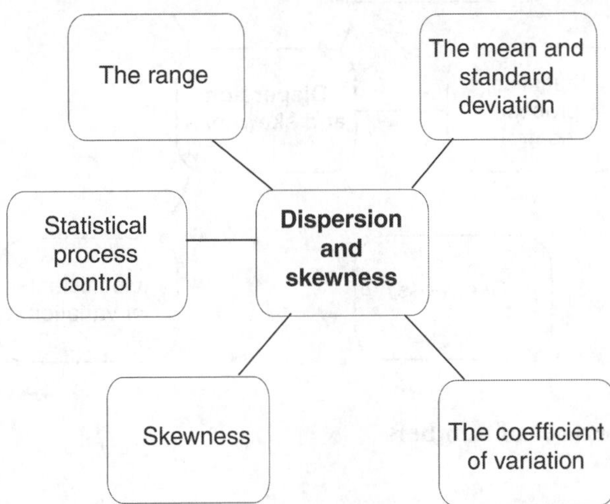

Introduction

As we have already seen, frequency distributions illustrate graphically how the values in the population of data are dispersed in the form of a shape. In order to use frequency distributions we need more information than just the shape. In the last chapter we discussed where the centre of the distribution is located, known as central tendency. We specifically looked at the averages: the arithmetic mean, median and mode.

An average is not in itself an adequate summary of a frequency distribution, we also need to know the dispersion of the data, that is, how spread out from the mean are the values (eg are they all closely clustered around the mean or are they well scattered). Measures of dispersion include the range, mean deviation, variance, standard deviation and the co-efficient of variation.

Your objectives

After completing this chapter you should:

(a) Understand the concept of dispersion

(b) Recognise that different measures of dispersion exist (range, quartile range, semi-interquartile range, standard deviation and variance) and calculate them

(c) Understand the idea of symmetry and how 'peaked' a distribution is

(d) Be able to explain statistical process control

1 THE RANGE

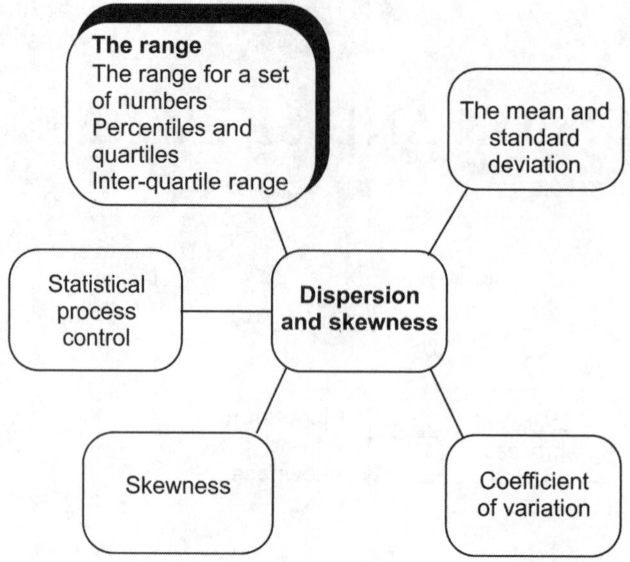

1.1 The range for a set of numbers

Definition

The **range** is the difference between the highest observation and the lowest observation

The range is the simplest measure of distribution and indicates the 'length' a distribution covers. It is determined by finding the difference between the lowest and highest value in a distribution.

Ungrouped data

The range for ungrouped data = highest extreme value – lowest extreme value. The range can be expressed as an interval such as 4-10, where 4 is the lowest value and 10 is highest. Often it is expressed as interval width; that is, the range of 4 – 10 is 6.

EXAMPLE

Suppose that the marks obtained in an examination were:

24, 27, 36, 48, 52, 52, 53, 53, 59, 60, 85, 90, 95

Lowest Value = 24 and Highest Value = 95

Thus the range = 95 – 24 = 71

The range is 71 marks.

Grouped data

The range for grouped data = highest upper class boundary – lowest lower class boundary

EXAMPLE

Consider the following data set of miles recorded by 120 sales people in one week

403	423	435	444	452	462	474	490	415	416	418	419	420	421	421
407	424	435	444	453	462	474	493	430	431	432	432	433	433	434
407	424	436	445	453	462	475	494	439	440	440	441	442	442	443
408	425	436	446	453	463	476	495	449	450	450	451	451	451	452
410	426	436	447	454	464	477	497	457	457	458	459	459	460	460
412	428	438	447	455	465	478	498	468	469	470	471	471	472	473
413	430	438	447	455	466	479	498	482	482	483	485	486	488	489
413	430	438	448	456	468	481	500	502	502	505	508	509	511	515

Grouping the data provides the following table:

Mileage	Frequency
400 – 419	12
420 – 439	27
440 – 459	34
460 – 479	24
480 – 499	15
500 – 519	8
	120

The highest upper class boundary = 509.5 – the lowest lower class boundary = 409.5

Thus the range = 509.5 – 409.5 = 100 miles

A great deal of information is ignored when computing the range, since only the largest and smallest data values are considered. The range value of a data set can be greatly influenced by the presence of just one unusually large or small value (outlier).

The disadvantage of using range is that it does not measure the spread of the majority of values in a data set –it only measures the spread between highest and lowest values. As a result, other measures are required in order to give a better picture of the data spread. The range is an informative tool used as a supplement to other measures such as the standard deviation or the inter-quartile range, but it should rarely be used as the only measure of spread.

The main properties of the range as a measure of dispersion are as follows.

(a) It is easy to find and to understand.
(b) It is easily affected by one or two extreme values.
(c) It gives no indication of spread between the extremes.
(d) It is not suitable for further statistical analysis.

Activity 1 **(10 minutes)**

Calculate the mean and the range of each of the following sets of data.

(a) x_1 = 4 8 7 3 5 16 24 5

(b) x_2 = 10 7 9 11 11 8 9 7

What do your calculations show about the dispersion of the data sets?

1.2 Percentiles and quartiles

A measure that expresses position in terms of a percentage is called a percentile for the data set.

Definition

Suppose a data set is arranged in ascending (or descending) order. The **pth percentile** is a number such that p% of the observations of the data set fall below and (100-p)% of the observations fall above it.

We have already defined the median as the 50th percentile. Other statistics can also be obtained from it and revolve around the idea of percentiles.

Deciles

In a similar way, a population could be divided into ten equal groups, and this time the value of each dividing point is referred to as a *decile*.

Quartiles

Quartiles are one means of identifying the range within which most of the values in the population occur. The lower quartile is the value below which 25% of the population fall and the upper quartile is the value above which 25% of the population fall. If there were 11 data items the lower quartile would be the third item and the upper quartile the ninth item. It follows that 50% of the total population fall between the lower and the upper quartiles.

The three quartiles, or the 25th percentile (Q1), the median (Q2) and 75th percentile (Q3) are often used to describe a data set because they divide the data set into four groups, with each group containing one-fourth (25%) of the observations. They would also divide the relative frequency distribution for a data set into four parts; each contains the same area (0.25), as shown below.

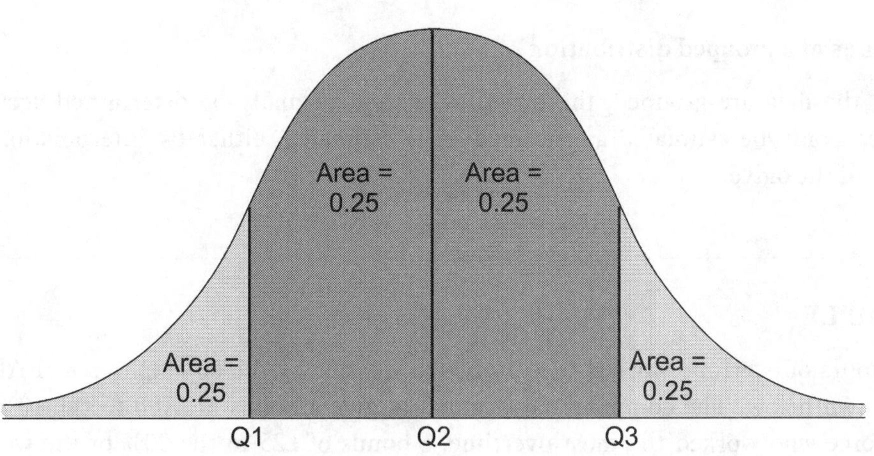

Figure 3.1: Inter-quartile range

The first part consists of values in the range from the 1st–25th percentiles, the second part consists of values in the range from the 26th–50th percentiles, the third part consists of values in the range from the 51st–75th percentiles, and the fourth part consists of values in the range from the 76th–100th percentiles.

EXAMPLE

Consider the marks of 19 students obtained in an examination arranged in the ascending order of magnitude.

20,	27,	29,	33,	37,	40,	42,	48,	50,	53,	55,	62,	81,	83,	88,	90,	91,	95,	100

To find Q1: n = 19 thus Q_1 is $(n+1)/4 = 20/4 = 5^{th}$ observation = 37 marks

Q2 is $(n + 1)/2 = 20/2 = 10^{th}$ observation (Median) = 53 marks

Q3 is $3(n + 1)/4 = 60/4 = 15^{th}$ observation = 88 marks

Also note that Q1 and Q3 are equidistant from the median. In any perfectly symmetrical distribution (normal distribution) Median – Q1 = Q3 – Median

---

Activity 2 **(10 minutes)**

From the data below calculate the median, the upper quartile and the lower quartile.

6, 47, 49, 15, 43, 41, 7, 39, 43, 41, 36

Quantiles

Quartiles, deciles, and percentiles and any other similar dividing points for analysing a frequency distribution are referred to collectively as quantiles.

The purpose of quantiles is to analyse the dispersion of data values. All quantiles can be found easily from an ogive.

Quartiles of a grouped distribution

When the data are grouped, the quartiles cannot normally be determined accurately; they can only be estimated as the median is estimated, either by interpolation or by means of the ogive.

EXAMPLE

The hours of overtime worked in a particular quarter by the 60 employees of ABC Ltd are shown below. The company has decided to give a bonus of £100 to the 10% of the workforce who worked the most overtime, a bonus of £25 to the 20% of the workforce who worked the least overtime and a £50 bonus to all other employees.

Hours		
More than	*Not more than*	*Frequency*
0	10	3
10	20	6
20	30	11
30	40	15
40	50	12
50	60	7
60	70	6
		60

Required

Calculate the range of overtime hours worked by those employees receiving a £50 bonus.

SOLUTION

Hours	*Cumulative frequency*
$> 0 \leq 10$	3
$>10 \leq 20$	9
$>20 \leq 30$	20
$>30 \leq 40$	35
$>40 \leq 50$	47
$>50 \leq 60$	54
$>60 \leq 70$	60

The 9th decile is at 60 – (10% of 60) = 54

The 2nd decile is at 20% of 60 = 12

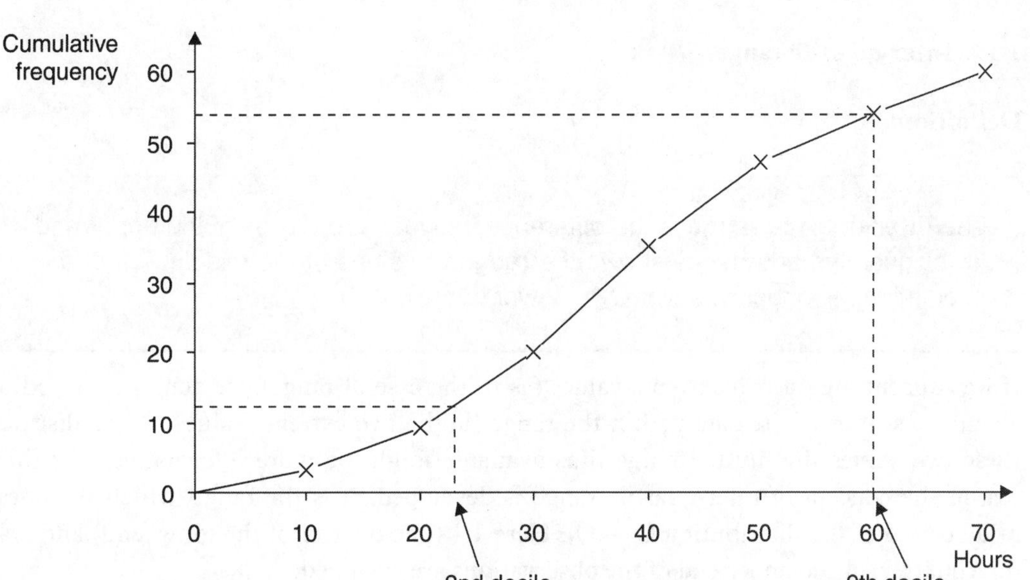

From the ogive the range of hours is approximately 23 to 60.

EXAMPLE

To find the quartiles of the height distribution we look at the cumulative frequency table given below:

Heights (cm)	*Number of children*	*Cumulative number of children*
<58	2	2
≥=58<60	5	7
≥=60<62	14	21
≥=62<64	60	81
≥=64<66	187	268
≥=66<68	304	572
≥=68<70	263	835
≥=70<72	121	956
≥=72<74	36	992
≥=74<76	7	999
≥=76	1	1000

Evidently Q_1 is in the range 64-66 cm. there are 250 items below Q_1, so we need to go 169/187 of the way along the class interval of 2 cm to reach Q_1.

$Q_1 = 64 + 2 \text{ x } (250 - 81)/187 = 65.81$ cm

Q_2 is in the range 66-68 cm and as there are 500 items below Q_2.

$Q_2 = 66 + 2 \text{ x } (500 - 268)/304 = 67.53$ cm

Similarly

$Q_3 = 68 + ((750 - 572)/263) \text{ x } 2 = 69.35$ cm

NOTES

1.3 Inter-quartile range

Definition

The **inter-quartile range** is the difference between the values of the upper and lower quartiles and hence shows the range of values of the middle half of the population, ie, upper quartile (Q_3) – lower quartile (Q_1)

If we concentrate on two extreme values (as in the case of range), we don't get any idea about the scatter of the data within the range (ie the two extreme values). If we discard these two values the limited range thus available might be more informative. For this reason the concept of inter-quartile range is developed. It is the range, which includes middle 50% of the distribution $Q_3 – Q_1$. Here 1/4 (one quarter of the lower end) and 1/4 (one quarter) of the upper end of the observations are excluded.

For example, if the lower and upper quartiles of a frequency distribution were 6 and 11, the inter-quartile range would be 11 – 6 = 5. This shows that the range of values of the middle half of the population is five units.

Dividing ($Q_3 – Q_1$) by 2 we get what is known as semi-inter-quartile range.

Activity 3 **(10 minutes)**

Find the values of the upper and lower quartiles of the frequency distribution detailed in the example below.

Class £	*Frequency*	*Cumulative frequency*
≥ 340 < 370	17	17
≥ 370 < 400	9	26
≥ 400 < 430	9	35
≥ 430 < 460	3	38
≥ 460 < 490	2	40
	40	

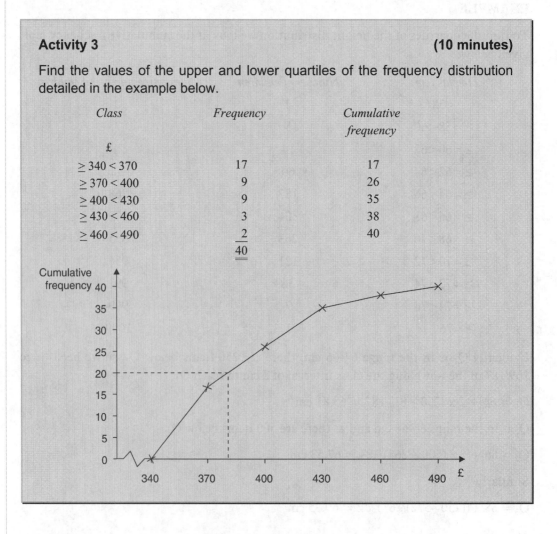

BPP LEARNING MEDIA

2 THE MEAN AND STANDARD DEVIATION

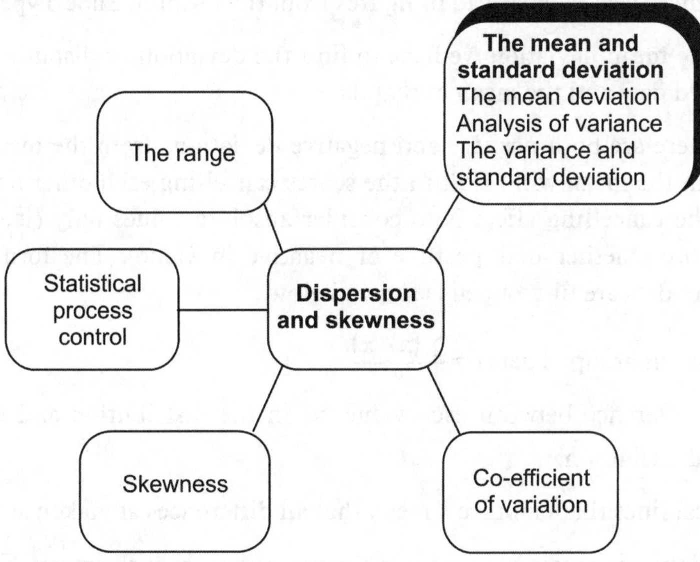

2.1 The mean deviation

Because it only uses the middle 50% of the population, the inter-quartile range is a useful measure of dispersion if there are extreme values in the distribution. If there are no extreme values which could potentially distort a measure of dispersion, however, it seems unreasonable to exclude 50% of the data. The mean deviation and the standard deviation are therefore often more useful measures.

Definition

> The **mean deviation** is a measure of the average amount by which the values in a distribution differ from the arithmetic mean.

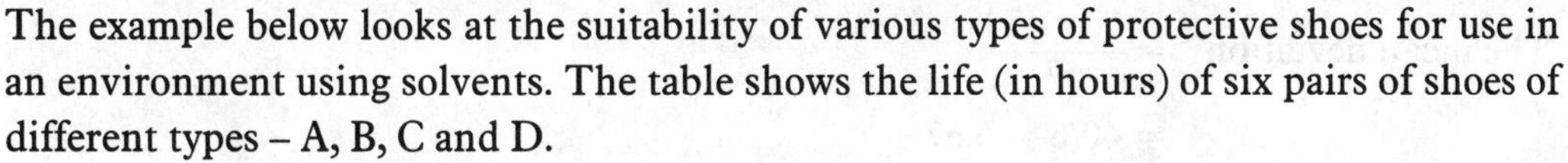

The example below looks at the suitability of various types of protective shoes for use in an environment using solvents. The table shows the life (in hours) of six pairs of shoes of different types – A, B, C and D.

Shoe life in hours			
Shoe type A	Shoe type B	Shoe type C	Shoe type D
50	60	60	90
50	50	60	70
50	50	50	50
50	50	50	50
50	50	40	20
50	40	40	20

Each of the types of shoes has a mean of 50 hours, however the spread is much bigger in Shoe Type D than the other types of shoes. We need to be able to measure the way in which the values disperse from the central measure. The most obvious way of measuring the spread is to examine the range.

NOTES

The range in Shoe Type D is 70 hours, whereas both Shoe Types B and C have a range of 20 hours, but there is greater spread in figures from the mean in Shoe Type C.

To calculate the mean deviation we have to find the deviation or distance between each item of observed data and the mean of that data.

However, as there are both positive and negative deviations from the mean, adding the deviations from the mean will result in the scores cancelling each other out. One way of allowing for the cancelling affect is to consider absolute values only (ie, only take the value and ignore whether it is positive or negative in value). The formula for mean deviation where data are ungrouped is shown below.

Mean deviation (ungrouped data) $= \frac{\Sigma(x-\overline{x})}{n}$

$(x-\overline{x})$ is the difference between each value (x) in the distribution and the arithmetic mean $\overline{x}$ of the distribution.

The two vertical lines that embrace x mean that all differences are taken as positive.

The mean deviation is obtained by adding the deviations from the mean. $\Sigma\ (x-\overline{x})$

Using the same shoe example as before and taking the values obtained for Shoe Type C we will get the following mean deviation.

Shoe type C	$(x-\overline{x})$	
60	60 – 50 =	10
60	60 – 50 =	10
50	50 – 50 =	0
50	50 – 50 =	0
40	40 – 50 =	10
40	40 – 50 =	10
Total		40

The mean deviation $= \frac{\Sigma(x-\overline{x})}{n}$

$= 40/6 = 6.67$

We can now state that the average distance of all values of Shoe Type C from the mean is 6.67 hours.

When calculating the mean distribution of a frequency distribution, the formula is:

Mean deviation (grouped data) $= \frac{\Sigma f(x-\overline{x})}{n}$

(a) When calculating the mean deviation for grouped data the deviations should be measured to the midpoint of each class: that is, x is the midpoint of the class interval.

(b) $f\ (x-\overline{x})$ is the value in (a) above, multiplied by the frequency for the class.

(c) $\Sigma f\ (x-\overline{x})$ is the sum of the results of all the calculations in (b) above.

(d) n (which equals Σf) is the number of items in the distribution.

EXAMPLE: THE MEAN DEVIATION

Calculate the mean deviation using the following frequency distribution of hours of overtime worked in a particular quarter by the 60 employees of ABC Ltd.

Hours		
More than	*Not more than*	Frequency
0	10	3
10	20	6
20	30	11
30	40	15
40	50	12
50	60	7
60	70	6
		60

SOLUTION

Midpoint *x*	*f*	*fx*	$(x-\bar{x})$	$f(x-\bar{x})$
5	3	15	32	96
15	6	90	22	132
25	11	275	12	132
35	15	525	2	30
45	12	540	8	96
55	7	385	18	126
65	6	390	28	168
	$\Sigma f =$ 60	$\Sigma fx =$ 2,220		780

$$\bar{x} = \frac{\Sigma fx}{\Sigma f} = \frac{2,220}{60} = 37$$

$$\text{Mean deviation} = \frac{780}{60} = 13 \text{ hours}$$

Therefore the mean is 37 hours and the mean deviation is 13 hours.

We will use this example again as we work through the topic.

Activity 4

Calculate the mean deviation of the following frequency distribution.

Value	*Frequency of occurrence*
5	4
15	6
25	8
35	20
45	**6**
55	6
	50

The usefulness of the mean deviation

The mean deviation is a measure of dispersion which shows by how much, on average, each item in the distribution differs in value from the arithmetic mean of the distribution.

Unlike quartiles, it uses all values in the distribution to measure the dispersion, but it is not greatly affected by a few extreme values because an average is taken.

The mean deviation is not, however, suitable for further statistical analysis.

2.2 Analysis of variance

Analysis of variance is best explained by means of an illustration.

The variance is a statistical parameter that shows the extent to which a set of values depart from uniformity, eg whether the weights of 1,000 men are closely clustered around a single value, eg around 120 kgs, or whether they are widely dispersed, eg from 60 to 180 kgs.

Suppose that we have weight data for 1,000 British men and 1,000 American men. We could calculate the total variance of all the men, but it would be more instructive to split this up into two components – the variance (extent of departure from the mean) between national weights and the variance within each national group, ie variance between samples and variance within samples. We could then determine whether it were true that there is a greater variation in the weights of British or American men. The analysis of variance provides answers to this kind of question. Similarly one could determine the extent to which the colour variations of a product were the result of processing temperature variations, processing time variations and inter-relationships between the two.

2.3 The variance and the standard deviation

Definitions

The **variance** is the average of the squared mean deviation for each value in a distribution.

The **standard deviation** is the square root of the variance.

Instead of taking the absolute value of the difference between the value and the mean to avoid the total of the differences summing to zero as we did with the mean deviation, we can square the differences. If we do this we get the variance and from that we get the most important measure of dispersion in statistics, the standard deviation. It is denoted by σ, the lower case Greek letter sigma.

Difference between value and mean	$x - \bar{x}$
Square of the difference	$(x - \bar{x})^2$
Sum of the squares of the difference	$\Sigma(x - \bar{x})^2$
Average of the sum (= variance = σ^2)	$\frac{\Sigma(x - \bar{x})^2}{n}$

The units of the variance are the square of those in the original data because we squared the differences. We therefore need to take the square root to get back to the units of the original data.

Square root of the variance = standard deviation = $\sqrt{\frac{\Sigma(x-\bar{x})^2}{n}}$

EXAMPLE: STANDARD DEVIATION

Calculate the standard deviation for the following ten lengths:

Values: 12, 9, 3, 10, 12, 22, 7, 11, 15 and 19cm.

Mean = 120 ÷ 10 = 12

	1	2	3	4	5	6	7	8	9	10	Sum
Values (cm)	12	9	3	10	12	22	7	11	15	19	**120**
Deviations	0	-3	-9	-2	0	10	-5	-1	3	7	**0**
Deviation squared	0	9	81	4	0	100	25	1	9	49	**278**

Sum of the deviations squared = 278

so the variance = 278 ÷ 10 = 27.8 cm and standard deviation = √27.8 = 5.27 cm

---

The same process can be applied to determine the standard deviation of data in a frequency distribution.

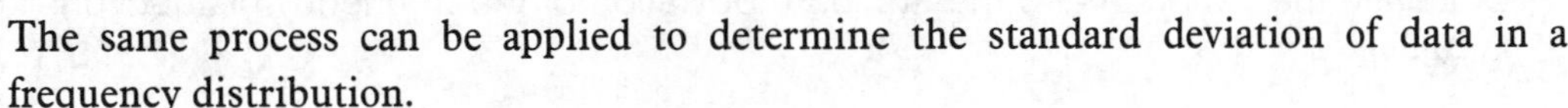

Square of the difference between value and mean $(x-\bar{x})^2$

Sum of the squares of the difference $\Sigma f(x-\bar{x})^2$

Average of the sum (= variance) $\frac{\Sigma f(x-\bar{x})^2}{\Sigma f}$

Square root = standard deviation = $\sqrt{\frac{\Sigma f(x-\bar{x})^2}{\Sigma f}}$

This formula can prove time-consuming to use. An alternative formula for the standard deviation is shown as follows.

Standard deviation = $\sqrt{\frac{\Sigma fx^2}{\Sigma f}-\bar{x}^2}$

Note that these formulae are appropriate if all the details are known of the whole population.

EXAMPLE: THE VARIANCE AND THE STANDARD DEVIATION

Calculate the variance and the standard deviation of the frequency distribution in the example under 2.1 concerning the hours of overtime worked by the employees of ABC Ltd.

NOTES

SOLUTION

Using the alternative formula for the standard deviation, the calculation is as follows.

Midpoint *x*	*f*	x^2	fx^2
5	3	25	75
15	6	225	1,350
25	11	625	6,875
35	15	1,225	18,375
45	12	2,025	24,300
55	7	3,025	21,175
65	6	4,225	25,350
	60		97,500

Mean = (from the example concerning ABC Ltd) = 37

$$\text{Variance} = \frac{\sum fx^2}{\sum f} - \bar{x}^2 = \frac{97{,}500}{60} - (37)^2 = 256 \text{ hours}$$

$$\text{Standard deviation} = \sqrt{256} = 16 \text{ hours}$$

Activity 5 **(10 minutes)**

Calculate the variance and the standard deviation of the frequency distribution in Activity 4.

The main properties of the standard deviation

Sigma (σ) is the mathematical symbol for standard deviation. As we have shown, it provides a measure of the dispersion, or variation, within the data set. The meaning of the standard deviation is most easily seen when the underlying population is a normal distribution, which graphically looks like a bell-curve. It is self-evident that in any normal distribution 50% of the population will be more than average; 50% will be lower. The standard deviation tells us more: it is known that 68.26% of the population (from which the sample is derived) lies within ± 1σ of the mean; 95.44% within ± 2σ and 99.73% within ± 3σ from the mean.

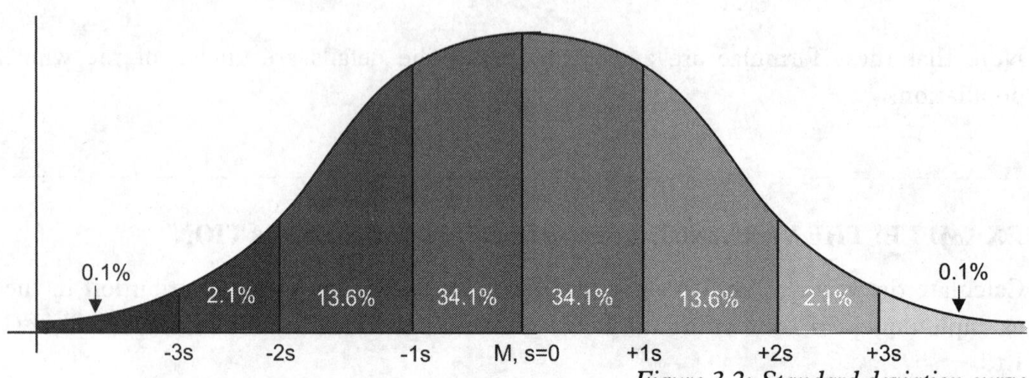

Figure 3.2: Standard deviation curve

The standard deviation's main properties are as follows:

(a) It is based on all the values in the distribution and so is more comprehensive than dispersion measures based on quantiles, such as the quartile deviation.

(b) It is suitable for further statistical analysis.

(c) It is more difficult to understand than some other measures of dispersion.

The importance of the standard deviation lies in its suitability for further statistical analysis.

3 THE COEFFICIENT OF VARIATION

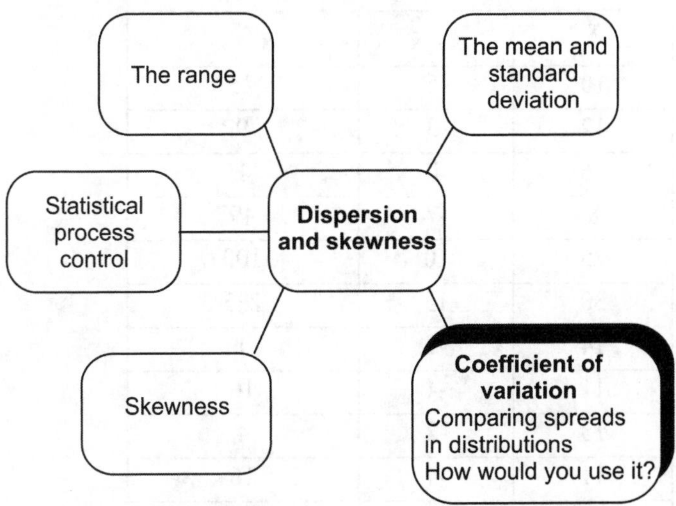

3.1 Comparing spreads in distributions

Definition

> The **coefficient of variation** compares the dispersion of two distributions.

The coefficient of variation indicates how large the standard deviation is in relation to the mean.

It is sometimes useful to be able to compare the spreads of two distributions. This comparison can be done using the coefficient of variation.

$$\text{Coefficient of variation} = \frac{\text{Standard deviation}}{\text{mean}}$$

The coefficient of variation is sometimes known as the coefficient of relative dispersion.

The bigger the coefficient of variation, the wider the dispersion. For example, suppose that two sets of data, A and B, have the following means and standard deviations.

	A	*B*
Mean	120	125
Standard deviation	50	51
Coefficient of variation	0.417	0.408

Although B has a higher standard deviation in absolute terms (51 compared to 50) its relative dispersion is a bit less than A's since the coefficient of variation is a bit smaller.

EXAMPLE

Calculate the standard deviation and its co-efficient from the following data.

Values: 10, 12, 16, 8, 25, 30, 14, 11, 13, 11

SOLUTION

Mean = 150 ÷ 10 = 15

x	$x - \bar{x}$	$(x - \bar{x})^2$
10	-5	25
12	-3	9
16	1	1
8	-7	49
25	10	100
30	15	225
14	-1	1
11	-4	16
13	-2	4
11	-4	16
Σx = 150		$\Sigma(x - \bar{x})^2$ = 446

Standard deviation = $\sqrt{\frac{\Sigma(x - \bar{x}^2)}{n}}$ = √ 446/10 = 6.7

Co-efficient of variation = $\frac{\text{Standard deviation}}{\text{mean}}$ = 6.7/15 = 0.45

Expressed as a percentage = 45%

3.2 How would you use it?

Many people who study the stock market calculate the stock's 'volatility' using the standard deviation (SD). Recording the closing price of a stock over several trading days, the SD would be equal to 0 if the stock's price never changed, it would be equal to a small number if the stock fluctuated just a little, and it would be equal to a large number of the stock's price jumped around wildly over the days studied.

However, the coefficient of variation does a better job of assessing volatility than does the standard deviation.

As an example, we will use two investors (A and B) who each have £1,000 to invest. Assume that A buys 100 shares of a stock that is selling for £10 a share, while B buys 20 shares of a different stock that is selling for £50 a share.

Over 5 days, suppose the price of the stocks moves like this:

	Day 1	Day 2	Day 3	Day 4	Day 5
Investor A	£10	£9	£13	£7	£11
Investor B	£50	£49	£53	£47	£51

The two stocks under consideration fluctuated by the same absolute amount. In each case, the SD of the five prices is equal to 2. However, this measure of volatility misrepresents the investors' 'ups and downs' over the five-day period under consideration. A's holdings fluctuated from £700 to £1,300 while B's investment fluctuated between £940 and £1,060.

Calculating the coefficient of variation (CV) instead of the SD, we get:

(i) For Investor A, the CV = 2/10 = 0.20;

(ii) For Investor B, the CV = 2/50 = 0.04. Comparing these CV indices, we see that Investor A's stock is five times as volatile as Investor B's stock.

This example shows how the coefficient of variation can be useful when trying to assess the degree of 'spread' within a set of numbers. As illustrated by the performance of the two hypothetical stocks, the SD disregards the level of the mean when it assesses variability. The SD computes how variable the scores are around the mean, but the size of the mean is not taken into consideration. In contrast, the coefficient of variation looks at the spread of scores (around the mean), adjusted for the size of the mean.

Activity 6 **(5 minutes)**

Calculate the coefficient of variation of the distribution in Activities 4 and 5.

4 SKEWNESS

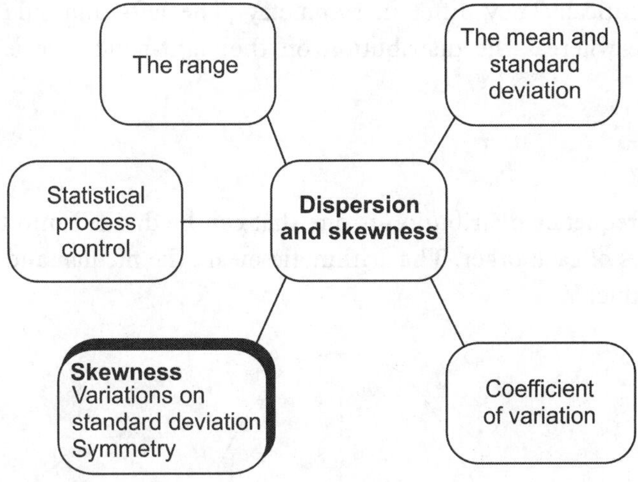

4.1 Variations on standard deviation

Since none of us can clearly see into the future, achieving an accurate assessment of risk and its related expected returns is a cornerstone of prudent investing. The most commonly used academic definition of risk is standard deviation — a measure of

volatility. But it is important to recognise that two investments with similar standard deviations can experience entirely different distribution of returns. While some investments exhibit normal distribution (ie, the familiar bell curve), others may exhibit 'skewness'.

Definition

Skewness is the asymmetry of a frequency distribution curve

In other words, the historical pattern of returns does not resemble a normal (ie, bell-curve) distribution.

As well as being able to calculate the average and spread of frequency distribution, you should be aware of the skewness. A frequency distribution must be either symmetrical or skewed (asymmetrical).

It may happen that two distributions have the same mean and standard deviations. For example, see the following diagram.

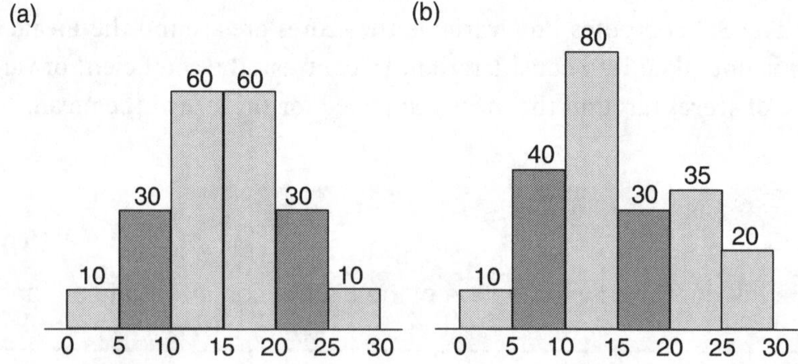

Figure 3.3: Distributions – (a) Symmetrical (b) Skewed

Although the two distributions have roughly the same means and standard deviations they are not identical. They differ in symmetry. The left-hand side distribution is a symmetrical one whereas the distribution on the right-hand side is asymmetrical or skewed.

4.2 Symmetry

A symmetrical frequency distribution is one that can be divided into two halves, which are mirror images of each other. The arithmetic mean, the median and the mode will all have the same value, M.

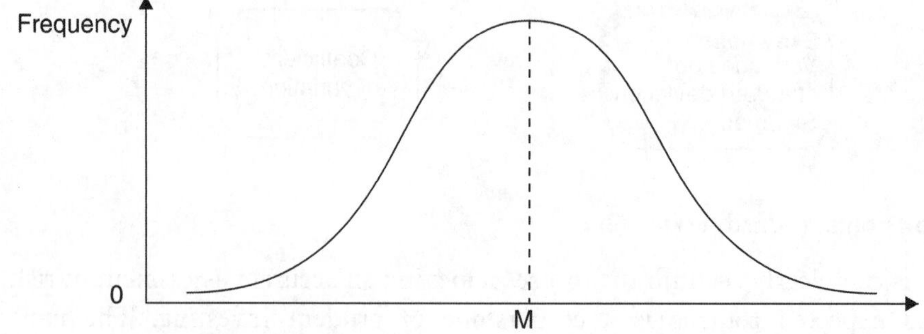

Figure 3.4: Symmetrical frequency distribution

A positively skewed distribution's graph will lean towards the left hand side, with a tail stretching out to the right. The mean, the median and the mode will have different values.

In a positively skewed distribution, the mode will have a lower value than the median and the mean will have a higher value than the median. The value of the mean is, in fact, higher than a great deal of the distribution.

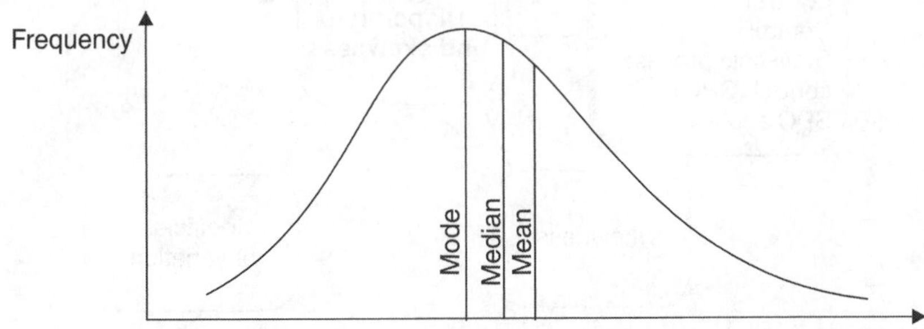

Figure 3.5: Positively skewed distribution graph

A negatively skewed distribution's graph will lean towards the right-hand side, with a tail stretching out to the left. Once again, the mean, median and mode will have different values.

In a negatively skewed distribution, the mode will have a higher value than the median and the mean will have a lower value than the median. The value of the mean is lower than a great deal of the distribution.

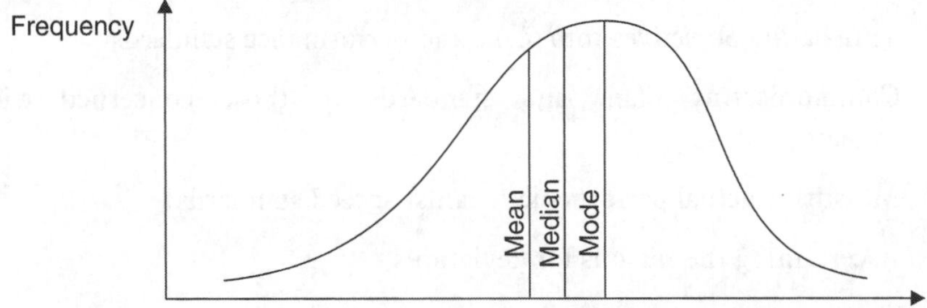

Figure 3.6: Negatively skewed distribution graph

It is a criticism of the mean as an average that for very skewed distributions its value may not be representative of the majority of the items in the distribution since it is affected by extreme values.

Behavioural finance studies have found that, in general, investors prefer assets with positive skewness. This is evidenced by their willingness to accept low or even negative expected returns when an asset exhibits positive skewness. A classic example is the lottery ticket, where the odds of winning the jackpot are extremely low, but the few times it does occur, the winnings are extremely high. At the same time investors generally avoid assets with negative skewness. High-risk asset classes such as junk bonds (so-called because they carry a high risk that the issuer will default on its borrowing commitments) or emerging markets, typically exhibit negative skewness, as do some investment vehicles such as hedge funds.

5 STATISTICAL PROCESS CONTROL

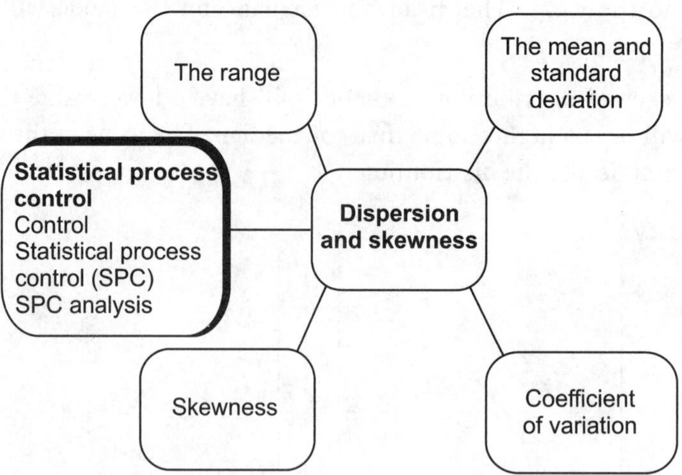

5.1 Control

Control is concerned with 'regulating the activities within an organisation so that the causes of deviations from standards specified in policies, plans and targets are identified and corrected'.

The main stages of the control process are:

(a) Determining and agreeing objectives

(b) Translating objectives into plans and performance standards

(c) Communicating plans and standards to those concerned with their implementation

(d) Measuring actual performance against agreed standards

(e) Ascertaining the reasons for deviations

(f) Taking appropriate corrective action

Uncertainty lies all around us and affects everything we do, making it impossible to predict with 100% accuracy what will occur in the future. The role of statistical methods is to bring some order to this scene of apparent chaos particularly when applied to the control of processes.

5.2 Statistical Process Control (SPC)

SPC is the continuous monitoring and charting of a process while it is operating, to warn when the process is moving away from predetermined limits. It means we can reliably assess the performance of any process, monitor it statistically and take steps to control it better. Typically the upper and lower control limits will be three standard deviations away from the mean. All points outside the control limits should be investigated and corrected.

SPC can be applied in a wider range of situations; some examples are given below.

(a) It can be used to process data to **optimise plant performance**. In its simplest form it is looking at the standard deviation of controlled variables and how close they are to the plant tolerance limits, and seeing if they can be pushed closer, making the plant more productive.

(b) It is an aspect of **Total Quality Management (TQM)**, which is a way of managing a business to ensure complete customer satisfaction internally and externally. It is accepted that it is not possible to achieve perfection in products because of the variations in raw material quality, operating skills, different types of machines used, wear and tear, etc. but quality control attempts to ascertain the amount of variation from perfect that can be expected in any operation. If the expected variation is acceptable according to engineering requirements, then production must be established within controlled limits and if the actual variation is too great then corrective action must be taken to bring it within acceptable limits.

(c) It can be used to **control buffer stocks** or inventories. These are an accumulation of stock, usually raw materials, for use in case of supply problems, or cash-flow difficulties that prevent purchase of new stock. A buffer stock, or safety stock, is an insurance against unexpected problems, but excessive hoarding ties up assets and limits supplies of the resource to other companies. The use of just-in-time techniques has reduced the requirement for buffer stock.

(d) It can involve the **use of control charts** to record and monitor the accuracy of the physical dimensions of products. Representational samples of an output manufacturing process may be taken daily or even hourly, and faults in the process which are revealed may be fairly simple to correct by adjusting the appropriate machinery. If output exceeds the control limits consistently then more urgent management action would be required because this could indicate some inadequacy in production methods or quality of raw materials and components. It could even be due to inefficiency in production or excessively tight tolerances in the first place.

(e) Control charts can also be applied to the **inspection of raw materials received** from suppliers in order to confirm that the supplier is supplying materials, which conform to the size and standard specified in the purchase contract.

5.3 SPC analysis

When data is collected regularly in predetermined subgroups for each feature of a particular job then SPC analysis is possible. This analysis uses either the mean and range of a group of readings, or the mean and standard deviation, to characterise a sub-group of readings.

These values can then be plotted on control charts using warning values to prevent the specification being compromised. The analysis is based on the normal distribution of data, the bell curve, and can be used to predict trends in the process away from the controlled condition.

Data obtained, manually or automatically, at the time of processing can be plotted graphically in order to provide a visual record of the performance of a process. Critical dimensions or other characteristics are measured. A typical control chart is shown in the diagram below. The horizontal axis is either time or a cumulative output volume. The vertical axis is a measure of a critical characteristic of the component such as its length or diameter.

NOTES

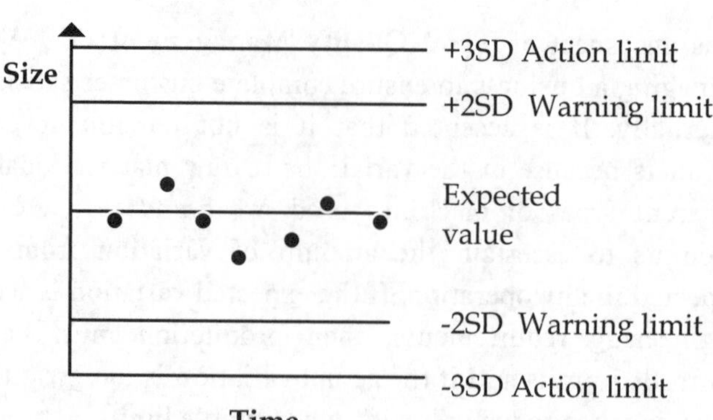

The objective value of the characteristic being measured is plotted as a horizontal line. This is the expected value. An analysis of past output will indicate the amount of random variation expected for the type of process being used. From this the standard deviation of the process from the mean (expected value) can be measured. Further horizontal lines can then be drawn on the graph at positions representing two and three standard deviations above and below the objective line. These values are derived from an analysis of the process and are control limits. It is expected that 67% of values will lie between ± 2 standard deviations hence within that part of the chart that lies between the warning limits. 99.75% will lie between ± 3 standard deviations and lie within the action limits. A control chart shows the limits within which output is expected.

As actual output is produced the value of the chosen dimension is plotted. This will show both random and gradual variations and also any deviations. Some output can be expected to be beyond the two standard deviation control limits. These are known are 'warning limits'. Some output of this type is not a problem since it is expected but successive values in this region indicate a problem that needs to be corrected. Virtually no output should occur beyond the three standard deviations limits. These are known as 'action limits'. If such values occur this indicates that the process is out of control and action is required to correct it.

No matter how good the equipment or how skilful the operative, a number of articles produced by the same process will never be exactly alike, although with imperfect measuring instruments they may appear so. There will always be a slight variation from one to another. The causes of variation may be divided into *assignable causes*, such as mechanical faults or abnormalities in the raw material, which can be identified and eliminated, and *chance causes*, which are either unknown or impossible to eliminate. When only chance causes are operating, the process is said to be 'under control'. The data recorded will then vary about the process average, with a standard deviation measuring the residual variation ie, the inherent variability of the process.

An empirical rule is used to assess whether a process is performing normally or is out of control if:

(a) 8 successive values are on the same side of the mean
(b) 4 out of 5 are beyond 1 standard deviation
(c) 2 out of 3 are beyond 2 standard deviations
(d) just 1 value is beyond 3 standard deviations

then it must be assumed that there is an assignable cause for this and that this could not occur if the process were in control. Such outputs therefore indicate a process out of control.

Chapter roundup

- This chapter has looked at measures of dispersion.
- Measures of dispersion give some idea of the spread of the variables about the average.
- The range is the difference between the highest and lowest observations.
- The quartiles and the media divide the population into four groups of equal size.
- The inter-quartile range is the difference between the upper and lower quartiles.
- The mean deviation is a measure of the average amount by which the values in a distribution different from the arithmetic mean.
- The standard deviation, which is the square root of the variance, is the most important measure of dispersion used in statistics. Make sure you know how to calculate the standard deviation of a set of data.
- The spreads of two distributions can be compared using the coefficient of variation.
- Skewness is the symmetry of a frequency distribution curve.

Quick quiz

1 What are quantiles?

2 When calculating the mean deviation for grouped data, to where should the deviations be measured?

3 Why are the differences between the value and the mean squared in the formula for the standard deviation?

4 Give a formula for the variance of data in a frequency distribution.

5 Define the coefficient of variation of a distribution.

6 Distinguish between positive skewness and negative skewness.

Answers to quick quiz

1 Quantiles is a collective term for dividing points for analysing a frequency distribution (eg quartiles, deciles and percentiles).

2 The deviations should be measured to the arithmetic mean.

3 In order to avoid the total of the differences summing to zero.

4 $\frac{\Sigma f(x-\bar{x})^2}{\Sigma f}$ or $\frac{\Sigma fx^2}{\Sigma f} - \bar{x}^{2}$

5 The coefficient of variation compares the dispersion of two distributions (and can be calculated by dividing the standard deviation by the mean).

NOTES

6 A positive skewed distribution's graph will lean towards the left hand side, with a tail stretching out to the right. The mean, median and the mode will have different values.

(a) The mode will have a lower value than the median.

(b) The mean will have a higher value than the median.

A negatively skewed distribution's graph will lean towards the right hand side, with a tail stretching out to the left. The mean, median and the mode will all have different values also.

(a) The mode will have a higher value than the median.

(b) The mean will have a lower value than the median.

Answers to activities

1 (a) $\bar{x}_1 = \frac{72}{8} = 9$

The figures have a mean of 9 and a range of 24 – 3 = 21.

(b) $\bar{x}_2 = \frac{72}{8} = 9$

The figures have a mean of 9 and a range of 11 – 7 = 4.

The set of data x_1 is more widely dispersed than the set of data x_2.

2

Data	6 47 49 15 43 41 7 39 43 41 36 (11 numbers)
Ordered data	6 7 15 36 39 41 41 43 43 47 49
Median = (11 + 1)/2 = 6th	= 41
Lower quartile (11 = 1)/4 = 3rd	= 15
Upper quartile 3 (11 + 1)/4 = 9th	= 43

3

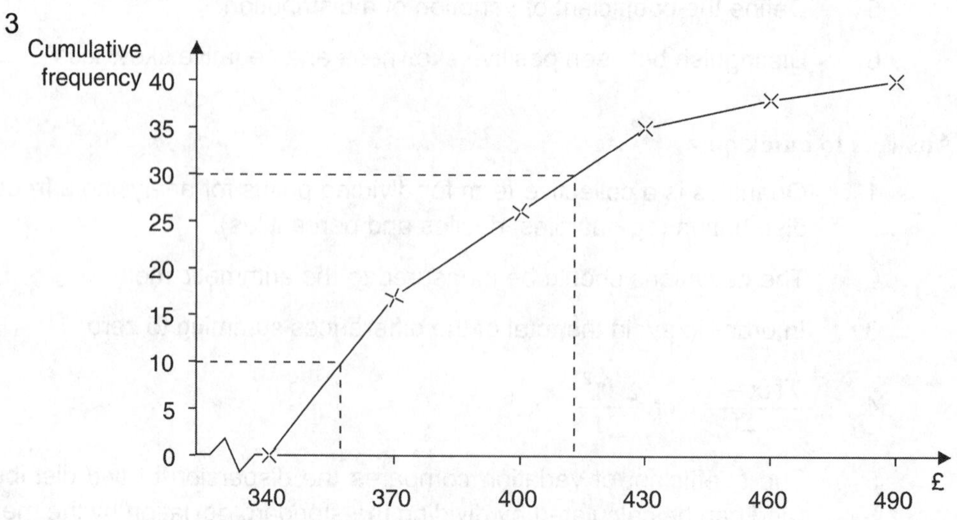

The upper quartile is the $^3/_4 \times 40 = 30^{th}$ value.

The lower quartile is the $^1/_4 \times 40 = 10^{th}$ value.

Reading off from the ogive these values are at approximately £358 and £412 respectively.

4

x	f	fx	$(x-\bar{x})$	$f(x-\bar{x})$
5	4	20	27.2	108.8
15	6	90	17.2	103.2
25	8	200	7.2	57.6
35	20	700	2.8	56.0
45	6	270	12.8	76.8
55	6	330	22.8	136.8
	50	1,610		539.2

Arithmetic mean $\bar{x} = \frac{1,610}{50} = 32.2$

Mean deviation $= \frac{539.2}{50} = 10.784$, say 10.8.

5

x	f	x^2	fx^2
5	4	25	100
15	6	225	1,350
25	8	625	5,000
35	20	1,225	24,500
45	6	2,025	12,150
55	6	3,025	18,150
	50		61,250

$\bar{x} = 32.2$ (from Activity 4)

Variance $= \frac{61,250}{50} - (32.2)^2 = 188.16$

Standard deviation $= \sqrt{188.16} = 13.72$

6 Coefficient of variation $= \frac{\text{Standard deviation}}{\text{Mean}} = \frac{13.72}{32.2} = 0.426$

NOTES

Chapter 4 :
CORRELATION AND REGRESSION

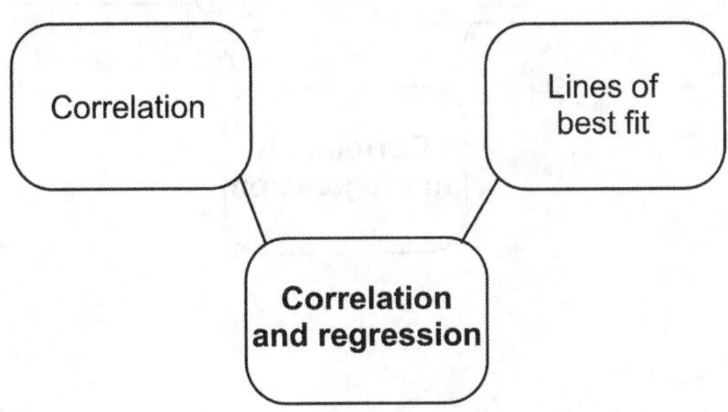

Introduction

We are now going to turn our attention to the statistical analysis of two-variable data (sales over time, advertising expenditure and sales revenue, output and costs and so on). Measures of correlation and regression can be thought of as the two-variable equivalents of the one-variable measures of location and dispersion: regression locates two-variable data in terms of a mathematical relationship which can be graphed as a curve or a line and correlation describes the nature of the spread of the items about the curve or line. The overall basic aim of correlation and regression is to ascertain the extent to which one variable is related to another.

Your objectives

After completing this chapter you should:

(a) Understand the concept of correlation

(b) Be aware of the difference between partial and perfect correlation and positive and negative correlation

(c) Be able to calculate and interpret the correlation coefficient

(d) Be able to calculate and interpret the coefficient of determination

(e) Be able to calculate and interpret Spearman's rank correlation coefficient and know when to use it

(f) Be able to construct a scattergraph and insert a line of best fit

(g) Be able to estimate a line of best fit using linear regression analysis

(h) Understand the meaning of 'least squares'

(i) Be able to interpret regression coefficients

(j) Be aware of the degree of reliance that can be placed on estimates.

1 CORRELATION

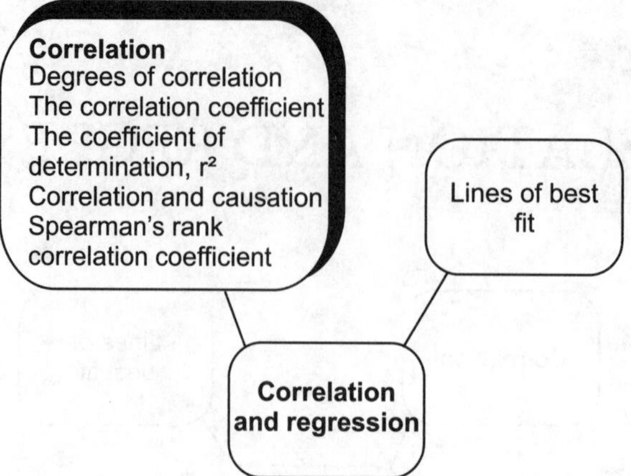

1.1 Introduction

Definition

Correlation means an inter-relationship or correspondence.

When the value of one variable is related to the value of another, they are said to be correlated.

Examples of variables which might be correlated are as follows.

(a) A person's height and weight
(b) The distance of a journey and the time it takes to make it

One way of showing the correlation between two related variables is on a scattergraph or scatter diagram, plotting a number of pairs of data on the graph.

For example, a scattergraph showing monthly selling costs against the volume of sales for a 12-month period might be as follows.

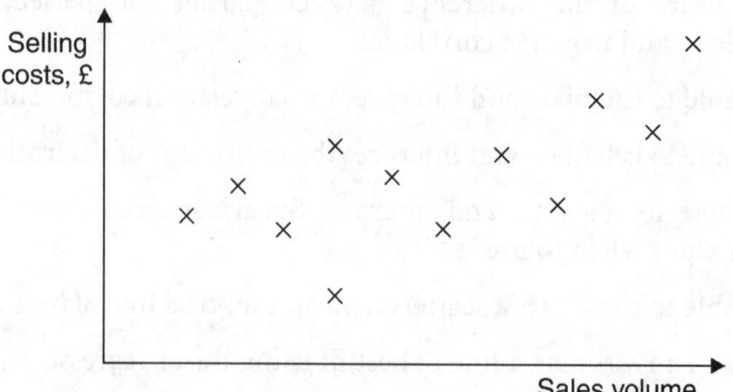

Figure 4.1: A scattergraph

This scattergraph suggests that there is some correlation between selling costs and sales volume, so that as sales volume rises, selling costs tend to rise as well.

1.2 Degrees of correlation

Two variables can be one of the following.

(a) Perfectly correlated
(b) Partly correlated
(c) Uncorrelated

These differing degrees of correlation can be illustrated by scatter diagrams.

Perfect correlation

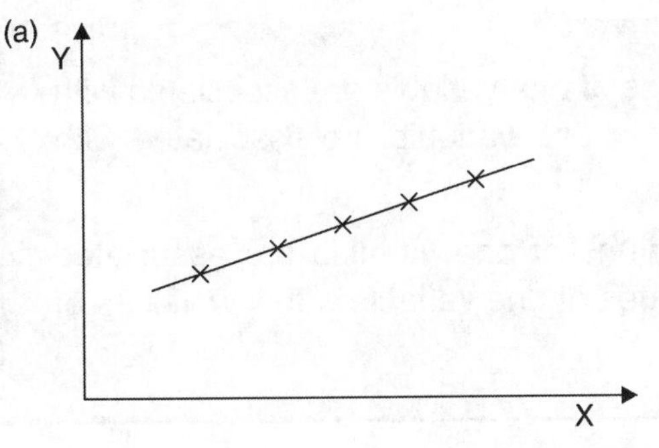

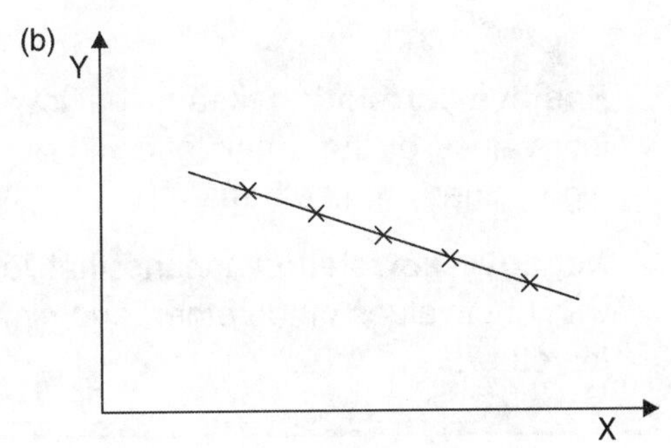

Figure 4.2: Perfect correlation

All the pairs of values lie on a straight line. An exact linear relationship exists between the two variables.

Partial correlation

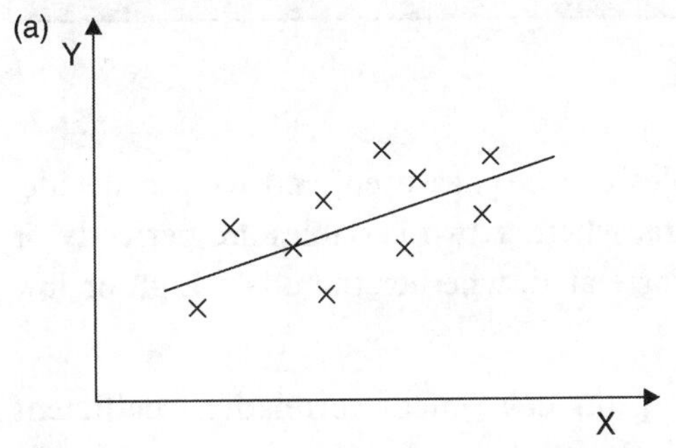

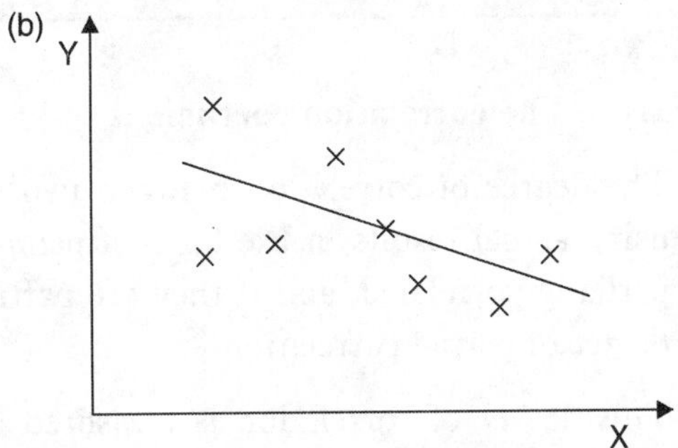

Figure 4.3: Partial correlation

In (a), although there is no exact relationship, low values of X tend to be associated with low values of Y, and high values of X with high values of Y.

In (b), again there is no exact relationship, but low values of X tend to be associated with high values of Y and *vice versa.*

No correlation

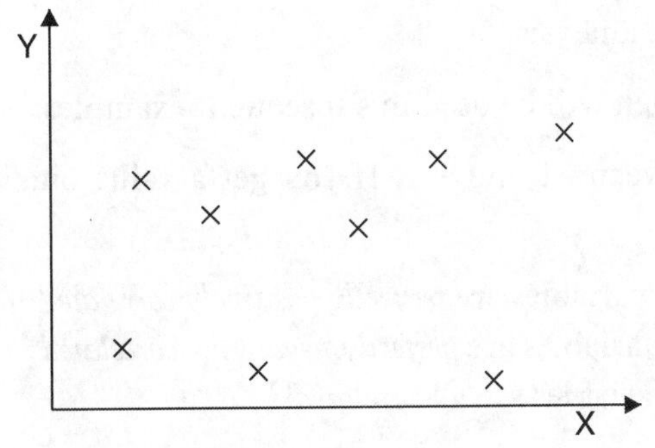

Figure 4.4 No correlation

The values of these two variables are not correlated with each other.

Positive and negative correlation

Correlation, whether perfect or partial, can be positive or negative.

Definitions

Positive correlation means that low values of one variable are associated with low values of the other, and high values of one variable are associated with high values of the other.

Negative correlation means that low values of one variable are associated with high values of the other, and high values of one variable with low values of the other.

Activity 1 **(5 minutes)**

Which of the four diagrams showing perfect and partial correlation demonstrate negative correlation?

1.3 The correlation coefficient

The degree of correlation between two variables can be measured, and we can decide, using actual results in the form of pairs of data, whether two variables are perfectly or partially correlated, and if they are partially correlated, whether there is a high or low degree of partial correlation.

This degree of correlation is measured by the product moment correlation coefficient (the coefficient of correlation), r (also called Pearson's product moment correlation coefficient).

There are several formulae for the correlation coefficient, although each formula will give the same value. These include the following.

$$\text{Correlation coefficient, } r = \frac{n\Sigma xy - \Sigma x\Sigma y}{\sqrt{[n\Sigma x^2 - (\Sigma x)^2][n\Sigma y^2 - (\Sigma y)^2]}}$$

where x and y represent pairs of data for two variables x and y, and n is the number of pairs of data used in the analysis.

This is the formula which will be used in subsequent examples.

r must always fall between –1 and +1. If you get a value outside this range you have made a mistake.

r = +1 means that the variables are *perfectly positively correlated*
r = –1 means that the variables are *perfectly negatively correlated*
r = 0 means that the variables are *uncorrelated*

EXAMPLE: THE CORRELATION COEFFICENT

The cost of output at a factory is thought to depend on the number of units produced. Data have been collected for the number of units produced each month in the last six months, and the associated costs, as follows.

Month	*Output* '000s of units	*Cost* £'000
	x	*y*
1	2	9
2	3	11
3	1	7
4	4	13
5	3	11
6	5	15

Required

Assess whether there is there any correlation between output and cost.

SOLUTION

$$r = \frac{n\Sigma xy - \Sigma x\Sigma y}{\sqrt{[n\Sigma x^2 - (\Sigma x)^2][n\Sigma y^2 - (\Sigma y)^2]}}$$

We need to find the values for the following.

(a) Σxy Multiply each value of x by its corresponding y value, so that there are six values for xy. Add up the six values to get the total.

(b) Σx Add up the six values of x to get a total. $(\Sigma x)^2$ will be the square of this total.

(c) Σy Add up the six values of y to get a total. $(\Sigma y)^2$ will be the square of this total.

(d) Σx^2 Find the square of each value of x, so that there are six values for x^2. Add up these values to get a total.

(e) Σy^2 Find the square of each value of y, so that there are six values for y^2. Add up these values to get a total.

Workings

x	*y*	*xy*	x^2	y^2
2	9	18	4	81
3	11	33	9	121
1	7	7	1	49
4	13	52	16	169
3	11	33	9	121
5	15	75	25	225
$\Sigma x = 18$	$\Sigma y = 66$	$\Sigma xy = 218$	$\Sigma x^2 = 64$	$\Sigma y^2 = 766$

$(\Sigma x)^2 = 18^2 = 324$ $(\Sigma y)^2 = 66^2 = 4{,}356$

$n = 6$

$$r = \frac{(6 \times 218) - (18 \times 66)}{\sqrt{(6 \times 64 - 324) \times (6 \times 766 - 4{,}356)}}$$

$$= \frac{1{,}308 - 1{,}188}{\sqrt{(384 - 324) \times (4{,}596 - 4{,}356)}}$$

$$= \frac{120}{\sqrt{60 \times 240}} = \frac{120}{\sqrt{14{,}400}} = \frac{120}{120} = 1$$

There is perfect positive correlation between the volume of output at the factory and costs.

Correlation in a time series

Correlation exists in a time series if there is a relationship between the period of time and the recorded value for that period of time. The correlation coefficient is calculated with time as the x variable although it is convenient to use simplified values for x instead of year numbers.

For example, instead of having a series of years 2005 to 2009, we could have values for x from 0 (2005) to 4 (2009).

Note that whatever starting value you use for x (be it 0, 1, 2, ..., 721, ..., 953), the value of r will always be the same.

Activity 2 **(20 minutes)**

Sales of product A between 20X7 and 20Y1 were as follows.

Year	*Units sold ('000s)*
20X7	20
20X8	18
20X9	15
20Y0	14
20Y1	11

Required

Determine whether there is a trend in sales. In other words, decide whether there is any correlation between the year and the number of units sold.

1.4 The coefficient of determination, r^2

Unless the correlation coefficient r is exactly or very nearly +1, –1 or 0, its meaning or significance is a little unclear. For example, if the correlation coefficient for two variables is +0.8, this would tell us that the variables are positively correlated, but the correlation is not perfect. It would not really tell us much else. A more meaningful analysis is available from the square of the correlation coefficient, r^2, which is called the coefficient of determination.

Definition

> The **coefficient of determination**, r^2 (alternatively R^2), measures the proportion of the total variation in the value of one variable that can be explained by variations in the value of the other variable.

In the activity above, r = –0.992, therefore r^2 = 0.984. This means that over 98% of variations in sales can be explained by the passage of time, leaving 0.016 (less than 2%) of variations to be explained by other factors.

Similarly, if the correlation coefficient between a company's output volume and maintenance costs was 0.9, r^2 would be 0.81, meaning that 81% of variations in maintenance costs could be explained by variations in output volume, leaving only 19% of variations to be explained by other factors (such as the age of the equipment).

Note, however, that if r^2 = 0.81, we would say that 81% of the variations in y can be explained by variations in x. We do not necessarily conclude that 81% of variations in y are caused by the variations in x. We must beware of reading too much significance into our statistical analysis.

Non-linear relationships

The formulae used above for r and r^2 only work for linear or near linear relationships. All the points on a scatter diagram might lie on a smooth curve as follows.

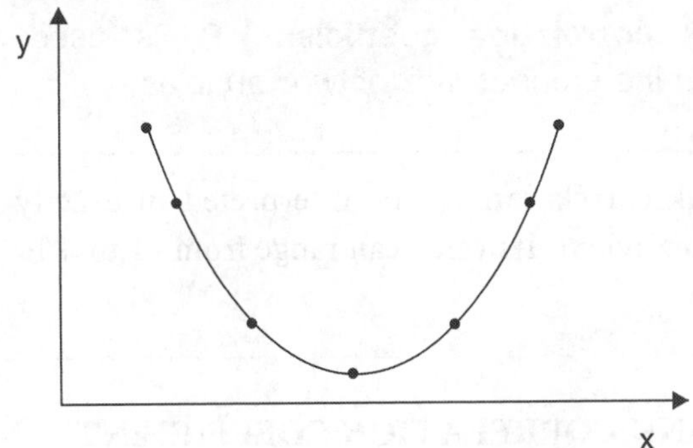

Figure 4.5: Non-linear relationship

If the formula for r were used in a situation such as this, a low value of r would be obtained, suggesting that very little correlation exists, whereas in fact the two sets of variables are perfectly correlated by a non-linear relationship. There are methods of testing correlations of this type, but they are outside the scope of this Course Book.

1.5 Correlation and causation

If two variables are well correlated, either positively or negatively, this may be due to pure chance or there may be a reason for it. The larger the number of pairs of data collected, the less likely it is that the correlation is due to chance, though that possibility should never be ignored entirely.

If there is a reason, it may not be causal. For example, monthly net income is well correlated with monthly credit to a person's bank account, for the logical (rather than causal) reason that for most people the one equals the other.

Even if there is a causal explanation for a correlation, it does not follow that variations in the value of one variable cause variations in the value of the other. For example, sales of ice cream and of sunglasses are well correlated, not because of a direct causal link but because the weather influences both variables.

Having said this, it is of course possible that where two variables are correlated, there is a direct causal link to be found.

1.6 Spearman's rank correlation coefficient

In the examples considered above, the data were given in terms of the values of the relevant variables, such as the number of units. Sometimes however, they are given in terms of order or rank rather than actual values. When this occurs, a correlation coefficient known as *Spearman's rank correlation coefficient, R*, should be calculated using the following formula.

$$\text{Spearman's rank correlation coefficient, } R = 1 - \left[\frac{6\Sigma d^2}{n(n^2-1)}\right]$$

where n = number of pairs of data

d = the difference between the rankings in each set of data.

Definition

Spearman's rank correlation coefficient, R, is used to measure the correlation between the order or rank of two variables.

The coefficient of rank correlation can be interpreted in exactly the same way as the ordinary correlation coefficient. Its value can range from –1 to +1.

EXAMPLE: THE RANK CORRELATION COEFFICIENT

The examination placings of seven students were as follows.

Student	*Statistics placing*	*Economics placing*
A	2	1
B	1	3
C	4	7
D	6	5
E	5	6
F	3	2
G	7	4

Required

Judge whether the placings of the students in statistics correlate with their placings in economics.

SOLUTION

Correlation must be measured by Spearman's coefficient because we are given the placings of students, and not their actual marks.

$$R = 1 - \left[\frac{6\Sigma d^2}{n(n^2 - 1)}\right]$$

where d is the difference between the rank in statistics and the rank in economics for each student.

Student	*Rank statistics*	*Rank economics*	*d*	*d^2*
A	2	1	1	1
B	1	3	2	4
C	4	7	3	9
D	6	5	1	1
E	5	6	1	1
F	3	2	1	1
G	7	4	3	9
				$\Sigma d^2 = 26$

$$R = 1 - \frac{6 \times 26}{7 \times (49 - 1)} = 1 - \frac{156}{336} = 0.536$$

The correlation is positive, 0.536, but the correlation is not strong.

Tied ranks

If in a problem some of the items tie for a particular ranking, these must be given an average place before the coefficient of rank correlation is calculated. Here is an example.

Position of students in examination			*Express as*
A	1 =	average of 1 and 2	1.5
B	1 =		1.5
C	3		3
D	4		4
E	5 =	average of 5, 6 and 7	6
F	5 =		6
G	5 =		6
H	8		8

Activity 3 **(10 minutes)**

Five artists were placed in order of merit by two different judges as follows.

Artist	*Judge P Rank*	*Judge Q Rank*
A	1	4 =
B	2 =	1
C	4	3
D	5	2
E	2 =	4 =

> *Required*
>
> Assess how the two sets of rankings are correlated.

2 LINES OF BEST FIT

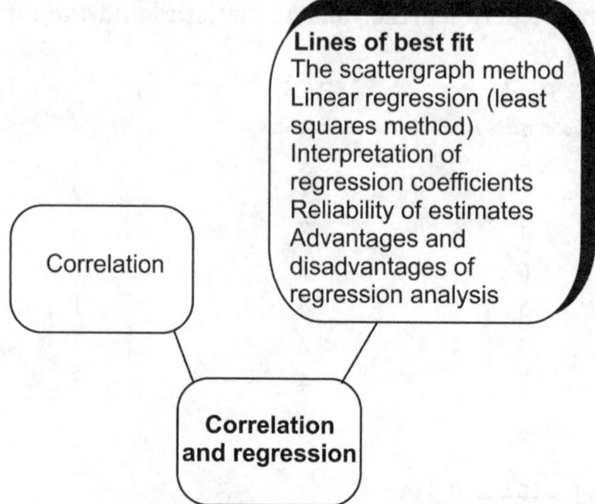

The correlation coefficient measures the degree of correlation between two variables, but it does not tell us how to predict values for one variable (y) given values for the other variable (x). To do that, we need to find a line which is a good fit for the points on a scattergraph, and then use that line to find the value of y corresponding to each given value of x.

We will be looking at two ways of doing this, the scattergraph method and linear regression using the least squares method.

2.1 The scattergraph method

Definition

> The **scattergraph method** is to plot pairs of data for two related variables on a graph, to produce a scattergraph, and then to **use judgement** to draw what seems to be a line of best fit through the data.

For example, suppose we have the following pairs of data about sales revenue and advertising expenditure.

Period	*Advertising expenditure*	*Sales revenue*
	£	£
1	17,000	180,000
2	33,000	270,000
3	34,000	320,000
4	42,000	350,000
5	19,000	240,000
6	41,000	300,000
7	26,000	320,000
8	27,000	230,000

BPP LEARNING MEDIA

These pairs of data would be plotted on a scattergraph (the horizontal axis representing the independent variable and the vertical axis the dependent) and a line of best fit might be judged as the one shown below. It was drawn to pass through the middle of the data points, thereby having as many data points below the line as above it.

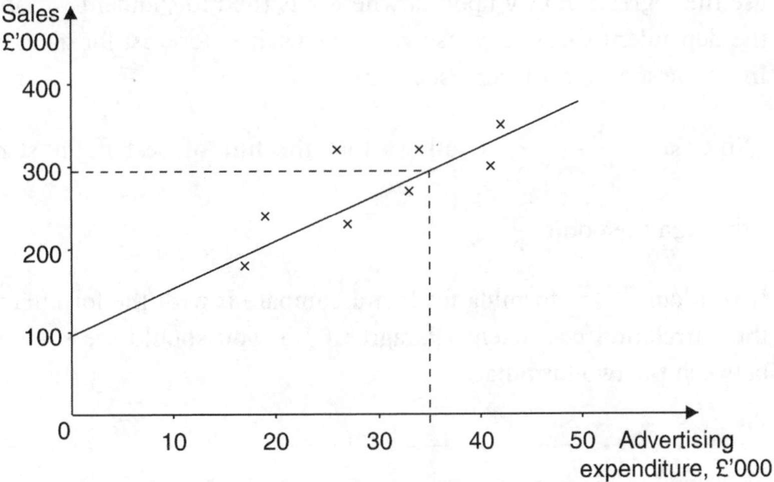

Figure 4.6: The scattergraph method

Suppose the company to which these data relate wants a forecast sales figure, given a marketing decision to spend £35,000 on advertising. An estimate of sales can be read directly from the scattergraph as shown (£290,000).

2.2 Linear regression using the least squares method

Definition

> The **least squares method of linear regression analysis** provides a technique for estimating the equation of a line of best fit.

The equation of a straight line has the form $y = a + bx$

where x and y are related variables
x is the independent variable
y is the dependent variable
a is the intercept of the line on the vertical axis
and b is the gradient of the line.

The least squares method provides estimates for the values of a and b using the following formulae.

$$b = \frac{n\Sigma xy - \Sigma x\Sigma y}{n\Sigma x^2 - (\Sigma x)^2}$$

$$a = \frac{\Sigma y}{n} - \frac{b\Sigma x}{n}$$

where n is the number of pairs of data.

There are some points to note about these formulae.

(a) The line of best fit that is derived represents the *regression of y upon x*.

A different line of best fit could be obtained by interchanging x and y in the formulae. This would then represent the *regression of x upon y* (x = a + by) and it would have a slightly different slope. For examination purposes, always use the regression of y upon x, where x is the independent variable, and y is the dependent variable whose value we wish to forecast for given values of x. In a time series, x will represent time.

(b) Since $a = \frac{\Sigma y}{n} - \frac{b\Sigma x}{n}$, it follows that the line of best fit must *always* pass through the point $\frac{\Sigma y}{n}, \frac{\Sigma x}{n}$.

(c) If you look at the formula for b and compare it with the formula we gave for the correlation coefficient (Paragraph 1.3) you should see some similarities between the two formulae.

EXAMPLE: THE LEAST SQUARES METHOD

You are given the following data for output at a factory and costs of production over the past five months.

Month	*Output*	*Costs*
	x	*y*
	'000 units	£'000
1	20	82
2	16	70
3	24	90
4	22	85
5	18	73

There is a high degree of correlation between output and costs, and so it is decided to calculate fixed costs and the variable cost per unit of output using the least squares method.

Task

(a) Calculate an equation to determine the expected level of costs, for any given volume of output.

(b) Prepare a budget for total costs if output is 22,000 units.

(c) Confirm that the degree of correlation between output and costs is high by calculating the correlation coefficient.

SOLUTION

(a) *Workings*

x	*y*	*xy*	x^2	y^2
20	82	1,640	400	6,724
16	70	1,120	256	4,900
24	90	2,160	576	8,100
22	85	1,870	484	7,225
18	73	1,314	324	5,329
$\Sigma x = 100$	$\Sigma y = 400$	$\Sigma xy = 8{,}104$	$\Sigma x^2 = 2{,}040$	$\Sigma y^2 = 32{,}278$

$$n = 5 \text{ (There are five pairs of data for x and y values)}$$

$$b = \frac{n\Sigma xy - \Sigma x\Sigma y}{n\Sigma x^2 - (\Sigma x)^2}$$

$$= \frac{(5 \times 8{,}104) - (100 \times 400)}{(5 \times 2{,}040) - 100^2}$$

$$= \frac{40{,}520 - 40{,}000}{10{,}200 - 10{,}000} = \frac{520}{200}$$

$$= 2.6$$

$$a = \frac{\Sigma y}{n} - \frac{b\Sigma x}{n}$$

$$= \frac{400}{5} - 2.6 \times \left(\frac{100}{5}\right)$$

$$= 28$$

$$y = 28 + 2.6x$$

where y = total cost, in thousands of pounds
x = output, in thousands of units.

(b) If the output is 22,000 units, we would expect costs to be

$28 + 2.6 \times 22 = 85.2 = £85{,}200$.

(c) $$r = \frac{520}{\sqrt{200 \times (5 \times 32{,}278 - 400^2)}}$$

$$= \frac{520}{\sqrt{200 \times 1{,}390}} = \frac{520}{527.3} = +\ 0.99$$

Activity 4 **(30 minutes)**

The expense claims and recorded car mileages on company business, relating to a particular day, of a sample of salesmen of a company are as follows.

Salesman	*Mileage*	*Expenses*
		£
A	100	60
B	80	48
C	20	20
D	120	55
E	70	38
F	50	38
G	80	44
H	40	30
I	50	40
J	60	50

Required

(a) Plot the data on a scatter diagram.

(b) Determine, by the method of least squares, a linear model to predict expenses, mileage having been given.

(c) Plot the model on your scatter diagram.

(d) Three further salesmen submit expense claims with mileages as follows

Salesman	*Mileage*	*Expenses*
		£
K	110	64
L	30	48
M	160	80

Discuss in each case whether or not the claim is reasonable.

Regression lines and time series

The same technique can be applied to calculate a regression line (a trend line) for a time series. This is particularly useful for purposes of forecasting. As with correlation, years can be numbered from 0 upwards.

Activity 5 **(20 minutes)**

Sales of product B over the seven year period from 20X1 to 20X7 were as follows.

Year	*Sales of B*
	'000 units
20X3	22
20X4	25
20X5	24
20X6	26
20X7	29
20X8	28
20X9	30

There is high correlation between time and the volume of sales.

Required

Calculate the trend line of sales, and forecast sales in 20Y0 and 20Y1.

The meaning of 'least squares'

The term 'squares' in 'least squares regression analysis' refers to the squares of the differences between actual values of the dependent variable (y) and predicted values given by the regression line of best fit. These differences are referred to as *residuals* or *residual errors*. 'Least squares' means that the line of best fit that is calculated is the one that minimises the sum of the squares of all the residuals. The differences are measured vertically on a graph, not at an angle to take the shortest route to the regression line.

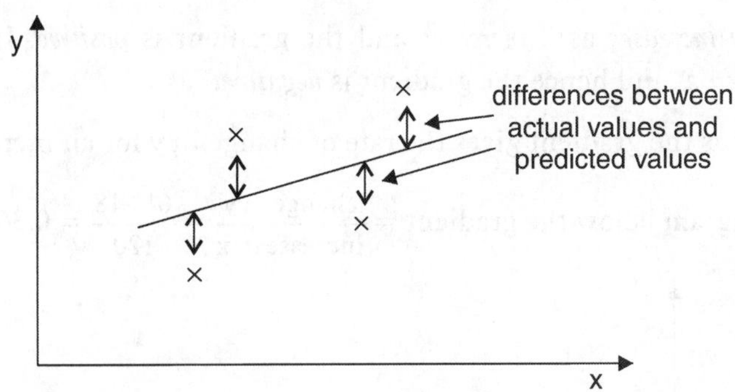

Figure 4.7: Graph showing 'least squares' method

2.3 Interpretation of the regression coefficients

We said earlier that the least squares method of linear regression analysis provides estimates for a and b and, given values for x and y, you should now be able to determine a and b yourself.

a and b are known as the coefficients of the regression line y = a + bx but what do they actually mean?

We explained in Section 2.2 that a is the intercept of the line of best fit on the vertical axis. The scatter diagram from Activity 4 has been reproduced below but the regression line has been extended so that it meets the y axis. The intercept of this line on the y axis would appear to be approximately 18 or 19; the value of a was calculated as 18.18 using linear regression analysis. This means that when mileage is zero, expenses are £18.00. In other words, there are other costs, unrelated to the distance travelled, of £18 per day. These might include subsistence costs.

b is the gradient or slope of the line of best fit. The slope of a line is dependent upon the change in y for an increase in x. In diagram (a) below, an increase in the value of x from 5 to 6 produces an increase in y of 10 from 10 to 20. In diagram (b), a similar increase in x produces an increase of 5 in y.

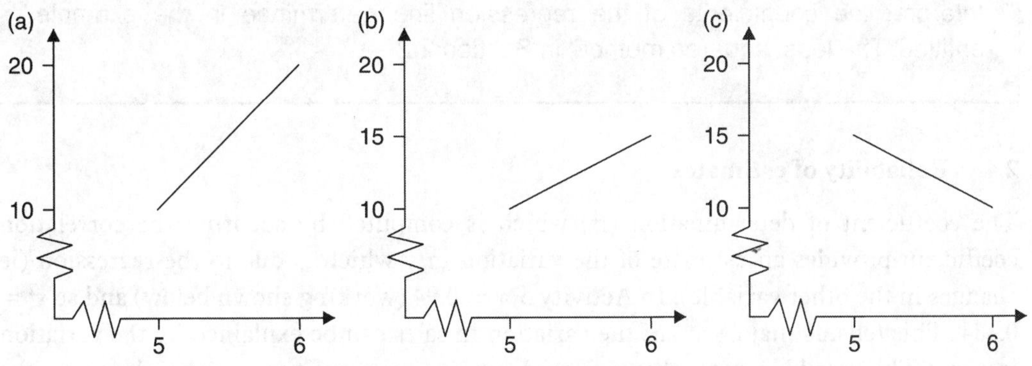

Figure 4.8: Graphs showing different gradients

$$\text{The gradient of the line in a} = \frac{\text{change in y}}{\text{increase in x}} = \frac{20-10}{6-5} = \frac{10}{1} = 10$$

$$\text{The gradient of the line in b} = \frac{\text{change in y}}{\text{increase in x}} = \frac{15-10}{6-5} = 5$$

$$\text{The gradient of the line in c} = \frac{\text{change in y}}{\text{increase in x}} = \frac{10-15}{6-5} = -5$$

In (a) and (b), y *increases* as x *increases* and the gradient is *positive*. In (c), however, y *decreases* as x *increases* and hence the gradient is *negative*.

In numerical terms the gradient gives the rate of change in y for an increase in x.

In the scatter diagram below the gradient $= \dfrac{\text{change in y}}{\text{increase in x}} = \dfrac{61-18}{120} = 0.36$

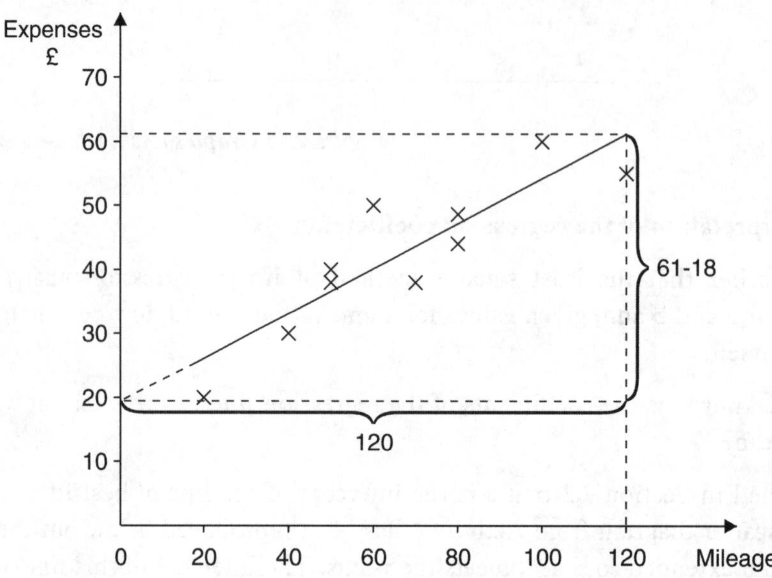

Figure 4.9: Scatter diagram of expenses and mileage

This means that an increase of one mile travelled produces an increase in costs of £0.36. The coefficient 0.36 therefore indicates that there is a variable motoring cost of 36p per mile on average.

Activity 6 **(5 minutes)**

Interpret the coefficients of the regression line determined in the example entitled 'The least squares method' in Section 2.2.

2.4 Reliability of estimates

The coefficient of determination (r^2) which is computed by squaring the correlation coefficient provides an estimate of the variation in y which is due to the regression (ie changes in the other variable). In Activity 5, r = 0.94 (working shown below) and so r^2 = 0.884. This tells us that 88.4% of the variation in sales can be explained by the variation in time. This would suggest that a fairly large degree of reliance can be placed on the estimate for 20X8 and 20X9.

We do not necessarily conclude that 88.4% of variations in y are caused by variations in time. It might be that high sales happened to coincide with a general economic boom, which was the real cause of increase.

$$r = \frac{(7 \times 587) - (21 \times 184)}{\sqrt{[(7 \times 91) - (21 \times 21)] \times [(7 \times 4{,}886) - (184 \times 184)]}}$$

$$= \frac{4{,}109 - 3{,}864}{\sqrt{(637 - 441) \times (34{,}202 - 33{,}856)}}$$

$$= \frac{245}{\sqrt{196 \times 346}} = \frac{245}{260.4}$$

$$= 0.94$$

If there is a perfect linear relationship between x and y ($r = \pm 1$) then we can predict y from any given value of x with great confidence.

If correlation is high (for example, $r = 0.9$) the actual values will all lie quite close to the regression line and so predictions should not be far out. If correlation is below about 0.7, predictions will only give a very rough guide as to the likely value of y.

As with any analytical process, the amount of data available is very important. Even if correlation is high, if we have fewer than about 10 pairs of values, we must regard any estimate as being somewhat unreliable.

When calculating a line of best fit, there will be a range of values for x. In the least squares method example following Section 2.2 the line $y = 28 + 2.6x$ was predicted from data with output values ranging from $x = 16$ to $x = 24$. Depending on the degree of correlation between x and y, we might safely use the estimated line of best fit to predict values for y, provided that the value of x remains within the range 16 to 24. We would be on less safe ground if we used the formula to predict a value for y when $x = 10$, or 30, or any other value outside the range 16 – 24, because we would have to assume that the trend line applies outside the range of x values used to establish the line in the first place.

(a) Interpolation means using a line of best fit to predict a value within the two extreme points of the observed range.

(b) Extrapolation means using a line of best fit to predict a value outside the two extreme points.

2.5 The advantages and disadvantages of regression analysis

The **advantages** of the least squares method of regression analysis are as follows.

(a) It can be used to estimate a line of best fit using all the data available. It is likely to provide a more reliable estimate than any other technique of producing a straight line of best fit (for example, estimating by eye).

(b) The reliability of the estimated line can be evaluated by calculating the correlation coefficient r.

The **disadvantages** of the method are as follows.

(a) It assumes a linear relationship between the two variables, whereas a non-linear relationship may exist.

(b) It assumes that what has happened in the past will provide a reliable guide to the future. For example, if a line is calculated for total costs of production, based on historical data, the estimate could be used to budget for future costs. However, if there has been cost inflation, a productivity agreement with the workforce, a move to new premises, the dismissal of large numbers of office

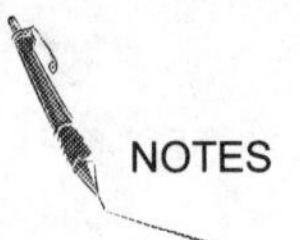

staff and the introduction of new equipment, future costs of production might bear no relation to costs in the past.

(c) The technique assumes that the value of one variable, y, can be predicted or estimated from the value of one other variable, x. In reality, the value of y might depend on several other variables, not just on x.

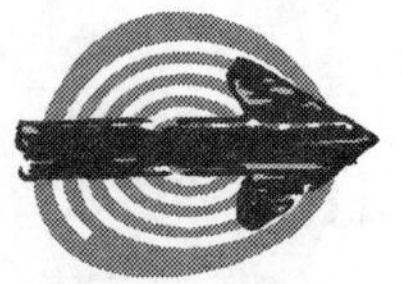

In this chapter we have looked at how the degree of correlation between two variables can be assessed. In the next chapter we shall be looking at how to use data that has been analysed over time to make forecasts about future values.

Chapter roundup

- When the value of one variable is related to the value of another, they are said to be correlated.
- Two variables might be perfectly correlated, partly correlated or uncorrelated. Correlation can be positive or negative.
- The degree of correlation between two variables is measured by the product moment correlation coefficient, r. The nearer r is to +1 or –1, the stronger the relationship.
- The coefficient of determination, r^2, measures the proportion of the total variation in the value of one variable that can be explained by the variation in the value of the other variable.
- Spearman's rank correlation coefficient is used when data is given in terms of order or rank rather than actual values.
- The scattergraph method involves the use of judgement to draw what seems to be a line of best fit through plotted data.
- Linear regression analysis (the least squares method) is one technique for estimating a line of best fit. Ensure that you know how to use the formulae to calculate a and b in y = a + bx.
- Correlation and regression analysis do not indicate cause and effect. Even if r = 1, the correlation could still be spurious, both variables being influenced by a third.

Quick quiz

1 Give some examples of variables which might be correlated.

2 Distinguish between positive and negative correlation.

3 What range of values can the product moment correlation coefficient take?

4 How should the coefficient of determination be interpreted?

5 When should Spearman's rank correlation coefficient be used?

6 What is the scattergraph method for finding a line of best fit?

7 When using the least squares method of linear regression, does it matter which variable is chosen as x?

8 What is a residual?

9 What are the advantages and disadvantages of the least squares method of linear regression?

Answers to quick quiz

1 (a) The person's height and weight.

(b) The distance of a journey and the time it takes to make it.

2 Positive correlation means that the low values of one variable are associated with low values of the other, and high values of one variable are associated with higher values of the other.

Negative correlation means that low values of one variable are associated with high values of the other, and high values of one variable with low values of the other.

3 The product moment correlation coefficient can take values in the range –1 to +1.

4 The coefficient of determination measures the proportion of the total variation in the value of one variable that can be *explained* (not caused) by the variations in the value of the other variable.

5 Spearman's rank correlation coefficient should be used when data are given in terms of order or rank rather than actual values.

6 The scattergraph method is to plot pairs of data for two related variables on a graph, to produce a scattergraph, and then to use judgements to draw what seems to be a line of best fit through the data.

7 Yes, it does matter. x should be the independent variable since the line of best fit that is derived in this type of analysis represents the regression of y upon x.

8 The term 'squares' in 'least squares regression analysis' refers to the squares of the differences between actual values of the dependent variable (y) and predicted values given by the regression line of best fit. These differences are referred to as *residuals.*

9 See Section 2.5.

Answers to activities

1 Diagrams (b) showing perfect correlation and (b) showing partial correlation both demonstrate negative correlation.

2 *Workings*

Let 20X7 to 20Y1 be years 0 to 4.

x	y	xy	x^2	y^2
0	20	0	0	400
1	18	18	1	324
2	15	30	4	225
3	14	42	9	196
4	11	44	16	121
Σx = 10	Σy = 78	Σxy = 134	Σx^2 = 30	Σy^2 = 1,266
$(\Sigma x)^2$ = 100		$(\Sigma y)^2$ = 6,084		

NOTES

$$n = 5$$

$$r = \frac{(5 \times 134) - (10 \times 78)}{\sqrt{(5 \times 30 - 100) \times (5 \times 1{,}266 - 6{,}084)}}$$

$$= \frac{670 - 780}{\sqrt{(150 - 100) \times (6{,}330 - 6{,}084)}} = \frac{-110}{\sqrt{50 \times 246}}$$

$$= \frac{-110}{\sqrt{12{,}300}} = \frac{-110}{110.90537} = -0.992$$

There is partial negative correlation between the year of sale and units sold. The value of r is close to –1, therefore a high degree of correlation exists, although it is not quite perfect correlation. This means that there is a clear downward trend in sales.

3

	Judge P	*Judge Q*		
	Rank	*Rank*	*d*	d^2
A	1.0	4.5	3.5	12.25
B	2.5	1.0	1.5	2.25
C	4.0	3.0	1.0	1.00
D	5.0	2.0	3.0	9.00
E	2.5	4.5	2.0	4.00
				28.50

$$R = 1 - \frac{6 \times 28.5}{5 \times (25 - 1)} = -0.425$$

There is a slight negative correlation between the rankings.

4 (a)

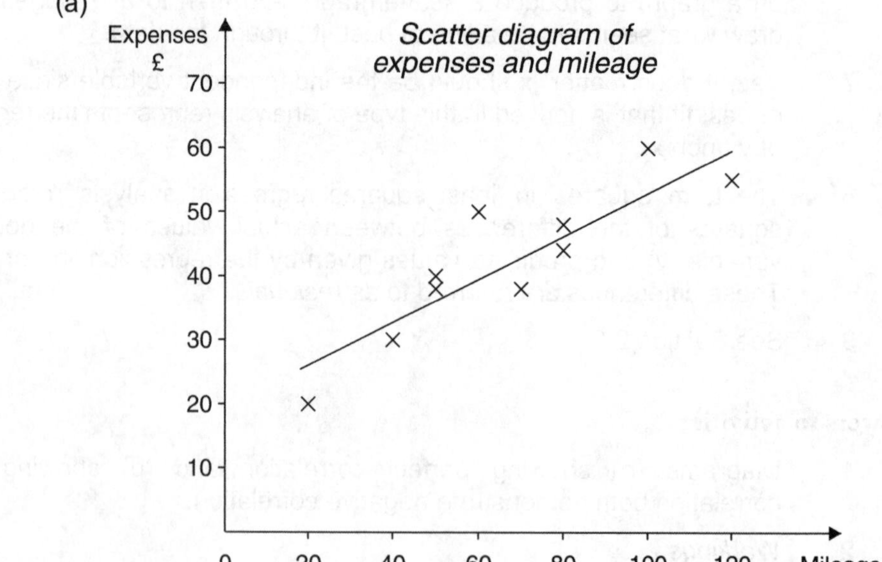

(b) The independent variable, x, is the mileage. The dependent variable, y, is the expenses in pounds.

x	y	x^2	xy
100	60	10,000	6,000
80	48	6,400	3,840
20	20	400	400
120	55	14,400	6,600
70	38	4,900	2,660
50	38	2,500	1,900
80	44	6,400	3,520
40	30	1,600	1,200
50	40	2,500	2,000
60	50	3,600	3,000
670	423	52,700	31,120

$$b = \frac{(10 \times 31{,}120) - (670 \times 423)}{10 \times 52{,}700 - 670^2}$$

$$= \frac{311{,}200 - 283{,}410}{527{,}000 - 448{,}900}$$

$$= \frac{27{,}790}{78{,}100}$$

$$= 0.36$$

$$a = \frac{423}{10} - 0.36 \times \frac{670}{10} = 18.18$$

The linear model is y = 18.18 + 0.36x.

(c) The line may be plotted using two points as follows.

x = 20, y = 25.38
x = 120, y = 61.38

The line is plotted on the graph above.

(d) For mileage of 110 miles, the model would predict expenses of 18.18 + (0.36 × 110) = £57.78, so K's claim of £64 is not unreasonably high.

For mileage of 30 miles, the model would predict expenses of 18.18 + (0.36 × 30) = £28.98, so L's claim of £48 is very high and should be investigated.

The model is based on data for mileages from 20 to 120 miles. It should not be used to extrapolate to 160 miles, but if it were to be so used it would predict expenses of 18.18 + (0.36 × 160) = £75.78. On this basis, M's claim for £80 is not unreasonable.

5 *Workings*

Year	*x*	*y*	*xy*	x^2
20X3	0	22	0	0
20X4	1	25	25	1
20X5	2	24	48	4
20X6	3	26	78	9
20X7	4	29	116	16
20X8	5	28	140	25
20X9	6	30	180	36
	Σx = 21	Σy = 184	Σxy = 587	Σx^2 = 91

NOTES

n = 7

where y = a + bx

$$b = \frac{(7 \times 587) - (21 \times 184)}{(7 \times 91) - (21^2)}$$

$$= \frac{245}{196}$$

$$= 1.25$$

$$a = \frac{184}{7} - \frac{1.25 \times 21}{7}$$

= 22.5357, say 22.5

y = 22.5 + 1.25x where x = 0 in 20X3, x = 1 in 20X4 and so on.

Using this trend line, predicted sales in 20Y0 (year 7) would be 22.5 + 1.25 × 7 = 31.25 = 31,250 units.

Similarly, for 20Y1 (year 8) predicted sales would be 22.5 + 1.25 × 8 = 32.50 = 32,500 units.

6 The coefficient a = 28 indicates that when there is no output costs of £28,000 will still be incurred. In other words, fixed costs are £28,000.

The coefficient b = 2.6 indicates as output levels increase by one unit, costs increase by £2.60. The variable cost per unit is therefore £2.60

Chapter 5 :

TIME SERIES ANALYSIS

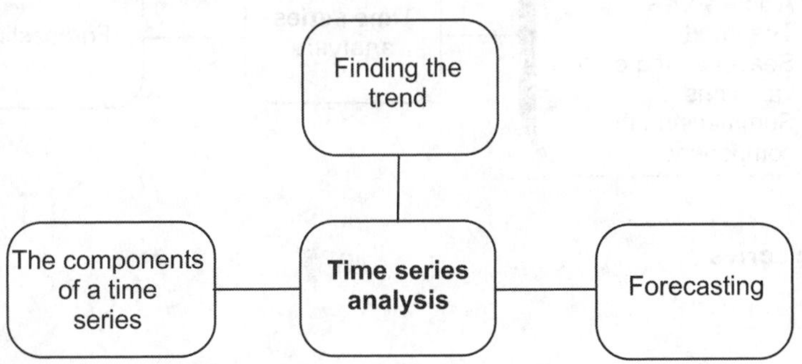

Introduction

In Chapter 4 we looked at how the relationship between two variables, and the strength of that relationship, can be assessed. This chapter looks at how the relationship between a variable (such as turnover, customer levels, output) and time can be analysed so as to forecast future values for the variable.

Your objectives

After completing this chapter you should:

(a) Know what a time series is

(b) Be able to describe the components of a time series

(c) Be able to find the trend using moving averages

(d) Be able to find seasonal variations using both the additive and multiplicative models

(e) Be able to forecast by extrapolating a trend and adjusting for seasonal variations

(f) Understand the concept of residuals

(g) Be aware of the concept of deseasonalisation.

1 THE COMPONENTS OF A TIME SERIES

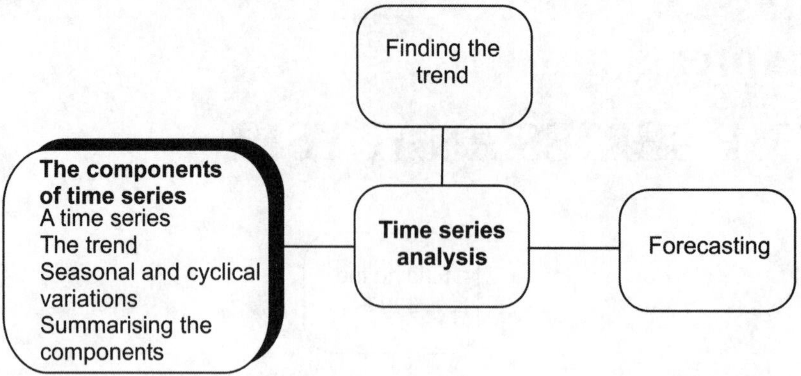

1.1 A time series

Definition

A **time series** is a series of figures or values recorded over time.

The following are examples of time series.

(a) Output at a factory each day for the last month

(b) Monthly sales over the last two years

(c) Total annual costs for the last ten years

(d) The Retail Prices Index each month for the last ten years

(e) The number of people employed by a company each year for the last twenty years

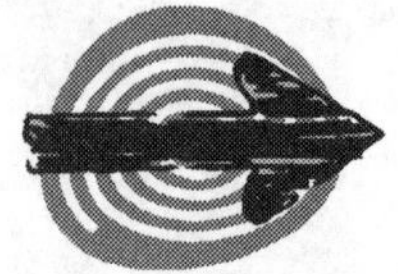

In Chapter 2 we briefly looked at a time series graph or historigram.

Consider the following time series.

Year	*Sales*
	£'000
20X0	20
20X1	21
20X2	24
20X3	23
20X4	27
20X5	30
20X6	28

The historigram is as follows.

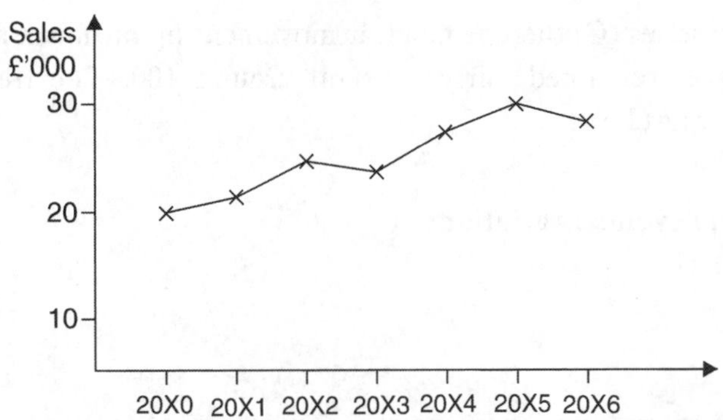

Figure 5.1: An historigram

The horizontal axis is always chosen to represent time, and the vertical axis represents the values of the data recorded.

There are several features of a time series which it may be necessary to identify.

(a) A trend

(b) Seasonal variations or fluctuations

(c) Cycles, or cyclical variations

(d) Non-recurring, random variations. These may be caused by unforeseen circumstances, such as a change in the government of the country, a war, the collapse of a company, technological change or a fire.

1.2 The trend

Definition

> The **trend** is the underlying long-term movement over time in the values of the data recorded.

In the following examples of time series, there are three types of trend.

	Output per labour hour	*Cost per unit*	*Number of employees*
	Units	£	
20X4	30	1.00	100
20X5	24	1.08	103
20X6	26	1.20	96
20X7	22	1.15	102
20X8	21	1.18	103
20X9	17	1.25	98
	(A)	(B)	(C)

(a) In time series (A) there is a downward trend in the output per labour hour. Output per labour hour did not fall every year, because it went up between 20X5 and 20X6, but the long-term movement is clearly a downward one.

(b) In time series (B) there is an upward trend in the cost per unit. Although unit costs went down in 20X7 from a higher level in 20X6, the basic movement over time is one of rising costs.

(c) In time series (C) there is no clear movement up or down, and the number of employees remained fairly constant around 100. The trend is therefore a static, or level one.

1.3 Seasonal and cyclical variations

Definition

Seasonal variations are short-term fluctuations in recorded values, due to different circumstances which affect results at different times of the year, on different days of the week, at different times of day, or whatever.

Here are some examples.

(a) Sales of ice cream will be higher in summer than in winter, and sales of overcoats will be higher in autumn than in spring.

(b) Shops might expect higher sales shortly before Christmas, or in their winter and summer sales.

(c) Sales might be higher on Friday and Saturday than on Monday.

(d) The telephone network may be heavily used at certain times of the day (such as mid-morning and mid-afternoon) and much less used at other times (such as in the middle of the night).

'Seasonal' is a term which may appear to refer to the seasons of the year, but its meaning in time series analysis is somewhat broader, as the examples given above show.

EXAMPLE: A TREND PLUS SEASONAL VARIATIONS

The number of customers served by a company of travel agents over the past four years is shown in the following historigram.

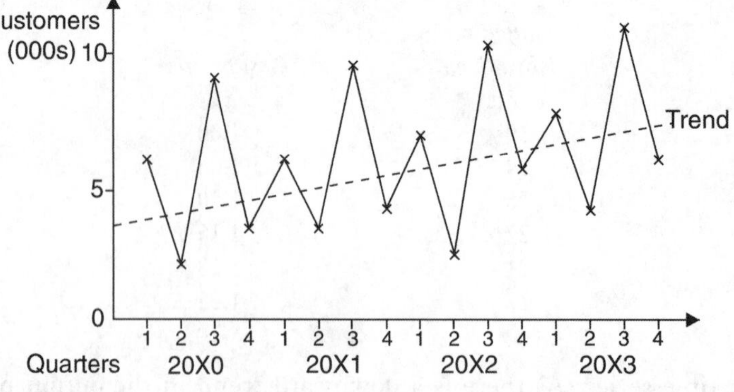

In this example, there would appear to be large seasonal fluctuations in demand, but there is also a basic upward trend.

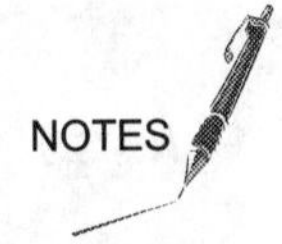

Activity 1 **(5 minutes)**

What seasonal variations would you expect to see in sales of DVD recorders?

Cyclical variations are medium-term changes in results caused by circumstances which repeat in cycles. In business, cyclical variations are commonly associated with economic cycles, successive booms and slumps in the economy. Economic cycles may last a few years. Cyclical variations are longer term than seasonal variations.

1.4 Summarising the components

In practice a time series could incorporate all four features and, to make reasonably accurate forecasts, the four features often have to be isolated. We can begin the process of isolating each feature by summarising the components of a time series by the following equation

$$Y = T + S + C + R$$

where: Y = the actual time series
T = the trend series
S = the seasonal component
C = the cyclical component
R = the residual component

Though you should be aware of the cyclical component, it is unlikely that you will be expected to carry out any calculation connected with isolating it. The mathematical model which we will use, the additive model, therefore excludes any reference to C and is

$$Y = T + S + R$$

We will begin by isolating the trend.

2 FINDING THE TREND

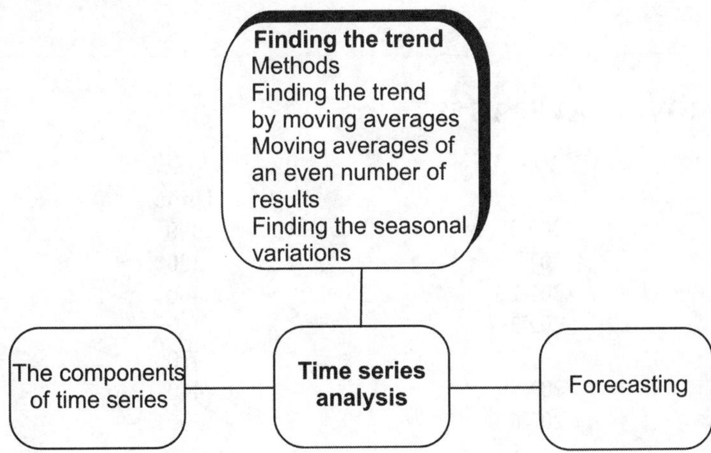

2.1 Methods

There are three principal methods of finding a trend.

(a) *Inspection*. As we saw in Chapter 4, the trend line can be drawn by eye on a graph in such a way that it appears to lie evenly between the recorded points, that is, a line of best fit is drawn by eye. It should be drawn to pass through the middle of the recorded points, thereby having as many data points below it as above it. The line on the historigram in the example in paragraph 1.1 is an example.

(b) *Regression analysis by the least squares method*. This method, which we looked at in Chapter 4, makes the assumption that the trend line, whether up or down, is a straight line. Periods of time (such as quarters for which sales figures are given) are numbered, commonly from 0, and the regression line of the data on those period numbers is found. That line is then taken to be the trend.

(c) *Moving averages*. This method attempts to remove seasonal (or cyclical) variations by a process of averaging and is looked at in detail in the next section.

2.2 Finding the trend by moving averages

Definition

Moving averages are consecutive averages of the results of a fixed number of periods.

Since a moving average is an average of several time periods, it is related to the mid-point of the overall period.

Moving averages could cover the sales of a shop over periods of seven days (Monday to the next Sunday for example) or a business's costs over periods of four quarters, or whatever else was appropriate to the circumstances.

EXAMPLE: MOVING AVERAGES

Year	*Sales*
	Units
20X0	390
20X1	380
20X2	460
20X3	450
20X4	470
20X5	440
20X6	500

Required

Take a moving average of the annual sales over a period of three years.

SOLUTION

(a) Average sales in the three year period 20X0 – 20X2 were

$$\left(\frac{390+380+460}{3}\right)=\frac{1,230}{3}=410$$

This average relates to the middle year of the period, 20X1.

(b) Similarly, average sales in the three year period 20X1 – 20X3 were

$$\left(\frac{380+460+450}{3}\right)=\frac{1,290}{3}=430$$

This average relates to the middle year of the period, 20X2.

(c) The average sales can also be found for the periods 20X2 – 20X4, 20X3 – 20X5 and 20X4 – 20X6, to give the following.

Year	*Sales*	*Moving total of 3 years' sales*	*Moving average of 3 years' sales (÷3)*
20X0	390		
20X1	380	1,230	410
20X2	460	1,290	430
20X3	450	1,380	460
20X4	470	1,360	453
20X5	440	1,410	470
20X6	500		

Note the following points.

(i) The moving average series has five figures relating to the years from 20X1 to 20X5. The original series had seven figures for the years from 20X0 to 20X6.

(ii) There is an upward trend in sales, which is more noticeable from the series of moving averages than from the original series of actual sales each year.

The above example averaged over a three-year period. Over what period should a moving average be taken? The answer to this question is that the moving average which is most appropriate will depend on the circumstances and the nature of the time series. Note the following points.

(a) A moving average which takes an average of the results in many time periods will represent results over a longer term than a moving average of two or three periods.

(b) On the other hand, with a moving average of results in many time periods, the last figure in the series will be out of date by several periods. In our example, the most recent average related to 20X5. With a moving average of five years' results, the final figure in the series would relate to 20X4.

(c) When there is a known cycle over which seasonal variations occur, such as all the days in the week or all the seasons in the year, the most suitable moving average would be one which covers one full cycle.

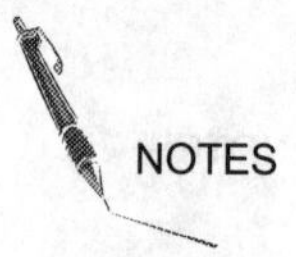

NOTES

Activity 2 **(5 minutes)**

Using the following data, what is the three-month moving average for April?

Month	*No of new houses finished*
January	500
February	450
March	700
April	900
May	1,250
June	1,000

2.3 Moving averages of an even number of results

In the previous example, moving averages were taken of the results in an odd number of time periods, and the average then related to the mid-point of the overall period.

If a moving average were taken of results in an even number of time periods, the basic technique would be the same, but the mid-point of the overall period would not relate to a single period. For example, suppose an average were taken of the following four results.

Spring	120	
Summer	90	average 115
Autumn	180	
Winter	70	

The average would relate to the mid-point of the period, between summer and autumn.

The trend line average figures need to relate to a particular time period; otherwise, seasonal variations cannot be calculated. To overcome this difficulty, we take a moving average of the moving average. An example will illustrate this technique.

EXAMPLE: MOVING AVERAGES OVER AN EVEN NUMBER OF PERIODS

Calculate a moving average trend line of the following results.

Year	*Quarter*	*Volume of sales* '000 units
20X7	1	600
	2	840
	3	420
	4	720
20X8	1	640
	2	860
	3	420
	4	740
20X9	1	670
	2	900
	3	430
	4	760

SOLUTION

A moving average of four will be used, since the volume of sales would appear to depend on the season of the year, and each year has four quarterly results.

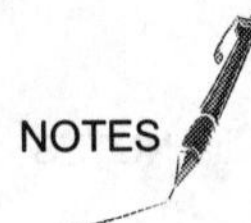

The moving average of four does not relate to any specific period of time; therefore we will take a moving total of pairs of four-quarter totals and divide that moving total by 8 (ie the number of data items which contributed to the total).

Year	*Quarter*	*Actual volume of sales* '000 units (A)	*Moving total of 4 quarters' sales* '000 units (B)	*Moving average of 4 quarters' sales* '000 units (B ÷ 4)	*Mid-point of 2 moving averages Trend line* '000 units (C)
20X7	1	600			
	2	840			
	3	420	2,580	5,200	650.00
	4	720	2,620	5,260	657.50
20X8	1	640	2,640	5,280	660.00
	2	860	2,640	5,300	662.50
	3	420	2,660	5,350	668.75
	4	740	2,690	5,420	677.50
20X9	1	670	2,730	5,470	683.75
	2	900	2,740	5,500	687.50
	3	430	2,760		
	4	760			

The final moving averages are related to specific quarters (from the third quarter of 20X7 to the second quarter of 20X9).

2.4 Finding the seasonal variations

Once a trend has been established, by whatever method, we can find the seasonal variations.

The additive model for time series analysis is Y = T + S + R. We can therefore write Y – T = S + R. In other words, if we deduct the trend series from the actual series, we will be left with the seasonal and residual components of the time series. If we assume that the residual component is relatively small, and hence negligible, the seasonal component can be found as S = Y – T, the de-trended series.

We will use an example to illustrate the process.

EXAMPLE: THE TREND AND SEASONAL VARIATIONS

Output at a factory appears to vary with the day of the week. Output over the last three weeks has been as follows.

	Week 1 '000 units	*Week 2* '000 units	*Week 3* '000 units
Monday	80	82	84
Tuesday	104	110	116
Wednesday	94	97	100
Thursday	120	125	130
Friday	62	64	66

NOTES

Required

Find the seasonal variation for each of the fifteen days, and the average seasonal variation for each day of the week using the moving averages method.

SOLUTION

Actual results fluctuate up and down according to the day of the week and so a moving average of five will be used. The difference between the actual result on any one day (Y) and the trend figure for that day (T) will be the seasonal variation (S) for the day.

The seasonal variations for the fifteen days are as follows.

		Actual (Y)	*Moving total of five days' output*	*Trend (T)*	*Seasonal variation (Y–T)*
Week 1	Monday	80			
	Tuesday	104			
	Wednesday	94	460	92.0	+2.0
	Thursday	120	462	92.4	+27.6
	Friday	62	468	93.6	–31.6
Week 2	Monday	82	471	94.2	–12.2
	Tuesday	110	476	95.2	+14.8
	Wednesday	97	478	95.6	+1.4
	Thursday	125	480	96.0	+29.0
	Friday	64	486	97.2	–33.2
Week 3	Monday	84	489	97.8	–13.8
	Tuesday	116	494	98.8	+17.2
	Wednesday	100	496	99.2	+0.8
	Thursday	130			
	Friday	66			

	Monday	*Tuesday*	*Wednesday*	*Thursday*	*Friday*
Week 1			+2.0	+27.6	–31.6
Week 2	–12.2	+14.8	+1.4	+29.0	–33.2
Week 3	–13.8	+17.2	+0.8		
Average	–13.0	+16.0	+1.4	+28.3	–32.4

You will notice that the variation between the actual results on any one particular day and the trend line average is not the same from week to week. This is because Y – T contains not only seasonal variations but random variations (residuals). In calculating the averages of the deviations, Y – T, for each day of the week, the residual components are expected to cancel out, or at least to be reduced to a negligible level.

Our estimate of the 'seasonal' or daily variation is almost complete, but there is one more important step to take. Variations around the basic trend line should cancel each other out, and add up to 0. In practice this is rarely the case because of random variation. The average seasonal estimates must therefore be corrected so that they add up to zero.

	Mon	*Tues*	*Wed*	*Thurs*	*Fri*	*Total*
Estimated average daily variation	–13.00	+16.00	+1.40	+28.30	–32.40	0.30
Adjustment to reduce ~ total variation to 0	–0.06	–0.06	–0.06	–0.06	–0.06	–0.30
Final estimate of average daily variation	–13.06	+15.94	+1.34	+28.24	–32.46	0.00

These might be rounded up or down as follows.

Monday –13; Tuesday +16; Wednesday +1; Thursday +28; Friday –32

Activity 3 **(20 minutes)**

Calculate a four-quarter moving average trend centred on actual quarters and then find seasonal variations from the following.

Sales in £'000

	Spring	*Summer*	*Autumn*	*Winter*
20X7	200	120	160	280
20X8	220	140	140	300
20X9	200	120	180	320

Seasonal variations using the multiplicative model

The method of estimating the seasonal variations in the above example was to use the differences between the trend and actual data. This is called the *additive model.*

Definition

The **additive model** for time series analysis assumes that the components of the series are independent of each other, an increasing trend not affecting the seasonal variations, for example.

The alternative is to use the *multiplicative model*. Sometimes this method is called the *proportional model.*

Definition

The **multiplicative** or **proportional model** for time series analysis expresses each actual figure as a proportion of the trend.

The model summarises a time series as $Y = T \times S \times R$. Note that the trend component will be the same whichever model is used but the values of the seasonal and residual components will vary according to the model being applied.

The previous example on the trend and seasonal variations can be reworked on this alternative basis. The trend is calculated in exactly the same way as before but we need a different approach for the seasonal variations.

The multiplicative model is Y = T × S × R and, just as we calculated S = Y – T for the additive model at the beginning of this Section we can calculate Y/T = S for the multiplicative model.

		Actual (*Y*)	*Trend* (*T*)	*Seasonal percentage* (*Y/T*)
Week 1	Monday	80		
	Tuesday	104		
	Wednesday	94	92.0	1.022
	Thursday	120	92.4	1.299
	Friday	62	93.6	0.662
Week 2	Monday	82	94.2	0.870
	Tuesday	110	95.2	1.155
	Wednesday	97	95.6	1.015
	Thursday	125	96.0	1.302
	Friday	64	97.2	0.658
Week 3	Monday	84	97.8	0.859
	Tuesday	116	98.8	1.174
	Wednesday	100	99.2	1.008
	Thursday	130		
	Friday	66		

The summary of the seasonal variations expressed in proportional terms is as follows.

	Monday %	*Tuesday* %	*Wednesday* %	*Thursday* %	*Friday* %
Week 1			1.022	1.299	0.662
Week 2	0.870	1.155	1.015	1.302	0.658
Week 3	0.859	1.174	1.008		
Total	1.729	2.329	3.045	2.601	1.320
Average	0.8645	1.1645	1.0150	1.3005	0.6600

Instead of summing to zero, as with the absolute approach, these should sum (in this case) to 5 (an average of 1).

They actually sum to 5.0045 so 0.0009 has to be deducted from each one. This is too small to make a difference to the figures above, so we should deduct 0.002 and 0.0025 from each of two seasonal variations. We could arbitrarily decrease Monday's variation to 0.8625 and Tuesday's to 1.162.

Activity 4 **(10 minutes)**

A company's quarterly sales figures have been analysed into a trend and seasonal variations using moving averages. Here is an extract from the analysis.

Year	*Quarter*	*Actual*	*Trend*
		£'000	£'000
20X8	1	350	366
	2	380	370
	3	400	380
	4	360	394
20X9	1	410	406
	2	430	414
	3	450	418
	4	370	423

Required

Find the average seasonal variation for each quarter, using the multiplicative model.

3 FORECASTING

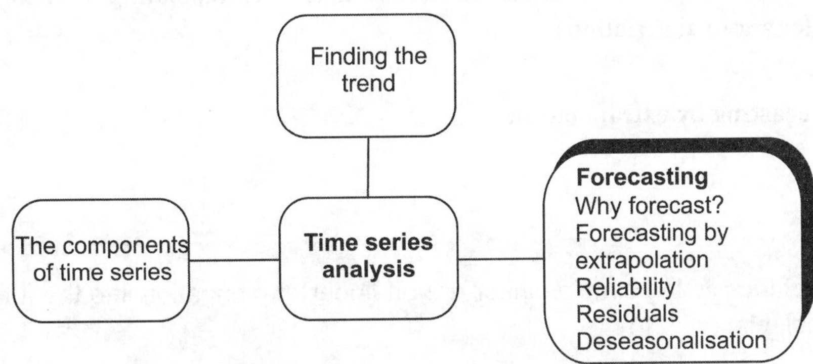

3.1 Why forecast?

Forecasting is an essential, but difficult, task of management. Many forecasts are made by guessing, but they are unlikely to be reliable.

The types of forecasting used by organisations include the following.

(a) **Costs**

- Raw materials
- Semi-finished goods
- Wage rates and overheads
- Interest rates

(b) **Sales/Activities**

- By industry, by region
- By market/product, market share
- By product category, by wholesaler, by retailer
- Competitive position – eg prices, exchange rates

- Competitive behaviour
- Price

(c) **Technology**

- New products
- New processes

(d) **Social and Political trends**

- Demographics
- Wealth profile
- Welfare and health provisions
- Impact of technology

(e) **Projects**

- Duration
- Costs

There are several mathematical techniques of forecasting which could be used. These techniques will not necessarily provide accurate forecasts but, on the whole, they are likely to provide more reliable estimates than guesswork. Techniques cannot eliminate uncertainty about the future, but they can help to ensure that managers take account of all currently-known facts in the preparation of their forecasts.

The technique which will be discussed here is that of extrapolating a trend and then adjusting for seasonal variations.

3.2 Forecasting by extrapolation

Definition

Extrapolation is the simple (linear or non-linear) prolongation into the future of historical relations.

Forecasts of future values should be made as follows.

(a) Calculate a trend line using moving averages or regression analysis. You may be asked to plot the trend line on a scatter diagram. It should be drawn as a straight line using the first and last available trend line figures.)

(b) Use the trend line to forecast future trend line values. (You can insert the appropriate value for x (= time) into a regression equation or calculate an average seasonal increase (or decrease) as the following example shows.)

(c) Adjust these values by the average seasonal variation applicable to the future period, to determine the forecast for that period. With the additive model, add (or subtract for negative variations) the variation. With the multiplicative model, multiply the trend value by the variation proportion.

Extending a trend line outside the range of known data, in this case forecasting the future from a trend line based on historical data, is known as extrapolation.

EXAMPLE: FORECASTING

Sales of product X each quarter for the last three years have been as follows (in thousands of units). Trend values, found by a moving averages method, are shown in brackets.

Year	*1st quarter*	*2nd quarter*	*3rd quarter*	*4th quarter*
1	18	30	20 (18.75)	6 (19.375)
2	20 (20)	33 (20.5)	22 (21)	8 (21.5)
3	22 (22.125)	35 (22.75)	25	10

Average seasonal variations for quarters 1 to 4 are –0.1, +12.4, +1.1 and –13.4 respectively.

Task

Use the trend line and estimates of seasonal variations to forecast sales in each quarter of Year 4.

SOLUTION

The trend line indicates an increase of about 0.6 per quarter. This can be confirmed by calculating the average quarterly increase in trend line values between the third quarter of Year 1 (18.75) and the second quarter of Year 2 (22.75). The average rise is

$$\frac{22.75-18.75}{7} = \frac{4}{7} = 0.57, \text{ say } 0.6$$

Taking 0.6 as the quarterly increase in the trend, the forecast of sales for Year 4, before seasonal adjustments (the trend line forecast) would be as follows.

Year	*Quarter*			*Trend line*
3	*2nd	(actual trend)	22.75, say	22.8
	3rd			23.4
	4th			24.0
4	1st			24.6
	2nd			25.2
	3rd			25.8
	4th			26.4

* last known trend line value.

Seasonal variations should now be incorporated to obtain the final forecast.

	Quarter	*Trend line forecast* '000 units	*Average seasonal variation* '000 units	*Forecast of actual sales* '000 units
Year 4	1st	24.6	–0.1	24.5
	2nd	25.2	+12.4	37.6
	3rd	25.8	+1.1	26.9
	4th	26.4	–13.4	13.0

If we had been using the multiplicative model, with an average variation for (for example) Quarter 3 of 1.057, our prediction for the third quarter of Year 4 would have been 25.8 × 1.057 = 27.3.

3.3 Reliability

Note that the multiplicative model is better than the additive model for forecasting when the trend is increasing or decreasing over time. In such circumstances, seasonal variations are likely to be increasing or decreasing too. The additive model simply adds absolute and unchanging seasonal variations to the trend figures whereas the multiplicative model, by multiplying increasing or decreasing trend values by a constant seasonal variation factor, takes account of changing seasonal variations.

All forecasts are, however, subject to error, but the likely errors vary from case to case.

(a) The further into the future the forecast is for, the more unreliable it is likely to be.

(b) The less data available on which to base the forecast, the less reliable the forecast.

(c) The pattern of trend and seasonal variations cannot be guaranteed to continue in the future.

(d) There is always the danger of random variations upsetting the pattern of trend and seasonal variation.

While all time series of data may be extrapolated, it is not meaningful to extrapolate in all cases. The following guidelines should improve the reliability.

(a) The extrapolation should preferably be based on the determining factor for the expected development and the trend of this factor.

(b) Data for an extrapolation should at least go five years back, preferably 10 years. However, when radical changes have taken place, which have altered or radically influenced the determining factors, it does not make sense to include data from before such changes.

(c) Any constraints on the extrapolation should be taken into account (e.g. physical or political boundaries for the development of the extrapolated factor). When approaching a constraint, the extrapolation will no longer be a good approximation.

Limitations of extrapolation in forecasting

Since extrapolation is based on historical data alone, and does not include combined effects of several developments, it can only be used for medium or short-term forecasts for smaller, specific areas, where no radical or untypical developments are expected.

In spite of its limitations, an extrapolation is a better forecast than an assumption of status quo. Thus, even when there is no time or resources to involve technical experts, it may be justified that a non-expert makes a simple extrapolation as a first approximation.

Activity 5 **(45 minutes)**

The percentage of employees absent from work was recorded over a four-week period as follows.

Week	*Mon*	*Tues*	*Weds*	*Thurs*	*Fri*
1	8.4	5.1	5.7	4.8	6.3
2	8.1	5.5	6.0	4.6	6.5
3	8.4	5.6	6.2	5.0	6.8
4	8.6	5.6	6.3	4.9	6.9

Task

(a) Draw a graph of the time series of absenteeism.

(b) By means of a moving average and the additive model, find the trend and the seasonal adjustments.

(c) Plot the trend line by eye and use it as a basis to forecast daily absenteeism for week 5.

(d) Personnel have suggested that the absenteeism figure for Friday of week 8 could be as high as 8%. Discuss whether or not you would support this.

3.4 Residuals

Definition

A **residual** is the difference between the results which would have been predicted (for a past period for which we already have data) by the trend line adjusted for the average seasonal variation and the actual results.

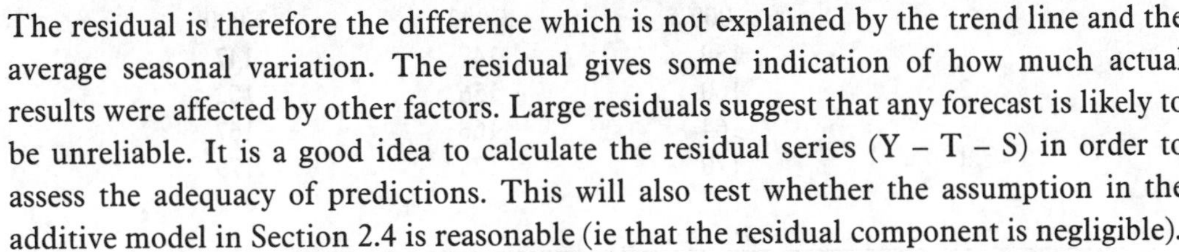

The residual is therefore the difference which is not explained by the trend line and the average seasonal variation. The residual gives some indication of how much actual results were affected by other factors. Large residuals suggest that any forecast is likely to be unreliable. It is a good idea to calculate the residual series (Y – T – S) in order to assess the adequacy of predictions. This will also test whether the assumption in the additive model in Section 2.4 is reasonable (ie that the residual component is negligible).

In the example above entitled 'Forecasting', the 'prediction' for the third quarter of year 1 would have been 18.75 + 1.1 = 19.85. As the actual value was 20, the residual was only 20 – 19.85 = 0.15. The residual for the fourth quarter of year 2 was 8 – (21.5 – 13.4) = 8 – 8.1 = –0.1. An analysis of all the residuals associated with a particular time series will indicate whether the predictions based on the time series are reliable.

3.5 Deseasonalisation

Economic statistics, such as unemployment figures, are often 'seasonally adjusted' or 'deseasonalised' so as to ensure that the overall trend (rising, falling or stationary) is clear. All this means is that seasonal variations (S) (derived from previous data) have been taken out, to leave a figure (Y – S) which might be taken as indicating the trend.

Definition

Deseasonalisation is the process of removing seasonal variations from data to leave a figure indicating the trend.

EXAMPLE: DESEASONALISATION

Actual sales figures for four quarters, together with appropriate seasonal adjustment factors derived from previous data, are as follows.

		Seasonal adjustments	
	Actual	*Additive*	*Multiplicative*
Quarter	*sales*	*model*	*model*
	£'000	£'000	
1	150	+3	1.02
2	160	+4	1.05
3	164	–2	0.98
4	170	–5	0.95

Required

Deseasonalise these data.

SOLUTION

We are reversing the normal process of applying seasonal variations to trend figures, so with the additive model we subtract positive seasonal variations (and add negative ones), and with the multiplicative model we divide by the seasonal variation factors (expressed as proportions).

		Deseasonalised sales	
	Actual	*Additive*	*Multiplicative*
Quarter	*sales*	*model*	*model*
	£'000	£'000	£'000
1	150	147	147
2	160	156	152
3	164	166	167
4	170	175	179

Chapter roundup

- A time series is a series of figures or values recorded over time.
- A time series has four features: a trend, seasonal variations, cyclical variations and random variations (residuals).
- A time series can be summarised by the additive model (Y = T + S + R) or the multiplicative (or proportional) model (Y = T × S × R).
- The most commonly used method in practice for finding the trend is the moving averages method. Once the trend has been established, the seasonal component can be calculated as Y – T (if the additive model is being used) or Y/T (if the multiplicative model is being used).
- A process of averaging and adjusting the individual seasonal components is necessary to remove the effect of any residuals and to arrive at seasonal components for each season of the year, day of the week as necessary.
- By extrapolating the trend line and adjusting the resulting figures for the seasonal component of the time series, forecasts can be obtained.
- Calculating the residuals of the time series assesses the adequacy and reliability of the predictions made using the trend and seasonal components.
- Deseasonalised data (Y – S) are often used by economic commentators.

Quick quiz

1. What is the definition of a time series?
2. What are the four components that combine to form a time series?
3. How can trend lines be found?
4. How are trend values calculated when moving averages of an even number of results are taken?
5. Why are average seasonal variations adjusted to sum to zero?
6. Distinguish between the additive model and the multiplicative model of time series.
7. In what circumstances should the proportional model rather than the additive model be used?
8. Describe how the additive model may be used in forecasting.
9. What is extrapolation?
10. What is the term for the difference which is not explained by the trend line and the average seasonal variation?

Answers to quick quiz

1 A time series is a series of figures or values recorded over time.

2 The trend, the seasonal component, the cyclical component and the residual component.

3 Trend lines can be found as follows.

(a) By inspection
(b) By regression analysis (least squares method)
(c) By moving averages

4 (a) A moving average of the even number of results is taken first.

(b) This is followed by taking a moving average of the moving average calculated in (a). This ensures that the trend line average figures are related to a particular time period.

5 Since variations around the basic trend line should cancel each other out, and add up to zero (this is rarely the case in practice because of random variations), average seasonal estimates must also be corrected so that they add up to zero.

6 The additive model for time series analysis assumes that the components of the series are independent of each other.

The multiplicative model, on the other hand, express each actual figure as a proportion of the trend.

7 The proportional model should be used when there is an increasing or decreasing trend over time.

8 (a) Find the trend by using the moving averages method or regression analysis. Forecast the trend for the required period.

(b) Calculate the seasonal component, s.

s = Y-T

(where Y = actual series and T= trend)

(c) Forecast future values by adding or subtracting seasonal variations from forecast trend values.

9 Extrapolation involves extending a trend line outside the range of known data.

10 A residual.

Answers to activities

1 Sales of DVD recorders might peak at Christmas and also before major sporting events such as the Olympic Games or the football World Cup.

2 $\frac{700+900+1{,}250}{3} = 950$

3

		Sales (Y)	4-quarter total	8-quarter total	Moving average (T)	Seasonal variation (Y-T)
20X7	Spring	200				
	Summer	120				
			760			
	Autumn	160		1,540	192.5	–32.5
			780			
	Winter	280		1,580	197.5	+82.5
			800			
20X8	Spring	220		1,580	197.5	+22.5
			780			
	Summer	140		1,580	197.5	–57.5
			800			
	Autumn	140		1,580	197.5	–57.5
			780			
	Winter	300		1,540	192.5	+107.5
			760			
20X9	Spring	200		1,560	195.0	+5.0
			800			
	Summer	120		1,620	202.5	–82.5
			820			
	Autumn	180				
	Winter	320				

We can now average the seasonal variations.

	Spring	Summer	Autumn	Winter	Total
20X7			–32.5	+82.5	
20X8	+22.5	–57.5	–57.5	+107.5	
20X9	+5.0	–82.5			
	+27.5	–140.0	–90.0	+190.0	
Average variation (in £'000)	+13.75	–70.00	–45.00	+95.00	–6.25
Adjustment so sum is zero	+1.5625	+1.5625	+1.5625	+1.5625	+6.25
Adjusted average variations	+15.3125	–68.4375	–3.4375	+96.5625	0

These might be rounded up or down to:

Spring £15,000, Summer –£68,000, Autumn –£43,000, Winter £96,000

4

Quarter	*1*	*2*	*3*	*4*
	%	%	%	%
Variation, 20X8	0.956	1.027	1.053	0.914
Variation, 20X9	1.010	1.039	1.077	0.875
Average variation	0.983	1.033	1.065	0.895
Adjustment	0.006	0.006	0.006	0.006
Adjusted average variation	0.989	1.039	1.071	0.901

5 (a)

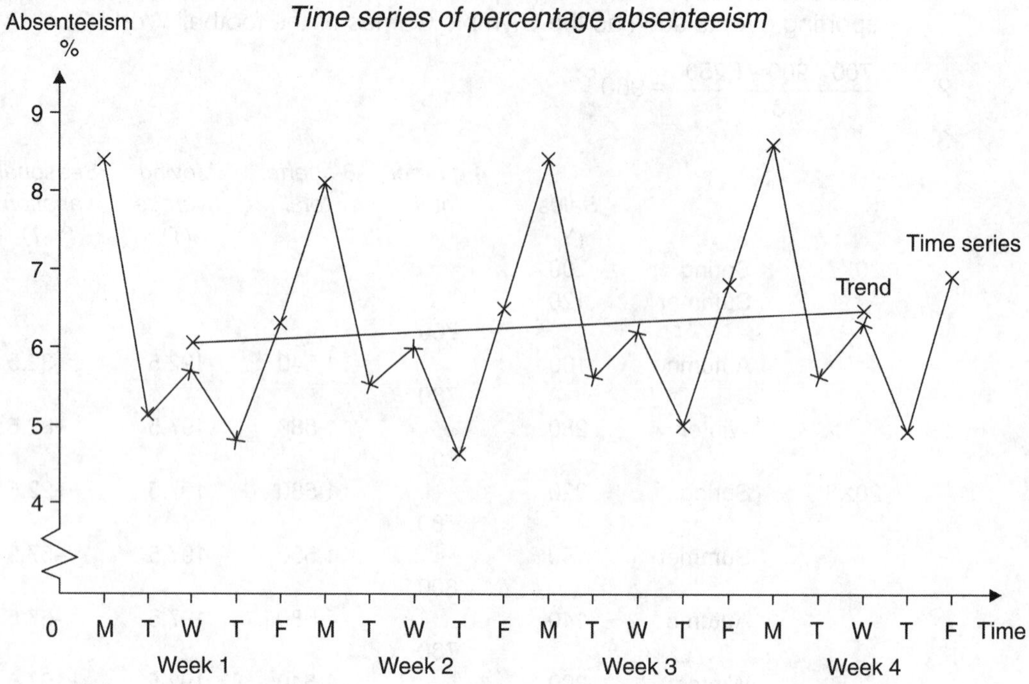

Time series of percentage absenteeism

(b)

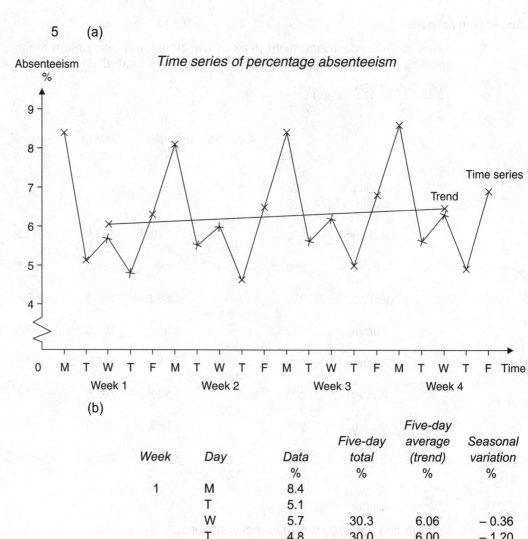

Week	*Day*	*Data* %	*Five-day total* %	*Five-day average (trend)* %	*Seasonal variation* %
1	M	8.4			
	T	5.1			
	W	5.7	30.3	6.06	– 0.36
	T	4.8	30.0	6.00	– 1.20
	F	6.3	30.4	6.08	+ 0.22
2	M	8.1	30.7	6.14	+ 1.96
	T	5.5	30.5	6.10	– 0.60
	W	6.0	30.7	6.14	– 0.14
	T	4.6	31.0	6.20	– 1.60
	F	6.5	31.1	6.22	+ 0.28
3	M	8.4	31.3	6.26	+ 2.14
	T	5.6	31.7	6.34	– 0.74
	W	6.2	32.0	6.40	– 0.20
	T	5.0	32.2	6.44	– 1.44
	F	6.8	32.2	6.44	+ 0.36
4	M	8.6	32.3	6.46	+ 2.14
	T	5.6	32.2	6.44	– 0.84
	W	6.3	32.3	6.46	– 0.16
	T	4.9			
	F	6.9			

Week	*M*	*T*	*W*	*T*	*F*	*Total*
	%	%	%	%	%	
1			– 0.36	– 1.20	+ 0.22	
2	+ 1.96	– 0.60	– 0.14	– 1.60	+ 0.28	
3	+ 2.14	– 0.74	– 0.20	– 1.44	+ 0.36	
4	+ 2.14	– 0.84	– 0.16			
	6.24	– 2.18	– 0.86	– 4.24	0.86	
Average	+ 2.08	– 0.73	– 0.22	– 1.41	+ 0.29	+ 0.01
Adjustment					– 0.01	– 0.01
Adjusted average	+ 2.08	– 0.73	– 0.22	– 1.41	+ 0.28	0.00

The seasonal adjustments are as shown in the last line of the above table.

(c) The trend line has been plotted on the graph above, using the figures for Wednesday of week 1 (6.06%) and Wednesday of week 4 (6.46%).

The trend rose by 0.4% over this period, an average daily rise of 0.4/15 = 0.027%. This average will be used to derive the trend for week 5.

Week 5 predictions

Day	*Trend*	*Seasonal variation*	*Prediction*	*Rounded prediction*
	%	%	%	%
Monday	6.541*	+ 2.08	8.621	8.6
Tuesday	6.568	– 0.73	5.838	5.8
Wednesday	6.595	– 0.22	6.375	6.4
Thursday	6.622	– 1.41	5.212	5.2
Friday	6.649	+ 0.28	6.929	6.9

* 6.46 + (3 × 0.027)

(d) A forecast for Friday of week 8, based on the above computations, would be 6.46 + (22 × 0.027) + 0.28 = 7.334%, which is significantly below the personnel department's forecast. It is probable that the personnel department have estimated a more steeply rising trend. However, no forecast so far into the future and based on only four weeks' data is likely to be reliable. The estimate of 8% cannot be supported.

Part C

Producing Information in Appropriate Formats

Chapter 6 :

PRODUCING INFORMATION WITH SPREADSHEETS

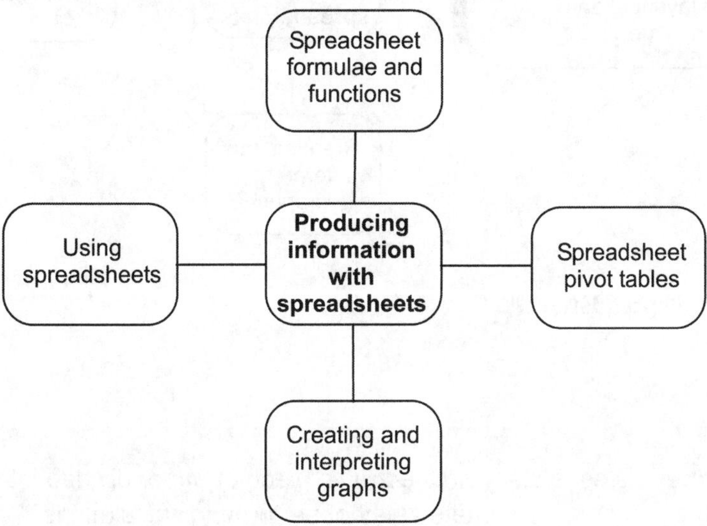

Introduction

In this chapter we explain the workings of some useful spreadsheet formulae and functions. In Chapters 2 and 5 we have already discussed the charts and graphs that are used when analysing data. In this chapter we are going to explain how to create and interpret these diagrams using a spreadsheet. Once you have mastered the basic graphs – line, pie, bar charts and histograms – using spreadsheet software, you can explore the many other features of a spreadsheet package for yourself. Remember, the online help facility provides an excellent source of information.

Your objectives

After completing this chapter you should:

(a) Be aware of the various uses of spreadsheets

(b) Understand the layout of an Excel page

(c) Know how to analyse data using pivot tables

(d) Be able to draw a range of graphs using a spreadsheet

(e) Be able to draw valid conclusions from the information derived

1 USING SPREADSHEETS

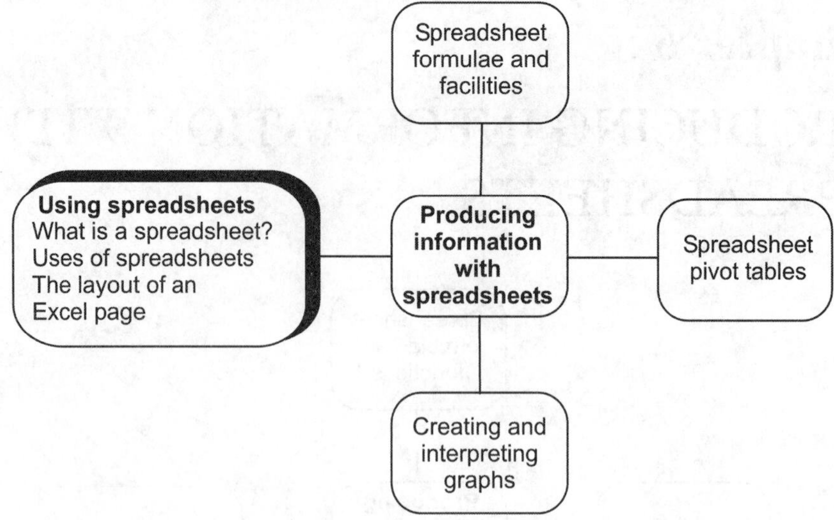

1.1 What is a spreadsheet?

Definition

A **spreadsheet** is essentially an electronic piece of paper divided into rows and columns. It provides an automated way of performing calculations.

It is a program that allows you to use data to forecast, manage, predict and present information. Below is a spreadsheet processing budgeted sales figures for three geographical areas for the first quarter of the year.

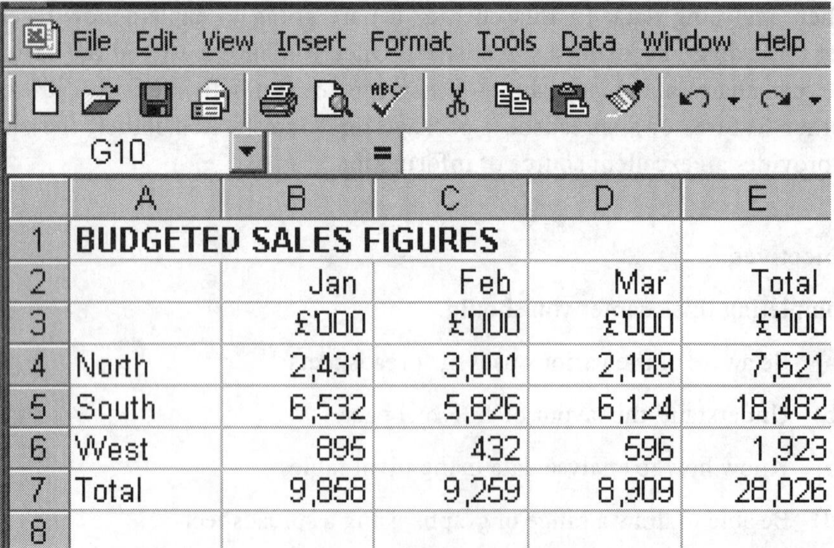

	A	B	C	D	E
1	BUDGETED SALES FIGURES				
2		Jan	Feb	Mar	Total
3		£'000	£'000	£'000	£'000
4	North	2,431	3,001	2,189	7,621
5	South	6,532	5,826	6,124	18,482
6	West	895	432	596	1,923
7	Total	9,858	9,259	8,909	28,026
8					

Spreadsheets save time. For example, the spreadsheet above has been set up to calculate the totals **automatically**, if you changed your estimate of sales in February for the North region to £3,296 the totals would change accordingly.

The main examples of spreadsheet packages are Lotus 1-2-3 and Microsoft Excel. We will be referring to Microsoft Excel, as this is the most widely used spreadsheet.

NOTES

1.2 Uses of spreadsheets

A spreadsheet, or worksheet, is a grid of rows and columns that help people keep track of numbers. It is an important financial analysis and decision-making tool. Since spreadsheets can be used to build a wide variety of models, spreadsheet packages are 'general purpose' software packages, as distinct from software packages which are designed for specific applications (for example a sales ledger package).

A spreadsheet can be something as simple as a tool which helps you keep track of your cheques, deposits and household expenses, or something as complex as a general ledger which a accountant uses to keep track of business transactions. They are used to create budgets, show trends and projections, or track performances and results.

Spreadsheets can be used to summarise data in many ways. For example, if we did a questionnaire survey, we could produce ordered or organised lists of responses, using some criteria (such as ordering the responses based upon age). We could summarise the information further by doing a count of respondents who gave similar responses. This translation from a textual (or verbal) response to a numerical one allows us to produce tables (e.g. one-way and two-way counts). Graphs can also be produced so we can see the ***distribution*** of responses. Information that is already in numerical form, such as age or income, can be summarised further by determining the statistical characteristics.

Some of the more **common applications** of spreadsheets are shown below:

• Management accounts	• Market share analysis and planning	• Stock control
• Cash-flow analysis and forecasting	• Budgets	• Profit and loss accounts (income statements)
• Reconciliations	• Sales and profit projections	• Balance sheets
• Job cost estimates	• Loan and depreciation schedules	• Product planning
• Individual and departmental statistics	• Payroll	• Pricing strategies
		• Investments

The best uses of electronic spreadsheets are for heavy number crunching and 'What if' analysis. This type of analysis refers to changing one or two numbers in a budget or pricing structure, for example, to see how it will affect the results. Excel's Solver and Report Manager enable you to explore a variety of sophisticated financial scenarios quickly and easily.

What all these have in common is that they all involve data processing with:

- Numerical data
- Repetitive, time-consuming calculations
- A logical processing structure

1.3 The layout of an Excel page

The 'workbook' (spreadsheet) is divided into columns identified with alphabetic headings, and rows, identified with numeric headings. The columns and rows divide the page into 'cells'. Its row number and column letter identify each cell. An example was shown in Section 1.1

The **cursor** shows the 'active' cell. At the top or bottom of the screen, the spreadsheet program will display information such as:

(a) The reference of the cell where the cursor lies.

(b) The width of the column where the cursor lies (you can alter column widths to suit yourself, without changing the total number of columns available on the spreadsheet).

(c) The contents of the cell where the cursor lies, if there is anything there.

The contents of any cell can be one of the following.

(a) **Text.** A cell so designated contains words or numerical data (e.g. a date) that will not be used in computations. On newer versions of all popular spreadsheets, text can be formatted in a similar way to what is possible using a word-processing package. Different fonts can be selected, text can be emboldened or italicised, and the point size of the lettering can be changed.

(b) **Values.** A value is a **number** that can be used in a calculation.

(c) **Formulae.** A formula **refers to other cells** in the spreadsheet, and performs some sort of computation with them. For example, if cell Cl contains the formula =Al-Bl this means that the contents of cell Bl should be subtracted from the contents of cell Al and the result displayed in cell Cl. Note that a formula starts with a specific command or choice or symbols in most packages to distinguish it from text. In Excel, a formula always begins with an equals sign: =

Laying-out a worksheet

- Leave the first row for the title of the worksheet.
- Data for the independent variable goes vertically down column A, starting with row 2, 3 or 4 depending on the dependent variable details.
- The description of the dependent variable goes on row 2, starting with column B. Use additional columns (C, D, etc.) if there is more than one variable (see example in Section 1.1).
- Data for each dependent variable goes vertically down the column under its description.

Adding cell information

- Move the cursor to a cell and click. A box forms around the cell and you can now type your data.
- When you have typed data into the cell, you have two options.
- TAB – to move to the next column on the same row.
- RETURN – to move to the next row in the same column.
- Continue until all data is added to the workbook page.
- When finished, click on a cell outside the range of your data. This will enter the data in the last cell.

Activity 1 **(20 minutes)**

This activity tests some basic ideas about spreadsheets.

(a) What is a spreadsheet?

(b) Give five uses of a spreadsheet.

(c) What is meant by the term 'active cell'?

(d) A cell in a spreadsheet can contain one of three things: text, values or formulae. Briefly explain the purpose of each of these.

2 SPREADSHEET FORMULAE AND FUNCTIONS

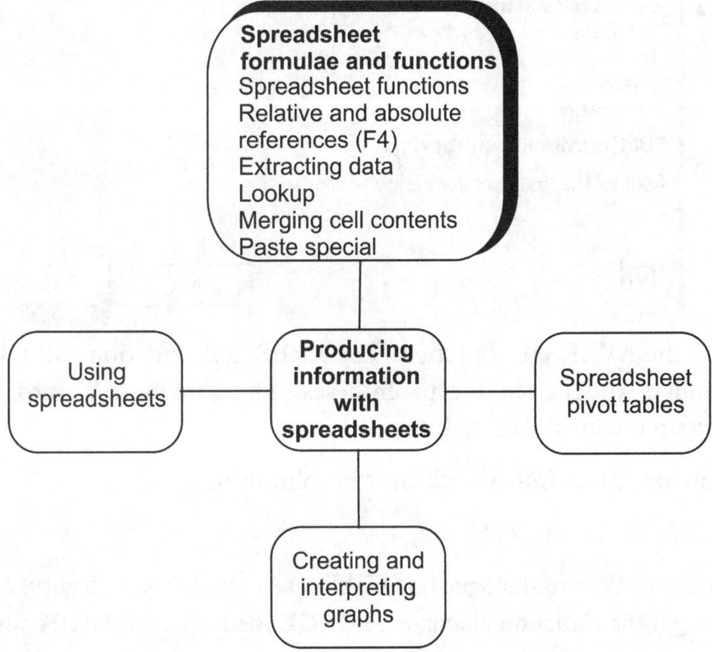

2.1 Spreadsheet functions

Functions are used to form all or part of a formula. Excel provides two general types of mathematical functions: those that are used in business applications and those that are oriented to higher mathematics. We will be focusing on those associated with business applications.

The Autosum function

One of the most commonly used functions is Autosum.

Whenever you click the **AutoSum** button (Σ) in the Standard toolbar, Excel inserts a SUM () function in the active cell. Not only will the SUM () function write the sum formula, but it will make a guess at what range of cells you desire to sum, and will leave you in edit mode so that you can correct the sum range.

Function wizard

Excel provides two ways for entering function names. You can type in the name of the function if you know it or you can use the ***Function Wizard***. To use the Function Wizard you can choose **Function** from the **Insert** menu or you can click on the **Function Wizard** button (*fx*) located on the Standard toolbar.

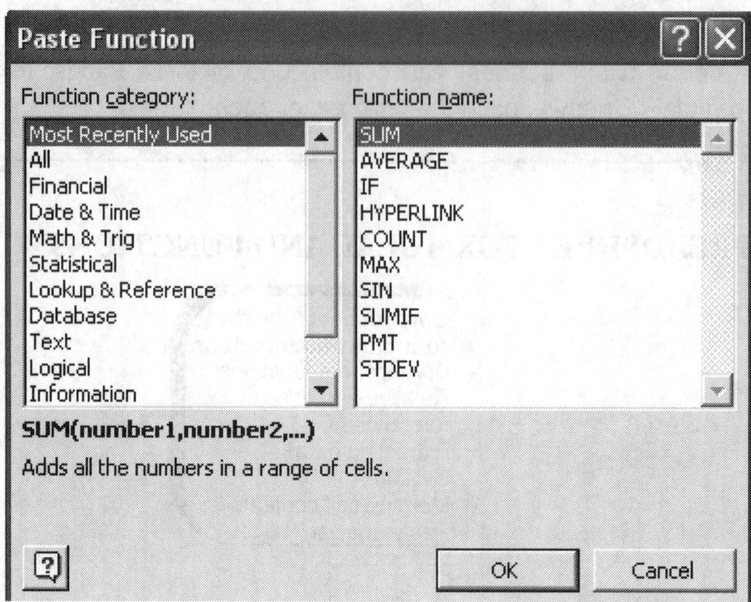

We want to use the AVERAGE function. The AVERAGE function will take the average of all the numbers you list in the parentheses. The Function Wizard will take you through setting up the formula step by step.

Enter the following grades into a worksheet in column B.

76. 89, 76, 100, 53, 89, 27, 65, 94, 57.

Within the **Function Wizard** dialogue box highlight the Function Category: **Most Recently Used** and highlight the Function Name: **AVERAGE** then click on the **OK** button.

The following dialog box should appear:

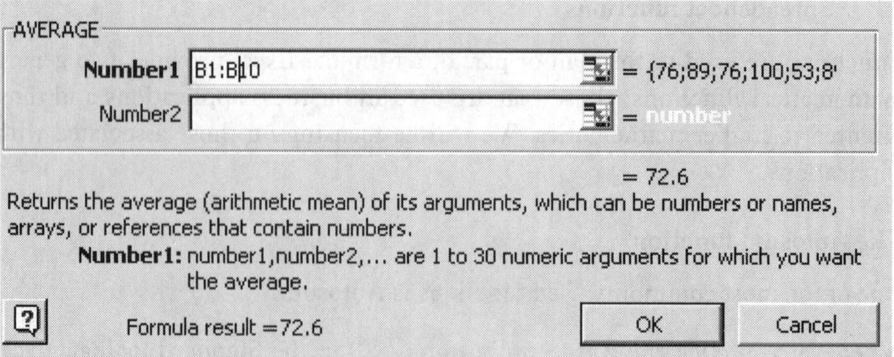

Enter the range B1:B10 in the Number 1 box of the dialogue box and then click on the **OK** button. Click on the **Enter** button or press the Return key to enter the formula.

Your workbook should look as follows.

File Edit View Insert Format Tools Data Window

C10 = =AVERAGE(B1:B10)

	A	B	C	D
1	Grades	76		
2		89		
3		76		
4		100		
5		53		
6		89		
7		27		
8		65		
9		94		
10		57	72.6	
11	Total	726		

EXAMPLE: CONSTRUCTING A CASH-FLOW PROJECTION

Suppose you wanted to set up a simple six-month cash-flow projection, in such a way that you could use it to estimate how the **projected cash balance** figures will **change** in total when any **individual item** in the projection is **altered**. You have the following information.

(a) Sales were £45,000 per month in 20X5, falling to £42,000 in January 20X6. Thereafter they are expected to increase by 3% per month (ie February will be 3% higher than January, and so on).

(b) Debts are collected as follows.

- (i) 60% in month following sale.
- (ii) 30% in second month after sale.
- (iii) 7% in third month after sale.
- (iv) 3% remains uncollected.

(c) Purchases are equal to cost of sales, set at 65% of sales.

(d) Overheads were £6,000 per month in 20X5, rising by 5% in 20X6.

(e) Opening cash is an overdraft of £7,500.

(f) Dividends: £10,000 final dividend on 20X5 profits payable in May.

(g) Capital purchases: plant costing £18,000 will be ordered in January. 20% is payable with order, 70% on delivery in February and the final 10% in May.

Headings and layout

The first job is to put in the various **headings** that you want on the cash-flow projection. At this stage, your screen might look as follows.

BPP LEARNING MEDIA

NOTES

	A	B	C	D	E	F	G
1	**EXCELLENT PLC**						
2	*Cash flow projection - six months ending 30 June X6*						
3		*Jan*	*Feb*	*Mar*	*Apr*	*May*	*Jun*
4		£	£	£	£	£	£
5	Sales						
6	*Cash receipts*						
7	1 month in arrears						
8	2 months in arrears						
9	3 months in arrears						
10	Total operating receipts						
11							
12	Cash payments						
13	Purchases						
14	Overheads						
15	Total operating payments						
16							
17	Dividends						
18	Capital purchases						
19	Total other payments						
20							
21	Net cash flow						
22	Cash balance b/f						
23	Cash balance c/f						
24							

A couple of points to note at this stage.

(a) We have **increased the width** of column A to allow longer pieces of text to be inserted. Had we not done so, only the first part of each caption would have been displayed (and printed).

(b) We have developed a **simple style for headings**. Headings are essential, so that users can identify what a spreadsheet does. We have **emboldened** the company name and *italicised* other headings.

(c) When **text** is entered into a cell it is usually **left-aligned** (as for example in column A). We have **centred** the headings above each column by highlighting the cells and using the relevant buttons at the top of the screen.

(d) **Numbers** should be **right-aligned** in cells.

(e) We have left **spaces** in certain rows (after blocks of related items) to make the spreadsheet **easier to use and read**.

Inserting formulae

The next stage is to put in the **calculations** you want the computer to carry out, expressed as **formulae**. For example, in cell B10 you want total operating receipts, so you move to cell B10 and put in the formula =SUM(B7:B9).

Look for a moment at cell C7. We are told that sales in January were £42,000 and that 60% of customers settle their accounts one month in arrears. We could insert the formula =B5*0.6 in the cell and fill in the other cells along the row so that it is replicated in each month. However, consider the effect of a change in payment patterns to a situation where, say, 55% of customer debts are settled after one month. This would necessitate a **change to each and every cell** in which the 0.6 ratio appears.

An alternative approach, which makes **future changes much simpler** to execute, is to put the relevant ratio (here, 60% or 0.6) in a cell **outside** the main table and cross-refer each cell in the main table to that cell.

This means that, if the percentage changes, the change need only be reflected in **one cell,** following which all cells which are dependent on that cell will **automatically use the new percentage**.

We will therefore input such values in separate parts of the spreadsheet, as follows over the page. Look at the other assumptions which we have inserted into this part of the spreadsheet.

	A	B	C	D	E	F	G
24							
25							
26	*This table contains the key variables for the*		*X6 cash flow projections*				
27							
28	Sales growth factor per month		1.03				
29	Purchases as % of sales		-0.65				
30							
31	Debts paid within 1 month		0.6				
32	Debts paid within 2 months		0.3				
33	Debts paid within 3 months		0.07				
34	Bad debts		0.03				
35							
36	Increase in overheads		1.05				
37							
38	Dividends (May)		-10000				
39							
40	Capital purchases		-18000				
41	January		0.2				
42	February		0.7				
43	May		0.1				
44							
45							
46	*This table contains relevant opening balance data as at Jan X6*						
47							
48	Monthly sales X5		45000				
49	January X6 sales		42000				
50	Monthly overheads X5		-6000				
51	Opening cash		-7500				
52							

Now we can go back to cell C7 and input =B5*C31 and then fill this in across the '1 month in arrears' row. (Note that, as we have no December sales figure, we will have to deal with cell B7 separately.) If we assume for the moment that we are copying to cells D7 through to G7 and follow this procedure, the contents of cell D7 would be shown as =C5*D31, and so on, as shown below.

	A	B	C	D	E	F	G
3		*Jan*	*Feb*	*Mar*	*Apr*	*May*	*Jun*
4		£	£	£	£	£	£
5	Sales						
6	*Cash receipts*						
7	1 month in arrears		=B5*C31	=C5*D31	=D5*E31	=E5*F31	=F5*G31
8	2 months in arrears						
9	3 months in arrears						
10	Total operating receipts						

NOTES

You may notice a problem if you look at this closely. While the formula in cell C7 is fine – it multiplies January sales by 0.6 (the 1 month ratio stored in cell C31) – the remaining formulae are useless, as they **refer to empty cells** in row 31. This is what the spreadsheet would look like (assuming, for now, constant sales of £42,000 per month).

	A	B	C	D	E	F	G
3		*Jan*	*Feb*	*Mar*	*Apr*	*May*	*Jun*
4		£	£	£	£	£	£
5	Sales	42000	42000	42000	42000	42000	42000
6	*Cash receipts*						
7	1 month in arrears		25200	0	0	0	0
8	2 months in arrears						
9	3 months in arrears						
10	Total operating receipts						

2.2 Relative and absolute references (F4)

There is a very important distinction between **relative** cell references and **absolute** cell references.

Usually, cell references are **relative.** A formula of =SUM(B7:B9) in cell B10 is relative. It does not really mean 'add up the numbers in cells B7 to B9'; it actually means '**add up the numbers in the three cells above this one**'. If the formula were copied to cell C10 (as we will do later), it would become =SUM(C7:C9).

This is what is causing the problem encountered above. The spreadsheet thinks we are asking it to 'multiply the number two up and one to the left by the number twenty-four cells down', and that is indeed the effect of the instruction we have given. But we are actually intending to ask it to 'multiply the number two up and one to the left by the number in cell C31'. This means that we need to create an **absolute** (unchanging) **reference** to cell C31. This is done by adding a pair of **dollar signs** ($) to the relevant formula, one before the column letter and one before the row number.

TIP

Don't type the dollar signs, add them as follows.

(a) Make cell C7 the active cell and press F2 to edit it.

(b) Note where the cursor is flashing: it should be after the 1. If it is not move it with the direction arrow keys so that it is positioned somewhere next to or within the cell reference C31.

(c) Press F4.

The **function key F4** adds dollar signs to the cell reference: it becomes $C$31. Press F4 again: the reference becomes C$31. Press it again: the reference becomes $C31. Press it once more, and the simple relative reference is restored: C31.

(a) A dollar sign **before a letter** means that the **column** reference stays the same when you copy the formula to another cell.

(b) A dollar sign **before a number** means that the **row** reference stays the same when you copy the formula to another cell.

EXAMPLE: BACK TO THE CASH-FLOW PROJECTION

In our example we have now altered the reference in cell C7 and filled in across to cell G7, overwriting what was there previously. This is the result.

(a) Formulae

	A	B	C	D	E	F	G
3		*Jan*	*Feb*	*Mar*	*Apr*	*May*	*Jun*
4		£	£	£	£	£	£
5	Sales	42000	42000	42000	42000	42000	42000
6	*Cash receipts*						
7	1 month in arrears		=B5*$C$31	=C5*$C$31	=D5*$C$31	=E5*$C$31	=F5*$C$31
8	2 months in arrears						
9	3 months in arrears						
10	Total operating receipts						

(b) Numbers

	A	B	C	D	E	F	G
3		*Jan*	*Feb*	*Mar*	*Apr*	*May*	*Jun*
4		£	£	£	£	£	£
5	Sales	42000	42000	42000	42000	42000	42000
6	*Cash receipts*						
7	1 month in arrears		25200	25200	25200	25200	25200
8	2 months in arrears						
9	3 months in arrears						
10	Total operating receipts						

Other formulae required for this projection are as follows.

(a) **Cell B5** refers directly to the information we are given – **sales of £42,000** in January. We have input this variable in cell C49. The other formulae in row 5 (sales) reflect the predicted sales growth of 3% per month, as entered in cell C28.

(b) Similar formulae to the one already described for row 7 are required in rows 8 and 9.

(c) **Row 10** (total operating receipts) will display simple **subtotals,** in the form =SUM(B7:B9).

(d) **Row 13 (purchases)** requires a formula based on the data in row 5 **(sales)** and the value in cell C29 (**purchases** as a % of sales). This model assumes no changes in stock levels from month to month, and that stocks are sufficiently high to enable this. The formula is B5 * $C$29. Note that C29 is negative.

(e) **Row 15** (total operating payments), like row 10, requires **formulae** to create **subtotals.**

(f) **Rows 17 and 18** refer to the **dividends and capital purchase data** input in cells C38 and C40 to 43.

(g) **Row 21** (net cash flow) requires a **total** in the form =B10 + B15 + B21.

(h) **Row 22** (balance b/f) requires the contents of the **previous month's closing cash** figure.

(i) **Row 23** (balance b/f) requires the **total** of the **opening cash** figure and the **net cash flow** for the month.

Once the formulae have been inserted, the following illustration shows the formulae the spreadsheet would contain. (Remember, it does not normally look like this on screen, as formulae are not usually displayed in cells.)

	A	B	C	D	E	F	G
1	EXCELLENT PLC						
2	Cash flow projection - six months						
3		*Jan*	*Feb*	*Mar*	*Apr*	*May*	*Jun*
4		£	£	£	£	£	£
5	Sales	=C49	=B5*$C$28	=C5*$C$28	=D5*$C$28	=E5*$C$28	=F5*$C$28
6	Cash receipts						
7	1 month in arrears	=$C$48*$C$31	=B5*$C$31	=C5*$C$31	=D5*$C$31	=E5*$C$31	=F5*$C$31
8	2 months in arrears	=$C$48*$C$32	=$C$48*$C$32	=B5*$C$32	=C5*$C$32	=D5*$C$32	=E5*$C$32
9	3 months in arrears	=$C$48*$C$33	=$C$48*$C$33	=$C$48*$C$33	=B5*$C$33	=C5*$C$33	=D5*$C$33
10	Total operating receipts	=SUM(B7:B9)	=SUM(C7:C9)	=SUM(D7:D9)	=SUM(E7:E9)	=SUM(F7:F9)	=SUM(G7:G9)
11							
12	Cash payments						
13	Purchases	=B5*$C$29	=C5*$C$29	=D5*$C$29	=E5*$C$29	=F5*$C$29	=G5*$C$29
14	Overheads	=$C$50*$C$36	=$C$50*$C$36	=$C$50*$C$36	=$C$50*$C$36	=$C$50*$C$36	=$C$50*$C$36
15	Total operating payments	=SUM(B13:B14)	=SUM(C13:C14)	=SUM(D13:D14)	=SUM(E13:E14)	=SUM(F13:F14)	=SUM(G13:G14)
16							
17	Dividends	0	0	0	0	=C38	0
18	Capital purchases	=C40*C41	=C40*C42	0	0	=C40*C43	0
19	Total other payments	=SUM(B17:B18)	=SUM(C17:C18)	=SUM(D17:D18)	=SUM(E17:E18)	=SUM(F17:F18)	=SUM(G17:G18)
20							
21	Net cash flow	=B10+B15+B19	=C10+C15+C19	=D10+D15+D19	=E10+E15+E19	=F10+F15+F19	=G10+G15+G19
22	Cash balance b/f	=C51	=B23	=C23	=D23	=E23	=F23
23	Cash balance c/f	=SUM(B21:B22)	=SUM(C21:C22)	=SUM(D21:D22)	=SUM(E21:E22)	=SUM(F21:F22)	=SUM(G21:G22)
24							

Negative numbers

In a spreadsheet, you must be very careful to sort out the approach which you wish to take when manipulating negative numbers. For example, if total operating payments in row 15 are shown as **positive**, you would need to **subtract** them from total operating receipts in the formulae in row 23. However if you have chosen to make them **negative**, to represent outflows, then you will need to **add** them to total operating receipts. This becomes even more important when you are dealing with accounts or balances which may be sometimes positive and sometimes negative, for example the cash balances rows.

Opening balances

It is important, in an exercise like this, to get the opening balances right. However good your budgeting of income and expenses is, if you have made a **poor estimate** of the opening cash balance, this will be **reflected right through the forecast**.

Integration

In practice, you might well **integrate** a cash-flow projection like this with a forecast profit and loss account (sometimes called an income statement) and balance sheet. This would give a high degree of **re-assurance** that the numbers '**stacked up**' and would enable you to present a 'cleaner' projection: for example, sales would appear on the profit and loss account, and the cash receipts formulae could refer direct to that part of the spreadsheet (or even to a separate spreadsheet in some packages). Similarly, cash not collected could be taken straight back into the profit and loss account as **bad debt expense**.

Here is the spreadsheet in its normal 'numbers' form.

	A	B	C	D	E	F	G
1	EXCELLENT PLC						
2	*Cash flow projection - six months ending 30 June X6*						
3		*Jan*	*Feb*	*Mar*	*Apr*	*May*	*Jun*
4		£	£	£	£	£	£
5	Sales	42000	43260	44558	45895	47271	48690
6	*Cash receipts*						
7	1 month in arrears	27000	25200	25956	26735	27537	28363
8	2 months in arrears	13500	13500	12600	12978	13367	13768
9	3 months in arrears	3150	3150	3150	2940	3028	3119
10	Total operating receipts	43650	41850	41706	42653	43932	45250
11							
12	*Cash payments*						
13	Purchases	-27300	-28119	-28963	-29831	-30726	-31648
14	Overheads	-6300	-6300	-6300	-6300	-6300	-6300
15	Total operating payments	-33600	-34419	-35263	-36131	-37026	-37948
16							
17	Dividends					-10000	
18	Capital purchases	-3600	-12600			-1800	
19	Total other payments	-3600	-12600			-11800	
20							
21	Net cash flow	6450	-5169	6443	6521	-4894	7302
22	Cash balance b/f	-7500	-1050	-6219	224	6746	1852
23	Cash balance c/f	-1050	-6219	224	6746	1852	9154
24							

This needs a little **tidying up**. We will do the following.

(a) Add in **commas** to denote thousands of pounds.

(b) Put **zeros** in the cells with no entry in them.

(c) Change **negative numbers** from being displayed with a **minus sign** to being displayed in **brackets**.

	A	B	C	D	E	F	G
1	EXCELLENT PLC						
2	*Cash flow projection - six months ending 30 June X6*						
3		*Jan*	*Feb*	*Mar*	*Apr*	*May*	*Jun*
4		£	£	£	£	£	£
5	Sales	42,000	43,260	44,558	45,895	47,271	48,690
6	*Cash receipts*						
7	1 month in arrears	27,000	25,200	25,956	26,735	27,537	28,363
8	2 months in arrears	13,500	13,500	12,600	12,978	13,367	13,768
9	3 months in arrears	3,150	3,150	3,150	2,940	3,028	3,119
10	Total operating receipts	43,650	41,850	41,706	42,653	43,932	45,250
11							
12	*Cash payments*						
13	Purchases	(27,300)	(28,119)	(28,963)	(29,831)	(30,726)	(31,648)
14	Overheads	(6,300)	(6,300)	(6,300)	(6,300)	(6,300)	(6,300)
15	Total operating payments	(33,600)	(34,419)	(35,263)	(36,131)	(37,026)	(37,948)
16							
17	Dividends	0	0	0	0	(10,000)	0
18	Capital purchases	(3,600)	(12,600)	0	0	(1,800)	0
19	Total other payments	(3,600)	(12,600)	0	0	(11,800)	0
20							
21	Net cash flow	6,450	(5,169)	6,443	6,521	(4,894)	7,302
22	Cash balance b/f	(7,500)	(1,050)	(6,219)	224	6,746	1,852
23	Cash balance c/f	(1,050)	(6,219)	224	6,746	1,852	9,154
24							

2.3 Extracting data

You may need to extract only specific characters from the data entered in a cell. For instance, suppose a set of raw materials codes had been entered into a spreadsheet as follows.

	A	B
1	6589D	
2	5589B	
3	5074D	
4	8921B	
5	3827B	
6	1666D	
7	5062A	
8	7121D	
9	7457C	
10	9817D	
11	6390C	
12	1148A	
13	4103A	
14	8988A	
15	6547C	
16	5390A	
17	6189D	
18	8331C	
19	1992B	
20	7587A	

The four **digits** are, say, a number derived from the supplier's reference number, while the **letter** indicates that the material is used to make Product A, B, C or D.

If you wanted to sort this data in **alphabetical** order of **Product** you would have a problem, because it is only possible to arrange it in ascending or descending **numerical** order, using the standard Sort method.

To get round this you can extract the letter from each cell using the **RIGHT** function, as follows.

	A	B
1	6589D	=RIGHT(A1,1)
2	5589B	=RIGHT(A2,1)
3	5074D	=RIGHT(A3,1)
4	8921B	=RIGHT(A4,1)
5	3827B	=RIGHT(A5,1)
6	1666D	=RIGHT(A6,1)

The formula in cell B1 means 'Extract the last (or rightmost) one character from cell A1'. If we wanted to extract the last **two** characters the formula would be **=RIGHT(A1,2)**, and so on.

The formula can then be filled down and then the data can be sorted by column B, giving the following results.

	A	B
1	5062A	A
2	1148A	A
3	4103A	A
4	8988A	A
5	5390A	A
6	7587A	A
7	5589B	B
8	8921B	B
9	3827B	B
10	1992B	B
11	7457C	C
12	6390C	C
13	6547C	C
14	8331C	C
15	6589D	D
16	5074D	D
17	1666D	D
18	7121D	D
19	9817D	D
20	6189D	D

The function **LEFT** works in the same way, except that it extracts the **first** (or leftmost) character or characters.

The function **MID**, as you might expect, extracts a character or characters from the **middle** of the cell, starting at the **position** you specify, counting from left to right:

=MID([Cell],[Position],[Number of characters]).

In Excel the first character extracted is the one at the position specified, so if you want to extract the **third** character you specify position 3. In Lotus 1-2-3 it is the next character after the position specified, so if you want to extract the third character you specify position 2.

Activity 2 **(10 minutes)**

Cell A1 contains the data: **12-D-496**

(a) What formula would you use to extract the **D** into a different cell?
(b) What formula would you use to extract the **12** into a different cell?

2.4 Lookup

The LOOKUP function allows you to enter data that corresponds to a value in one cell in a column and return the data in the corresponding row in a different column. A simple example will make this clearer.

	A	B	C	D	E	F	G
1	1	Red					
2	2	Green					
3	3	Blue					
4	4	Yellow					
5							
6					1	Red	
7							
8							

Here the user enters a figure between 1 and 4 in cell E6 and the spreadsheet returns the corresponding colour from the range A1:B4. If the user had entered **3** then cell F6 would say **Blue**.

Here is the formula that is used to do this.

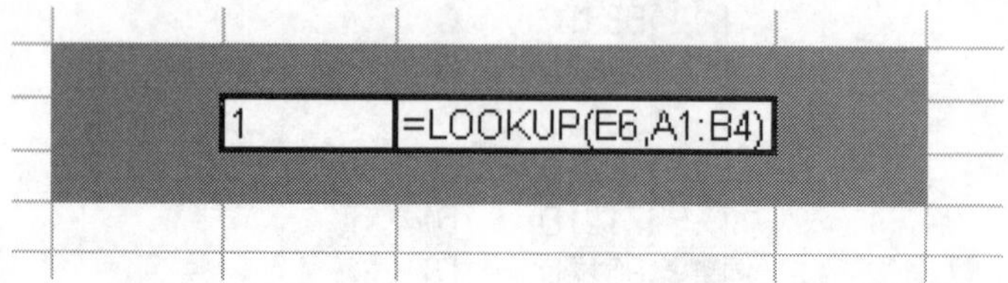

2.5 Merging cell contents

The next formula is only available in Excel 97 and above.

	A	B	C	D
1	21	A	64	
2	62	P	14	
3	87	T	26	
4				

Suppose data had been entered into a spreadsheet as follows.

What if you wanted the data in cells A1, B1 and C1 in a single cell: 21A64? To do this in Excel 97 you can simply join the contents of individual cells together using the **&** symbol, as follows. The formula could be filled down to give the same results for the rest of the list.

	A	B	C	D
1	21	A	64	=A1&B1&C1
2	62	P	14	
3	87	T	26	
4				

2.6 Paste special

Sometimes you may wish to convert a formula into an absolute value, for example you may want the contents of cell D1 in the above example to be '21A64', not a formula that gives this result.

To convert a formula to an absolute value, copy the relevant cell or cells in the normal way, then highlight another cell (say, E1 in the above example) and **right click**. From the menu that appears, choose **Paste Special.** The following dialogue box will appear.

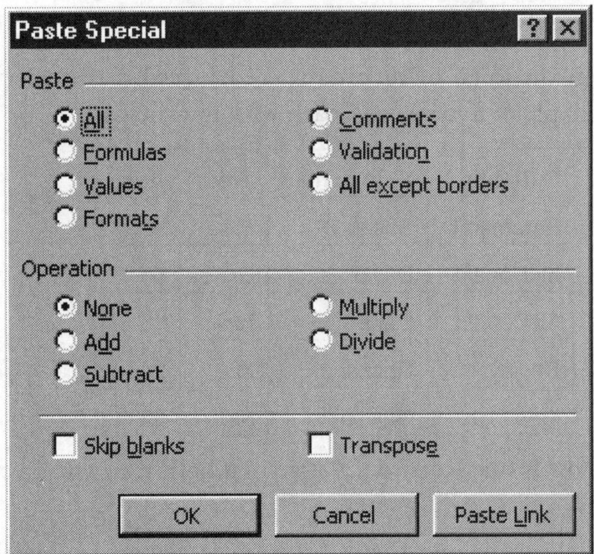

Here, if you choose **Values** then what will be pasted into cell E1 is the value '21A64', not the formula in cell D1.

3 SPREADSHEET PIVOT TABLES

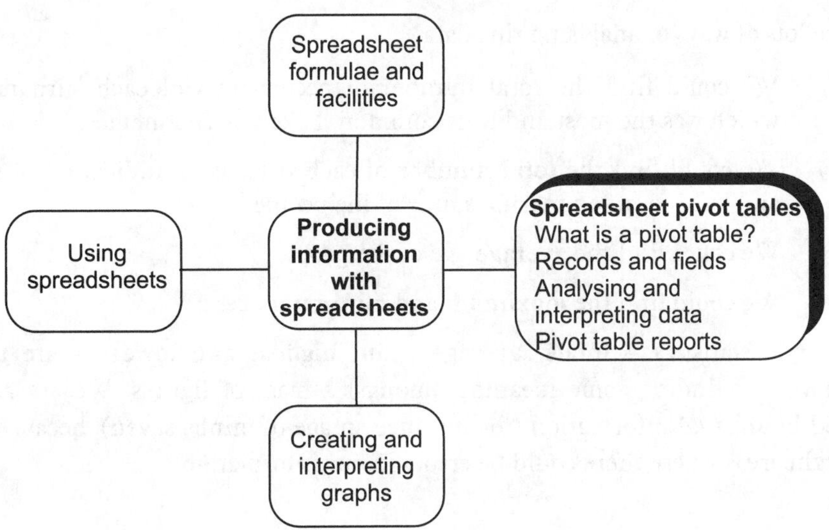

3.1 What is a pivot table?

Definition

> A **pivot table** is an interactive table that summarises and analyses data from lists and tables.

To understand pivot tables we first need to get a little bit more understanding of records and fields.

3.2 Records and fields

A typical database is made up of **records** and each record is made up of a number of **fields**. Here's an example of five records, each with four fields.

Surname	First name	Title	Age
Foreman	Susan	Miss	42
McDonald	David	Dr	56
McDonald	Dana	Mrs	15
Sanjay	Rachana	Ms	24
Talco	Giovanni	Mr	32

(a) Each **Row** is one **Record**. (Notice that both Row and Record begin with the letter R.)

(b) Each **Column** is one **Field**. (If you can remember that Rows are Records, this shouldn't be too hard to work out!)

The example above has records for five people, and each record contains fields for the person's surname, first name, title and age.

3.3 Analysing and interpreting data

There are lots of ways of analysing this data.

(a) We could find the **total number** of occurrences of each surname to see which was the most and least common. Likewise first names.

(b) We could find the **total number** of each title, as an indication of the most and least common marital status of the people.

(c) We could find the **average** age of the people

(d) We could find the **maximum** and **minimum** ages.

These simple statistics – **totals, averages, and highest and lowest** – are the most common way of finding some meaning amongst a mass of figures. We are also often interested in **unusual** information (for instance an age of minus seven), because it tends to highlight areas where there could be errors in our information.

3.4 Pivot table reports

To extract information quickly and easily from a table in Excel we can simply highlight it and click on **Data** and then **Pivot Table Report**. This starts up a Wizard which first asks you to confirm the location of the data you want to analyse and then offers you the following options.

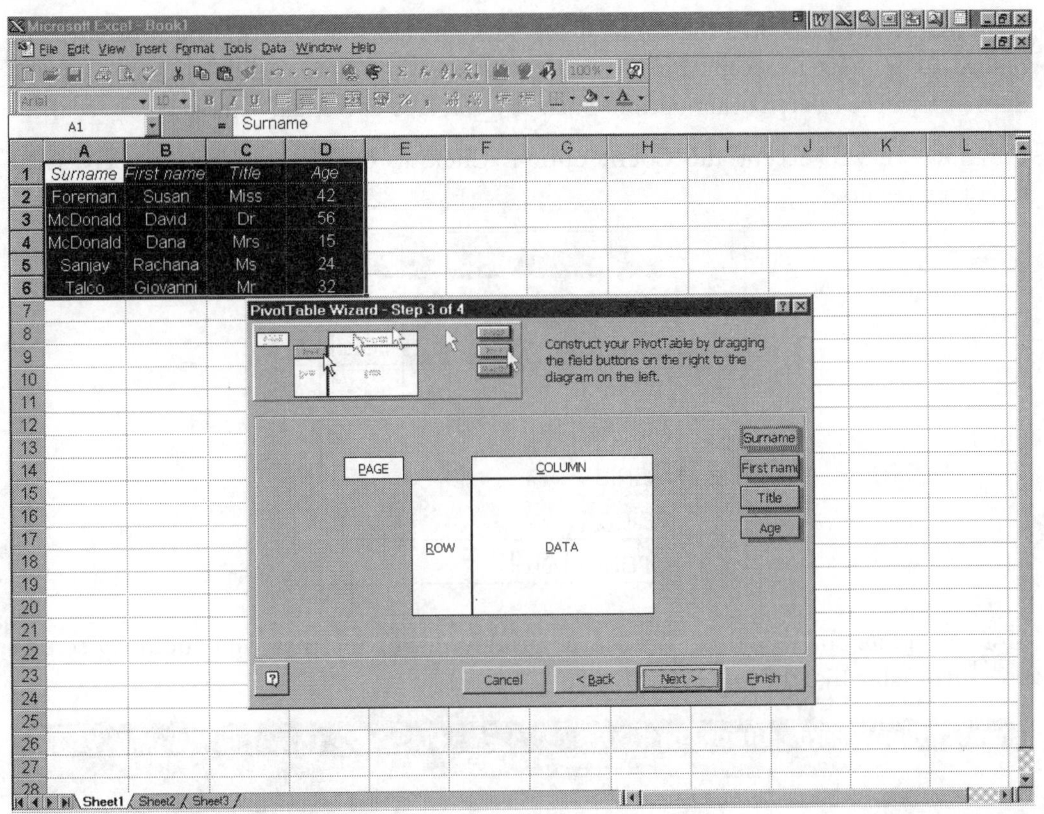

All you have to do to analyse the data is drag any of the labelled buttons on the right into the appropriate part of the white area. For instance, if we wanted to know the total number of surnames of each type we could drag the Surname label into the row area and then drag another instance of the surname label into the Data area. This is what you would see.

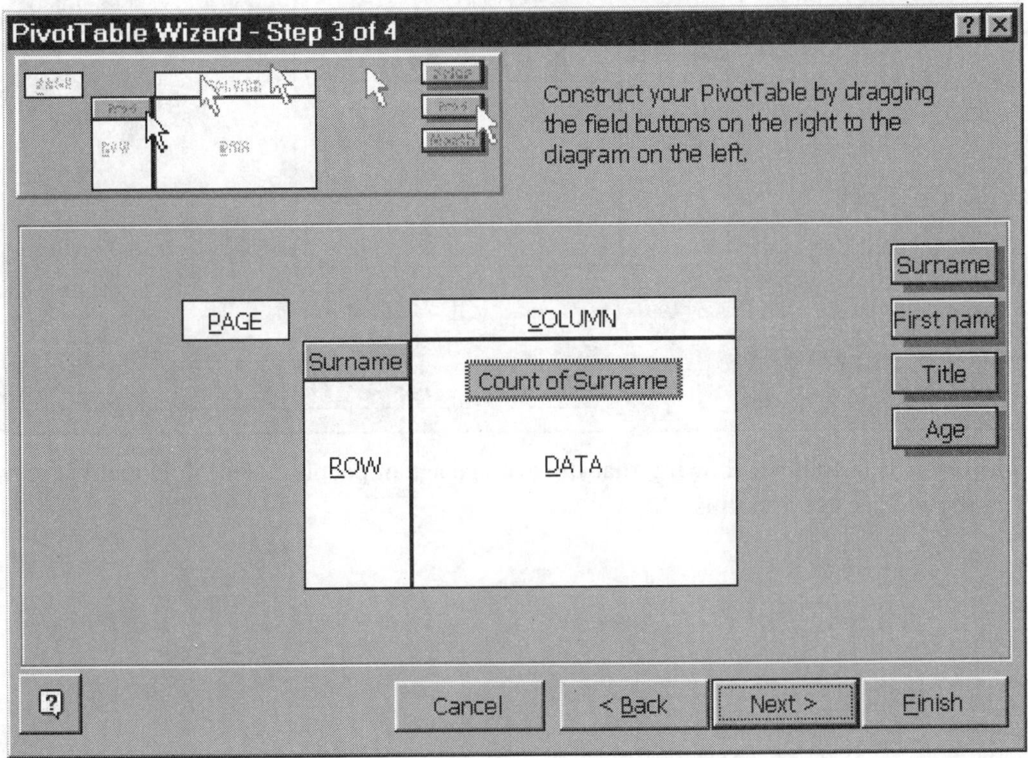

Note that in the Data area the name of the Surname label changes to Count of Surname but we do not have to accept this if it is not what we want. If we double-click on Count of Surname we are offered other options such as Sum, Average, Max, Min.

For now we will accept the Count option. Clicking on Next and Finish gives the following results.

	A	B
1	Count of Surname	
2	Surname	Total
3	Foreman	1
4	McDonald	2
5	Sanjay	1
6	Talco	1
7	Grand Total	5

More elaborate analyses than this can be produced. For instance, you could try setting up a pivot table like this.

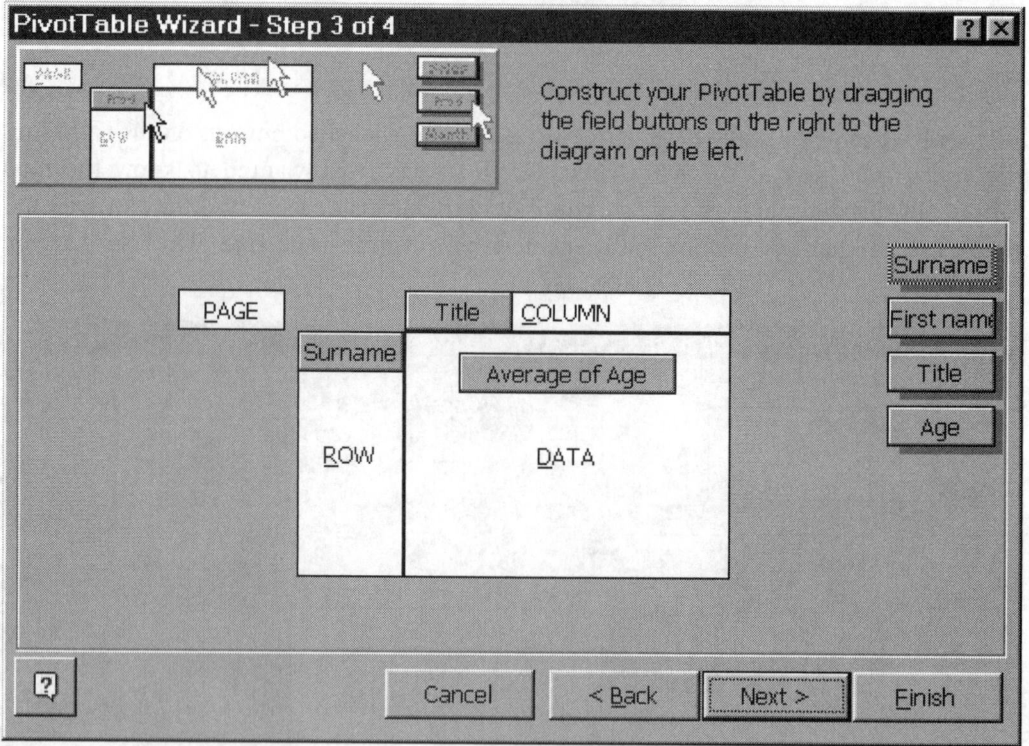

The result is as follows, showing that the average age of people called McDonald is 35.5 and the average age overall is 33.8.

	A	B	C	D	E	F	G
1	Average of Age	Title					
2	Surname	Dr	Miss	Mr	Mrs	Ms	Grand Total
3	Foreman		42				42
4	McDonald	56			15		35.5
5	Sanjay					24	24
6	Talco			32			32
7	Grand Total	56	42	32	15	24	33.8

This arrangement of the data also draws attention to the fact that the data includes a 'Mrs' who is only 15 years old. This is not impossible, but it is quite unusual and should be checked because it could be an inputting error.

If we don't happen to like the way Excel arranges the data it can be changed in a flash, simply by dragging the labels in the results to another part of the table. For instance if Title is dragged down until it is over cell B3 the data is automatically rearranged as follows.

	A	B	C
1	Average of Age		
2	Surname	Title	Total
3	Foreman	Miss	42
4	Foreman Total		42
5	McDonald	Dr	56
6		Mrs	15
7	McDonald Total		35.5
8	Sanjay	Ms	24
9	Sanjay Total		24
10	Talco	Mr	32
11	Talco Total		32
12	Grand Total		33.8

FOR DISCUSSION

What other features of spreadsheets do people in your group find useful?

4 CREATING AND INTERPRETING GRAPHS

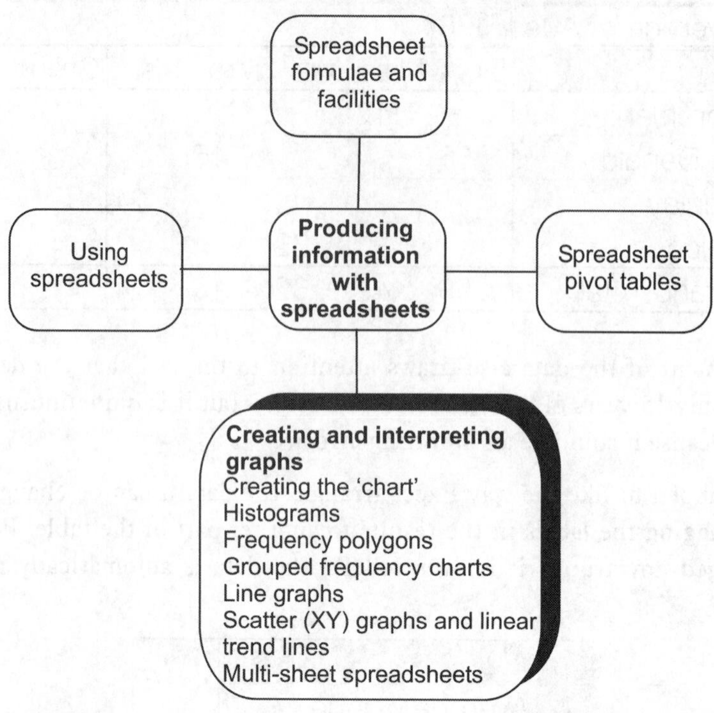

4.1 Creating the 'chart'

Data can be represented visually, and the way this is done is through graphs, which are pictorial representations of the data. Most commonly the graphs used are bar, pie, histograms, frequency polygons and line graphs.

The current spreadsheet trend is to call graphs, charts. Whether it is called a picture, chart or graph it is almost always easier to analyse than a set of numbers. This is especially true when a large amount of data has been collected. Also a picture that shows information will communicate better than numbers alone. The old saying is true: 'a picture is worth a thousand words'.

Knowing how to convey information by chart is important in the presentation of statistics. The following is a list of some general rules to keep in mind. A graph should:

(a) Be simple and not too cluttered

(b) Show data without changing the data's message

(c) Clearly show any trend or differences in the data, and

(d) Be accurate in a visual sense (if one chart value is 15 and another 30, then 30 should appear to be twice the size of 15).

It is also important to know what type of graph to use when presenting statistics. There are several types of graph you can use, which are outlined in the following pages.

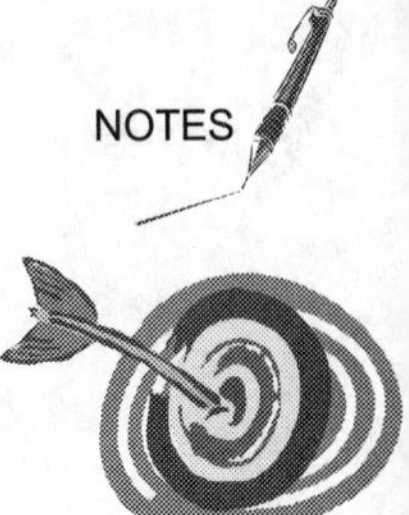

EXAMPLE: CREATING A CHART

We are going to use the Discount Traders Ltd example shown below to generate a number of charts showing the net sales to different customers.

File Edit View Insert Format Tools Data Financial Manager

C5 = =IF($B5>=1000,$B5*0.05,0)

	A	B	C	D
1	**Discount Traders Ltd**			
2	*Sales analysis - April 200X*			
3	Customer	Sales	5% discount	Sales (net)
4		£	£	£
5	Arthur	956.00	0	956.00
6	Dent	1423.00	71.15	1351.85
7	Ford	2894.00	144.7	2749.30
8	Prefect	842.00	0	842.00

Enter this information into your own computer so that you can work through the example yourself.

Note the formula in C5 to calculate the discount of 5% on sales of £1,000 or over.

It is usually possible to convert tabulated data in a spreadsheet into a variety of bar chart or graphical formats. Impressive looking charts can be generated simply by selecting the range of figures to turn into a chart and then clicking on a chart icon and following the step-by-step instructions on screen.

The basic steps to creating a chart in Excel are as follows:

- Use the mouse to highlight the block of cells containing your data, and then click the Chart. In this example the relevant data to select is in cells A5 to A8 and D5 to D8. Start by selecting A5:A8 in the normal way and hold down **Crtl** and then select D5:D8
- Click the chart wizard button on the tool bar and follow the steps.

Step 1 of 4: Pick the appropriate chart type.

A bar chart (or graph) may be either horizontal or vertical. To differentiate between the two, a vertical bar chart is called a *column* chart. An important point about bar charts is the *length* of the bars: the greater the length, the greater the value. Column charts are good for comparing values. One disadvantage of the column chart is lack of room for a written label at the foot of each bar; so it is best to use a column graph when the label is short, as in our example.

A single click on a Chart type will give us a choice of sub-types and a description of the type highlighted. Click Next> to go to step 2.

NOTES

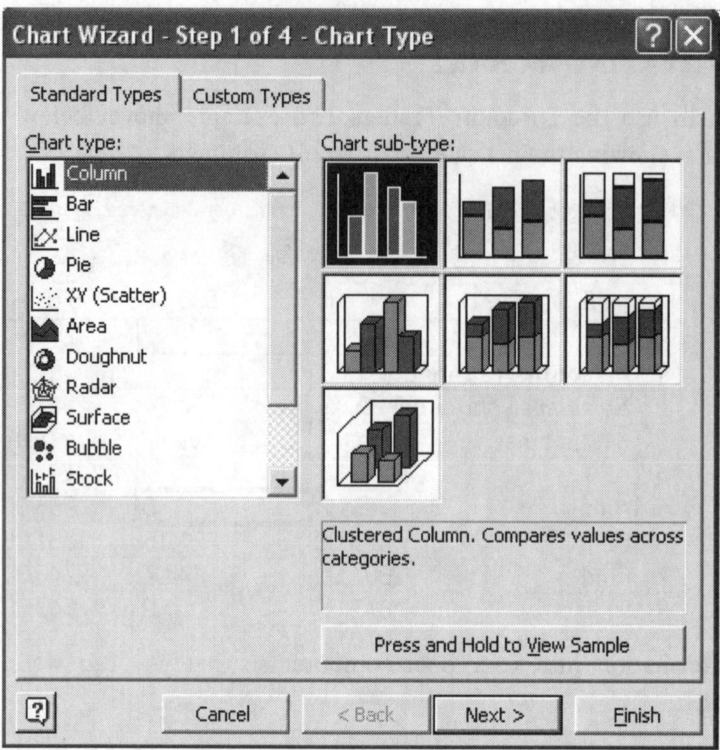

Step 2 of 4: This gives us the opportunity to confirm that the data we selected earlier was correct and to decide on how the **data series** should be shown: **in** other words whether the chart should be based on **columns** (eg Customer, Sales, Discount etc) or **rows** (Arthur, Dent etc).

A data series is a group of related data points plotted in a chart that originate from rows or columns on a single worksheet. Each data series in a chart has a unique colour or pattern. You can plot one or more data series in a chart. Pie charts have only one data series.

In this case, because there is only one data series – net sales – it makes no difference whether we choose the rows or column option.

NOTES

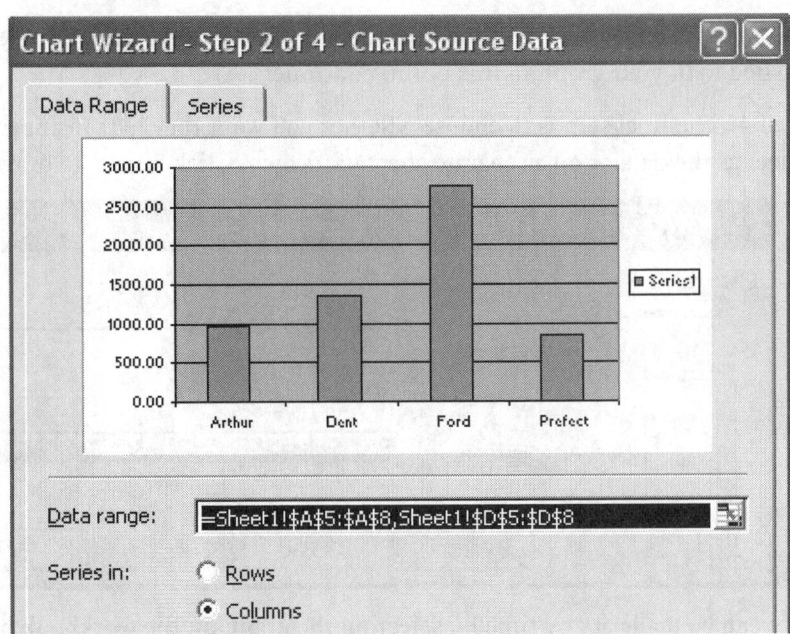

Step 3 of 4: As you can see, there are several operations available in this step on the wizard. You can see the effect of selecting or deselecting each one in **preview** – experiment with these options as you like.

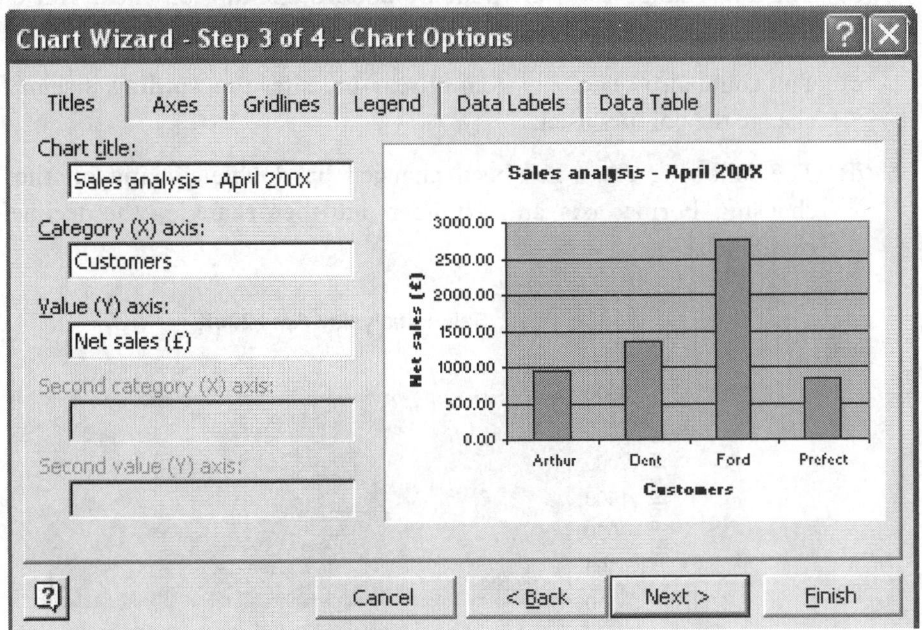

(a) **Titles** – type a chart title in the space provided.

(b) **Axes** – the category (Customers) is the X-axis and the value (Net sales in £) is the Y-axis.

(c) **Gridlines** – for most line graphs, you will want to show the major gridlines for both X and Y-axis.

(d) **Legend** – your choice here depends on the data. Do not show two legends. The data table will show a legend unless you tell it not to do so.

(e) **Data labels** – show data labels only if they will not clutter the graph.

(f) **Data table** – show the data table if there is room. Do not show the data table if it makes your print of the graph take more than one page.

You can make changes back and forth in the chart wizard without a problem. When you are satisfied with your graph to this point, continue.

Step 4 of 4: The final step is to choose whether you want the chart to appear on the same worksheet as the data or on a separate sheet of its own. Click 'finish' to draw the graph.

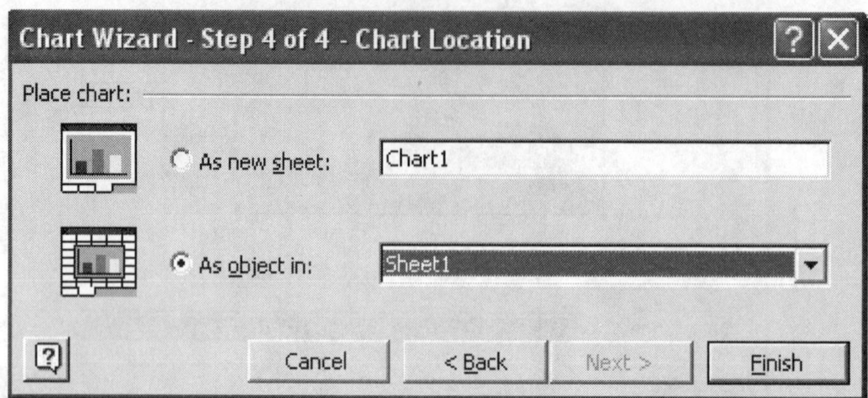

Changes can be made at any time by selecting the graph on the workbook page (click just inside the graph page margin), then clicking on the chart wizard button on the toolbar.

(a) You can **resize it** simply by selecting it and dragging out its borders.

(b) You can change **each element** by **double clicking** on them and choosing from a variety of further options.

(c) You could also select any item of **text** and alter the wording, size or font, **or** change the **colours** used.

(d) The following chart has been changed by double-clicking on the Y-axis, choosing 'Format axis' and 'Number' and then changing the decimal places from 2 to zero.

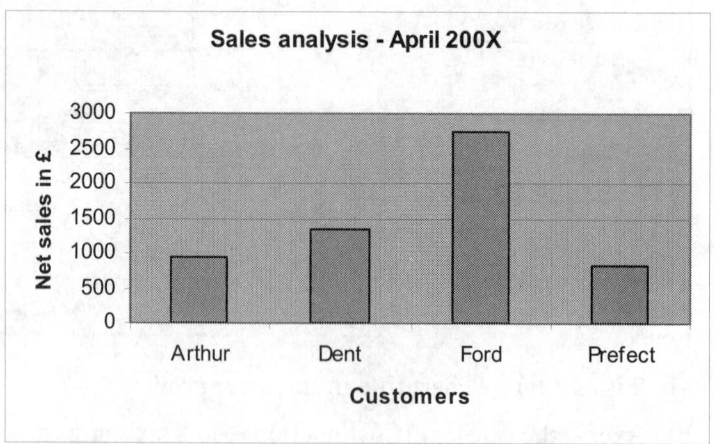

Bar charts are flexible and are most commonly used to display data from multiple-select, rank order, single-select matrix and numerical questions.

Special forms of the bar chart allow the percentage on the vertical axis to be shown. Several data sets can be plotted for each class or rank on the horizontal axis or the data sets can be stacked one on top of the other. A rotated bar chart can also be produced which rotates the position of the horizontal and vertical axes.

NOTES

The example shown above used an Excel Column chart to display the data. The diagram below shows the Discount Traders Ltd data as an Excel 3-D Bar chart.

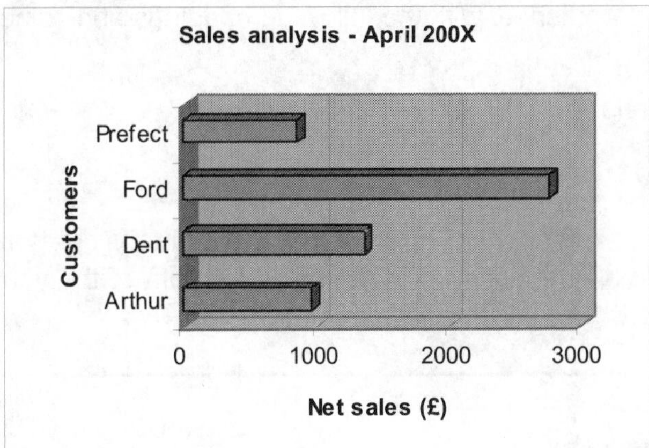

As you are aware, we had various options, including 3-D displays, which we could have used with the data from Discount Traders Ltd. We can also use a pie chart to display the data.

A pie chart is appropriate when the data are in a *nominal* form and the frequency count, proportion or percentage for each class must be shown. It is a simple, visually effective way to show percentage, showing the relative size of a number of items that are part of one larger item. Step 3 of 4 of the chart Options below is a 3-D pie chart showing the title but no legend and displaying both the label and the percent.

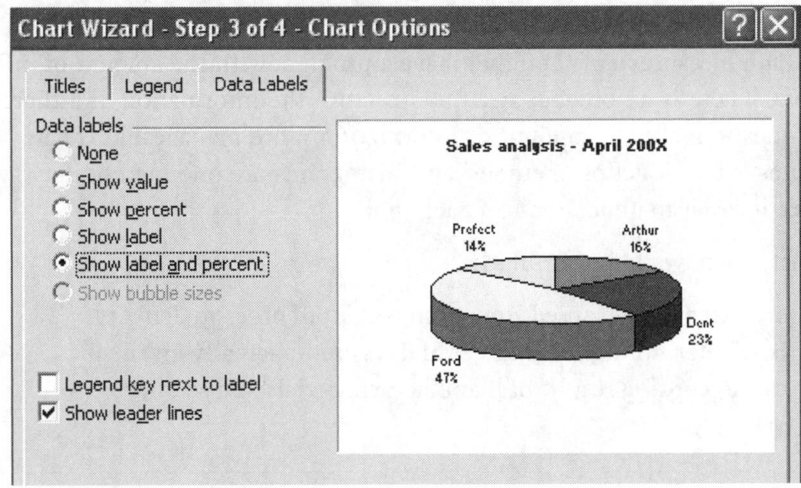

When comparing two sets of data using a pie chart, it is important to make sure the colours used for each response option remain consistent in each chart. This way, a side-by-side visual comparison can quickly be made. Pie charts are not appropriate for multiple-select questions because each respondent can answer more than one option, and the sum of the option percentages will exceed 100%.

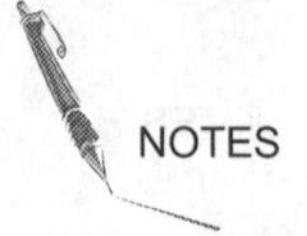

Activity 3 **(15 minutes)**

Set up a worksheet with the following headings and values.

Sales £m	*20X3*	*20X7*
Lemonade	80	120
Cola	90	100
Water	28	160

Use your spreadsheet to draw two pie charts – one for each year – showing the percentage make up of the sales for both of the years. Copy both of them to a Word file.

4.2 Histograms

You should remember from Chapter 2 that a histogram is a bar graph that charts the relationship between value and frequency (number of occurrences).

In general, the values are plotted on the horizontal axis and the frequencies on the vertical axis. The width of the bars represents the intervals, and the height of the bars represents the frequency of scores in each interval. It is used for continuous variables such as height and weight, and the bars of the graph touch.

Histograms can structure data to make it easier to understand and act upon. Whenever we produce something and measure it, be it in manufacturing or in any other process, the value that is measured will vary over time. One problem we all have is that we make many such measurements and then have a problem with the amount of information that we have. There is an obvious need to structure the information and there is a need for techniques to make the amount of information more manageable. These techniques are known as 'data reduction methods' and histograms are one method for structuring data to make it easier to understand and act upon.

The histogram would be useful in:

(a) Recording elapsed time from receipt of order to delivery,
(b) Determining the number of days credit actually given, or
(c) Recording results of manufacturing trials and so on.

EXAMPLE: HISTOGRAM

Consider the following measurements of litres of petrol consumed by similar models of car travelling from London to Chesterfield by the same 150-mile route.

20.1	20.0	19.7	19.4	19.5	19.9	19.3	19.8	19.3	19.4	19.5
19.5	19.6	19.7	19.1	20.2	19.6	19.7	19.0	19.6	19.4	19.2
20.0	19.9	19.8	19.9	19.4	20.1	19.7	19.5	19.6	19.6	20.0
19.8	19.7	20.0	19.9	19.5	19.4	19.9	19.8	19.5		

This data does not tell us much as we tend to concentrate on individual numbers and fail to see an overall pattern. Instead of data we want information. At this stage, if we were drawing a histogram manually we would be reducing the data using a 'tally sheet' where

individual measurements are marked as they are recorded but this can be done automatically using Excel.

Step 1 – We make a start when using Excel by entering the 42 items of data (shown above) onto the spreadsheet (all in column A). This is the **Input Range**. Before we begin we need to highlight the Input Range and make sure that we have the Data Analysis tools on the **Tools** menu. If you can't find Data Analysis then click on Add-ins and enable the Analysis ToolPak by clicking in the box (see below) and then OK. It should now appear in your Tools menu.

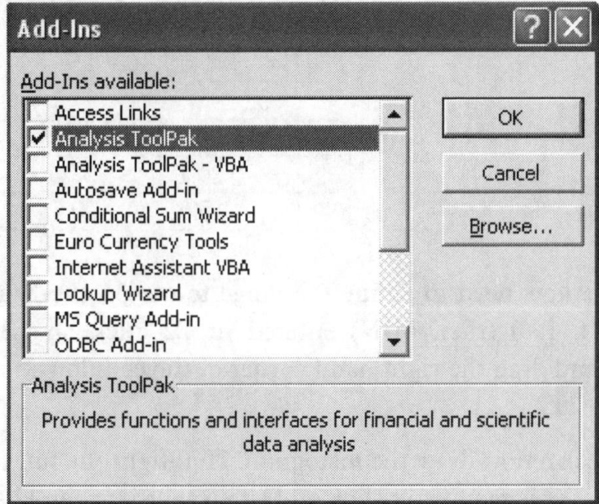

Step 2 – Because there is only a small range in the data we do not need to group it before analysing it further but we do need to find the smallest and the largest variable – the maximum and the minimum – so we can plot the data on a histogram. We can do this two ways:

(i) Click on Tools, then Data Analysis and then Descriptive Statistics. Click on Summary Statistics and specify the input range by highlighting our cells containing data. Then click on Output Range under Output Options. Click on the box into which the Output Range will be specified, and then specify the Output Range by dragging the cursor from about D19 to E33 then press OK. This tells the computer where we want it to record our output data. You should get quite a lot of information about the data (see below) including the Maximum and Minimum.

Mean	19.65476
Standard error	0.043404
Median	19.65
Mode	19.5
Standard deviation	0.281288
Sample variance	0.079123
Kurtosis	–0.17358
Skewness	1.2
Range	19
Minimum	20.2
Maximum	825.5
Count	42

(ii) To find the MAX and MIN separately:

- To find the MAX click on an empty cell (say, B2) and enter the formula: =MAX(A1:A42) . When you press enter you should see the value 20.2 in the cell.
- To find the MIN click on an empty cell (say, C2) and type in the formula: =MIN(A1:A42) and you should get the value 19.0 as the lowest.

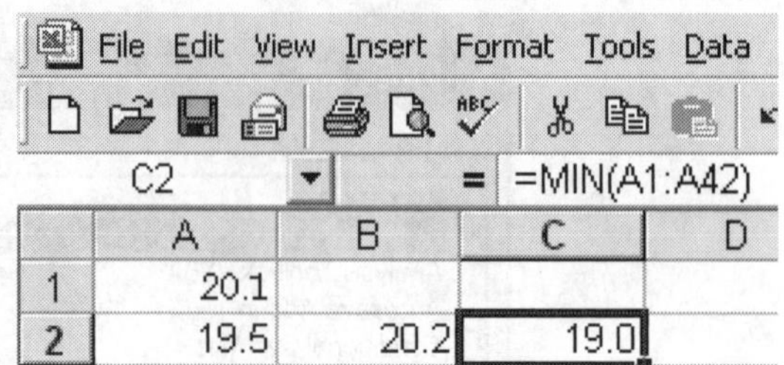

Step 3 – We now need to define the range to use on the X-axis – this is called the **Bin Range**. With 19.0 (then MIN) entered in C2 click on C3 and put in the formula: =$C2+0.1 and drag the right hand corner of the cell down to C14 so that the range goes from 19.0 to 20.2.

Step 4 – We can now draw the histogram. Highlight the full range of variables – all 42 of them. Go to Tools menu and click on Data Analysis , then Histogram then OK.

The Histogram Wizard then requires some input. For the Input Range we start at the first variable in our Input Range (A1) and drag the cursor down to the last (A42). For the Bin range we do the same with the range of numbers we will be using (C2 – C14). For the output Range we need to specify where we want the frequency count to be. Drag the cursor from E2 to F14 and then press OK.

Ensure that the cursor is in the box where the required range is recorded before you try and drag the cursor, otherwise you will either change a range you have already specified or you won't be able to drag the cursor at all.

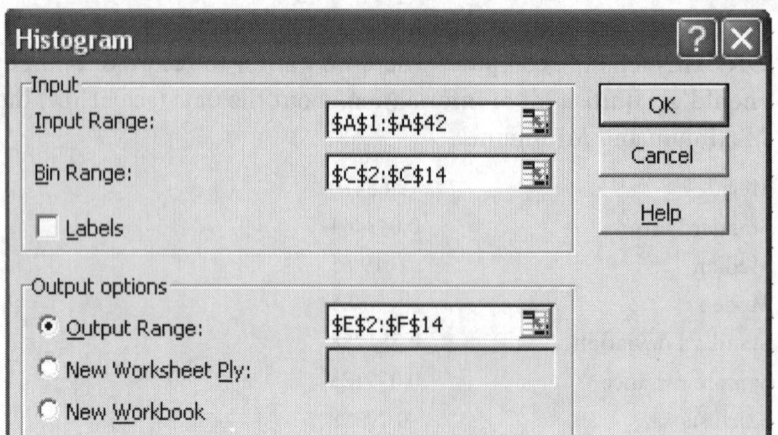

In the area you have specified you should now see the frequencies of each variable. Highlight the area and click on the Chart Wizard. Choose 'Clustered Column' and then continue to the Finish putting in a title and labels.

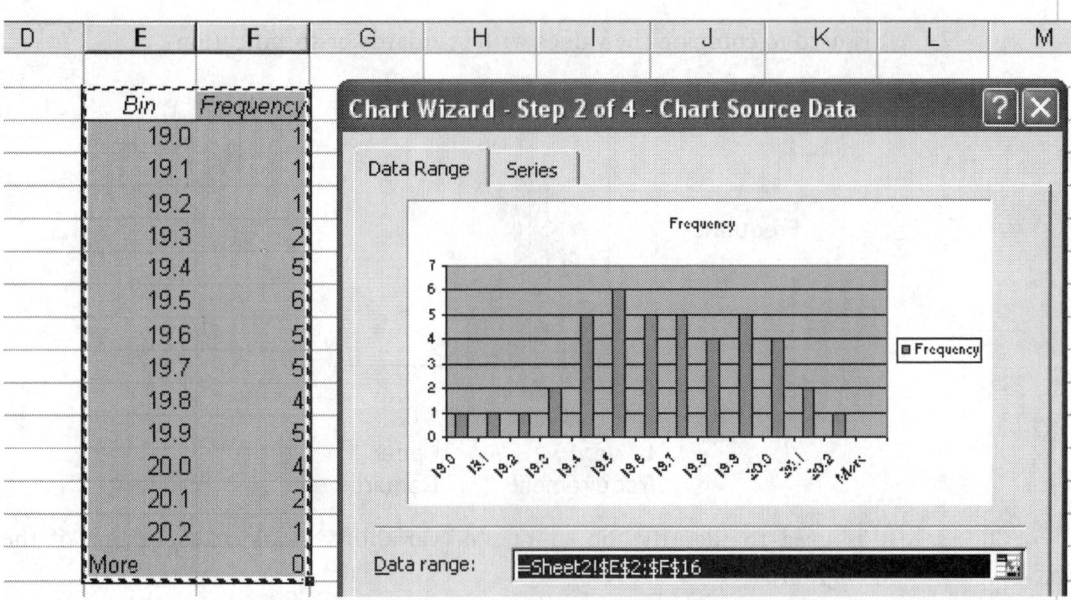

If you want to join the columns, when the chart is finished right click on one of the bars and then click on Format Data Series and Options. Reduce the Gap Width to 0 – thus joining up the columns. Your chart should look something like the one below:

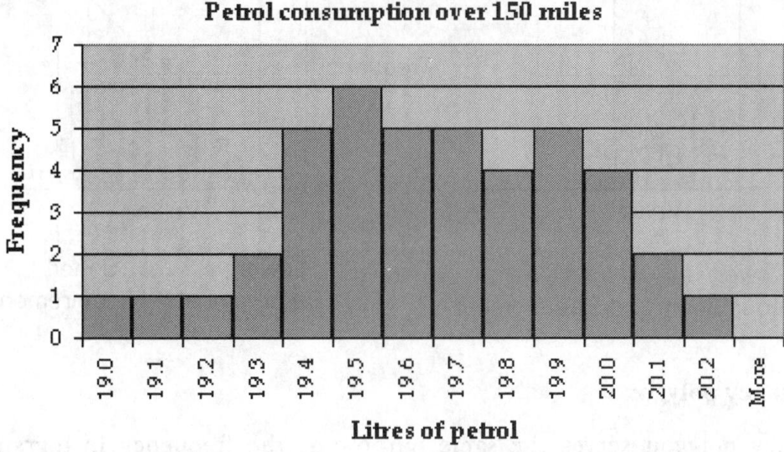

Save your histogram worksheet as we will refer to it again shortly.

The histogram has many uses:

1 It is used to find abnormalities in the distribution

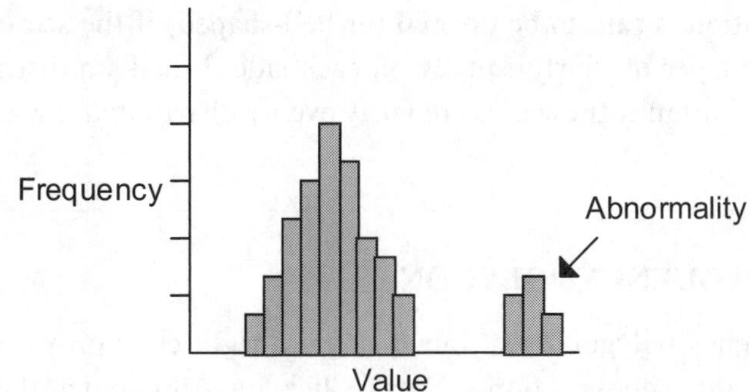

2 It is used to compare the values with standards or specifications.

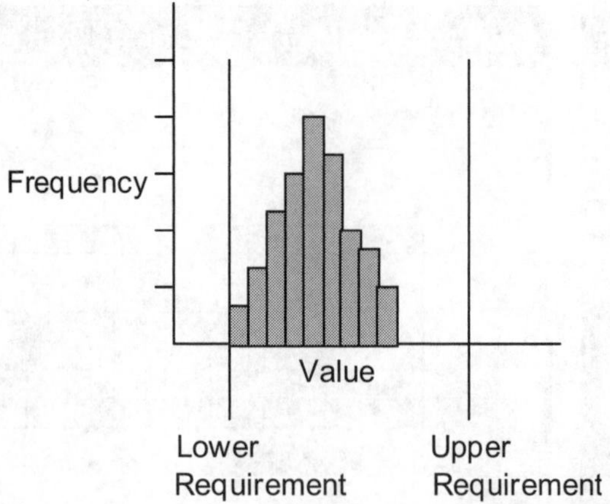

3 It is used to identify the sources of variability (look at the shape of the histogram).

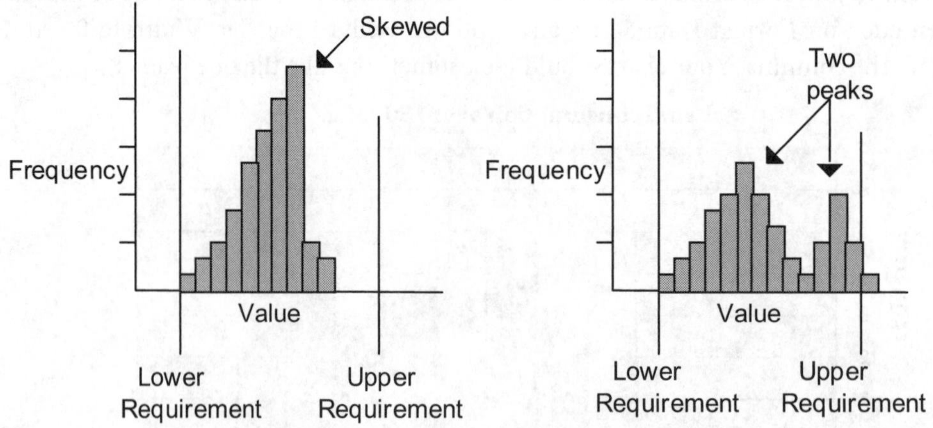

4.3 Frequency polygon

The frequency polygon serves the same purpose as the frequency histogram and is obtained by joining the midpoints of the bars in a histogram with a line

There are a few shapes that a frequency polygon can take. A graph in which scores bunch up toward either end of the x-axis is said to be skewed. The skewness of a graph is in the direction of its 'tail.' If the scores bunch up toward the high end, the graph has a **negative skew**. If the scores bunch up toward the low end, the graph has a **positive skew**. A distribution is said to be **normal** (or bell-shaped) if the scores bunch up in the middle and then taper off fairly equally on each side. Finally, a distribution is called a rectangular distribution if the scores are fairly evenly distributed throughout the graph.

EXAMPLE: FREQUENCY POLYGON

To draw a frequency polygon over your histogram right click on your finished chart in your worksheet and choose 'Source Data'. Click on Add under the Series box. You should now have a Series 2. Clear the Name box and enter the Bin Range from your worksheet. Clear the Values box and enter the frequency details.

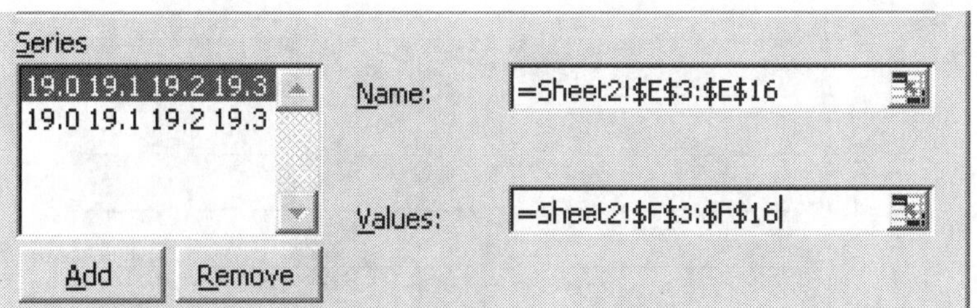

When you press Finish your chart should show two series of bar charts. Right click on one of the bars of the latest one and choose Chart Type. Click on 'Line' and the chart should display both chart types in one – similar to the one below.

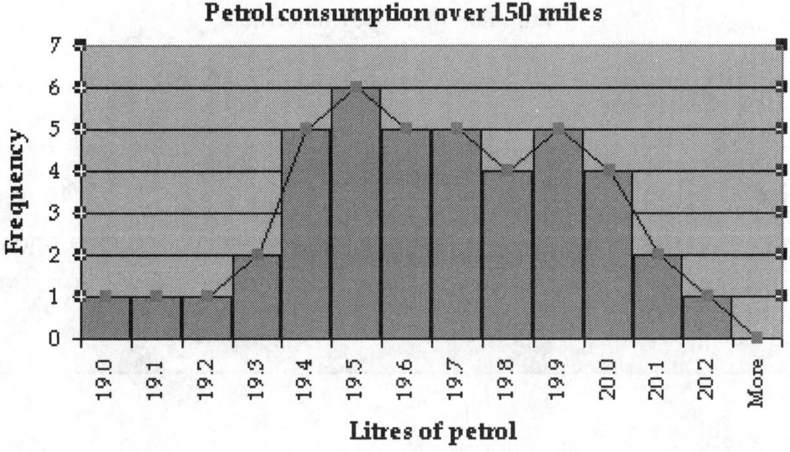

4.4 Grouped frequency charts

With some data, typically when the difference between the highest and the lowest variable is greater than 15, you might prefer to use a grouped frequency distribution. The variables are grouped into intervals, and the frequency of each interval is listed in a separate column. The intervals can be of any size, but, for ease of construction, a grouped frequency distribution should end up with no more than about 10 groups. This type of distribution provides less precise information than does an ungrouped one, because the individual scores are lost. However, the benefit is that one can understand any trends in the data at a quick glance.

EXAMPLE: GROUPED FREQUENCY CHARTS

Below is a list of the number of DVDs owned by the 23 members of a student society.

43, 15, 52, 24, 84, 36, 75, 70, 98, 44, 56, 60, 48, 41, 38, 7, 62, 49, 32, 71, 25, 46, 58.

Enter the data onto your worksheet. By scanning the data or doing a Summary Statistics we can see the minimum is 7 and the maximum is 98. If we group the data into intervals of 10 starting at 9 and ending in 99, these ten intervals will be the Bin Range.

Continue as before by clicking on Tools/Data analysis and Histogram putting in the Input data and the Bin Range to get the frequency. You can then plot the bin range and the frequency using a Column Chart. When the chart is complete close the gaps between the bars as before.

NOTES

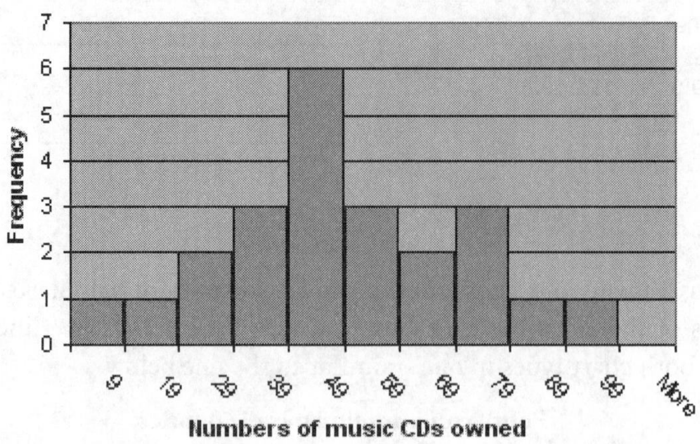

Activity 4 **(10 minutes)**

What shape is the DVD ownership distribution chart? What would have made the distribution take on a positive skew? A negative skew? A rectangular shape?

4.5 Line graphs

The pie graphs, the frequency histograms and the frequency polygons are useful for plotting frequency data, and the **line graph** is useful for displaying how things change over a period of time. It is a way to summarise how two pieces of information are related and how they vary depending on one another. The horizontal axis usually shows a period of time while the vertical axis shows the amount of change. It is extremely important that the variable plotted on the x-axis (eg time) has an equal increment between values, otherwise select an X-Y graph or scatter graph.

Line graphs can be used for *ordinal, interval or ratio* data. They do not have to start at zero. Some do, but others start at a number closest to the lowest number recorded. For example, if you were recording daily summer temperatures that are generally in the 70's the first number on the vertical axis of your line graph might be 65 and not zero.

As we have already noted, line charts in Excel can be used as an alternative to the histogram with the frequency plotted at the midpoint of each class and a line used to join the midpoints. This is not a problem with the type of data used in the next example.

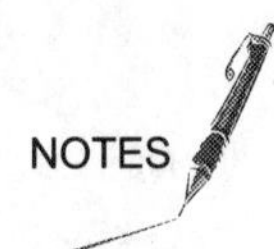

EXAMPLE: LINE GRAPHS

From a survey done on a particular train's punctuality, a record was kept of the number of times it left late from the station. The findings are shown below.

Sep	6
Oct	9
Nov	13
Dec	20
Jan	21
Feb	23
Mar	15
Apr	13
May	7
Jun	4
Jul	3
Aug	1

To create the graph using Excel, enter the data onto your spreadsheet. Click on the chart wizard and select the Line chart. The chart below used the chart sub-type with lines and markers displayed at each data value. At step 2, enter the Data Range i.e., the days late each month then click on Series and enter the months in the Category (X) axis labels. The rest of the procedure is as before.

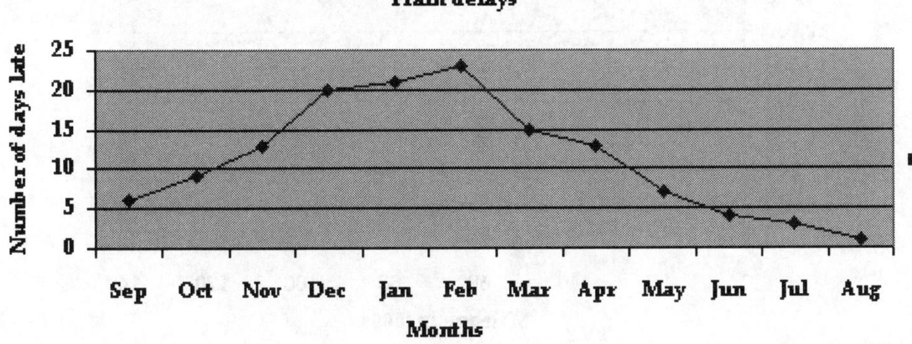

There is quite a bit of information that is easily available from this chart. For example:

- The number of trains that were late during the month of November
- The two months that showed the biggest increase in train delays
- The two months that had the same number of trains late
- The difference between the month with the most number of trains late and the month with the least number of trains late

X-Y graph

An x-y graph is created when two variables, as data pairs (x, y) are plotted one against the other. Always plot the independent variable on the x-axis and the dependent variable on

NOTES

the y-axis. Only data measured on an *interval* or *ratio* scale can be plotted using this form of graph since both axes are continuous.

EXAMPLE: X-Y GRAPH

We are going to plot the value of a commercial van as the mileage on its clock increases. You need to enter the following details on your spreadsheet:

Value	*Mileage in '000s*
14,000	0
12,000	20
8,000	40
5,000	60
4,000	80
3,400	100
2,900	120

Click on the Chart Wizard and select XY (Scatter) and then the sub-chart with smoothed lines without markers. At the 2 of 4 stage select 'Series' and clear the boxes showing the X and Y-values and enter the mileage in '000s in the X-values box by highlighting the data on the worksheet and then enter the value data in the Y-values box.

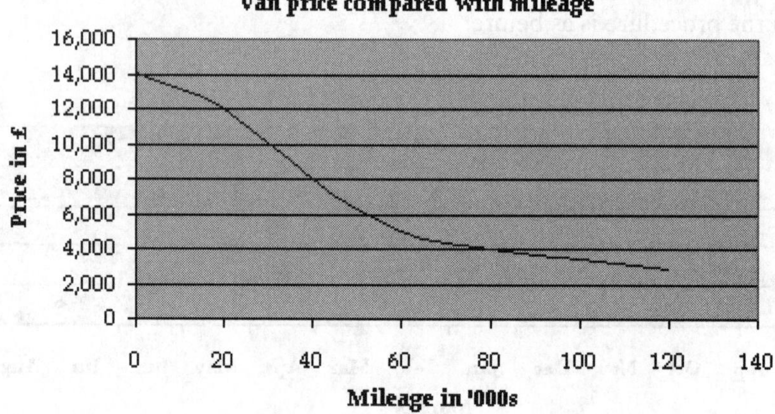

The line graph shows that when the van is new, it costs £14,000. The more it is driven, the more its value falls according to the curve shown on the graph. Its value falls £2000 the first 20,000 miles it is driven. When the mileage is 80,000, the van's value is about £4000.

Ogive

An ogive is a line graph that is produced by cumulating the class data in a frequency polygon. If we go back to the CDs example, we can add a column to the worksheet where we manually calculate the cumulative frequency. Once this is calculated we continue as a line chart using the cumulative frequency data in the Data Range box.

Bin	*Frequency*	*Cumulative frequency*
9	1	1
19	1	2
29	2	4
39	3	7
49	6	13
59	3	16
69	2	18
79	3	21
89	1	22
99	1	23

The ogive below is created using the Line Chart with the chart sub-type that displays the trend over time or categories.

Survey of 23 people in the accounting department

Frequency

0 5 10 15 20 25

9 19 29 39 49 59 69 79 89 99

Numbers of music CDs owned

4.6 Scatter (XY) graphs and linear trend lines

A scatter graph is very similar to a line graph. It allows you to investigate links between two variables and encourages the viewer to assess possible causal relationships between them. For example, there might be a correlation between people's heights and their shoe sizes. Data connecting two variables is known as ***bivariate*** data. Although it does not tell you anything you could not work out from the numbers in the results table a (good) visual image can often make the job much easier.

Scatter graphs can be used to visualise the degree of correlation between two aspects of data. When the points form a random pattern then we say there is no correlation between the aspects of the data. This means there is very little or no relationship between the two aspects of the data. When the points are loosely gathered together we say there is a poor correlation – or weak correlation – between the aspects of the data. This means there is a slight relationship between the two aspects of the data.

When the points more or less form what looks like a straight line we say there is a good correlation – or strong correlation – between the two aspects of the data. This means the two aspects are closely related to each other.

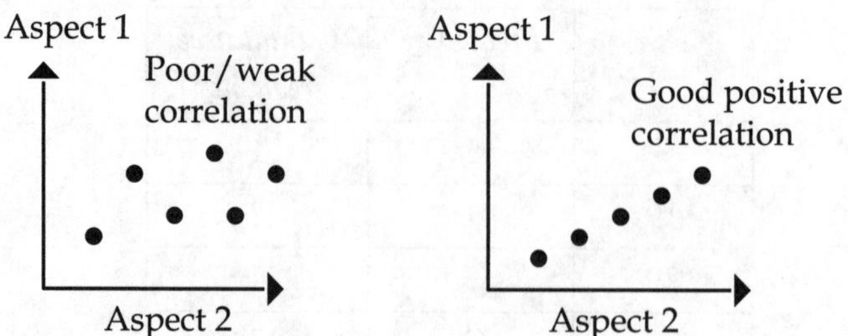

The correlation of the data can be positive or negative depending on the general slope of the points.

Line of Best Fit (trend line)

If the points on the scatter graph lie within a narrow band – i.e. there is a good correlation between the 2 aspects of data – it may be possible to draw a line of best fit that shows graphically the trend of the correlation. A line of best fit may be straight or curved. It is an approximation or estimate – and may go through most of the points or the points may be more or less evenly scattered on either side of the line. If there is a perfect correlation between two aspects of the data, then all the points will lie on a line – this is automatically the line of best fit. If the correlation is not so exact, then the line of best fit matches the slope of the points scattered on the graph

Caution!

There is a maxim in statistics that says, 'Correlation does not imply causality.' In other words, your scatter plot may show that a relationship exists, but it does not and cannot prove that one variable is causing the other. There could be a third factor involved which is causing both, some other systemic cause, or the apparent relationship could just be a fluke. Nevertheless, the scatter plot can give you a clue that two things might be related, and if so, how they move together.

EXAMPLE: CREATING A SCATTER PLOT AND LINE OF BEST FIT USING EXCEL

The data we will use for this example shows test scores received by 20 students.

Information on the hours each student studied for the test is provided. We will attempt to determine if hours studied has a strong linear correlation to test scores.

Student test scores and hours of study

Student	Hours of Study	Test Scores
1	5	54
2	10	56
3	4	63
4	8	64
5	12	62
6	9	61
7	10	63
8	12	73
9	15	78
10	12	72
11	12	78
12	20	83
13	16	83
14	14	86
15	22	83
16	18	81
17	30	88
18	21	87
19	28	89
20	24	93

All scatter plots require two matching sets of data. Enter the corresponding measurements in adjacent columns on your worksheet.

Highlight all of the data values (ignore the student numbers). Click on the Chart Wizard and select the **XY (Scatter)** and the **unconnected points icon** for the Chart sub-type. Click Next for Step 2 of 4 under Chart Options.

Under Titles fill in the Chart title, Value X and Value Y and under Legend click off the legend box. Click Next

Under Chart Location click either new sheet or object, then Finish.

To add a trend line

Place cursor on one of the data plot points and Right Click. Next Left Click on *Format Data Series*.

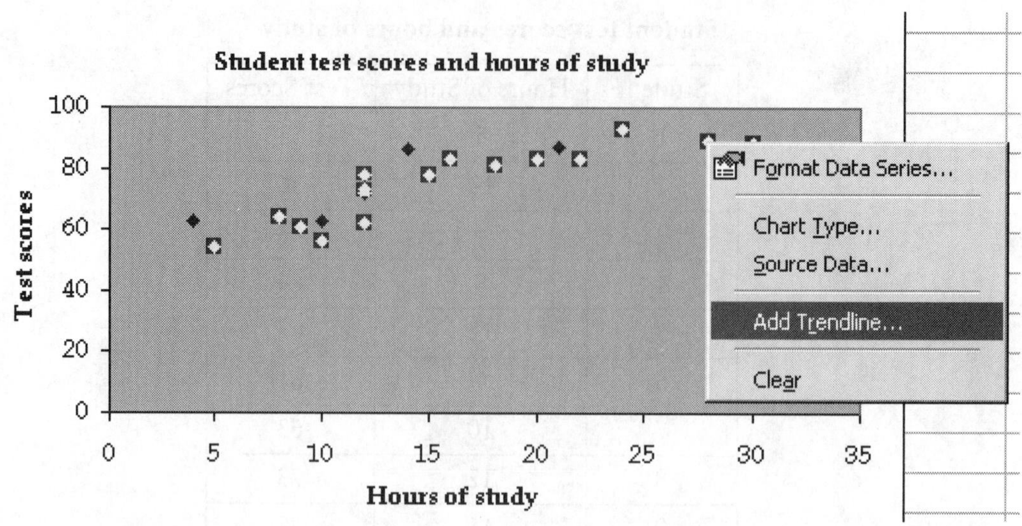

Click on Add Trend line and select the first type of Trend line, which is labelled Linear. Click on the Options Tab. Click the Display Equation on Chart box and then OK

The equation for the straight line in the form y = mx+b. Where m is the slope of the line and b is the y intercept.

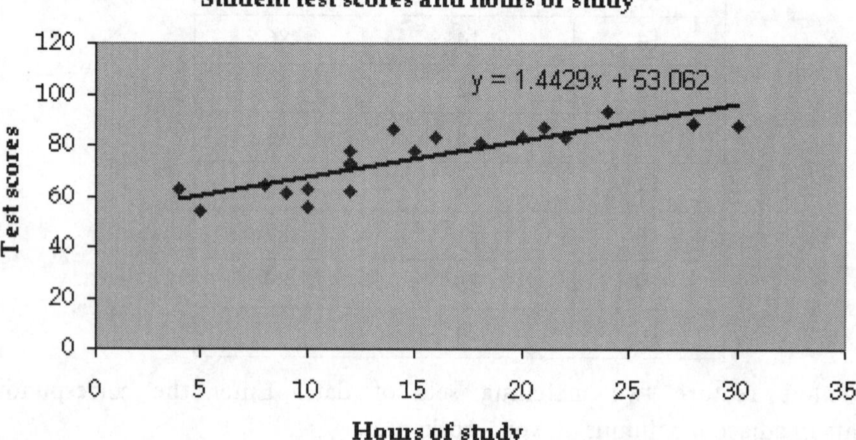

There is a clear trend on this graph; the points form a line diagonally across the graph. Students who spend more time studying achieve higher test scores. The points all fall close to a straight line so they are said to show a linear correlation. The graph rises from left to right so this is known as a positive correlation; a line that falls from left to right shows a negative correlation. Although the trend could be clearly seen by any viewer before adding a trend line, the relationship can be quantified by it.

Activity 5 **(15 minutes)**

Interpret the 'Student test scores and hours of study chart' above by answering the following questions.

(a) How would you describe the correlation between test scores and hours of study?

(b) What is the equation of the line of best fit?

(c) What is the slope of the line of best fit?

(d) What is the y-intercept of the line of best fit?

(e) What does this y-intercept tell you?

(f) Using the trend line on the scatter plot, estimate the mark of a student who studied for 25 hours.

(g) Using the equation of the line of best fit for the trend line, calculate the mark a student who studied 25 hours might receive.

Summary of trends

Some of the simpler trends are listed below; more complex relationships may be a combination of two or more of these. Remember that it is the analysis of these trends, and explaining them, that provides the information required.

Straight-line (linear) graphs

y x	• the line passes through the origin • y increases at a constant rate • y is directly proportional to x • equation: y=mx
y x	• positive gradient, *m* • y increases at a constant rate • y is proportional to x plus a constant • equation: y=mx+b
y x	• negative gradient, *m* • y decreases at a constant rate • y is proportional to –x plus a constant • equation: y=mx+b (m is negative)
y x	• y is not dependent on the value of x i.e. y is constant • equation: y=b

NOTES

Curved (non-linear) graphs

y, x	• y increases at an increasing rate • possible equations: $y=mx^2$, $y=mx^3$, etc • eg y is proportional to x squared
y, x	• y increases at a decreasing rate • possible equation: $y=a-m(x-b)^2$
y, x	• y decreases at an increasing rate • possible equation: $y=a-mx^2$
y, x	• y decreases at a decreasing rate • possible equations: $y=m/x$, etc • eg y is inversely proportional to x
y, x	• y has a minimum value • possible equation: $y=a+m(x-b)^2$
y, x	• y has a maximum value • possible equation: $y=a-m(x-b)^2$

4.7 Multi-sheet spreadsheets

In early spreadsheet packages, a spreadsheet file consisted of a single worksheet. Excel provides the option of multi-sheet spreadsheets, consisting of a series of related sheets.

For example, suppose you were producing a profit forecast for two regions, and a combined forecast for the total of the regions. This situation would be suited to using separate worksheets for each region and another for the total. This approach is sometimes referred to as working in **three dimensions**, as you are able to flip between different sheets stacked in front or behind each other. Cells in one sheet may **refer** to cells in another sheet. Excel has a series of 'tabs', one for each worksheet at the foot of the spreadsheet.

Sheet1 / Sheet2 / Sheet3 /

Excel can be set up so that it always opens a fresh file with a certain number of worksheets ready and waiting for you. Click on **Tools ... Options** ... and then the **General** tab and set the number *Sheets in new workbook* option to the number you would like each new spreadsheet file to contain (Sheets may be added or deleted later).

If you subsequently want to insert more sheets you just **right click** on the index tab after which you want the new sheet to be inserted and choose **Insert** ... and then **Worksheet**. By default sheets are called **Sheet 1, Sheet 2** etc. However, these may be changed. To **rename** a sheet in **Excel, right click** on its index tab and choose the rename option. You can then simply type the new name on the tab.

NOTES

When building a spreadsheet that will contain a number of worksheets with identical structure, users often set up one sheet, then copy that sheet and amend the sheet contents. This can be done by clicking on any ell on the worksheet, select Edit, Move or Copy sheet, and ticking the Create a Copy box. A 'Total' sheet would use the same structure, but would contain formulae totalling the individual sheets.

Formulae on one sheet may refer to data held on another sheet. The links within such a formula may be established using the following steps.

Step 1 In the cell that you want to refer to a cell from another sheet, type =.

Step 2 Click on the index tab for the sheet containing the cell you want to refer to and select the cell in question.

Step 3 Press Enter or Return.

We'll look at a very simple example. Start with a blank spreadsheet and ensure that it contains at least two sheets.

Type the number 1,746, 243 in cell A1 of the first sheet. Then select the tab for the second sheet and select A1 in that sheet (this is step 1 from the three steps above). Type =. Follow steps 2 and 3 above. The same number will display in cell A1 of both sheets. However, what is actually contained in cell A1 of the second sheet is the formula **=Sheet1!A1**

Cell A1 in the second sheet is now linked to cell A1 in the first sheet. This method may be used regardless of the cell addresses – the two cells **do not have to be in the same place** in their respective sheets. For instance cell Z658 of one sheet could refer to cell P24 of another. If you **move cells** or insert **extra rows** or columns on the sheet with the original numbers the cell references on the other sheet will **change automatically**.

There are a wide range of situations suited to the multi-sheet approach. A variety of possible uses follow.

(a) A model could use one sheet for variables, a second for calculations, and a third for outputs.

(b) To enable quick and easy **consolidation** of similar sets of data, for example the financial results of two subsidiaries or the budgets of two departments.

(c) To provide **different views** of the same data. For instance you could have one sheet of data sorted in product code order and another sorted in product name order.

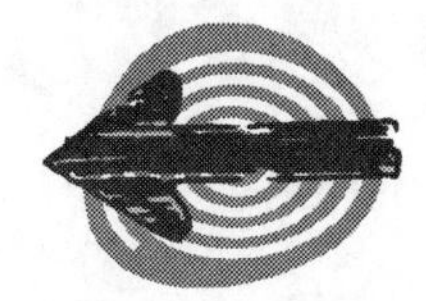

We will be drawing some charts in the next chapter when preparing a business presentation and a formal business report.

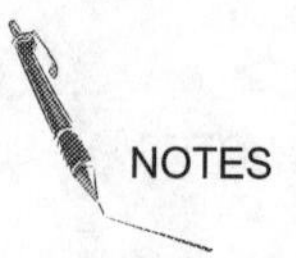

Chapter roundup

- A spreadsheet is an electronic piece of paper divided into rows and columns
- In this chapter we looked at some useful spreadsheet formulae and functions including: Left, right and mid, Lookup and Pivot tables.
- We prepared a range of graphs using spreadsheets – line, pie, bar charts and histograms and drew conclusions based on the information derived
- We looked at some practical uses of spreadsheets.

Quick quiz

1 Name three functions from the Insert menu in Excel.

2 When would you use the left, right or mid function provided in Excel?

3 What does the lookup function do?

4 What is a pivot table?

Answers to quick quiz

1 There are many to choose from: SUM, AVERAGE, MAX, MIN, STDEV, SUMIF AND COUNT.

2 You would use the left, right or mid function to extract specific characters from the data entered in a cell. The left function extracts the first character or characters; the mid extracts from the middle of the cell and the right extracts the last from the cell.

3 The lookup function allows you to enter data that corresponds to a value in one cell in a column and return the data in the corresponding row in a different column.

4 A pivot table is an interactive table that summarises and analyses data from lists and tables.

Answers to activities

1 (a) A spreadsheet is like an electronic piece of paper divided into rows and columns. It provides an easy way of performing numerical calculations. The principal feature of a spreadsheet is that, once it is set up, a change in any one of the values means that the others change automatically.

(b) Any five of the following (although you might have thought of other valid uses).

(i) Cash-flow projections
(ii) Balance sheets
(iii) Profit forecasts
(iv) Sales forecasts
(v) General ledger
(vi) Stock records
(vii) Job cost estimates

(c) The cell (or range of cells) that will be changed by keyboard or mouse input.

(d) (i) 'Text' means words or numerical data, such as a date, that cannot be used in computations.

(ii) A value is a number that can be used in a calculation.

(iii) A formula operates on other cells in the spreadsheet and performs calculations with them. For example, if cell B4 has to contain the total of the values in cells B2 and B3, a formula that could be entered in B4 is =B2+B3.

2 (a) =MID(A1,4,1) – the starting position is 4 because the hyphen between the 2 and the D counts as position 3.

(b) =LEFT(A1,2)

3

Sales of soft drinks in 20X3

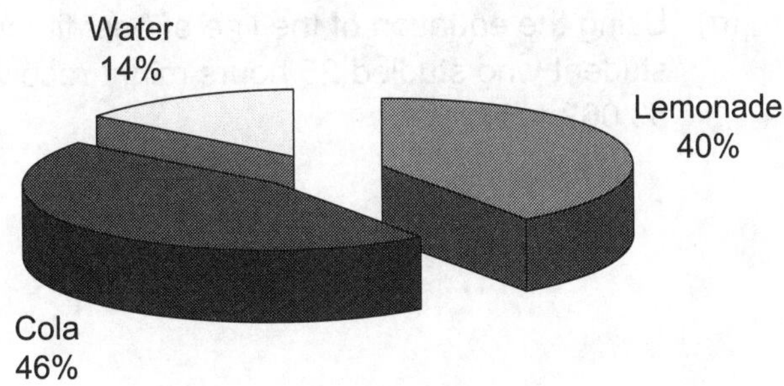

Sales of soft drinks in 20X7

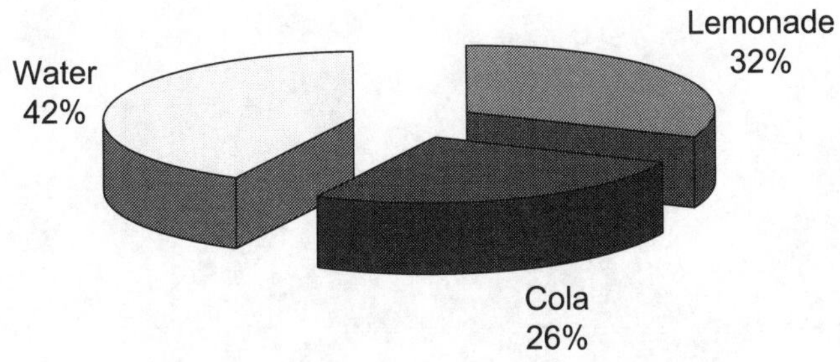

4 The shape is a normal (or bell) shaped distribution. If many of the participants had stated that they owned 70 – 90 DVDs and very few reported owning in the 0 – 20 range, then the distribution would have been negatively skewed. If many had reported owning between 0 and 20 DVDs and only a few reported owning between 70 and 90 DVDs, then the distribution would have had a positive skew. To get a rectangular distribution, there would have to be roughly equal number of DVDs reported for each interval.

5 (a) There is a strong linear correlation between the test scores and the hours of study

(b) The equation of the line of best fit is y = 1.4429x+53.062

(c) The slope is m = 1.4429

(d) The y intercept is 53.062

(e) This y intercept forecasts that a student who does no studying at all will achieve a score of around 53

(f) Using the chart, an estimate of the mark of a student who studied for 25 hours is 85

(g) Using the equation of the line of best fit for the trend line, the mark a student who studied 25 hours might receive would be 1,4429 × 25 + 53.062 = 89

Chapter 7 : REPORTING

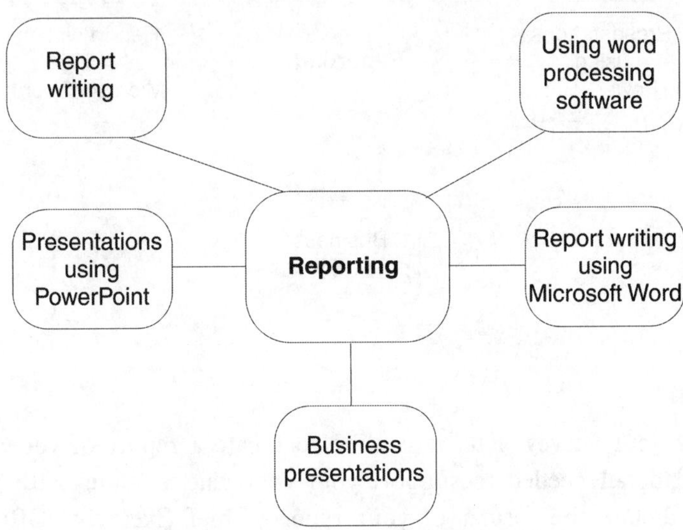

Introduction

Having done all of your planning, research and analysis, you may now feel that you are facing the hardest task of all, which is to write a formal business report and prepare a business presentation using suitable software and techniques to disseminate information effectively and persuasively.

There are certain skills attached to report writing and presentations and this chapter aims to familiarise you with them.

We will be looking at Microsoft Word and PowerPoint and examining the techniques you will need to complete the report on your business problem.

Your objectives

After completing this chapter you should be able to:

(a) Write a formal business report

(b) Understand how to use word processing software to produce the report

(c) Prepare a business presentation

(d) Use suitable software and techniques to disseminate information effectively and persuasively

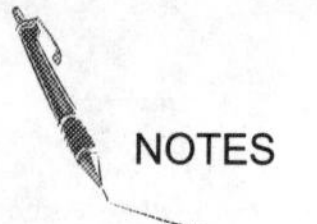

1 REPORT WRITING

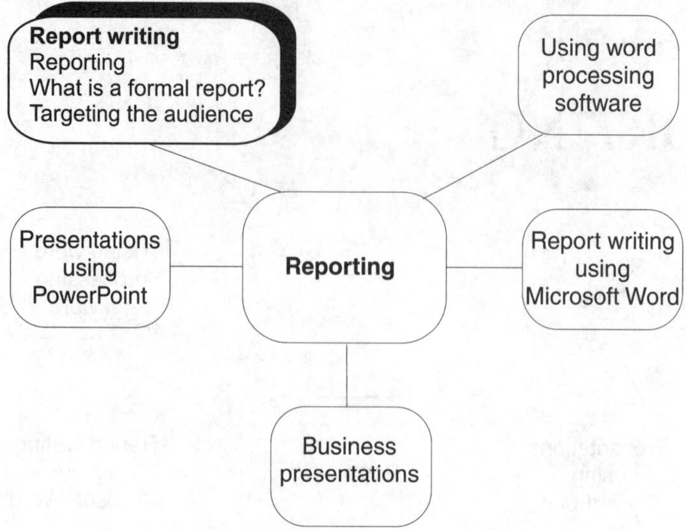

1.1 Reporting

After analysing your survey data, it is time to create a report of your findings. The complexity and detail needed to support your conclusions, along with your intended audience, will dictate the format of your report. Chief Executive Officers require a different level of detail than line managers, so for maximum results consider who is going to receive your report and tailor it to meet their unique needs.

Visual reports, such as an HTML document or Microsoft PowerPoint presentation, are suitable for simple findings. These graphical reports are best when they are light on text and heavy on graphs and charts. They are reviewed quickly rather than studied at length, and most conclusions are obvious, so detailed explanations are seldom required. For more complex topics, a detailed report created in Microsoft Word or Adobe Acrobat is often required. Reports created using Word often include much more detailed information, report findings that require significant explanation, are extremely text heavy, and are often studied at great length and in significant detail.

No matter which type of report you use, always remember that information can be more powerfully displayed in a graphic format verses a text or tabular representation. Often, trends and patterns are more obvious and recommendations more effective when presented visually. Ideally, when making comparisons of one or more groups of respondents, it is best to show a chart of each group's responses side-by-side. This side-by-side comparison allows your audience quickly to see the differences you are highlighting and will lead to more support for your conclusions.

At the beginning of your report, you should review your survey objective and sampling method. This will help your audience understand what the survey was about, and enable you to avoid many questions that are outside your original objectives. Your report should have a description of your sampling method, including who was invited to participate, over what time frame results were collected, and any issues that might exist relative to your respondent pool. Next, you should include your analysis and conclusions in adequate detail to meet the needs of your audience. Include a table or graph for each area of interest and explain why it is noteworthy. After your analysis section, you should make recommendations that relate back to your survey objectives. Recommendations can be as simple as 'conduct further studies' to a major shift in company direction.

In either case, your recommendation must be within the scope of your survey objective and supported by the data collected. Finally, you can include a copy of your survey questions and a summary of all the data collected as an appendix to your report.

1.2 What is a formal report?

A formal report is a report for a specific target audience. The purpose of the report is to answer questions that are being asked by someone else. This may be your manager or a director in an organisation, or the intended audience may be a group of people.

There are two types of formal report that are most likely to be requested in a business environment.

(a) **Analytical reports** which focus on investigations into events, organisations, situations, issues and processes. Their purpose is often to provide the reader with information that can be used to make decisions and take further action.

(b) **Practical/Scientific reports** which give an account of what has happened in a test situation, a practical session or as part of an experiment.

In a formal report there is a different style of writing to that in a technical or academic report, and a difference in the language you would use when talking or sending emails to friends/colleagues.

Whether the report is 'one-off' or routine, there is an obligation on the part of the person requesting the report to state the use to which it will be put. In other words, the purpose of the report must be clear to both its writers and its users. There is also an obligation on the part of the report writer to communicate information in an unbiased way. The report writer knows more about the subject matter of the report than the report user (otherwise there would be no need for the report in the first place). It is important that this information should be communicated impartially, so that the report users can make their own judgements. It is important that the report contains the following.

(a) Clearly stated assumptions, evaluations and recommendations by the report writer.

(b) Points that are not over-weighted or omitted as irrelevant, without honestly evaluating how objective the selection is.

(c) Facts and findings which are balanced against each other.

(d) A firm conclusion, if possible. It should be clear how and why it was reached.

The elements of a formal report are shown in the table below.

ELEMENTS OF A FORMAL REPORT	
Title	Subject of report
Terms of reference	Clarify what has been requested
Introduction	Who the report is from and to How the information was obtained
Main body	Divided into sections with sub-headings to aid reader Logical order
Conclusions	Summarises findings
Recommendations	Based on information and evidence May be combined with conclusion
Signature	Of writer
Executive summary	Saves time for managers receiving a long report No more than one page

One example of a short formal report is shown below.

REPORT ON PROPOSED UPDATING OF COMPANY POLICY MANUAL

To: Board of Directors, BCD Ltd
From: J Thurber, Opus Management Consultants
Status: Confidential
Date: 3 October 20X8

I INTRODUCTION AND TERMS OF REFERENCE

This report details the results of an investigation commissioned by the Board on 7 September 20X8. We were asked to consider the current applicability of the company's policy manual and to propose changes needed to bring it into line with current practice.

II METHOD

The following investigatory procedures were adopted:

1 Interview of all senior staff regarding use of the policy manual in their departments

2 Observation of working practices in each department

III FINDINGS

The manual was last updated ten years ago. From our observations, the following amendments are now needed:

1 The policy section on computer use should be amended. It deals with safe storage of disks, which is no longer applicable as data is now stored on a server. Also, it does not set out the company's e-mail policy.

2 The company's equal opportunities policy needs to be included.

3 The coding list in the manual is now very out of date. A number of new cost centres and profit centres have been set up in the last ten years and the codes for these are not noted in the manual.

4 There is no mention of the provisions of the Data Protection Act as they relate to the company.

IV CONCLUSIONS

We discovered upon interviewing staff that very little use is made of the policy manual. When it has been amended as above, it can be brought back into use, and we recommend that this should be done as soon as possible.

Signed J Thurber, Opus Management Consultants

A formal report like this will be **word-processed**. We will look into some of the facilities offered by Microsoft Word that can help when writing a formal report in the next two sections.

Activity 1 **(5 minutes)**

Can you think of two valid purposes for a formal report?

1.3 Targeting the audience

There is an obligation on the part of the report writer to recognise the needs and abilities of the report user. Beware of jargon, overly technical terms, and specialist knowledge the user may not share. Keep your vocabulary, sentence and paragraph structures as simple as possible, for clarity, without patronising an intelligent user. Bear in mind the type and level of detail that will interest the user and be relevant to his/her purpose. In a business context, the user may range from senior manager to junior supervisor, to non-managerial employee (such as in the case of minutes of a meeting, or general bulletin) to complete layman (customer, press and so on). Your vocabulary, syntax and presentation, the amount of detail you can go into, the technical matter you can include and the formality of your report structure should all be influenced by such concerns.

As with all information, a report may be of no use at all if it is not produced on time, however well researched and well presented it is. There is no point in presenting a report to influence a decision if the decision has already been made by the time the report is issued. The timescales within which the report user is working must be known, and the time available to produce the report planned accordingly.

2 USING WORD PROCESSING SOFTWARE

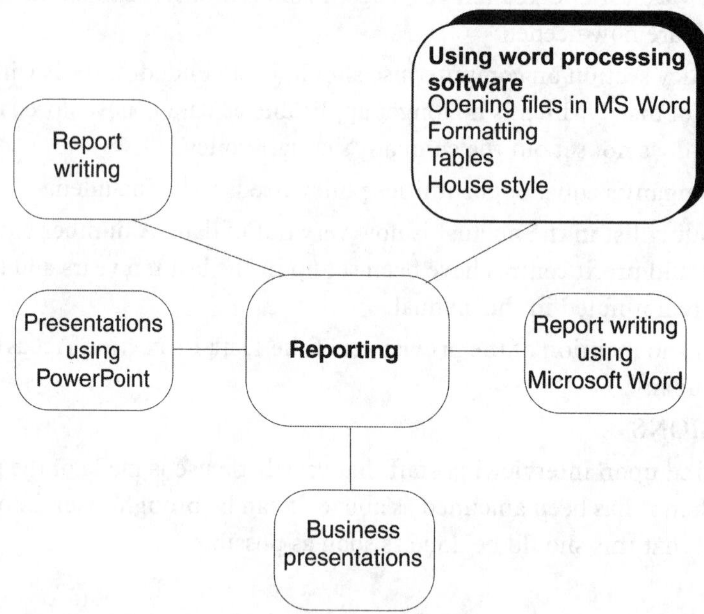

2.1 Introduction

Much of the information used for management control today is analysed or presented using spreadsheet or word processing software.

Definition

Word processing software enables you to use a computer to create a document, store it electronically, display it on-screen, modify it by entering commands and characters from the keyboard, and print it using a printer.

In this section, we cover some basic functions of Microsoft Word, the most popular word processing software package. If you have little experience with this software, you should work through this section hands-on, at a computer that has Microsoft Word available. Alternatively, if you feel that you are at ease using the basic facilities offered by a word processing package, then skip this section and go onto the next.

After working through this section, you may wish to experiment with other functions of word processing software – explore the Microsoft Word online Help facility (**Help** from the Word main menu) for detailed guidance.

2.2 Opening files in Microsoft Word

Microsoft Word is launched by double-clicking on the Word **icon** or button, or by choosing Microsoft Word from the **Start** menu (maybe from within the **Microsoft Office** option). When **W**ord starts, you are presented with a blank document. To open an existing document, you select File, Open from the main menu.

The document itself displays in the centre part of the screen. Above the document is a bank of toolbar buttons. These buttons serve a variety of functions. In recent versions of Word, if you let the mouse pointer linger over a particular button (without clicking on it) a little label soon pops up telling you what it does. The menu choices just below the title bar offer a range of further functions and options. We are going to look at several of the most commonly used.

File: Open

Click on the word **File** and a menu will drop down which includes the item **Open.** If you click on this, a window like the following will appear.

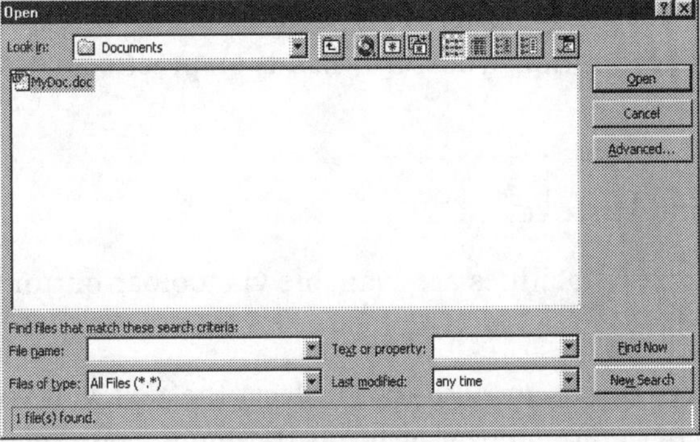

To open a particular existing file, you click on the **Look in** box arrow and then locate the file by navigating through the folder structure. When you locate the document, click on the file name and then click on OK to open the file. *Double-clicking* on a file name has the effect of both selecting it and clicking on OK to open it.

File: Save As

If you open an existing file (that will obviously already have an existing file name), and then you make some changes to it which you want to save, but you also wish to leave the original document intact, you should use the File, Save As option, and give the amended file a new name.

The file you originally opened will remain in its original form, and the file with the new name will include all of your changes. For example, you could open a file containing a letter to Mrs Smith called Smith.Doc, change the name and address details, and save it as Jones.Doc. You would end up with *two* files – one called Smith.Doc and the other called Jones.Doc.

File: Close

To close a Word file simply select **File** and then **Close**. If you haven't already done so you will be asked if you want to save any changes you made.

File: Print

If you have a document open and you wish to print it, click on the **Print** option in the **File** menu. The following box will appear.

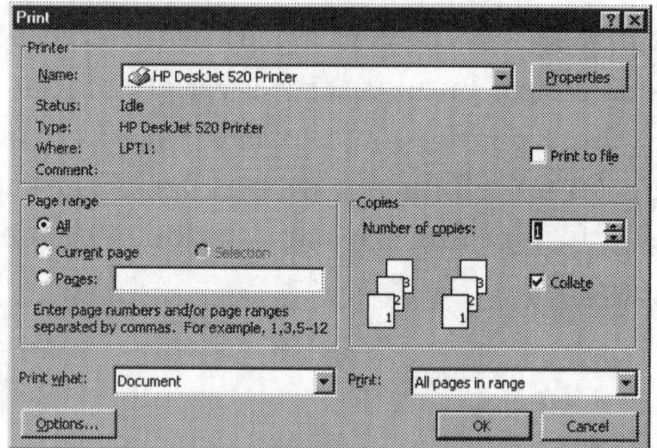

There are options to select a different printer (if you are on a network and have other printers available), to print more than one copy, to print only the current page, to print only text you have already selected by highlighting or to print specific pages only. Experiment with these options yourself – hands on practice is essential.

Edit: Cut, Copy and Paste 

The cut, copy and paste facilities are available via toolbar buttons or as menu items. The menu is used as follows.

(a) The first step is to highlight (select) the text you wish to format. To select text using your mouse, position the mouse pointer at the beginning of the first word, then hold down the left mouse button and move the pointer across the text you wish to select. Then release the mouse button. The portion of text will now be highlighted as shown below.

This·text·is·selected.·This·text·isn't·selected.

To select using the keyboard, move the cursor to the beginning of the area to be selected. Hold down the Shift key, and while holding it down, use the navigation (arrow) keys to highlight the required area. (To unselect text, click anywhere in your document except inside the selected region.)

(b) With the required text highlighted, click on **Edit** from the main menu.

(i) To retain the highlighted text in its current place and also to make a copy of it which is retained temporarily on the computer's 'clipboard', click on **Copy**.

(ii) To remove the highlighted text from its current place, but also place it temporarily on the computer's clipboard, click on **Cut**. The highlighted text will disappear.

(c) Move the cursor to the point in your document where you want to place the text.

(d) Click on Edit again and choose **Paste**. The text you highlighted will reappear here.

The toolbar buttons may prove a little quicker, and are used as follows.

(a) Select the text by highlighting

(b) Click on (*cut*) or (*copy*)

(c) Move the cursor to the destination required.

(d) Click on (*paste*)

Note also that there are keyboard shortcuts for cutting, copying and pasting. These are listed on the **Edit** menu –for example pressing the Ctrl and V keys at the same time is the same as selecting Paste from the Edit menu. Another option, that achieves the same as cutting and pasting, is to *drag* the selected text and *drop* it in the new place. Try doing this yourself.

2.3 Formatting

Formatting options are accessed either via the Format menu or through the Formatting tool bar (shown below). If you can't see these options available on-screen, select View, Toolbars, Formatting from the main menu.

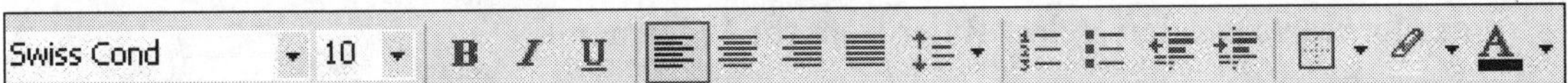

The formatting toolbar allows you to select a font, a font size, to apply bold, italic and underline options, to justify text, apply numbers or bullets or outlines and to select font colour options.

To change the font, click the down arrow of the font name box. A list of the currently available fonts appears in the box. You may select any one of the fonts listed. The name of the newly selected font will appear in the font name box. Any selected text will have the new format, any text entered after the font selection will have the new format. This same procedure works for the font size as well.

The bold (**B**), italic (*I*) and underline (U) buttons do exactly that, they bold, italicise, or underline the current selection, or make the appropriate settings for the text typed in at the cursor. Font colour can be modified by using the underlined capital A button at the end of the tool bar. Click on the down arrow next to the A, the colour you then select is the colour that will be applied to selected text.

Explore these same options using the items available under the Format menu rather than using the toolbar buttons.

Format: Paragraph

This item on the **Format** menu offers you (amongst other things) a consistent and professional way of spacing out paragraphs. You should use this option rather than pressing return several times to leave blank lines.

Clicking on the **Paragraph** option in the **Format** menu brings up the Indents and Spacing tab. The Spacing option allows you to specify the number of 'points' (small units of vertical space) before paragraphs and after them. For example there are '6 pts' between this paragraph and the previous one.

Paragraph Justification refers to how the text is laid out on the screen.

(a) Left justification has the left side of the text even and aligned, while the right side remains jagged.

(b) Right justification is just the opposite, where the right margin is smooth and the left margin is left jagged.

(c) Centre justification has each line is positioned in the centre of the page.

(d) Full justification forces both right and left margins to be even and aligned by putting very small spaces between the words to make up for the extra space you would normally find at the end of a line.

All of these options are also available from the toolbar buttons shown here.

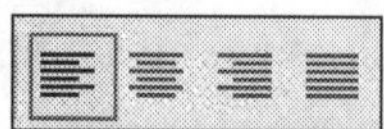

Ruler bars

The Ruler bars are located above and to the left of your document. They display the arrangement of your margins, your paragraph indents, tab settings, and page layout information. If the ruler bars do not appear, they have simply been turned off. If you cannot see your rulers, select Ruler from the View menu.

The horizontal ruler bar (shown above) allows you to set tabs, indents and margins. The white areas of the ruler bar determine where text can be placed. The margin is shown where white meets grey. No text will be displayed beyond the white area. You can adjust the margin simply by moving the mouse over the separator line between white and grey, then when the pointer becomes a two-pointed arrow, click and drag the margin to the required position.

The triangle like shapes on the horizontal ruler bar are used for paragraph indents. These may be dragged to indent paragraphs as required. The top-left triangle (pointing down) is the First Line Indent – the position where the first line will start. The left edge of all other lines in the paragraph are aligned with the bottom triangle on the left side of the ruler bar. This is the Hanging Indent. Below the Hanging Indent triangle is a small rectangle. This is the Left Indent control – if you drag this rectangle it will move the First Line Indent and the Hanging Indent in unison. The triangle on the right side of the ruler bar is for right indentation.

The vertical ruler bar is similar to the horizontal ruler bar. You adjust the vertical margins by using the same procedure you used with the horizontal ruler bar. Note that changes to margins affect the entire page, while indent settings apply only to the current paragraph.

Tabs

Tabs are used to space text across the page. The Tab tool is shown on-screen in the top left corner of the page. There are four main types of Tab, each representing a different type of alignment. Clicking on the Tab tool changes the type of Tab to be inserted.

To place a tab in your document, click on the ruler bar where you want the tab stop to go. A symbol, identical to the one in the tab box, will appear on the ruler bar. To move the tab, drag the tab marker to the left or right. To remove a tab, drag the marker down and drop it anywhere below the ruler.

As with all of the features we have covered, you should experiment using Tabs yourself hands-on.

Tools: Spelling and grammar

Finally we come to one of the most popular features of word processing software. Click on **Tools** and then on **Spelling and Grammar** in the drop down menu. Word will work right through your document seeing if the spelling matches the spelling of words in the computer's dictionary. If not it suggests alternatives from which you choose the correct one. For example, if you type 'drp', the choices you are offered include 'drip', 'drop', 'dry' and 'dip'.

The spell-checker will identify all words that don't appear in the word processing package's dictionary. Remember that not all of the words highlighted will actually be mistakes, for example the word 'spreadsheeting' (eg 'this job requires good spreadsheeting skills') is suggested as a mistake.

Also, some mistakes won't be highlighted as the incorrect spelling matches another word. For example, you may type 'form' when you meant 'from' – this won't be highlighted as a spelling mistake.

So, when using the spell checker always take your time before deciding whether to accept or ignore the suggested change. Also, ensure the correct dictionary is being used, for example English UK rather than English US.

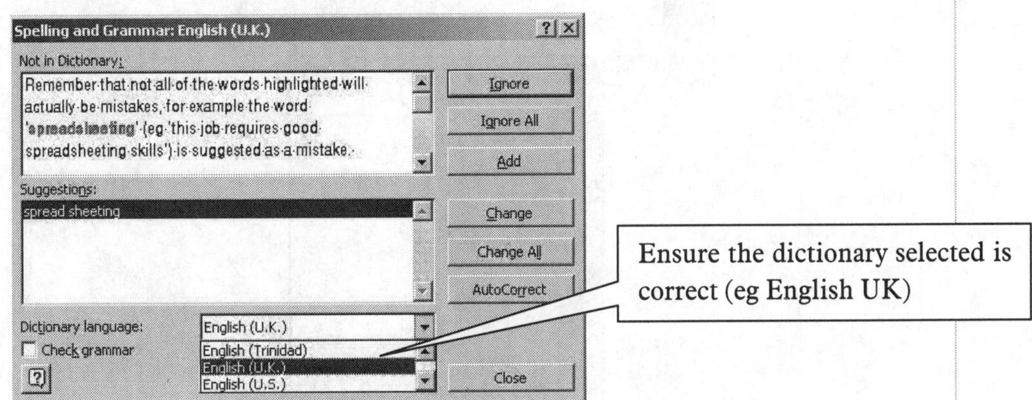

The grammar check will perform tasks such as:

- Detecting sentences where you have omitted the verb
- Detecting sentences where you have used mixed singular and plural subject and verb (eg, 'two of the main reasons for the development of the multinational company is...')
- Indicating sentences that are unduly long or have too many clauses, potentially confusing the reader.

You can specify in the grammar check what style of language you are using, such as 'standard', 'formal', 'casual', and 'technical'. You can also use a grammar option that gives the readability statistics of your work. This is a useful tool in that it can indicate when your language is becoming obscure.

If you think your use of words is becoming repetitive, try using a Thesaurus. This will suggest alternatives and can also supply meanings.

2.4 Tables

Some information to be included in a report, letter, memo or other document may best be presented in a table. We will briefly explain how to create and format a table using menu items. As with many Microsoft Word functions, the same process could be performed using toolbar buttons (if you wish to experiment using toolbar buttons, activate the Tables and Borders toolbar by selecting View, Toolbars, Tables and Borders from the main menu).

To create a simple table follow the following steps.

Step 1 Click where you want to create a table within your document.

Step 2 From the main menu select, Table, Insert, Table.

Step 3 The Insert Table dialogue box will appear as shown (if you are using an earlier version of Word the box will appear slightly different). Enter the required number of vertical columns and the number of horizontal rows (don't worry if you are not 100% sure as these options may be changed later). Accept the column width default setting of Auto. Click OK.

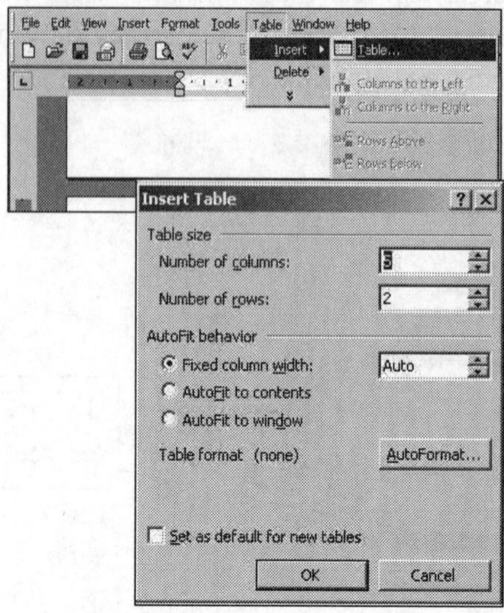

Step 4 You should now have a Table in your document.

Step 5 The table you have created is a starting point only. As you add data to your table you may decide to format the contents of particular cells in a certain way, or to insert or delete columns or rows.

Instructions for some useful actions associated with tables are shown in the table below.

Table action	Explanation
Entering text and moving around the table	Click into the appropriate cell (individual area of the table) and start typing. When you reach the end of the cell the text will continue on the next line, and the cell height will adjust automatically. Move to a different cell by using your mouse to click the cursor in the new cell. If you prefer, you can move around the table using the following keys. Tab – takes you to the next cell. Shift + Tab – takes you 'back' a cell. (The Shift key is above the Ctrl key) Up or Down direction arrow key – takes you up or down a row. Return or Enter – takes you to a new line within the same cell.
Aligning text	The default is to align text in tables to the left. To align text in the centre or to the right, use the alignment buttons on the standard toolbar.
Formatting text	You format text in a table just as you would format normal text – by selecting it then using toolbar buttons or the Format menu.
Selecting rows	Position the cursor to the left of the row you wish to select. The cursor will become an arrow pointing towards the top of the row. Click to select the row. If you prefer, click into the row you wish to select, then choose Table, Select, Row from the menu.
Selecting columns	Position the cursor just above the column you wish to select. The cursor will become a black, downward pointing arrow. Click to select the column. If you prefer, click into the column you wish to select, then choose Table, Select, Column from the menu.
Selecting a single cell	Position the cursor just inside the left border of the cell you wish to select. The cursor will become a black arrow pointing towards the top of the cell. Click to select the cell. If you prefer, click into the row you wish to select, then choose Table, Select, Cell from the menu.
Selecting the entire table	Click in any cell in the table. Choose Table, Select, Table from the menu.

Table action	Explanation
Changing row height and column width	Move the cursor over the border you wish to move until it becomes two lines with arrows pointing up and down (rows) or left and right (columns). Hold down the mouse button and drag the boundary to the required height or width.
Deleting rows and columns	Select the row or column as above. Then chose Table, Delete, Rows or Table, Delete, Columns from the menu.
Deleting the contents of rows and columns	To clear the contents of a row or column select the area to be cleared then press the Delete key.
Adding rows and columns	To add an extra row, select the row below where you wish the new row to be then chose Table, Insert, Rows from the menu. To add an extra column, select the column to the right of where you wish the new column to be then chose Table, Insert, Columns from the menu.
Merging cells	Joining two cells together to contain text that spans two or more columns is called merging cells. This is useful, for example, to provide a cell at the top of a table suitable for a heading that spans across all columns. To merge cells, you must first select the cells you wish to merge – then choose Table, Merge Cells from the menu.
Borders and shading	Word inserts a simple line border around all cells in a new table. You may change some or all borders, or add shading, or remove all border lines, by using the options available under Format, Borders and Shading. You should experiment with these options.

2.5 House style

With such a wide range of fonts, formats and other options available, it is possible to produce documents with a vast range of appearances. To present a consistent, professional image, some organisations specify the same font and formatting options for all documents. This ensures consistency and presents a professional image. For example, the headings and areas of text within this book use the same fonts each time they appear – and each chapter uses the same styles, headers and footers.

If your organisation has a house style, ensure you know how to apply it to your documents.

NOTES

3 REPORT WRITING USING MICROSOFT WORD

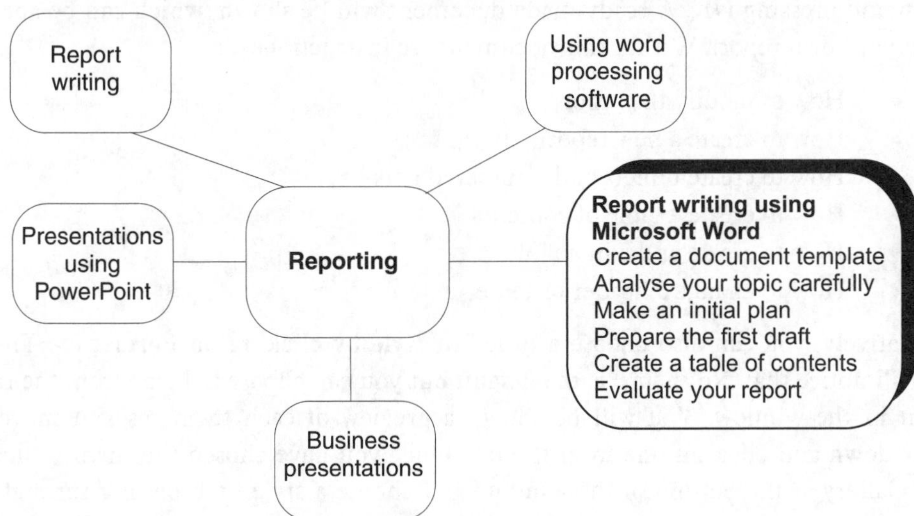

Once you have your topic, you should follow a series of steps for writing analytical reports.

3.1 Create a document template

Various display techniques may be used to make the content of a report easy to identify and digest. For example, the relative importance of points should be signalled, each point may be referenced, and the body of text should be broken up to be easy on the eye.

Early in your process of planning the report it is important to choose a set of formatting and style guidelines.

Every Microsoft Word document is based on a template; it determines the basic structure for a document and contains document settings such as AutoText entries, fonts, key assignments, macros, menus, page layout, special formatting, and styles. Microsoft Office provides Basic Styles such as Heading 1 and Normal, all which can be accessed through the Format -> Styles and Formatting menu option, and all containing settings available to all documents. Document templates, such as the report templates in the **New** dialog box, contain settings that are available only to documents based on that template. For example, if you create a report using one of the report templates, it can use the settings from both the report template as well as the settings in any global template.

Open a new folder or file for your report and label it. You can use an existing template or create an alternative report format on the File menu, select New -> More new templates and then select the type you want. Choosing 'Reports' offers a choice.

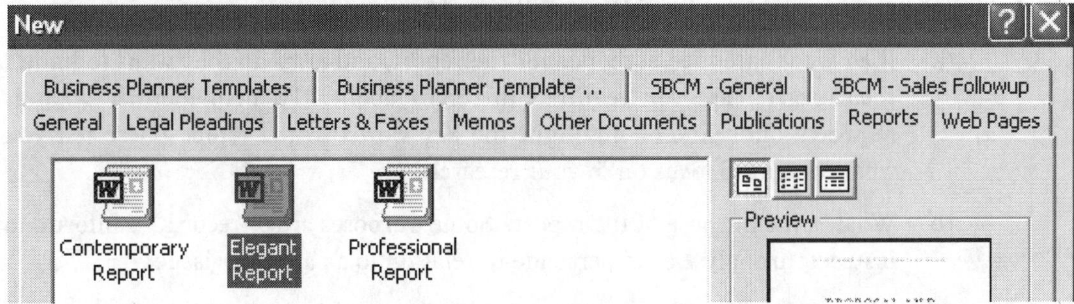

Clicking on one shows a preview that, if you like, you can use by enabling the document button and pressing OK. A ready-made document will be shown, which can be adapted to suit your own report. Within this document are instructions on:

- How to modify the report
- How to create a new report
- How to create bullets and numbered lists
- How to create a table of contents
- How to create and edit a table
- How to change a header or footer

Alternatively, you can also choose a different style by clicking on Format -> Theme. You will notice that 'No theme' is the default but you can choose a theme from the range shown in the window. You will be shown a preview of each theme as you move the cursor down and click on one from the list. Once you have chosen the theme, click on Style Gallery at the bottom of the window and choose a style by browsing through the drop-down menu–there are many to choose from, including one for a professional report.

3.2 Analyse your topic carefully

Either key in the outline and requirements for your report or import the details from another source. If you are inserting part of a file into your document go to the file and highlight the portion you want to copy and do a copy and paste into the new document. For the whole file go to Insert ->File and then browse for the file you want to import. Click on Insert and then OK. For a certain type of file you may want to insert it as a link. By doing this, if the file is updated or changed in any way, your link in your document can be updated as well by clicking on it and right clicking to show the 'Update field' command.

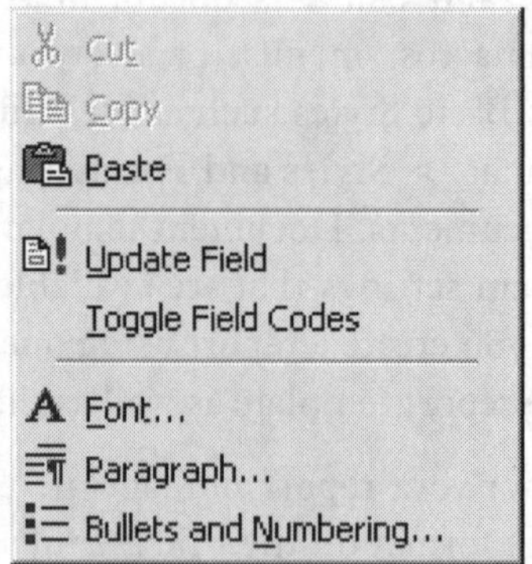

In analysing your topic, you can ask yourself a series of questions:

(a) *Who* is the intended audience for the report, and *what* do they want to know? *What* exactly are you required to report about? To help identify what is required, underline or highlight the key words in the topic. These tell you what content to focus on in your research.

(b) What is the purpose of the report? Some purposes are to record, to inform, to instruct, to analyse or to persuade in relation to a particular issue.

(c) What is the *scope* of your report? What aspects of the topic are you to cover?

(d) What are the *limits* of the report? There are *three kinds* of 'limits' you need to consider here. These include limits to the *information* part of the topic, which confine it to a particular place, time or group. Also, there are limits placed on the *number of words* and the *time* you have available. Sometimes, too, there are limits on the *resources* available.

If you are limited to a word count this only refers to the *main section* of your report. The Executive Summary, Letter of Authorisation, Acknowledgements, Glossary, Appendices and Reference List/Bibliography are not normally included in the word count. You can keep tabs on your word count by highlighting the relevant areas of the document then clicking on Tools -> Word Count, which gives you a statistical breakdown.

Plan in advance how much time you have available to research and complete your report. You may find it helpful to draw up a timeline and set planning goals.

3.3 Make an initial plan

To develop your initial plan follow through the steps below.

(a) Brainstorm your ideas. Develop a technique for doing this effectively - for example, by mind mapping or by asking questions such as what, who, where, when, how and why in relation to your topic

(b) Select the ideas relevant to the aims of your report and to the questions your reader/s want answered

(c) Organise these ideas into a preliminary plan, grouping related ideas together into headings and sub-headings. These different levels are indicated by different font sizes and styles. A decimal numbering system is commonly used, with single numerals (1, 2, 3,...) for the main headings, one decimal (1.1, 1.2, 1.3,...) for the second level of headings and two decimals (1.1.1, 1.1.2,...) for any third level headings.

(d) Consider how best to investigate your topic. For example, do you need to draw your information mainly from journal articles or books, etc? Or are you required to prepare and/or conduct a survey or interview with individuals/groups, and then report on your findings? Gather the information you require, keeping in mind the aim and structure of your report. Record the sources of your information, including full bibliographic details, in a systematic way.

3.4 Prepare the first draft

An example of a report outline, given below, shows the three different sections (Preliminary, Main and Supplementary), and how the stages in the main section have been developed into three levels of numbered headings. Note that only the main section is numbered.

Section	Heading and numbering	Purpose
Preliminary Section	Report on the proposal to establish a National Music Centre in East Grinstead Table of Contents Executive Summary	This page should include the title and date of the report, the name of person or organisation for whom the report has been prepared and your name (or for a group report, the names of all those in the group who prepared the report) The Table of Contents outlines the different sections of the report, and shows the reader where to find them. The Executive Summary needs to be written last, because it summarises the information contained in the whole report. It gives the reader a general *overview/summary* of the *whole* report without them having to read the entire document. It should be able to stand alone as a separate document if required.
Main Section: Stage 1	**1 Introduction** 1.1 Background to the initiative 1.1.1 Summary of 20X8 survey 1.1.2 Summary of the State Arts Council's proposal 1.1.3 Aims and objectives of the proposal	The purpose is to orientate your reader to the whole document, and to give your report a context. You can do this by including: • a clear statement of purpose – *why* this topic is being investigated; • background to the report – *why* the report was requested and *by whom*; • scope and limits of the report – *what* issues are covered in it, what issues are not covered and why; and • the methods of investigation – *how* you investigated this topic.

Section	Heading and numbering	Purpose
Main Section: Stage 2	**2 Key Findings and Analysis** 2.1 National need for a Music Training and Resource Centre 2.1.1 Musicians 2.1.2 Current facilities 2.1.3 Current venues 2.1.4 Community response 2.1.5 Analysis of findings	This stage is central to your report as it includes both the *presentation* and the *analysis* of your findings. Here you describe *what you found out* from your investigation, and analyse *what those findings mean.*
Main Section: Stage 3	**3 Conclusion** 3.1 Feasibility 3.2 Funding 3.3 Location	The purpose of the Conclusion is to restate in a shortened form the *most significant points* from your investigation and analysis and to make a general statement about the significance of these. This prepares the reader for any recommendations you go on to make. Note that no new information should be included in this section.
	4 Recommendations 4.1 Establishment of links at: 4.1.1 Local level 4.1.2 National level 4.1.3 International level	The purpose of this section is to make suggestions about the action(s) or future direction(s) that should be taken as a result of your conclusions. These should be written in order of priority.
Supplementary Section	**Reference List** **Appendices** Appendix I Appendix II	This section has additional information that allows the reader to verify your sources and check more detailed data. The Reference List contains a list of all the sources you have either used or referred to in your report. To keep the main body of the report short enough to hold the reader's interest, detailed explanations, calculations, charts and tables of figures should be put into appendices. The main body of the report should make cross-references to the appendices in appropriate places.

Main section

The main section is usually the best place to start. Once you have written that, you can go on to write the other sections.

Add any diagrams (eg. graphs, tables, figures, etc) to support and present your material visually. Each diagram must have a title, and be numbered consecutively. You can do this automatically with a Word caption by clicking on Insert -> Caption and then AutoCaption. This is a numbered label, such as 'Figure 1,' that you can add to a table, figure, equation, or other item. You can vary the caption label and number format for different types of items eg, 'Table II' and 'Equation 1-A.' If you later add, delete, or move captions, you can easily update the caption numbers all at once.

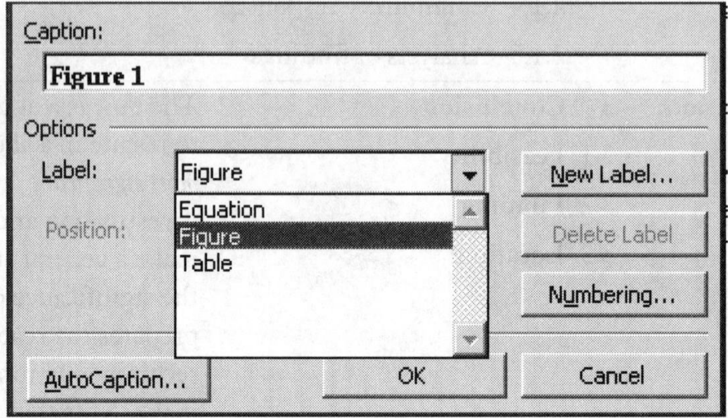

There are various ways of editing and formatting captions. You can change the label and/or the number format for one or more captions eg, change 'Table 6' to 'Figure 6', or create a new caption label, such as 'Photo'.

If your document includes chapter numbers, you can include these numbers in the captions eg, 'Figure 1-A'.

Conclusions

Conclusions come at the end of a report. They are where any decisions or recommendations that you make are discussed, and any 'next steps' that will be required are discussed. A conclusion is not a summary of the whole report; it is the major output of the report and should be your strongest point. A busy executive or manager should be able to read the executive summary and conclusion and be able to have a good understanding of what the report covers, what is decided, and what the executive (or someone else) needs to do next.

Executive summary

An executive summary is positioned at the beginning of a report, but it can only be written once the rest of the report is completed. The executive summary needs to be a piece of work which can stand alone … the formal report should make sensible reading without the executive summary, and the executive summary could be read in isolation without recourse to the rest of the report and still be a legitimate document.

The executive summary condenses the whole report into a page of text, usually of around 250 – 500 words. It should set the scene, why the report was commissioned and who the intended audience is. It should then outline the rest of the report. While it is difficult to

give precise definitions, as a good rule of thumb each page of the report should be condensed to one or two simple sentences.

The idea of an executive summary is that people who are too busy to read the whole report can read the executive summary (and the conclusions, see above), and from this be able to get the main thrust of the arguments presented. Because of this, the executive summary should not contain any material that is not mentioned elsewhere in the report, though if a particularly pithy or relevant reference by someone well respected in the field can provide a good start or finish to the executive summary, this is acceptable.

3.5 Create a table of contents

The Table of Contents outlines the different sections of the report, and shows the reader where to find them. It contains a list of all the headings, sub-headings, tables/figures, appendices, etc, and their corresponding page numbers.

Once all of the text has been entered and your document has built-in heading styles (use a maximum of three levels: one level for the major headings, one level for the sub-headings, and one for further sub-headings) as headings you want to include in your table of contents, you may begin to generate the table of contents. Choose Insert -> Reference -> Index and Table and choose the Table of Contents tab. A message box will be displayed that will allow you to specify the Styles that will be used to generate the table of contents. By choosing 'Modify', it is possible to change the levels each style holds in the table. Also, it allows you to add or subtract styles from the table of contents. Pressing OK will create a Table of Contents based on your preferences. You will see the headings listed in the Table along with the corresponding pages that they appear on.

It is important to note that the table of contents will not automatically update page number and report information as it is added to the document. In order to update the table, it is necessary to right click on the table and choose 'Update Field'. This will cause Word to rescan the document and reflect the changes made to the document in the Table.

3.6 Evaluate your report

Once you have completed your first draft you will need to check the following.

(a) That you have followed the guidelines given to you by the report instigator. Check particularly the requirements relating to *word length, format*, *layout*, *presentation* and *referencing*.

(b) That your writing style is appropriate. Analytical reports are written in a formal style using relatively short sentences.

(c) That you have connected your points logically, and used appropriate linking words and phrases.

(d) That each paragraph deals with one main idea.

(e) That your claims are supported by evidence, using references where appropriate.

(f) That your examples are relevant to the points being made.

(g) That you have referenced your work appropriately.

(h) That your grammar, spelling and punctuation are correct.

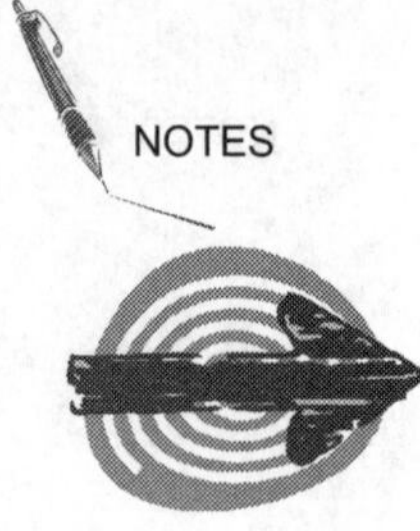

In the next part of this chapter we look at the steps involved in preparing a business presentation.

4 BUSINESS PRESENTATIONS

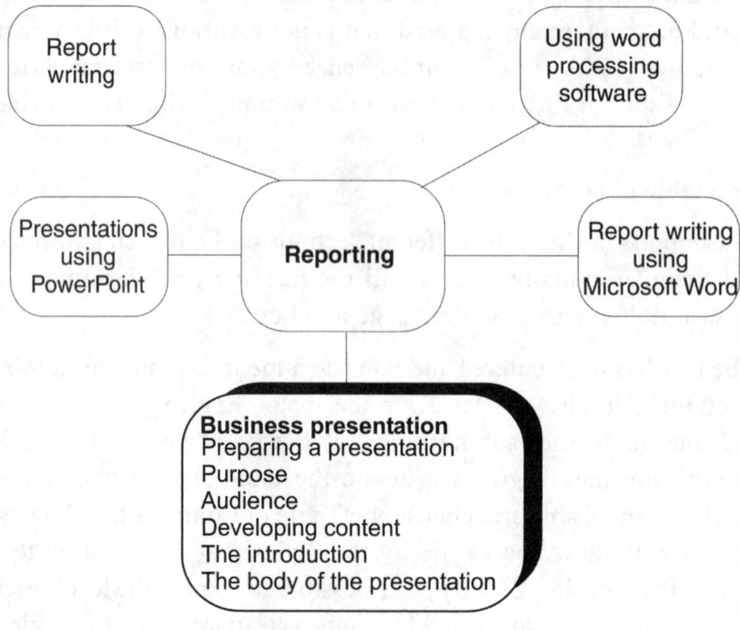

4.1 Preparing a presentation

Definition

A **presentation** is the act of making something (eg information) available to an audience. Presentations are usually planned acts of communication.

A **business presentation** could be made in a wide range of contexts, which may vary in terms of a number of aspects.

(a) The **size and composition of the audience**. This could range from a single manager to a small group of decision-makers or a large conference. The audience may be known to you or be complete strangers. They may have prior knowledge of the area you are speaking about or be complete 'laymen'. All these factors will affect the audience's ability to accept your message.

(b) The **purpose and approach** of the presentation. You may be offering:

   (i) Technical information
   (ii) Instruction
   (iii) A comparison
   (iv) A recommendation
   (v) Persuasion

(c) The **complexity** of the subject matter

(d) The **level of formality**. A staff briefing may be informal while a presentation to senior management is likely to be formal.

(e) The **time available**. The purpose of the presentation should be a guide as to time required – but time available may be different, placing constraints on your content and style.

4.2 Purpose

As a starting point in your preparation you should devise **clear objectives for your presentation**. If your objectives are going to help you plan your presentation they need to be **specific** and **measurable**.

Your objectives should be stated in terms of what the audience will do, or how they will be changed, at the end of the presentation: eg they will believe, be persuaded, agree, be motivated, do, understand, be able – or something similar.

Start with your primary objective, then move on to secondary objectives you will need to achieve along the way. This hierarchy of objectives provides a useful aid to planning the content and structure of your presentation.

4.3 Audience

You are likely to have a fair idea of the audience composition – from senior decision-makers to trainees.

The **audience's motivations and expectations** will influence their perceptions of you and your message. Why might they be at your presentation?

(a) Attendance may be compulsory. Unless interest can be stimulated by the presentation, compulsory attendance may create resistance to the message.

(b) Attendance may be recommended by a superior. Participants may be motivated because they perceive it to be in their own interest to do so.

(c) They are interested in the topic of the presentation. This often means there is a fine line to tread between telling the audience what they already know, and losing them by assuming more knowledge than they possess.

(d) They need specific information. An audience that is deliberately seeking information, and intending to use it to further their own objectives, is highly motivated.

Taking into account audience needs and expectations, your message needs to have the following qualities.

(a) **Relevance**. It should be relevant to the audience's needs and interests, eg making a difficult decision easier, or satisfying a need.

(b) **Credibility**. It should be consistent in itself, contain known facts, apparently objective, and from a source perceived to be trustworthy.

(c) **Accessibility**

(i) It should be audible and visible. Do you need to be closer to the audience? Do you need a microphone? Enlarged visual aids?

(ii) It should also be understandable. What is the audience's level of knowledge of the topic? What technical terms or 'jargon' will need to be avoided or explained?

4.4 Developing content

Armed with your clearly stated objectives and audience profile, you can plan the content of your presentation.

One approach, which may help to clarify your thinking, is as follows.

Step 1 **Brainstorm**. Think laterally about the subject, noting down your thoughts. Do not worry about the order or relevance of the ideas - just keep them coming, until your brain 'dries up'.

Step 2 **Prioritise**. Select the **key points**, and a **storyline** or theme that gives your argument a unified sense of 'direction'. The fewer points you make (with the most emphasis) and the clearer the direction in which your thoughts are heading, the easier it will be for the audience to grasp and retain your message. Discard – or de-emphasise – points which do not further your simple design.

Step 3 **Structure/Outline**. Make notes that show the selected main points and how they link to each other. Then flesh out your message. The outline should include an introduction; supporting evidence, examples and illustrations; notes of where (and what) visual aids will be required; signals of logical progressions and a conclusion.

Step 4 **Practise**. Learn the basic outline, or sequence of ideas, rather than a word-for-word 'script': if you repeat a speech by rote, it will sound stilted and mechanical. You should attempt **at least one full, timed 'dress' rehearsal,** preferably in front of a mock audience.

Step 5 Develop your cue and visual aids. Your outline may be too unwieldy to act as a cue or aide for the talk itself. Cards small enough to fit into the palm of your hand are ideal memory 'joggers'. If you are using slides, either on an overhead projector or via a PC and presentation software (eg Microsoft PowerPoint), these will also guide you and the audience. They should contain very brief, clear notes (verbal or pictorial), which provide:

- Key words for each topic and the logical links between them, and
- The full text of any (brief) detailed information you wish to quote.

4.5 The Introduction

You only get one chance to make a good first impression!

Purpose of the Introduction	Suggested approach(es)	Example
Establish your credibility on the subject	Very briefly (eg two sentences) outline your qualifications and / or experience, emphasising the parts most relevant to the topic. An 'old' **un**successful anecdote may demonstrate the need for proficiency in the subject.	'My first experience of an accounting package was not an enjoyable experience - due in equal measures to the quality of the package and the quality of my skills! However, the last decade has seen rapid developments in accounting packages, and hopefully a steady development of my knowledge and skills.'
Gain the audience's attention and interest	Establish the relevance of the topic to the audience – problems or opportunities they may be able to apply the material to. Surprise them with an interesting fact.	'In 1985 60% of management accountants used a computer less than three times a week!'
Establish a rapport with the audience	Anecdote, humour or identify with them.	
Prepare the audience for the content and structure of your presentation	Define and describe the topic. Make it clear why the presentation is being made. What are the objectives? Set the scene, introduce the topic and state your 'theme'.	'The techniques explained in this session have the potential to save you on average ten hours a week.'

4.6 The 'body' of the presentation – clarifying the message

Your structured notes and outline should contain cues that clarify the shape and progression of your information or argument. This will help keep you 'on track' and enable the audience to:

(a) Maintain a sense of purpose and motivation
(b) Follow your argument, so that they arrive with you at the conclusion.

Logical cues indicate the links between one topic or statement and the next. Here are some examples.

(a) You can simply begin each point with **linking words or phrases** like:

This has led to...

Therefore ... [conclusion, result or effect, arising from previous point]

So...

As a result...

However...

But ... [contradiction or alternative to previous point]

On the other hand...

Similarly ... [confirmation or additional example of previous point]

Again...

Moreover ... [building on the previous point]

(b) You can set up a **framework** for the whole argument, giving the audience an overview and then filling in the detail. For example:

'There are three main reasons why ... First ... Second ... Third....'

'So what's the answer? You could take two sides, here. On the one hand.... On the other hand....'

'Let's trace how this came about. On Monday 17th.... Then on Tuesday....'

'Of course, this isn't a perfect solution. It has the advantages of.... But there are also disadvantages, in that....'

'You might like to think of communication in terms of the five C's. That's: concise, clear, correct, complete, and courteous. Let's look at each of these in turn'.

(c) You can use devices that **summarise or repeat the previous point** and lead the audience to the next. These have the advantage of giving you, and the listener, a 'breather' in which to gather your thoughts.

Other ways in which content can be used to clarify the message include the following.

(a) **Examples** and illustrations – showing how an idea works in practice.

(b) **Anecdotes** – inviting the audience to relate an idea to a real-life situation.

(c) **Questions** – rhetorical, or requiring the audience to answer, raising particular points that may need clarification.

(d) **Explanation** – showing how or why something has happened.

(e) **Description** – helping the audience to visualise the setting you are describing.

(f) **Definition** – explaining the precise meaning of terms that may not be understood.

(g) The use of facts, **quotations** or **statistics** – to 'prove' your point.

Your **vocabulary** and style should contribute to the clarity of the message. Use short, simple sentences. Avoid jargon, unexplained acronyms, colloquialisms, double meanings and vague expressions.

Adding emphasis

Emphasis is the 'weight', importance or impact given to particular words or ideas. This can be achieved through delivery – the tone and volume of your voice, eye contact and gestures. Emphasis can also be provided through the following techniques:

Technique	Comment
Repetition	'If accuracy in income estimation is vital to our investment decisions, then accurate income estimation techniques must be developed.'
Rhetorical questions	'Do you know how many of our departmental heads are unhappy with the management information we provide? Fifty percent. Do you think that's acceptable?'
Quotation	'Information overload is the number one issue in the information we are producing. That's the conclusion of our survey.'
Statistics	'One in two of our internal customers have complained this year: that's 20% more complaints than last year. If the trend continues, we will soon have more complainers than satisfied customers!'
Exaggeration	'We have to look at our quality control system, because if the current trend continues, we are going to end up without any customers at all.'

Adding interest

Simple, clear information may only be interesting to those already motivated by the subject. You should strike a balance between the need for clarity and the need to make your message vivid, attention grabbing and memorable.

Here are some further suggestions:

(a) **Analogy.** Comparing something to something else which is in itself more colourful or interesting.

(b) **Anecdote or narrative**. Telling a story that illustrates the point, using suspense, humour or a more human context.

(c) **Curiosity or surprise**. For example, 'If you put all the widgets we've sold this year end to end, they would stretch twice around the equator.'

(d) **Humour**. Used well, this will add entertainment value, and serve as a useful 'breather' for listeners. Be careful, humour may not travel well; the audience may not be on the speaker's wavelength. Use with caution!

(e) **Emotion**. You may wish to appeal to the audience's emotions. As with humour you have to be sure of your audience before you attempt this. Your appeal may come across as patronising, manipulative or just irrelevant. Emotion does add human interest, and can be used to stress the humanity and involvement of the speaker.

'When I first heard about this technique, I was sceptical about it: *surely* it couldn't be as effective as they were trying to claim? But when I tried it for myself – Wow! I was just ... so excited. So impressed. Perhaps I can share some of that with you today.'

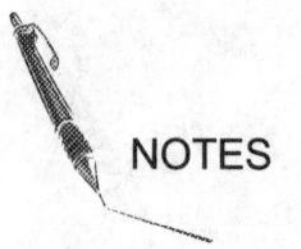

Activity 2 **(10 minutes)**

You are preparing a presentation to management on the benefits of flexitime hours. What techniques might you use?

5 PRESENTATIONS USING POWERPOINT

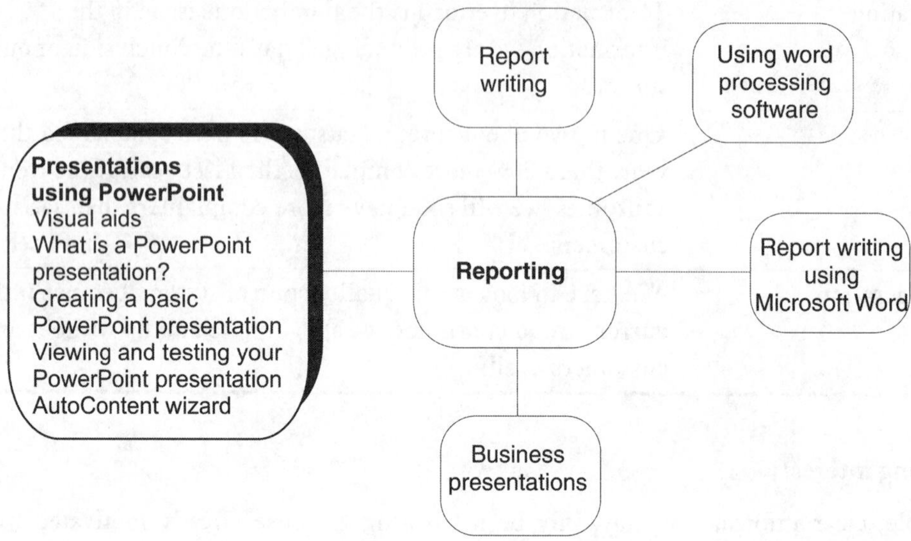

5.1 Visual aids

Visual aids use a visual image to aid communication. The purpose of visual aids is not to look good for their own sake, but to support the message. Michael Stevens *(Improving Your Presentation Skills)* notes:

'The proper use of aids is to achieve something in your presentation that you cannot do as effectively with words alone. They are only *a means to an end*, for instance to clarify an idea, or prove a point. A good aid is one that does this efficiently.'

Slides (Used with an overhead projector or PC and projector)

Slides may include photographs, text, diagrams and other images projected onto a screen or other surface. Slides have several useful features.

(a) They allow the use of images that can be used to create a mood or impression. As they are perceived as an image of reality, they are also powerful tools if you wish to 'prove a point'.

(b) They are pre-prepared. The slides for a business presentation would now usually be prepared using presentation software. This allows careful planning and execution, and slides can be finished to a very high degree of style, quality and 'professionalism'.

(c) The sequence and timing of slides is controlled by the presenter, allowing the synchronisation of images with relevant points in the presentation. Slides are therefore flexible in keeping pace with the presenter and audience.

(d) The swiftness with which one image follows another is particularly suited to messages of contrast or comparison: two products, say, or before and after scenarios.

Before you start up the presentation software, you need to review your speech outline and identify the points that can be illustrated with PowerPoint:

- Definitions
- Charts
- Graphs
- Statistics etc.

5.2 What is a PowerPoint presentation?

A PowerPoint presentation is a selection of slides, handouts, speaker's notes and your outline.

(a) **Slides** – these are the pages of a presentation and can contain text, images, graphs and sounds. As well as being used as a PowerPoint slide show the slides can be printed as overhead transparencies.

(b) **Handouts** – these are smaller printed versions of your slides with 2, 3 or 6 slides on an A4 page.

(c) **Speaker's notes** – you can produce these to be used alongside your presentation.

(d) **Outline** – this shows the title and main text of the whole presentation but not images

There are five views you can use when creating a PowerPoint presentation. You can switch between views using the buttons in the **bottom left** corner of the PowerPoint window. Each view gives you different editing capabilities and a different way of looking at your work.

(a) **Slide view** – Working on one slide at a time you can add text, draw shapes, add graphics and change the layout of your slide.

(b) **Outline view** – This can be used to organise your presentation. You work only with slide titles and the main text.

(c) **Slide Sorter view** – This gives you an overall view of all the slides in your presentation. You can rearrange the order of the slides, add transitions and set timings for electronic presentations

(d) **Notes Page view** – You can add speaker's notes to any of the slides in your presentation.

(e) **Slide Show view** – This gives you an overall view of all the slides in your presentation. You can rearrange the order of the slides, add transitions and set timings for electronic presentations.

PowerPoint has four toolbars - standard, format, draw and common tasks (shown in this order below).

To give an idea of how efficient this presentation media is, here's an example. A traditional text heavy report may contain 100 pages of text and graphics, and wading through this material can be time-consuming and hard to understand. However when organized in a slide format, this massive amount of information can be reduced down to a 20-50 page slide presentation, with concise bullet points and compelling visuals.

5.3 Creating a basic PowerPoint presentation

We are going to begin by creating and viewing a basic PowerPoint presentation and then go on to add some embellishments. Like any creative package, once you have the confidence to explore, there are many extras that you can do on your own. This section in a study pack will only be sufficient to get you started.

1. Open Microsoft PowerPoint by either double-clicking on the PowerPoint shortcut on the Windows desktop or select it from the Start Menu.
2. Select 'Design Template' from the PowerPoint window (we will look at the AutoContent Wizard later in this section) and click the Slide Design button on the Formatting toolbar. PowerPoint displays a gallery of designs that include co-ordinated colours, fonts, and layouts Scroll through the gallery to find a design you think you would like and click the design to apply it to your slide show.

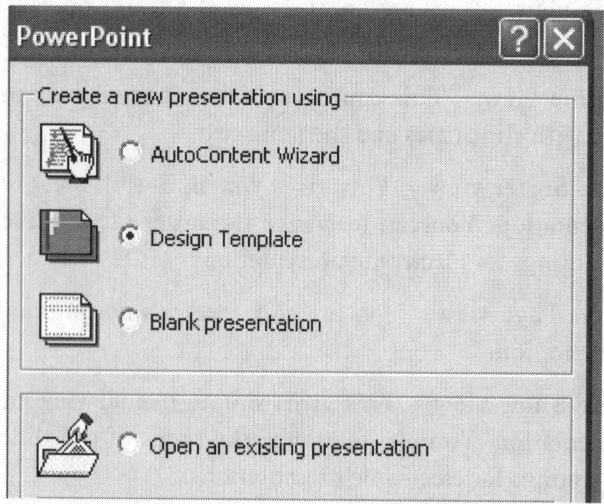

A template can be applied to a new or existing presentation. Once a design has been applied to a presentation you can change the design but not revert to using no design.

You can change the design any time, even after you have created an entire slide show. However, by default PowerPoint changes the design for all slides

in the presentation, and changes later may make it necessary to edit the slide show to make text and other objects fit the new layout. For example, a title that fits nicely in one design layout might be too long for another. If possible, try to select a design that you will stick with for the entire presentation.

3. PowerPoint will take you directly to choose an AutoLayout for your new slide. You need to choose a slide layout from those offered in the preview box. Helpfully the default is a title slide. Click on OK. A template for your first slide appears to which you can add a title and sub title.

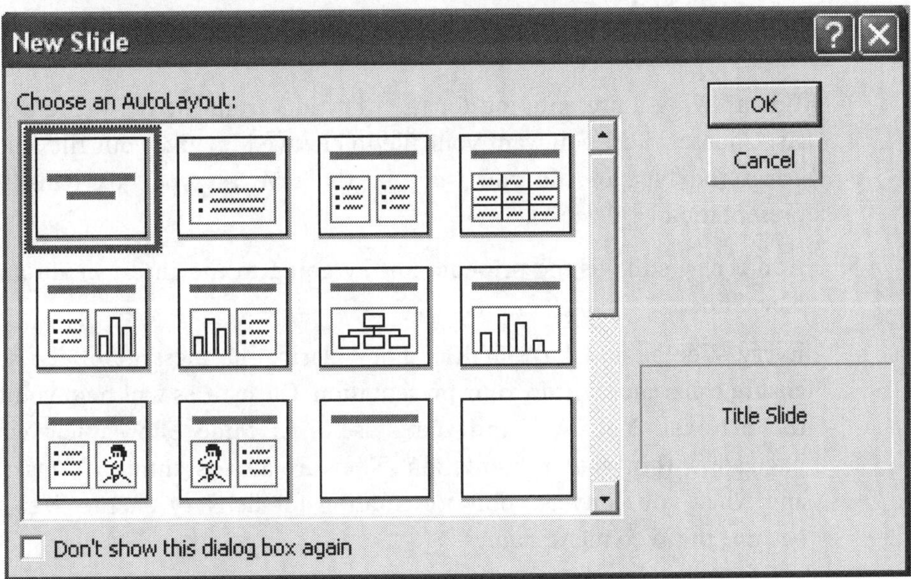

The other options are:

Title slide	Bulleted list	Bulleted list with 2 columns	Table
Bulleted list + chart	Chart + bulleted list	Organisational chart	Chart
Bulleted list + image	Image + bulleted list	Blank with title	Blank

4. Enter your title ***Introduction to PowerPoint*** and subtitle - this can be your name or the date that you (or someone else) will be showing the presentation. If you do not want the subtitle you can click on it and delete it.

Introduction to PowerPoint

Practise moving, removing and resizing a body box. Click on it once and grab the edges to make it a different size. The text will reset itself to match the size and shape you create. Move the title and sub-title boxes wherever on the page you want them. Practise changing the characteristics of the title and text – this could be the title, the body or all of the text – highlight what you want to change. Choose Format from the Menu bar and then Font. In this window, you can change the face, style, size and colour of the font. Click on the Colour bar and choose More Colours if none of the standard colours appeal to you.

You can use Undo to reverse nearly anything. But Undo is not only a tool that you use to correct mistakes. Because creating PowerPoint slides is akin to an artistic experience, consider the Undo tool as a way to try things out. You can do, undo, and do again until you get just what you want.

You can also delete slides or slide information. To delete information from a slide, simply click the object you want to remove (for example, a graph or graphic image) and press Delete. To delete an entire slide, click the slide icon in the outline area at the left and press Delete. PowerPoint does *not* warn you that you're about to lose an entire slide. If you accidentally delete a slide, simply click the Undo button on the toolbar.

When saving a presentation for the first time from the file menu select Save As. Choose where you want your file to be saved in, give your file a name and select the type of file you want in the save as type box (this is set to presentation by default).

5. Add a new slide to the presentation by going to the Insert menu and select New Slide.

   Every slide should have a title. They clarify the message of the slide and ensure coherence within your presentation. Clear titles will help you organise the material. You will find them useful in Slide Show View when you navigate within your presentation. They are also essential in PowerPoint if and when you convert your presentation for delivery on the Web, as they become the Web menu names.

   It is a good idea to make a preview slide to let your audience know what is in store for the session so, in the New Slide window, select the 'bulleted list' layout and do the following:

Elements of a Presentation
What a PowerPoint presentation contains
PowerPoint toolbars
PowerPoint views

   Save the presentation by selecting Save from the File menu.

   You can change the design of the bullet points using Format > Bullets and Numbering. To avoid a cluttered look, try to limit slides to the title line and six lines per slide and a maximum of six words per line. If your main idea or theme requires more than this, add an additional slide (or two or three) rather than trying to fit all the necessary text onto one slide. A good rule of thumb is to leave 10–15% around all edges of the slide free of text and graphics. Only use key words or phrases when making titles and sub-headings on your slides.

6. Add a new slide by clicking on the New Slide button on the Standard Toolbar. In the New Slide window, select the 2 column text layout and do the following.

What a PowerPoint presentation contains

- ✓ Slides
- ✓ Presentations
- ✓ Handouts
- ✓ Outlines

7. Add a new slide as before and in the New Slide window, select the Text & Clip Art layout, and do the following:

PowerPoint Toolbars

- Standard
- Formatting
- Drawing
- Common tasks

To insert ClipArt – double click on the image on the slide. Select the one you want and then click the grey 'Insert' button on the right. ClipArt images can be moved and re-sized just like AutoShapes.

8. Add the last new slide as before and in the **New Slide** window, select the **Chart & Text** layout, and do the following:

PowerPoint Views

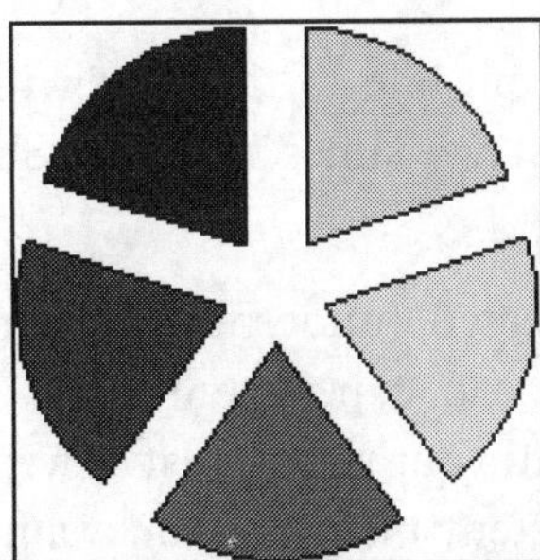

- Outline view
- Slide Sorter view
- Notes Page view
- Slide Show view
- Slide view

Graphs can be inserted by double clicking on the chart image on the slide. A Datasheet will also appear which you can edit to include your own graph information. If you right click within the chart area, but not on the chart itself, a menu appears, allowing you to edit your chart. The chart will be automatically inserted into your presentation and can be edited similar to graphs.

Tips on formatting your slides:

- Experiment with type styles, sizes and colours. Don't be afraid to embolden text, underline or italicise if you are trying to emphasise a point.
- Keep titles short. About five to seven words will get your point across.
- Make good use of the space available on the slide. Enlarge the graphs and have the text large enough that it is easy to read across a room.
- Format your slides horizontally (landscape) and not vertically (portrait). You don't want part of your slide to be below eye level.
- Try not to put too much data on one slide. One idea per slide is ideal. If you have many graphs and data in one place, the audience may lose interest. In addition, the increased amount of text will most likely require you reduce your font size, which will make it harder to read from a distance.
- Two graphs maximum per slide. This will make your data easier to understand. If you must have two visuals, make sure the text accompanying it is simple.
- Avoid busy slide backgrounds. Multiple colours or gradients can make text hard to read.

Activity 3 **(20 minutes)**

Produce a presentation slide and supporting notes that could be used to start a presentation entitled 'What is the Internet?'

5.4 Viewing and testing your PowerPoint presentation

After completing all your slides, select View Show from the Slide show menu to review your presentation. This menu gives you control over all aspects of the slideshow, and allows you to use animation, slide transition and alter the order in which items appear on slides. Transitions occur *between* slides, whereas animation happens *on* the slides.

By default, the slides in your show snap from one to the next without any transition between them. To add a transition between two slides, click on Slide Show - > Slide Transition.

Note that 'No Transition' is currently selected (underneath the picture) but arrows indicate choices of transitions, which you can experiment with. You can apply the transition to one of the slides, or apply it to all your slides. Just as with colour schemes, it is a good idea to use transitions in a consistent manner - for example, use one or two throughout the presentation to help create visual unity. Also notice that the slides can advance when you click the mouse or you can set them to automatically advance every set number of seconds. This latter option is especially good for looping slides used for advertising or public information.

If you wish you can even add sound effects – but these will only play if a sound output has been connected up when giving the presentation. Press Escape button on keyboard to end slide show.

To add animation, choose the text you want to animate and select Preset Animation from the Slide Show menu, and click on one of the different styles. For a more comprehensive choice of animation, right click on the highlighted text you want to animate, and select custom animation. This will give you endless options with the facility to preview the animation itself.

Testing is one of the most important parts of making a successful presentation, and, often one of the things that is overlooked. You should test your slide show to make sure that everything is just the way you want it. At any point it is possible to change the way the whole show looks by using the options in the Format menu. Don't forget to save your work afterwards.

Printing

You can print your entire presentation – the slides, outline, speaker's notes, and audience handouts – in colour or in black and white. All printing features are available from the File >Print menu. No matter what you print, the process is basically the same. You open the presentation you want to print and choose whether you want to print slides, handouts, notes pages, or an outline.

Then you identify the slides to be printed and the number of copies you want.

You can make colour or black-and-white overhead transparencies from your slides. When you print audience handouts, you can print one, two, three, or six slides on a page.

Creating speaker's notes

To type notes while working on a presentation:

- On the View menu, click Notes Page.
- Click the notes box, and then enter your notes for the current slide.
- Use the scroll bar to move to other slides you want to add notes to.

To enlarge the view of the notes box, click the Zoom box. You can also add notes by entering them in the Speaker Notes dialog box. Click Speaker Notes on the View menu, and then type your notes. The notes are added to your notes page.

5.5 AutoContent Wizard

Instead of going the route of Blank Presentation or Design Template, we can opt for letting the Wizard do most of the work.

NOTES

Click on AutoContent Wizard, and PowerPoint displays the AutoContent Wizard dialog box. Click Next to get started. The AutoContent Wizard leads you through the steps required to prepare presentations with specific content.

The first step is to select a presentation type. You can choose from various categories, or you can select All to see all the templates you can choose from. When you find the one you want, select it and then click Next.

The second step is to choose the presentation style. Typically, you'll be making an onscreen presentation, but you can also create a presentation targeted for the Web, for printed overhead transparencies, or for 35mm slides. Stick with the onscreen presentation for now. After you select it, click Next.

The third step is to choose certain basic options, which include the following.

- Title
- Footer – this is text that appears at the bottom of each slide. An example might be your company logo or department name.
- Date – by default, PowerPoint automatically generates the date your slide show was last updated (that is, saved) and places it at the bottom of each slide. Uncheck the Date Last Updated box if you don't want it
- Slide numbers - PowerPoint assumes that you want slide numbers. Uncheck the Slide Number check box if you don't.

After you make your choices, click Next, and then on the final wizard screen, click Finish. PowerPoint displays the title slide with the options you chose.

You can scroll through the outline to get a sense of suggested elements for a successful presentation on the topic you chose. For example, if you chose a marketing plan, you see slides showing market summary, production definition, competition, and so on. You may or may not use all the sample slides, and you'll likely add others. To change a slide's text content, you go to the left side of the screen and select the slide that you want to change by clicking on it.

Chapter roundup

- In this chapter we identified the types of formal report and the elements that are included when writing one.
- The basic functions of Word include opening files, entering and formatting data, creating tables, saving your work and closing the files when you have finished.
- Report writing includes some newer skills such as creating templates, using headings and adding captions and tables of contents.
- We discussed how to prepare a presentation and keep the audience interested.
- Using presentation software helps to disseminate information effectively and persuasively.

Quick quiz

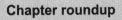

1 What types of reports are suitable for simple findings?

2 Identify the elements of a formal report.

3 If text is left justified in a Word document, what does the right-hand side look like?

4 Give an example of a mistake that would not be picked up by the spelling checker.

5 Which sections of a formal report are numbered?

6 Give three techniques for adding emphasis to a presentation.

7 Identify the parts in a presentation that can be illustrated by PowerPoint.

Answers to quick quiz

1 Graphical reports

2 Title, Terms of reference, Introduction, Main Body, Conclusion, Recommendations and Executive Summary

3 Ragged

4 Manger instead of manager

5 Only the main section

6 Repetition, Rhetorical Questioning, Quotations, Statistics or Exaggeration.

7 Definitions, Charts, Graphs and Statistics

Answers to activities

1 Valid purposes for a formal report include:

- To investigate an area of interest on behalf of someone
- To produce a business case or other argument for or against a proposal that someone is considering
- To make a recommendation to management. Note this does not mean that the recommendation will be followed, the purpose of the report is simply to make a recommendation, but you may need to discuss the 'next steps' that would be required by management should the recommendations be acted upon.
- In all cases a report will cause something to happen, even if this is 'to find out more facts' or 'do nothing for the time being'.

2 Some options are outlined below. The **techniques** listed below are applicable to a range of presentations.

(a) As part of your **introduction**, **explain** what flexitime is and the philosophy behind it.

(b) Include **statistics** on staff absenteeism and turnover to support your argument.

(c) Offer a **case study** of another organisation that introduced flexitime to their benefit.

(d) Present **quotes and opinions** of staff who are working 9 to 5, and others in a flexitime scheme.

(e) Present a **series of scenarios** (from the organisation's and employees' points of view) in which a problem – seasonal demand, dentist's appointment, travel delays etc – would be solved by flexitime.

(f) Compare flexitime, in **an analogy**, with a school day of fixed hours, with pupils completing homework outside those hours.

NOTES

3

What is the Internet?

- Technology
- www
- Web browsers
- Websites
- Internet service providers

Technology. The Internet is the name given to the technology that allows any computer with a telecommunications link to exchange information with any other suitably equipped computer.

The Internet is also called the ***World Wide Web*** (**www**), information superhighway or cyberspace, although technically it is the 'Web' that makes the Internet easy to use.

Web browsers are the software loaded on Internet-enabled computers to allow them to view information from the Internet.

Internet information is contained on ***websites***, which range from a few pages about one individual to large sites offering a range of services such as Amazon.co.uk and Lastminute.com.

Access to the Internet is provided by ***Internet Service Providers***. An Internet connection may be made via a telephone line (or an ISDN or broadband line) to the ISP and then onto the world wide web.

Part D

Software Generated Information

Chapter 8 :

MANAGEMENT INFORMATION SYSTEMS

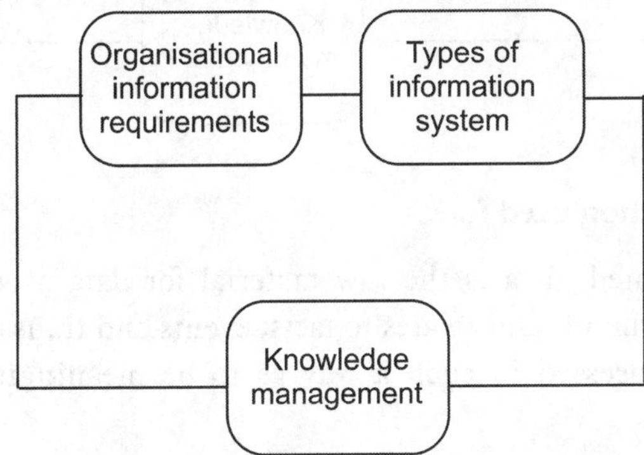

Introduction

In this chapter we introduce the concept of an information system. We start with the information requirements of the modern organisation and consider various aspects of the use of information systems to address corporate needs and make decisions.

Although a large number of people are employed to design and operate information systems, many more individuals are involved as users or 'consumers' of information systems. Users include individuals from a broad spectrum of occupations, ranging from workers in a factory to the top management of an organisation. Use of an information system includes the receipt of a report, the submission of input for a system, and the operation of a terminal or a similar activity.

In today's complex society, a knowledge of computer-based information systems is vital for an educated individual and for most organisations in the future, if not already, the determining factor in competition will be the processing and analysis of information.

Your objectives

After completing this chapter you should:

(a) Appreciate the information requirements of a range of organisations

(b) Be able to identify information processing tools for operational, tactical and strategic levels of the organisation

(c) Know the main features of different types of management information system (MIS) and appreciate the various IT systems that deliver information to different levels in the organisation (eg Transaction Processing, Decision Support and Executive Information/Support Systems)

(d) Understand how databases and planning models help the strategic planning process, (eg external databases, economic models, forecasting and modelling packages / applications)

1 ORGANISATIONAL INFORMATION REQUIREMENTS

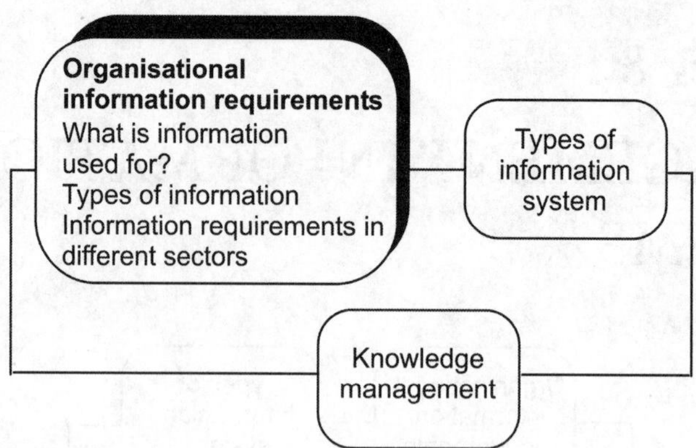

1.1 What is information used for?

As we have already noted, data is the raw material for data processing. It consists of numbers, letters and symbols and relates to facts, events and transactions. Information is data that has been processed in such a way as to be meaningful to the person who receives it.

All organisations require information for a range of purposes. These can be categorised as follows information for:

- Planning
- Controlling
- Recording transactions
- Performance measurement
- Decision-making

Planning

Planning requires a knowledge of the available resources, possible time-scales and the likely outcome under alternative scenarios. Information is required that helps decision making, and how to implement decisions taken.

Controlling

Once a plan is implemented, its actual performance must be controlled. Information is required to assess whether it is proceeding as planned or whether there is some unexpected deviation from plan. It may consequently be necessary to take some form of corrective action.

Recording transactions

Information about each transaction or event is required. Reasons include:

(a) Documentation of transactions can be used as evidence in a case of dispute.

(b) There may be a legal requirement to record transactions, for example for accounting and audit purposes.

(c) Operational information can be built up, allowing control action to be taken.

Performance measurement

Just as individual operations need to be controlled, so overall performance must be measured. Comparisons against budget or plan are able to be made. This may involve the collection of information on, for example, costs, revenues, volumes, time-scale and profitability.

Decision-making

Good quality information should lead to better informed decisions.

1.2 Types of information

Strategic information

Strategic information is used to plan the objectives of the organisation, and to assess whether the objectives are being met in practice. Such information includes overall profitability, the profitability of different segments of the business, future market prospects, the availability and cost of raising new funds, total cash needs, total manning levels and capital equipment needs.

Strategic information is:

- Derived from both internal and external sources
- Summarised at a high level
- Relevant to the long-term
- Concerned with the whole organisation
- Often prepared on an '*ad hoc*' basis
- Both quantitative and qualitative
- Uncertain, as the future cannot be predicted

Tactical information

Tactical information is used to decide how the resources of the business should be employed, and to monitor how they are being and have been employed. Such information includes productivity measurements (output per man hour or per machine hour) budgetary control or variance analysis reports, and cash-flow forecasts, manning levels and profit results within a particular department of the organisation, labour turnover statistics within a department and short-term purchasing requirements.

Tactical information is:

- Primarily generated internally (but may have a limited external component)
- Summarised at a lower level
- Relevant to the short- and medium-term
- Concerned with activities or departments
- Prepared routinely and regularly
- Based on quantitative measures

Operational information

Operational information is used to ensure that specific tasks are planned and carried out properly within a factory or office.

In the payroll office, for example, operational information relating to day-rate labour will include the hours worked each week by each employee, his rate of pay per hour, details of his deductions, and for the purpose of wages analysis, details of the time each man spent on individual jobs during the week. In this example, the information is required weekly, but more urgent operational information, such as the amount of raw materials being input to a production process, may be required daily, hourly, or in the case of automated production, second by second.

Operational information is:

- Derived from internal sources
- Detailed, being the processing of raw data
- Relevant to the immediate term
- Task-specific
- Prepared very frequently
- Largely quantitative

Activity 1 **(5 minutes)**

Of what type of information are the following examples?

- Listings of debtors and creditors
- Payroll details
- Raw materials requirements and usage
- Listings of customer complaints
- Machine output statistics
- Delivery schedules

1.3 Information requirements in different sectors

The tables opposite provide examples of the typical information requirements of organisations operating in different sectors.

(a) **Manufacturing sector**

Information type	Example(s)	General comment
Strategic	Future demand estimates New product development plans Competitor analysis	The information requirements of commercial organisations are influenced by the need to make and monitor profit. Information that contributes to the following measures is important: • Changeover times • Number of common parts • Level of product diversity • Product and process quality
Tactical	Variance analysis Departmental accounts Stock turnover	
Operational	Production reject rate Materials and labour used Stock levels	

(b) **Service sector**

Information type	Example(s)	General comment
Strategic	Forecast sales growth and market share Profitability, capital structure	Organisations have become more customer and results– orientated over the last decade. As a consequence, the difference between service and other organisations' information requirements has decreased. Businesses have realised that most of their activities can be measured, and many can be measured in similar ways regardless of the business sector.
Tactical	Resource utilisation such as average staff time charged out, number of customers per hairdresser, number of staff per account Customer satisfaction rating	
Operational	Staff timesheets Customer waiting time Individual customer feedback	

(c) **Public sector**

Information type	Example(s)	General comment
Strategic	Population demographics Expected government policy	Public sector (and non-profit making) organisations often don't have one overriding objective. Their information requirements depend on the objectives chosen. The information provided often requires interpretation (eg, student exam results are not affected by the quality of teaching alone). Information may compare actual performance with: • Standards • Targets • Similar activities • Indices • Activities over time as trends
Tactical	Hospital occupancy rates Average class sizes Percent of reported crimes solved	
Operational	Staff timesheets Vehicles available Student daily attendance records	

(d) **Non-profit/charities sector**

Information type	Example(s)	General comment
Strategic	Activities of other charities Government (and in some cases overseas government) policy Public attitudes	Many of the comments regarding Public Sector organisations can be applied to not-for-profit organisations. Information to judge performance usually aims to assess economy, efficiency and effectiveness. A key measure of efficiency for charities is the percentage of revenue that is spent on the publicised cause, (eg, rather than on advertising or administration).
Tactical	Percent of revenue spent on administration Average donation 'Customer' satisfaction statistics	
Operational	Households collected from / approached Banking documentation Donations	

2 TYPES OF INFORMATION SYSTEM

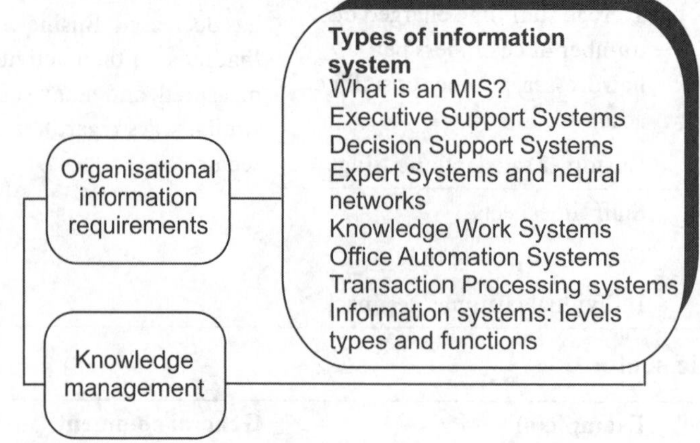

2.1 What is an MIS?

Definitions

Two definitions of the term Management Information System (MIS) are shown below.

'A **Management Information System (MIS)** converts data from internal and external sources into information, and communicates that information in an appropriate form to managers at all levels. This enables them to make timely and effective decisions for planning, directing and controlling the activities for which they are responsible.'

(Lucey T; *Management Information Systems*)

> 'A computer system or related group of systems which collects and presents management information to a business in order to facilitate control.'
>
> (Chartered Institute of Management Accountants, *Computing Terminology*)

We have talked a good deal about the need to gather and analyse *information* in the preceding chapters without stopping to consider how that information can be organised. Information is a key business resource. Drucker suggests the executive's tool kit has four **types of information.**

(a) **Foundation information,** such as profitability or cash flow, is only useful insofar that, if abnormal, when it tells us something is wrong.

(b) **Productivity information** is only slowly being developed for *knowledge* and *service* work.

(c) **Competence information:** competence is the ability 'to do something others cannot do at all or find difficult to do even poorly'. A firm should meticulously track down what it does best. This need not be a production technique; it might be the use of customer information or expertise in logistics.

(d) **Resource-allocation information** tells us how resources are used.

These four kinds of information relate to **tactics** and the **current business**. For **strategy** organised information about the **environment** is necessary: 'at least half the important new technologies that have transformed an industry in the past 50 years came from outside the industry itself'. Such information is unpredictable, informal or unstructured.

While a **management information system** (MIS) may not, in principle, be able to provide all the information used by management, it should however be sufficiently flexible to enable management to incorporate unpredictable, informal or unstructured information into decision-making processes. For example, many decisions are made with the help of financial models such as spreadsheets, so that the effect of new situations can be estimated easily.

A modern organisation requires a **wide range of systems** to hold, process and analyse information. We will now examine the various information systems used to serve organisational information requirements.

Organisations require different **types of information system** to provide different **levels of information** in a range of **functional areas**. One way of portraying this concept is shown on the following diagram (taken from *Laudon* and *Laudon*, *Management Information Systems*).

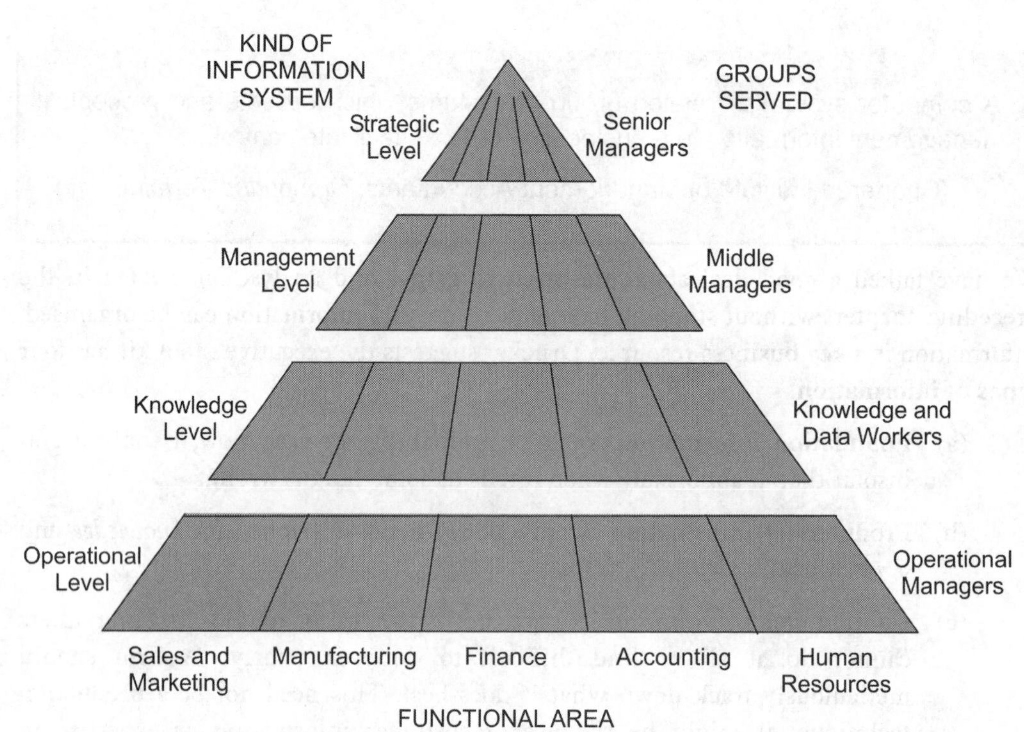

Figure 8.1: Types of information system

System level	System purpose
Strategic	To help senior managers with long-term planning. Their main function is to ensure changes in the external environment are matched by the organisation's capabilities. At this level the information system is likely to be informal, in the sense that it is not possible always to quantify or program strategic information, and much of the information might come from environmental sources. The MIS will provide summary level data from transactions processing. Human judgement is used more often at this level, as many strategic decisions cannot be programmed. Highly sophisticated, large-scale integrated corporate systems known as *enterprise resource planning* (ERP) systems eg, SAP are used at this level. They may in fact be essential, depending on the complexity of the undertaking and the degree of competition.
Management	To help middle managers monitor and control. These systems check if things are working well or not. Some management– level systems support non-routine decision-making such as 'what if?' analyses. The MIS will interact with the same systems as that at operational level, and in fact tactical information may be generated in the same processing operation as operational level information. For example, tactical level information comparing actual costs incurred to budget can be produced by a system in which those costs are recorded. Functional MIS at tactical level are typically related to other functional MIS. Information from the sales MIS will affect the financial accounting system, for example.

System level	System purpose
Knowledge	To help knowledge and data workers design products, distribute information and perform administrative tasks. These systems help the organisation integrate new and existing knowledge into the business and to reduce the reliance on paper documents.
Operational	To help operational managers track the organisation's day-to-day operational activities. Operational decisions are essentially small-scale and programmed, and operational information is often highly formal and quantitative. Many operational decisions can be incorporated into routine computer processing, for example allowing a sale subject to a credit limit. Most MIS are used at this level for enabling routine queries to be answered, processing and tracking transactions, updating files and so forth.

Example: the finance subsystem

In a finance subsystem, the operational level would deal with cash receipts and payments, bank reconciliations and so forth. The tactical level would deal with cash flow forecasts and working capital management. Strategic level financial issues are likely to be integrated with the organisation's commercial strategy, but may relate to the most appropriate source of finance.

2.2 Executive Support Systems (ESS)

Definition

An **Executive Support System (ESS)** pools data from internal and external sources and makes information available to senior managers in an easy-to-use form. ESS help senior managers make strategic, unstructured decisions.

An ESS should provide senior managers with easy access to key **internal and external** information. The system summarises and tracks strategically critical information, possibly drawn from internal MIS and DSS, but also including data from external sources eg competitors, legislation, external databases such as Reuters.

An ESS is likely to have the following **features**.

(a) Flexibility
(b) Quick response time
(c) Sophisticated data analysis and modelling tools

A model of a typical ESS is shown below.

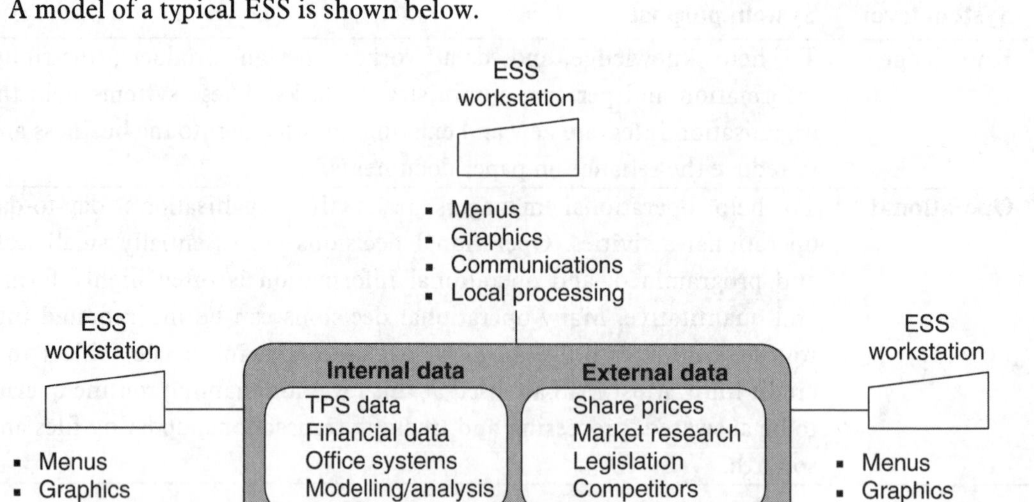

Figure 8.2: An Executive Support System (ESS)

2.3 Decision Support Systems (DSS)

Definition

> **Decision Support Systems (DSS)** combine data and analytical models or data analysis tools to support semi-structured and unstructured decision making.

Decision support systems (DSS) are used by management to aid in making decisions on issues which are unstructured, with high levels of uncertainty about the true nature of the problem, or the various responses which management could undertake or the likely impact of those actions.

They are intended to provide a wide range of alternative information gathering and analytical tools with a major emphasis upon flexibility and user-friendliness. DSS include a range of systems, from fairly simple information models based on spreadsheets to expert systems. They have more analytical power than any other systems, enabling them to analyse and condense large volumes of data into a form that aids managers make decisions.

Although called decision support systems, they do not make decisions. The objective is to allow the manager to consider a number of alternatives and evaluate them under a variety of potential conditions. A key element in the usefulness of these systems is their ability to function interactively.

Databases in DSS

Definition

> A **database** is a collection of structured data with minimum duplication, which is common to all users of the system but is independent of programs that use the data.

The database can grow and change and is built up stage by stage within the organisation. It will actually comprise several databases, each providing the anticipated information for several logically related management information systems where the data can be accessed, retrieved and modified with reasonable flexibility. Some companies have designed marketing databases to gain faster access to the required data, whether from internal sources, such as customers' sales details or from external sources through networks such as the Internet, which allow access to a wide variety of databases.

The following diagram shows the importance of databases to the decision support systems.

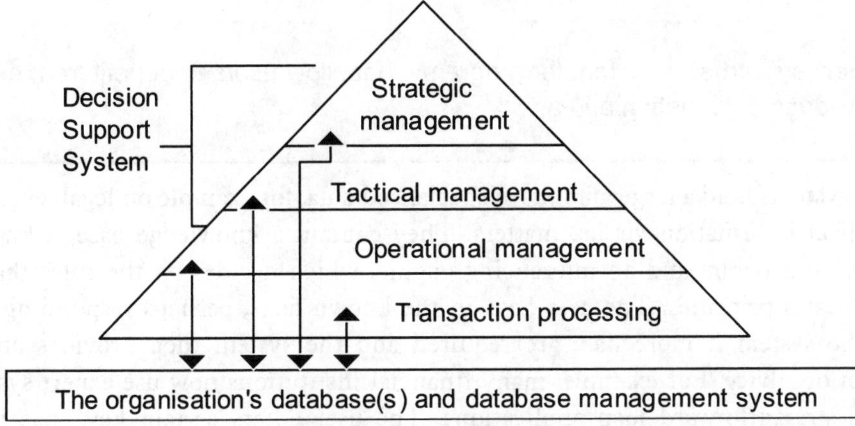

Figure 8.3: Databases to support Decision Support Systems

The database system provides a number of advantages.

(a) Data is used for a wide range of reasons, but is only input to the database and stored once.

(b) Data is used in the knowledge that all departments concerned are using identical data, whereas if each department has its 'own' data, it is possible that the facts and figures used may conflict with those of another user.

(c) The database supports management requirements – especially at the strategic level, although all levels need access – and provides both routine and *ad hoc* reports.

What kind of data will be held in the database? The mix is likely to contain the following.

(a) Transaction data in detail (resulting from processing through application programs).

(b) Data needed by current and probable future programs.

(c) By-product data (from other processing).

The database and the Database Management System (DBMS) allow the manager to interrogate and access a mass of data at will. An enormous range of packages is available to use this data in exploring alternatives and making decisions. For example, for:

(a) Modelling and simulation
(b) Spreadsheets
(c) Statistical analysis of all types
(d) Forecasting
(e) Non-linear and linear programming
(f) Regression analysis
(g) Financial modelling
(h) Sensitivity and risk analysis
(i) Expert systems.

Activity 2 **(15 minutes)**

Imagine a retail business consisting of multiple locations. What type of questions might the directors want answers to?

2.4 Expert systems and neural networks

Definition

Expert systems are computer programs that allow users to benefit from expert knowledge, information and advice.

Expert systems hold a large amount of specialised data, for example on legal, engineering or medical information, or tax matters. They contain a knowledge base, a knowledge acquisition program and an inferencing engine, which decides on the rules that apply and allocates priorities. The user keys in the known facts, perhaps responding to cues from the system if more data are required and the system then provides an expert solution or advice. For example, many financial institutions now use expert systems to process straightforward loan applications. The user enters certain key facts into the system such as the loan applicant's name and most recent addresses, their income and monthly outgoings, and details of other loans. The system will then work through the following.

(a) Check the facts given against its database to see whether the applicant has a good previous credit record.

(b) Perform calculations to see whether the applicant can afford to repay the loan.

(c) Make a judgement as to what extent the loan applicant fits the lender's profile of a good risk (based on the lender's previous experience).

(d) Suggest a decision.

Examples of other applications of expert systems are given below.

(a) Tax advice – a user without much tax knowledge could consult an expert system for taxation for guidance on particular matters of tax.

(b) Legal matters – a user without a legal background can obtain guidance on the law without having to consult a solicitor – for example, on property purchase matters, or for company law guidance.

(c) Forecasting of economic or financial developments, or of market and customer behaviour.

(d) Surveillance, for example of the number of customers entering a supermarket, in order to decide shelves which need restocking and how many checkouts need to be open, or machines in a factory, to determine when they need maintenance.

(e) Diagnostic systems, to identify causes of problems, for example in production control in a factory, or in healthcare.

(f) Education and training, for example in diagnosing a student's or worker's weaknesses and providing or recommending extra instruction as appropriate.

NOTES

Expert systems are not suited to high-level unstructured problems, as these require information from a wide range of sources rather than simply deciding between a few known alternatives.

Activity 3 **(10 minutes)**

What do you consider is the importance of some of the management information systems discussed above for organisation hierarchy?

Neural networks

Neural networks are another application of Artificial Intelligence (AI), seen by some as the 'next step' in computing. Neural computing is modelled on the biological processes of the human brain.

Neural networks can **learn from experience**. They can analyse vast quantities of complex data and **identify patterns** from which predictions can be made. They have the ability to cope with incomplete or 'fuzzy' data, and can deal with previously unspecified or **new situations**.

Neural techniques have been applied to similar areas as expert systems eg credit risks. Neural techniques are more advanced in that they don't rely on a set of hard rules, but develop a 'hidden' layer of experience and come to a decision based on this hidden layer.

A diagram showing a neural network follows.

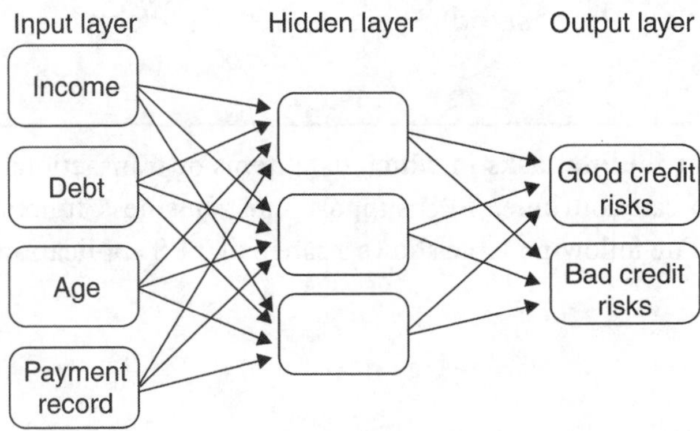

Figure 8.4: Neural network

2.5 Knowledge Work Systems (KWS)

Definitions

Knowledge Work Systems (KWS) are information systems that facilitate the creation and integration of new knowledge into an organisation.

Knowledge workers are people whose jobs consist of primarily creating new information and knowledge. They are often members of a profession such as doctors, engineers, lawyers and scientists.

KWS help knowledge workers create new knowledge and expertise. Examples include:

- Computer-aided design (CAD)
- Computer-aided manufacturing (CAM)
- Specialised financial software that analyses trading situations

2.6 Office Automation Systems (OAS)

Definition

> **Office Automation Systems (OAS)** are computer systems designed to increase the productivity of data and information workers.

OAS support the major activities performed in a typical office such as document management, facilitating communication and managing data. Examples include:

- Word processing, desktop publishing, and digital filing systems
- E-mail, voice mail, videoconferencing, groupware, intranets, schedulers
- Spreadsheets, desktop databases

2.7 Transaction Processing Systems (TPS)

Definition

> A **Transaction Processing System (TPS)** performs and records routine transactions.

TPS are used for **routine tasks** in which data items or transactions must be processed so that operations can continue. TPS support most business functions in most types of organisations. The following table shows a range of TPS applications.

Transaction processing systems					
	Sales/marketing systems	**Manufacturing/ production systems**	**Finance/ accounting systems**	**Human resources systems**	**Other types (eg university)**
Major functions of system	• Sales management • Market research • Promotion • Pricing • New products	• Scheduling • Purchasing • Shipping/ receiving • Engineering • Operations	• Budgeting • General ledger • Billing • Management accounting	• Personnel records • Benefits • Salaries • Labour relations • Training	• Admissions • Student academic records • Course records • Graduates
Major application systems	• Sales order information system • Market research system • Pricing system	• Materials resource planning • Purchase order control • Engineering • Quality control	• General ledger • Accounts receivable/ payable • Budgeting • Funds management	• Payroll • Employee records • Employee benefits • Career path systems	• Registration • Student record • Curriculum/ class control systems • Benefactor information system

Batch processing and online processing

A TPS will process transactions using either **batch** processing or **online** processing.

Batch processing involves transactions being **grouped** and **stored** before being processed at regular intervals, such as daily, weekly or monthly. Because data is not input as soon as it is received the system will not always be up-to-date.

The lack of up-to-date information means batch processing is usually not suitable for systems involving customer contact. Batch processing is suitable for internal, regular tasks such as payroll.

On-line processing involves transactions being input and processed immediately. An airline ticket sales and reservation system is an example.

2.8 Information systems: levels, types and functions

Examples of the levels and types of information system we have discussed in this section are shown in the following diagram.

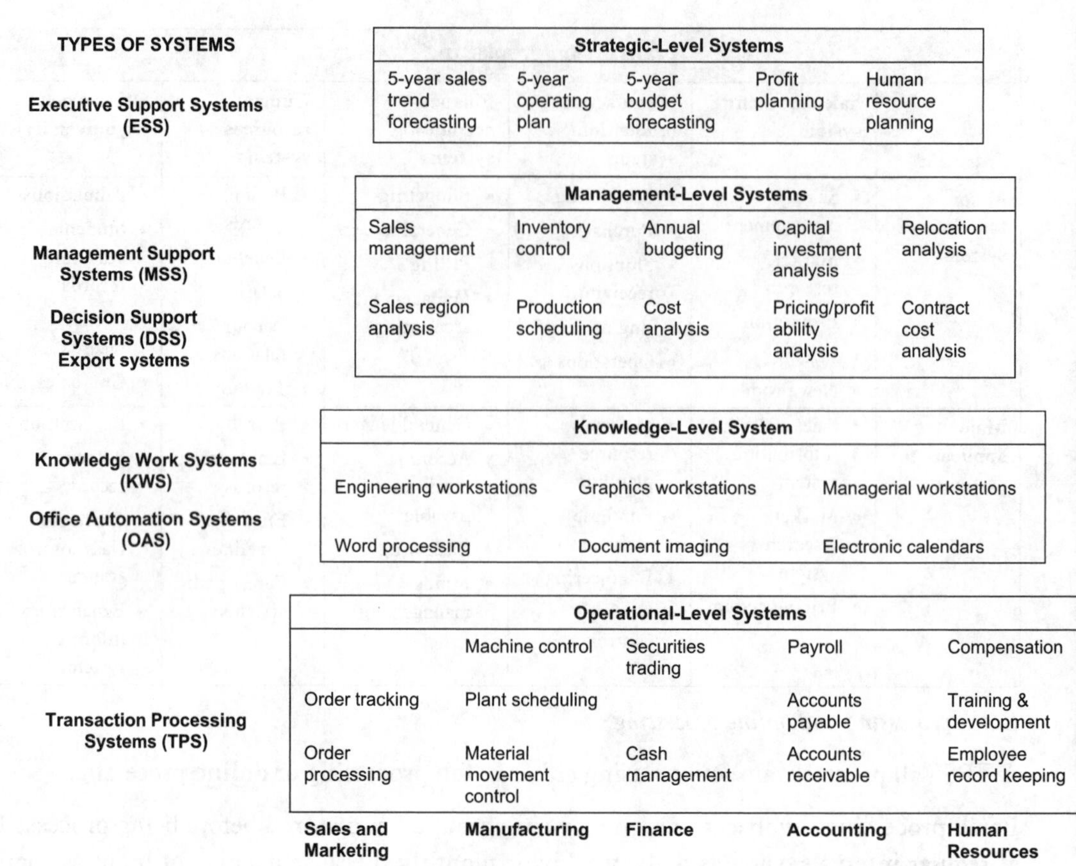

Figure 8.5: Information systems: levels, type and functions

3 KNOWLEDGE MANAGEMENT

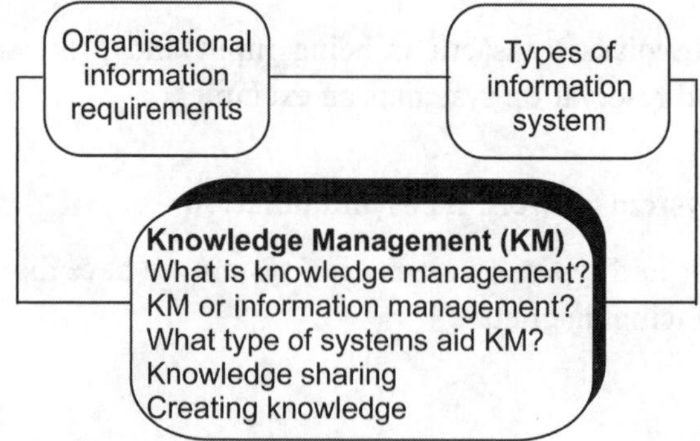

3.1 What is knowledge management?

Studies have indicated that 20 to 30 per cent of company resources are wasted because organisations are not aware of what **knowledge they already possess**. Lew Platt, Chief executive of Hewlett Packard, has articulated this in the phrase 'If only HP knew what HP knows, we would be three times as profitable'.

Definitions

> **Knowledge** is information within people's minds.
>
> **Knowledge management** describes the process of collecting, storing and using the knowledge held within an organisation.

Knowledge is now commonly viewed as a sustainable source of **competitive advantage,** and one that it is essential f or companies to tap. In an era of rapid change and uncertainty, companies need to **create new knowledge, nurture it and disseminate it** throughout the organisation, and **embody it in technologies, products and services.** Several sectors – for example, the financial services industries – depend on knowledge as their principal means of value creation.

Knowledge is valuable because humans use it to create new ideas, insights and interpretations and apply these to information use and decision making. However knowledge, like information, is of no value unless it is applied to decisions and actions in a purposeful business context.

People in organisations are constantly **converting knowledge into various forms of information** (memos, reports, e-mails, briefings) and **acquiring information for others to improve their knowledge.**

Knowledge management programmes are attempts at:

(a) Designing and installing techniques and processes to create, protect and use **explicit knowledge** (that is knowledge that the company knows that it has). Explicit knowledge includes facts, transactions and events that can be clearly stated and **stored in management information systems.**

(b) Designing and creating environments and activities to discover and release **tacit knowledge** (that is, knowledge that the company does not know it has). Tacit knowledge is implied or inferred, it concerns the feelings and experiences **stored in peoples minds.**

Organisations should encourage people to share their knowledge. This can be done through **improved management of information** about **where knowledge resides,** how it can be **deployed and reused** and when it can create greater business value through **new ideas and innovations.**

A range of **technology** is available to support KM. The three main threads are information retrieval, document management and workflow processing.

The process by which an organisation develops its store of knowledge is sometimes called organisational learning. A learning organisation is centred on the **people** that make up the organisation and the **knowledge** they hold. The organisation and employees feed off and into the central pool of knowledge. The organisation uses the knowledge pool as a tool to teach itself and its employees.

3.2 Knowledge management or information management?

There are dozens of **different approaches** to KM, including document management, information management, business intelligence, competence management, information

systems management, intellectual asset management, innovation, business process design, and so on.

You might be forgiven for thinking, therefore, that 'knowledge management' is just a different, more up-market **label** for information management?

(a) It is true that many KM projects have a significant element of information management. After all, people need information about where knowledge resides, and to share knowledge they need to transform it into more or less transient forms of information.

(b) But beyond that, KM does have two distinctive tasks: to facilitate the **creation** of knowledge and to **manage the way people share and apply it**. Companies that prosper with KM will be those that realise that it is as much about **managing people** as about information and technology.

3.3 What type of systems aid knowledge management?

Information systems play an important role in knowledge management, helping with **information flows** and helping formally **capture** the knowledge held within the organisation.

Any system that encourages people to work together and share information and knowledge will aid knowledge management. Examples are shown in the following table.

What the systems facilitate	Examples	
Knowledge distribution	**Office automation systems** As we learnt earlier, an OAS is any application of information technology that increases productivity within an office. KW is dependent on the efficient production and distribution of documents and other forms of communication such as voice messaging systems. Document imaging systems convert documents and images to digital form, reducing the amount of paper required.	Word processing Electronic schedulers Desktop databases Web publishing Voice mail E-mail
Knowledge sharing	**Group collaboration systems**	Groupware Intranets Extranets
Knowledge creation	**Knowledge work systems**	CAD Virtual Reality Investment workstations
Knowledge capture and codification	**Artificial Intelligence (AI) systems** AI is the development of computer-based systems designed to behave as humans. AI systems are based on human expertise, knowledge and reasoning patterns.	Expert systems Neural Nets Fuzzy logic Intelligent agents Robotics 'Natural language' programming tools

3.4 Knowledge sharing

Groupware

Definition

> **Groupware** is a term used to describe software that provides functions for the use of collaborative work groups.

Typically, groups utilising groupware are small project-oriented teams that have important tasks and tight deadlines Perhaps the best-known groupware product at present is **Lotus Notes**. However, there are many related products and technologies.

Features might include the following.

(a) A **scheduler** (or diary or calendar), allowing users to keep track of their schedule and plan meetings with others.

(b) An electronic **address book** to keep personal and business contact information up-to-date and easy to find. Contacts can be sorted and filed in any way.

(c) **To do** lists. Personal and business to-do lists can be kept in one easy-to-manage place, and tasks can quickly be prioritised.

(d) A **journal**, which is used to record interactions with important contacts, record items (such as e-mail messages) and files that are significant to the user, and record activities of all types and track them all without having to remember where each one was saved.

(e) A **jotter** for jotting down notes as quick reminders of questions, ideas, and so on.

There are clearly advantages in having information such as this available from the desktop at the touch of a button, rather than relying on scraps of paper, address books, and corporate telephone directories. However, it is when groupware is used to **share information** with colleagues that it comes into its own. Here are some of the features that may be found.

(a) **Messaging**, comprising an **e-mail** in-box which is used to send and receive messages from the office, home, or the road and **routing** facilities, enabling users to send a message to a single person, send it sequentially to a number of people (who may add to it or comment on it before passing it on), or sending it to every one at once.

(b) Access to an **information database**, and customisable '**views**' of the information held on it, which can be used to standardise the way information is viewed in a workgroup.

(c) **Group scheduling**, to keep track of colleagues' itineraries. Microsoft Exchange Server, for instance offers a 'Meeting Wizard', which can consult the diaries of everyone needed to attend a meeting and automatically work out when they will be available, which venues are free, and what resources are required.

(d) **Public folders**. These collect, organise, and share files with others on the team or across the organisation.

(e) One person (for instance a secretary or a stand-in during holidays or sickness) can be given '**delegate access**' to another's groupware folders and send mail on their behalf, or read, modify, or create items in public and private folders on their behalf.

(f) **Conferencing**. Participation in public, online discussions with others.

(g) **Assigning tasks**. A task request can be sent to a colleague who can accept, decline, or reassign the task. After the task is accepted, the groupware will keeps the task status up-to-date on a task list.

(h) **Voting** type facilities that can, say, request and tally responses to a multiple-choice question sent in a mail message (eg 'Here is a list of options for this year's Christmas party').

(i) **Hyperlinks** in mail messages. The recipient can click the hyperlink to go directly to a Web page or file server.

(j) **Workflow management** (see below) with various degrees of sophistication.

Workflow is a term used to describe the defined series of tasks within an organisation to produce a final outcome. Sophisticated workgroup computing applications allow the user to define different **workflows** for different types of jobs. For example, in a publishing setting, a document might be automatically routed from writer to editor to proofreader to production.

At **each stage** in the workflow, **one individual** or group is **responsible** for a specific task. Once the task is complete, the workflow software ensures that the individuals responsible for the **next** task are notified and receive the data they need to do their stage of the process.

Workflow systems can be described according to the type of process they are designed to deal with. There are three common types.

(a) **Image-based workflow systems** are designed to automate the flow of paper through an organisation, by transferring the paper to digital "images". These were the first workflow systems that gained wide acceptance. These systems are closely associated with 'imaging' (or 'document image processing' (DIP)) technology, and help with the routing and processing of digitised images.

(b) **Form-based workflow systems** (formflow) are designed to route forms intelligently throughout an organisation. These forms, unlike images, are text-based and consist of editable fields. Forms are automatically routed according to the information entered on them. In addition, these form-based systems can notify or remind people when action is due.

(c) **Co-ordination-based workflow systems** are designed to help the completion of work by providing a framework for **co-ordination** of action. Such systems are intended to improve organisational productivity by addressing the issues necessary to **satisfy customers**, rather than automating procedures that are not closely related to customer satisfaction.

Intranets

Definition

> An **intranet** is an internal network used to share information. Intranets utilise Internet technology and protocols. The firewall surrounding an internet fends off unauthorised access.

The idea behind an 'intranet' is that companies set up their own **mini version of the Internet.** Intranets use a combination of the organisation's own networked computers and Internet technology. Each employee has a browser, used to access a server computer that holds corporate information on a wide variety of topics, and in some cases also offers access to the Internet.

Potential applications include company newspapers, induction material, online procedure and policy manuals, employee web pages where individuals post up details of their activities and progress, and **internal databases** of the corporate information store.

Most of the **cost** of an intranet is the **staff time** required to set up the system.

The **benefits** of intranets are diverse.

(a) Savings accrue from the **elimination of storage, printing** and **distribution** of documents that can be made available to employees online.

(b) Documents on-line are often **more widely used** than those that are kept filed away, especially if the document is bulky (eg manuals) and needs to be searched. This means that there are **improvements in productivity** and **efficiency**.

(c) It is much **easier to update** information in electronic form.

(d) Wider access to corporate information should open the way to **more flexible working patterns**, eg material available on-line may be accessed from remote locations.

Extranets

Definition

> An **extranet** is an intranet that is accessible to authorised outsiders.

Whereas an intranet resides behind a firewall and is accessible only to people who are members of the same company or organisation, an extranet provides various levels of accessibility to outsiders.

Only those outsiders with a valid username and password can access an extranet, with varying levels of access rights enabling control over what people can view. Extranets are becoming a very popular means for **business partners to exchange information**.

Extranets therefore allow better use of the knowledge held by an organisation – by facilitating access to that knowledge.

3.5 Creating knowledge

Knowledge work systems (KWS)

Knowledge Work Systems (KWS) are information systems that facilitate the creation and integration of new knowledge into an organisation. They provide knowledge workers with tools such as:

- Analytical tools
- Powerful graphics facilities
- Communication tools
- Access to external databases
- A user-friendly interface

The workstations of knowledge workers are often designed for the specific tasks they perform. For example, a design engineer would require sufficient graphics power to manipulate 3-D Computer-aided design (**CAD**) images; a financial analyst would require a powerful desktop computer to access and manipulate a large amount of financial data (an **investment workstation**).

The components of a KWS are shown in the following diagram.

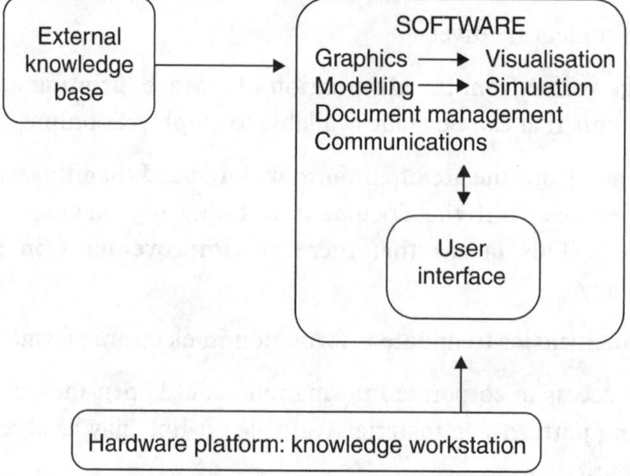

Figure 8.6: Knowledge work system

Virtual reality systems are another example of KWS. These systems create computer generated simulations that emulate real-world activities. Interactive software and hardware (eg special headgear) provide simulations so realistic that users experience sensations that would normally only occur in the real world.

EXAMPLES

Virtual reality

Burger King has used virtual reality stores to test new store designs.

Volvo has used virtual reality test drives in vehicle development.

Chapter roundup

- Organisations require information for recording transactions, measuring performance, making decisions, planning and controlling.
- An organisation's information requirements will be influenced by the sector they operate in.
- Information may be strategic, tactical or operational.
- There are many systems available to hold, process and analyse information. Examples include Executive Support Systems (ESS), Decision Support Systems (DSS), Knowledge Work Systems (KWS), Office Automation Systems (OAS) and Transaction Processing Systems (TPS).
- An information system should be designed to obtain information from all relevant sources – both internal and external
- Effective information systems are vital at all levels of an organisation to assist in decision-making.
- Decision support systems allow managers to consider a number of alternatives and evaluate them under a variety of potential conditions.
- Executive information systems have summary level data and more detailed levels and other data manipulation and analysis facilities, graphics and templates.
- Expert systems are computer programs that allow users to benefit from expert knowledge and information.

Quick quiz

1 Distinguish between strategic, tactical and operational information.

2 Give two examples of strategic, tactical and operational information relevant to an organisation operating in the manufacturing sector.

3 Distinguish between batch processing and online processing

4 Decision support systems are used for routine decisions.
TRUE or FALSE?

5 What are decision support systems used for?

6 What are some applications of expert systems?

Answers to quick quiz

1 Strategic information is used to plan the objectives of the organisation.

Tactical information is used to decide how the resources of the business should be employed, and to monitor how they are being and have been employed.

Operational information is used to ensure that specific tasks are planned and carried out properly.

2 Two examples of strategic information:

(i) Communication of corporate objectives to the management of the business expressed in terms of profit targets and measures of wealth such as earnings per share.

(ii) Communicating information on strategy for future acquisitions of companies in different fields as a hedge against risk.

Two examples of tactical information:

(i) A twelve-month budget of sales analysed by product group.

(ii) A manufacturing plan for the next twelve months.

Two examples of operational information:

(i) An 'aged' analysis of debts showing all customers whose deliveries have been stopped pending settlement of overdue balance.

(ii) A list of all purchase orders outstanding with the financial evaluation of total purchase order commitment.

3 Batch processing remains a common form of processing and the basic principle involved is that related transactions are stored together and processed as one batch of input so that the various programs and routines which need to be performed are performed in the most efficient way by one run rather than several. A system is referred to as 'online' when the data is input directly to the computer from the point of origination, and where the output is transmitted to the user's location. This involves data communications.

4 False

5 A Decision Support System (DSS) is normally an interactive system that helps people make decisions, use judgement and work in ill-defined areas. It supports decision-making in semi-structured and unstructured situations and provides information, models, or tools for manipulating and/or analysing information. It enables managers to focus on the real business problems, by automating the process of gathering, summarising and analysing information relevant to a particular decision area, and enables one-off *ad hoc* problem situations to be resolved. Its most likely usage is in the area of producing information to aid in tactical decision-making.

6 The ES will be used for:

- Diagnosing problems
- Strategic planning
- Internal control planning
- Maintaining strategies.

The system is able to make complex and unstructured decisions. It can offer managers advice and explanation, and is able to integrate with other systems such as MIS, DSS and EIS.

Examples of expert systems include:

- Advice on legal implications during labour-management negotiations
- Tax computations
- Selection of training methods

Answers to activities

1 They are examples of operational information.

2 The directors might want to know:

- The most profitable store so far this year
- Which product delivered the most profit in the previous year
- How efficient the warehouse system is
- The average time taken to fulfil a back order
- The most effective promotion in generating sales across all regions last year
- The most effective location in the South of England
- Region(s) which declined in profitability over the last six months
- Region(s) which grew fastest in the same time.

3 (a) Expert systems bring the power of expertise to the desk. Say a person wants a loan from a bank. An expert system can be used for credit scoring, so the request will not have to be directed back to a superior.

(b) Executive information systems mean that senior management can focus easily on operations so the middle management function of information processing might disappear.

This points to delayering of management hierarchies, counterbalanced by the creation of new jobs in information management.

Chapter 9 :
STOCK (INVENTORY) CONTROL

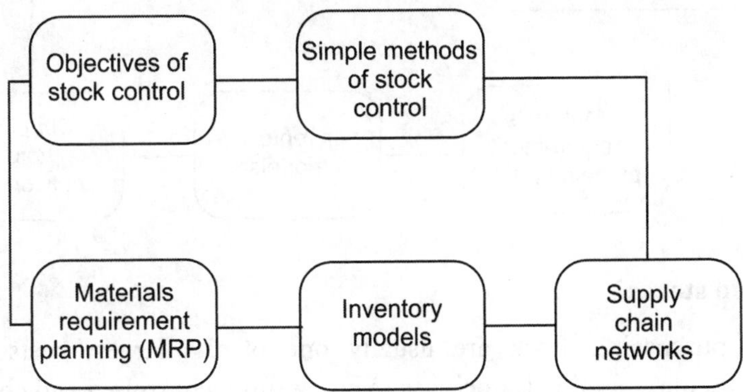

Introduction

Inventory (stock) is traditionally one of the key concerns of a business. This chapter considers a variety of methods by which it may be 'controlled'. In effect this means minimising the cost but not running out.

Your objectives

After completing this chapter you should:

(a) Know the different costs associated with stock

(b) Understand the methods of stock control including JIT

(c) Be able to calculate the reorder level and reorder quantity

(d) Have an understanding of the basic economic quantity order (EOQ) model

(e) Have an understanding of the economic batch quantity (EBQ) model

(f) Understand the effect of discounts on the total cost of an order

(g) Use software-generated information to prepare a spreadsheet to calculate economic order quantities

(h) Understand the implications for supply chain management of supply chain networks

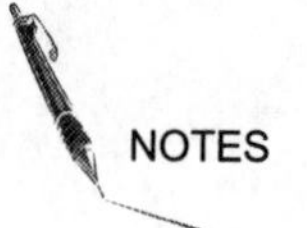

1 OBJECTIVES OF STOCK CONTROL

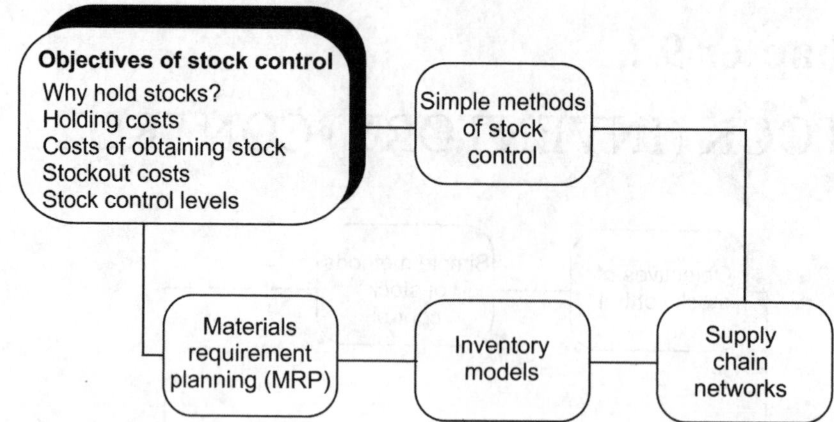

1.1 Why hold stocks?

The costs of purchasing stock are usually one of the largest costs faced by an organisation and, once obtained, stock has to be carefully controlled and checked.

The main reasons for holding stocks can be summarised as follows.

- To ensure sufficient goods are available to meet expected demand
- To provide a buffer between processes
- To meet any future shortages
- To take advantage of bulk purchasing discounts
- To absorb seasonal fluctuations and any variations in usage and demand
- To allow production processes to flow smoothly and efficiently
- As a necessary part of the production process (such as when maturing cheese)
- As a deliberate investment policy, especially in times of inflation or possible shortages

1.2 Holding costs

If stocks are too high, **holding costs** will be incurred unnecessarily. Such costs occur for a number of reasons.

(a) **Costs of storage and stores operations**. Larger stocks require more storage space and possibly extra staff and equipment to control and handle them.

(b) **Interest charges**. Holding stocks involves the tying up of capital (cash) on which interest must be paid.

(c) **Insurance costs**. The larger the value of stocks held, the greater insurance premiums are likely to be.

(d) **Risk of obsolescence**. The longer a stock item is held, the greater is the risk of obsolescence.

(e) **Deterioration**. When materials in store deteriorate to the extent that they are unusable, they must be thrown away with the likelihood that disposal costs would be incurred.

1.3 Costs of obtaining stock

On the other hand, if stocks are kept low, small quantities of stock will have to be ordered more frequently, thereby increasing the following **ordering** or **procurement costs.**

(a) **Clerical and administrative costs** associated with purchasing, accounting for and receiving goods

(b) **Transport costs**

(c) **Production run costs,** for stock which is manufactured internally rather than purchased from external sources

1.4 Stockout costs

An additional type of cost which may arise if stocks are kept too low is the type associated with running out of stock. There are a number of causes of **stockout costs.**

- Lost contribution from lost sales
- Loss of future sales due to disgruntled customers
- Loss of customer goodwill
- Cost of production stoppages
- Labour frustration over stoppages
- Extra costs of urgent, small quantity, replenishment orders

The overall objective of stock control is, therefore, to maintain stock levels so that the total of holding costs, ordering costs and stockout costs is minimised.

1.5 Stock control levels

Based on an analysis of past stock usage and delivery times, a series of control levels can be calculated and used to maintain stocks at their optimum level (in other words, a level which minimises costs). These levels will determine 'when to order' and 'how many to order'.

(a) **Reorder level**. When stocks reach this level, an order should be placed to replenish stocks. The reorder level is determined by consideration of the following.

- The maximum rate of consumption
- The maximum lead time

The maximum lead time is the time between placing an order with a supplier, and the stock becoming available for use

Reorder level = maximum usage × maximum lead time

(b) **Minimum level**. This is a warning level to draw management attention to the fact that stocks are approaching a dangerously low level and that stockouts are possible.

Minimum level = reorder level – (average usage × average lead time)

(c) **Maximum level**. This also acts as a warning level to signal to management that stocks are reaching a potentially wasteful level.

Maximum level = reorder level + reorder quantity – (minimum usage × minimum lead time)

(d) **Reorder quantity**. This is the quantity of stock which is to be ordered when stock reaches the reorder level. If it is set so as to minimise the total costs associated with holding and ordering stock, then it is known as the economic order quantity.

(e) **Average stock**. The formula for the average stock level assumes that stock levels fluctuate evenly between the minimum (or safety) stock level and the highest possible stock level (the amount of stock immediately after an order is received, ie safety stock + reorder quantity).

Average stock = safety stock + ½ reorder quantity

We will look at some of these stock levels again in the next section of this chapter when we look at methods of inventory control.

Definitions

- The **lead time** is the time which elapses between the beginning and end of something, in this case between the placing of an order for stock and its eventual delivery. Thus, a supply lead time of two months means that it will take two months from the time an order is placed until the time it is delivered.
- **Stockouts** arise when there is a requirement for an item of stock, but the stores or warehouse is temporarily out of stock.
- **Buffer stocks** are safety stocks held in case of unexpectedly high demand. Buffer stocks should only be required from time to time during the lead time between ordering fresh quantities of an item and their delivery. If there is excessive demand, or a delay in delivery, the buffer stocks might be used.
- The **order quantity** is the number of units of an item in one order. A fixed size is usually estimated for the order quantity.
- The **reorder level** is the balance of units remaining in stock, at which an order for more units will be placed.

Activity 1 **(10 minutes)**

A manufacturing firm holds an average of 40,000 items of stock. This is typically one month's supply. Stock items are bought for an average of £2.50 each. Further possibly relevant information from last year's financial and management accounts is as follows.

	£
Warehouse rent	8,000
Delivery charges (goods in)	24,000
Purchase department wages	45,400
Stores department wages	75,600
Purchase department overheads	31,400
Stores department overheads	34,800
Warehouse contents insurance	4,800

(a) What is the average cost of acquiring and holding a single item of stock?

(b) Would any other information be relevant?

2 SIMPLE METHODS OF STOCK CONTROL

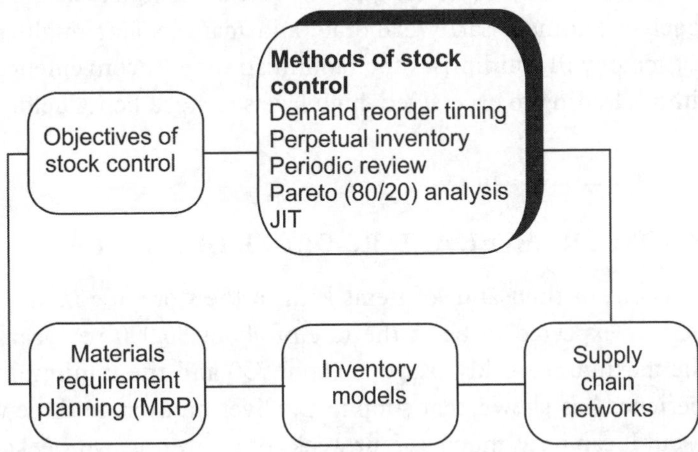

2.1 Introduction

A business needs to ensure that stock levels are high enough to avoid production stoppages. At the same time, it is undesirable that stock levels should be kept higher than necessary because management will wish to keep storage costs to a minimum. There are also administration and handling costs associated with ordering materials and accepting delivery from suppliers. An inventory control system can be instituted to minimise the combined costs of holding and ordering stocks, while maintaining high enough stock levels to avoid customer dissatisfaction.

Simple methods of inventory control are as follows.

- Demand reorder timing
- Perpetual inventory
- Periodic review

2.2 Demand reorder timing

Control of stock levels is often achieved by collecting, for each stores item, details of the amounts used in an **average period**, an **exceptionally busy period** and an **exceptionally slack period**. We will call these usage levels the **average level, maximum level** and **minimum level** respectively. **Suppliers' delivery period** or **lead time** would be analysed in the same way and a **maximum, average** and **minimum delivery time** ascertained.

With this information it is possible to calculate a level of stock (a **re-order level**) which will trigger a fresh purchase. If stockouts are to be avoided, a prudent re-order level could be calculated as follows.

Re-order level = maximum delivery period × maximum usage

It is unnecessary to keep detailed records of stock levels at every moment. It is enough to perform occasional checks to ensure that stock has not fallen to the *re-order level*. This makes the method a suitable one to use for stock items of comparatively low value, where up-to-the-minute information on stock levels is an unnecessary luxury.

Another problem is to decide a re-order quantity, that is the quantity of the stock item which should be ordered when stocks have fallen to the re-order level. As we shall see, mathematical models can be used to calculate an optimum re-order quantity (one which minimises the combined costs of holding stocks and ordering stocks). For small value items such models are unnecessarily elaborate and management might choose a level which they estimate will minimise the administrative inconvenience of frequent re-ordering, without leading to excessively high levels of stock being held.

EXAMPLE: RE-ORDER LEVEL AND RE-ORDER QUANTITY

Component 697 is one of thousands of items kept in the store of a manufacturer. Usage of the component is expected to be at the rate of about 30,000 per year. Management believes that the maximum weekly usage is about 750 and the minimum weekly usage about 400. Experience has shown that suppliers deliver on average three weeks after an order is placed, but it can be as much as four weeks or as little as two weeks.

Suggest a re-order level and a re-order quantity for component 697.

SOLUTION

(a) Average weekly usage is approximately 600 per week. The average usage between the time an order is placed and the time delivery is received is equal to 600 × 3 = 1,800. The maximum usage during the supplier's lead time is 750 × 4 = 3,000. Management would be likely to fix a re-order level nearer to the maximum usage than to the average usage. A stock of 3,000 might be regarded as an acceptable re-order level.

(b) Assuming that component 697 is not a particularly valuable stock item, management will take a simple approach to fixing a re-order quantity. Perhaps six orders a year would be considered a suitable number, so that each order would be for two months' stock. The re-order quantity would then be 30,000/6 = 5,000.

2.3 Perpetual inventory

Definitions

A **perpetual inventory** method involves knowing stock levels of all items at all times. A record is kept of all items showing receipts, issues and balances of stock. Since in practice physical stocks may not agree with recorded stocks, (because of clerical errors, storekeepers' errors, pilferage etc) it is necessary to check the inventory by **continuous stocktaking**. Here a number of items are counted and checked daily or at frequent intervals and compared with the bin cards. Each item is checked at least once a year and any discrepancies are investigated and corrected immediately.

Perpetual inventory systems usually involve the upkeep of two sets of records.

(a) **Bin cards**. These show the physical balance of units in stock at any time.

(b) **Stores ledger records**. These show both the physical balance of units in stock at any time and also their valuation.

The physical balances on the bin cards and the stores ledger record should agree at all times, unless there has been a clerical error on one of the records.

A perpetual inventory system uses the same system of re-order levels to trigger a fresh purchase of stock as with the demand and supply system.

2.4 Periodic review

Periodic stocktaking is a process that involves physically counting and valuing all stock times at one set point in time, usually at the end of an accounting period.

Periodic stocktaking has a number of disadvantages when compared with continuous stocktaking.

The advantages of continuous stocktaking compared to periodic stocktaking are as follows.

(a) The annual stocktaking is unnecessary and the disruption it causes is avoided.

(b) Regular skilled stocktakers can be employed, reducing likely errors.

(c) More time is available, reducing errors and allowing investigation.

(d) Deficiencies and losses are revealed sooner than they would be if stocktaking were limited to an annual check.

(e) Production hold-ups are eliminated because the stores staff are at no time so busy as to be unable to deal with material issues to production departments.

(f) Staff morale is improved and standards raised.

(g) Control over stock levels is improved, and there is less likelihood of overstocking or running out of stock.

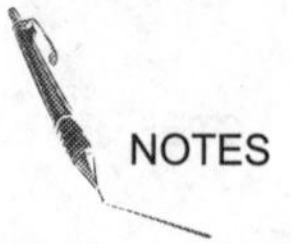

Activity 2 **(5 minutes)**

A firm needs regular supplies of a material that has to be imported from South America. Lead time for delivery is typically nine weeks but it can be between five and 13 weeks. The firm uses a minimum of about 2,000 kg per week and never more than 4,000 kg. It does not expect any increase or decrease in production levels in the foreseeable future. There is not room to store more than 60,000 kg at any one time. What re-order level and re-order quantity would you suggest?

2.5 Pareto (80/20) analysis

Another approach to stock control is Pareto (80/20) analysis**,** based on the finding that in many stores, 80% of the value of stock is accounted for by only 20% of the stock items. In purchasing, 80 per cent of the value of purchasing expenditure is purchased from only 20 per cent of suppliers. Stocks of these more expensive items should be controlled more closely.

EXAMPLE: PARETO ANALYSIS

A company holds ten items in stock, which it uses in various products. The value of the stock parts is as follows.

Stock parts	£
A	231
B	593
C	150
D	32
E	74
F	17
G	1,440
H	12
I	2
J	19
	2,570

Rearranging value in descending order and calculating cumulative figures and percentages gives us the following analysis.

Stock parts	£	*Cumulative value (W1)* £	*Cumulative value (W2)* %
G	1,440	1,440	56.0
B	593	2,033	79.1
A	231	2,264	88.1
C	150	2,414	93.9
E	74	2,488	96.8
D	32	2,520	98.1
J	19	2,539	98.8
F	17	2,556	99.5
H	12	2,568	99.9
I	2	2,570	100.0
	2,570		

Workings

1. This is calculated as follows:
   1,440 + 593 = 2,033
   2,033 + 231 = 2,264 and so on.
2. (1/2,570 × 1,440 × 100)% = 56.0%

   (1/2,570 × 2,033 × 100)% = 79.1% and so on.

   (Enter 1/2,570 into your calculator as a constant – do the calculation and then tap the multiplication button twice until 'k' appears on the screen – and then simply enter each cumulative revenue figure and press the 'equals' button to get the percentage as a decimal.)

In the example above, the Pareto rule applies – almost 80% of value of stock is accounted for by just two stock parts, G and B. The point of Pareto analysis is to highlight the fact that the effort that is put into a company's stock control is often barely worth the trouble in terms of its value.

In many ways the application of the 80:20 rule is instinctive and we know that it is right when it feels right. The important point is that when you can separate the vital few from the trivial many then you can begin to concentrate your efforts where the rewards are greatest.

2.6 ABC Analysis

In ABC analysis, the application of the Pareto 80/20 rule has been slightly modified resulting in three classifications of inventory and purchased items: A, B and C.

These percentages may vary somewhat between organisations but the principle is powerful in inventory control and purchasing effectiveness because it enables concentration of effort in the areas of highest payoffs – it pays to spend far more managerial time and effort on the high value items (A and B) and simply ensure sufficient inventory of the low value (C) category.

NOTES

2.7 Just-in-time (JIT)

Just-in-time is an approach to operations planning and control based on the idea that goods and services should be produced only when they are needed – neither too early (so that inventories build up) nor too late (so that the customer has to wait). JIT is also known as 'stockless production'.

In its extreme form, a JIT system seeks to hold zero inventories. JIT disruption at any part of the system becomes a problem for the whole operation to resolve. Supporters of JIT management argue that this will improve the likelihood that the problem will be resolved, because it is in the interest of everyone to resolve it.

JIT requires the following characteristics in operations.

(a) **High quality**. Disruption in production due to errors in quality will reduce throughput and reduce the dependability of internal supply.

(b) **Speed**. Throughput in the operation must be fast, so that customer orders can be met by production rather than out of inventory.

(c) **Reliability**. Production must be reliable and not subject to hold-ups.

(d) **Flexibility**. To respond immediately to customer orders, production must be flexible, and in small batch sizes.

(e) **Lower costs**. As a consequence of high quality production, and with a faster throughput and the elimination of errors, costs will be reduced.

A consequence of JIT is that if there is no immediate demand for output, the operation should not produce goods for inventory.

2.8 JIT techniques

JIT is a **collection of management techniques.** Some of these relate to basic working practices.

(a) **Work standards**. Work standards should be established and followed by everyone at all times.

(b) **Flexibility in responsibilities**. The organisation should provide for the possibility of expanding the responsibilities of any individual to the extent of his or her capabilities, regardless of the individual's position in the organisation. Grading structures and restrictive working practices should be abolished.

(c) **Equality of all people working in the organisation**. Equality should exist and be visible. For example, there should be a single staff canteen for everyone, without a special executive dining area; and all staff including managers might be required to wear the same uniform. An example of this is car manufacturer Honda.

(d) **Autonomy.** Authority should be delegated to the individuals responsible directly in the activities of the operation. Management should support people on the shop floor, not direct them.

(e) **Development of personnel.** Individual workers should be developed and trained.

(f) **Quality of working life**. The quality of working life should be improved, through better work area facilities, job security and involvement of everyone in job-related decision-making.

(g) **Creativity**. Employees should be encouraged to be creative in devising improvements to the way their work is done.

(h) **Use several small, simple machines**, rather than a single large and more complex machine. Small machines can be moved around more easily, and so offer greater flexibility in shop floor layout. The risk of making a bad and costly investment decision is reduced, because relatively simple small machines usually cost much less than sophisticated large machines.

(i) **Work floor layout and work flow**. Work can be laid out to promote the smooth flow of operations. Work flow is an important element in JIT, because the work needs to flow without interruption in order to avoid a build-up of inventory or unnecessary down-times.

(j) **Total productive maintenance (TPM)**. Total productive maintenance seeks to eliminate unplanned breakdowns and the damage they cause to production and work flow. Staff operating on the production line are brought into the search for improvements in maintenance.

(k) **JIT purchasing.** With JIT purchasing, an organisation establishes a close relationship with trusted suppliers, and develops an arrangement with the supplier for being able to purchase materials only when they are needed for production. The supplier is required to have a flexible production system capable of responding immediately to purchase orders from the organisation.

3 INVENTORY MODELS

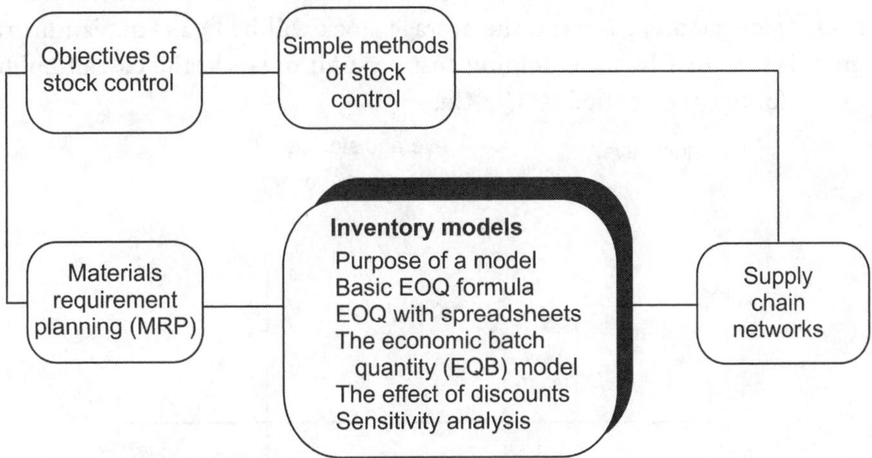

3.1 The purpose of an inventory model

The purpose of an inventory model is to help management to decide how to **plan** and **control** stocks efficiently, so as to minimise costs. Models may therefore estimate the following.

(a) The optimal size of an order for a particular item
(b) Whether the offer of a bulk purchase discount for large orders should be accepted
(c) The optimal re-order level for an item of stock
(d) How frequently orders should be placed

3.2 The basic EOQ formula

Definition

The **economic order quantity (EOQ)** or *economic batch quantity (EBQ)* is the order quantity for an item of stock which will minimise costs.

The assumptions used in the model are as follows.

(a) Demand is certain, constant and continuous over time.
(b) Supply lead time is constant and certain, or else there is instantaneous re-supply.
(c) Customers' orders cannot be held while fresh stocks are awaited.
(d) No stock-outs are permitted.
(e) All prices are constant and certain and there are no bulk purchase discounts.
(f) The cost of holding stock is proportional to the quantity of stock held.

At this stage, some symbols must be introduced.

Let D = the usage in units for one time period (demand)

Co = the cost of making one order (relevant costs only)

Ch = the holding cost per unit of stock for one time period (relevant costs only)

Q = the re-order quantity

Average stock

If the lead time is zero or is known with certainty, then fresh stocks can be obtained when stocks fall to zero. When fresh stocks arrive, stocks will be at their maximum level which is Q. As demand is constant, the average stock will be Q/2. This is illustrated in the diagram below. As Ch is the holding cost per unit of stock, the cost of holding the average stock for one time period is (Q/2)Ch.

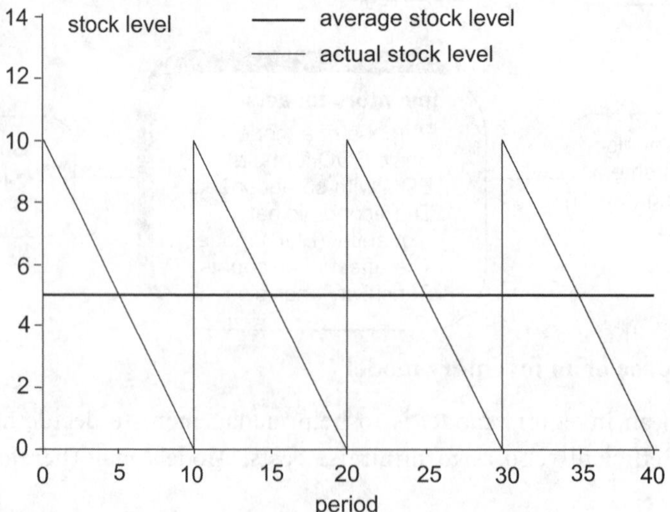

Figure 9.1: Average stock

NOTES

The number of orders for stock made in a time period depends upon the annual usage (D) and the re-order quantity (Q). The number of orders made in a time period will, equal D/Q. If the cost of making one order is Co then total ordering costs for the time period will equal CoD/Q.

The total cost per time period, T, equals

The objective is to minimise T.

Since there are no stock-out costs, no buffer stocks and no bulk purchase discounts, these are the only items of cost which vary with the size of the order.

The formula for the **economic order quantity,** (EOQ), can be derived from the above using elementary calculus. For now you should simply accept that

$$EOQ = \sqrt{\frac{2CoD}{Ch}}$$

EXAMPLE: THE EOQ FORMULA

The demand for a commodity is 40,000 units a year, at a steady rate. It costs £20 to place an order, and 40p to hold a unit for a year. Find the order size to minimise stock costs, the number of orders placed each year, and the length of the stock cycle.

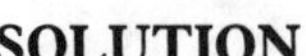

SOLUTION

$$Q = \sqrt{\frac{2 \times 20 \times 40{,}000}{0.4}}$$

= 2,000 units

This means that there will be

$\frac{40{,}000}{2{,}000}$ = 20 orders placed each year, so that the stock cycle is

$\frac{52 \text{ weeks}}{20 \text{ orders}}$ = 2.6 weeks.

Activity 3 **(5 minutes)**

Placing an order for an item of stock costs £170. The stock costs £30 a unit, and annual storage costs are 15% of purchase price. Annual demand is 600,000 units. What is the economic order quantity?

A graphical approach

The variation of costs with order size can be represented by the following graph.

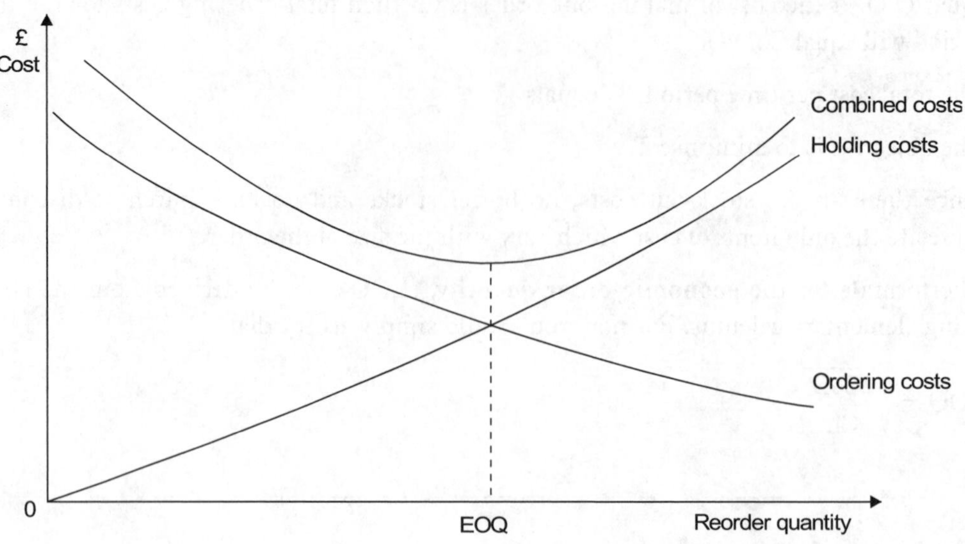

Figure 9.2: EOQ: variation of cost and order size

At the EOQ level of order size, ordering costs per period will equal stock holding costs:

$$\frac{QCh}{2} = \frac{CoD}{Q}$$

In the example on the previous page, where the EOQ was 2,000 units, costs were as follows.

	£
Annual ordering costs £20 × 20	400
Annual stock holding costs 2,000/2 × £0.40	400
Total annual costs of having stock	800

Buffer stock

Imagine that the EOQ model is to be employed by a firm but the management is worried by the fact that the mathematics implies that stocks will be allowed to fall to zero. Given that, in reality, demand will not be constant as is implied by the regular fall in stocks as sales take place, it is quite likely that management would like to have a buffer stock (or safety stock) so that stock levels were never allowed to fall below a certain level. Assume that this safety level is given as *S*. If all of the other assumptions of the model hold, the path that stocks will follow will be that given by the diagram below where safety stocks of two units are assumed.

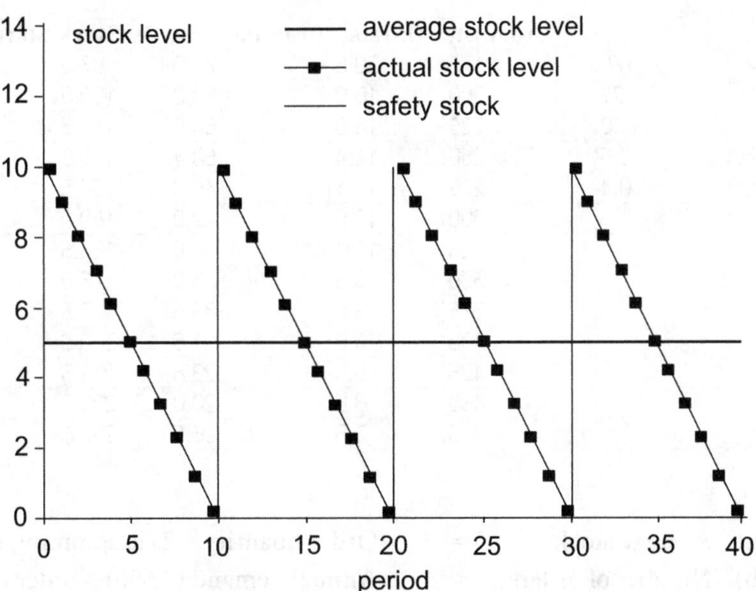

Figure 9.3: Buffer stocks

Thus, Q (10 units in the example) will be ordered but stocks will not fall to zero before the firm restocks. Rather stocks fall to S and then new stocks arrive at the warehouse. The question that is posed, therefore, is 'does this have any effect on the value of the economic order quantity?' The answer is 'no'.

The use of buffer stocks leaves many features of the model unchanged. The cost of holding **one unit** of stock has not altered. Similarly, the cost of reordering stock has not changed. The only effect has been to increase the average stock level for any reorder quantity. In the simple case shown in earlier, when safety stocks were zero, a reorder quantity of Q implied that stocks start at a level of Q and then fall to zero at which time a new order arrives. Thus, the **average** stock level was $Q/2$. However, in the new case, shown in the figure above, stocks start at a level of $Q+S$ (10 +2) and fall to S (2 units of buffer stock). At this time a new delivery of Q arrives and is added to the existing safety stock of S. This returns the stock level to $Q+S$.

In effect there is a permanent stock of two units in this example and a revolving stock that starts at *10* and falls to zero· The average level of the permanent stock is obviously S and the average level of the revolving stock is the same as that in the simple model: $Q/2$. The only difference now is that holding (storage) costs have increased because, at any time, more stock will be held. This does not affect the EOQ as it applies to all ordering frequencies.

3.3 EOQ with spreadsheets

Suppose a company purchases goods for resale. The annual demand for the goods is 3,600 units and the minimum order quantity is 175 units and they are sold in boxes of 25. The holding (store) cost per unit is £0.40 and the cost of placing an order is £3.50.

We can use Excel and tabulate the annual relevant costs for various order quantities as follows.

			Order Qty	Orders	Ordering Cost	Av Stock	Store Cost	Total	
First Qty	175		175	20.6	72.0	87.5	35.0	107.0	
Qty Inc	25		200	18.0	63.0	100.0	40.0	103.0	
Sales	3600		225	16.0	56.0	112.5	45.0	101.0	
Order Cost	3.5		250	14.4	50.4	125.0	50.0	100.4	<<<
Store Cost	0.4		275	13.1	45.8	137.5	55.0	100.8	
			300	12.0	42.0	150.0	60.0	102.0	
			325	11.1	38.8	162.5	65.0	103.8	
			350	10.3	36.0	175.0	70.0	106.0	
			375	9.6	33.6	187.5	75.0	108.6	
			400	9.0	31.5	200.0	80.0	111.5	
			425	8.5	29.6	212.5	85.0	114.6	
			450	8.0	28.0	225.0	90.0	118.0	
			475	7.6	26.5	237.5	95.0	121.5	

Notes

(a) Average stock = Order quantity ÷ 2 (ie assuming no buffer stock)

(b) Number of orders = Annual demand (3,600) ÷ order quantity

(c) Store cost = Average stock × £0.40

(d) Annual order cost = Number of orders × £3.5

You will see that the economic order quantity is 250 units. At this point the total annual relevant costs are at a minimum.

When setting up your worksheet keep the data that you enter initially separate from the calculation area but refer to them in the formulae so that any amendments eg, to the cost of ordering or storing can be added easily.

The graph (below) shows that, as the average stock level and order quantity increase, the storage cost increases. On the other hand, the ordering costs decline as stock levels and order quantities increase. The total cost line represents the sum of both the storage and the ordering costs

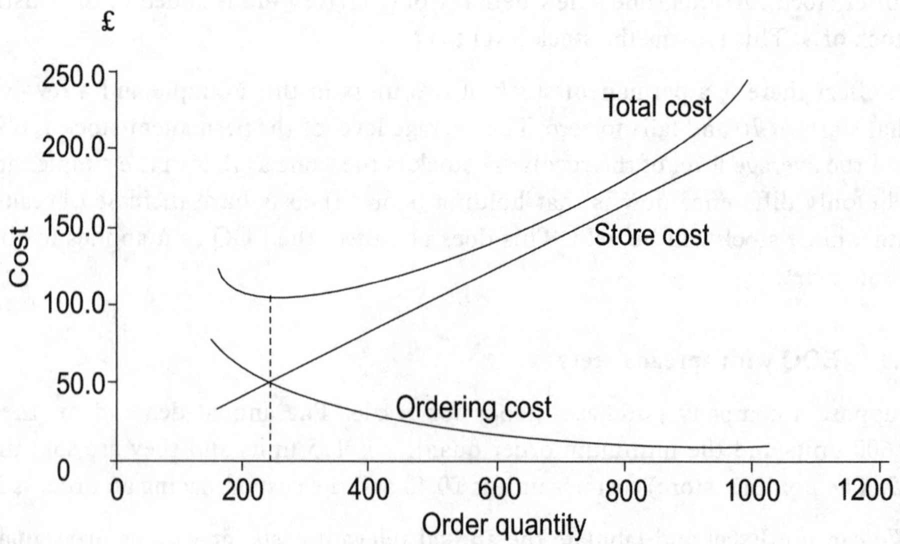

Figure 9.4: EOQs and storage costs

Note that the total cost line is at a minimum for an order quantity of 250 units and occurs at the point where the ordering cost curve and holding cost curve intersect. The EOQ is therefore found at the point where holding costs equal ordering costs.

3.4 The economic batch quantity (EBQ) model

You may come across a problem in which the basic EOQ formula requires modification because re-supply is **gradual**, instead of instantaneous. Typically, a manufacturing company might hold stocks of a finished item, which is produced in batches. Once the order for a new batch has been placed, and the production run has started, finished output might be used before the batch run has been completed.

For example suppose that the daily demand for an item of stock is ten units, and the storekeeper orders 100 units in a batch. The rate of production is 50 units a day.

On the first day of the batch production run, assuming no previous stocks, re-supply will begin. 50 units will be produced during the day, and ten units will be consumed. The closing stock at the end of day 1 will be 50 – 10 = 40 units.

On day 2, the final 50 units will be produced and a further ten units will be consumed. Closing stock at the end of day 2 will be (40 + 50 – 10) = 80 units.

In eight more days, stocks will fall to zero.

The **minimum stock** in this example is zero, and the **maximum stock** is 80 units. The maximum stock is the quantity ordered (Q = 100) minus demand during the period of the batch production run which is Q × D/R, where

D	is the rate of demand
R	is the rate of production
Q	is the quantity ordered.

In our example, the **maximum stock** is $(100 - \frac{10}{50} \times 100) = 100 - 20 = 80$ units.

The **maximum stock** level, given gradual re-supply, is thus $Q - \frac{QD}{R} = Q(1 - D/R)$.

The position can be represented graphically as follows.

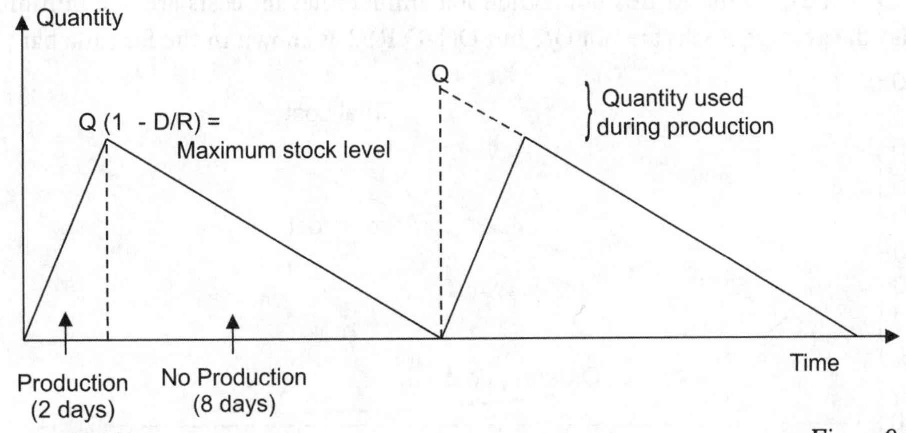

Figure 9.5: EBQ

An amended EOQ formula is required because average stocks are not Q/2 but Q(1 – D/R)/2.

The amended formula is known as the **Economic Batch Quantity** or the EBQ formula, and is written as:

$$Q = \sqrt{\frac{2CoD}{Ch(1 - D/R)}}$$

where Q = the amount produced in each batch
D = the usage per time period
Co = the set up cost per batch
Ch = the holding cost per unit of stock per time period
R = the production rate per time period (see below)

When carrying out EBQ calculations (or EOQ calculations) make sure that the figures you use are compatible. For example do not mix in a usage figure per *month* with a production rate per **day**.

The 'production' rate may actually be a 'supply' rate: for example if X Ltd were only able to obtain 100 units of raw materials per day and one unit were needed per widget they could only **make** 100 widgets per day.

Using the same example that we used for the EOQ on spreadsheet and adding a production rate of 18,000 we can show the effects on the average stock and on the orders.

H2 = =E2*(1-Sales/ProdRate)/2

	A	B	C	D	E	F	G	H	I	J	K
1					Order Qty	Orders	Ordering Cost	Av Stock	Store Cost	Total	
2					175	20.6	72.0	70.0	28.0	100.0	
3					200	18.0	63.0	80.0	32.0	95.0	
4					225	16.0	56.0	90.0	36.0	92.0	
5		First Qty	175		250	14.4	50.4	100.0	40.0	90.4	
6		Qty Inc	25		275	13.1	45.8	110.0	44.0	89.8	<<<
7		Sales	3600		300	12.0	42.0	120.0	48.0	90.0	
8		Order Cost	3.5		325	11.1	38.8	130.0	52.0	90.8	
9		Store Cost	0.4		350	10.3	36.0	140.0	56.0	92.0	
10		Production Rate	18000		375	9.6	33.6	150.0	60.0	93.6	
11					400	9.0	31.5	160.0	64.0	95.5	

The EBQ is at 275 units. At this point the total annual relevant costs are at a minimum. Note that the average stocks are not Q/2 but Q(1-D/R)/2 as shown in the formula bar.

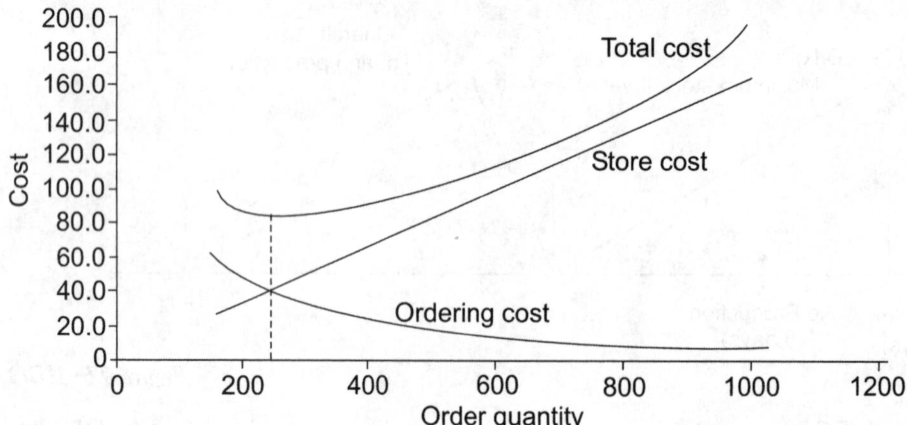

Figure 9.6: EBQ and storage costs

Activity 4 **(5 minutes)**

A company is able to manufacture its own components for stock at the rate of 4,000 units a week. Demand for the component is at the rate of 2,000 units a week. Set up costs for each production run are £50. The cost of holding one unit of stock is £0.001 a week. Calculate the economic production run.

3.5 The effect of discounts

A **quantity discount** is a price discount on an item if predetermined numbers of units are ordered. Many manufacturing companies receive price discounts for ordering materials and supplies in high volume, and retail stores receive price discounts for ordering merchandise in large quantities.

The basic EOQ model can be used to determine the optimal order size with quantity discounts; however, the application of the model is slightly altered. The total inventory cost function must now include the purchase price of the item being ordered.

Purchase price was not considered as part of our basic EOQ formulation earlier because it had no impact on the optimal order size. In the EOQ formula *the price and demand* would not alter the basic shape of the total cost curve; that is, the minimum point on the cost curve would still be at the same location, corresponding to the same value of *Q*. Thus, the optimal order size is the same no matter what the purchase price is. However, when a discount price is available, it is associated with a specific order size, which may be different from the optimal order size, and the customer must evaluate the trade-off between possibly higher carrying costs with the discount quantity versus EOQ cost. As a result, the purchase price does affect the order-size decision when a discount is available.

We can use Excel to calculate the effect of discounts. Using the same example as before, we can add a unit price and a discount structure.

	A	B	C	D	E	F	G	H	I	J	K	L	M
1					**Order Qty**	**Orders**	**Ordering cost**	**Discount**	**Net Price**	**Av Stock**	**Store Cost**	**Total**	
2					175	20.6	72.0	0.0	540.0	87.5	35.0	647.0	
3					200	18.0	63.0	0.0	540.0	100.0	40.0	643.0	
4					225	16.0	56.0	0.0	540.0	112.5	45.0	641.0	
5		First Qty	175.0		250	14.4	50.4	0.0	540.0	125.0	50.0	640.4	
6		Qty inc	25.0		275	13.1	45.8	0.0	540.0	137.5	55.0	640.8	
7		Sales	3600.0		300	12.0	42.0	0.0	540.0	150.0	60.0	642.0	
8		Order cost	3.5		325	11.1	38.8	0.0	540.0	162.5	65.0	643.8	
9		Store cost	0.4		350	10.3	36.0	72.0	468.0	175.0	70.0	574.0	
10					375	9.6	33.6	72.0	468.0	187.5	75.0	576.6	
11					400	9.0	31.5	72.0	468.0	200.0	80.0	579.5	
12		Unit price	0.2		425	8.5	29.6	72.0	468.0	212.5	85.0	582.6	
13		Discount Qry 1	350.0		450	8.0	28.0	72.0	468.0	225.0	90.0	586.0	
14		Discount percentage	2.0		475	7.6	26.5	72.0	468.0	237.5	95.0	589.5	
15		Discount Qty 2	600.0		500	7.2	25.2	72.0	468.0	250.0	100.0	593.2	
16		Discount percentage	3.0		525	6.9	24.0	72.0	468.0	262.5	105.0	597.0	
17					550	6.5	22.9	72.0	468.0	275.0	110	600.9	
18					575	6.3	21.9	72.0	468.0	287.5	115.0	604.9	
19					600	6.0	21.0	108.0	432.0	300.0	129.0	573.0	<<<
20					625	5.8	20.2	108.0	432.0	312.5	125.0	577.2	
21					650	5.5	19.4	108.0	432.0	325.0	130.0	581.4	
22													
23					=IF(E2>=DiscQty2,Sales*Disc2/100,IF(E2>=DiscQty1, Sales*Disc1/100,0)								

The optimal order quantity may or may not occur at the quantity where total ordering cost equals total holding cost. Finding the optimal order quantity involves calculating the total annual cost (including purchase cost) for each of these quantities, and picking the quantity that gives the lowest total cost.

It can be seen from the graph below that differing bulk discounts are given at 350 units and 600 units. The minimum total cost, in this case, is when 600 units are ordered - total cost =£573, rather than when the EOQ is ordered (250 units with a total cost of £640.40)

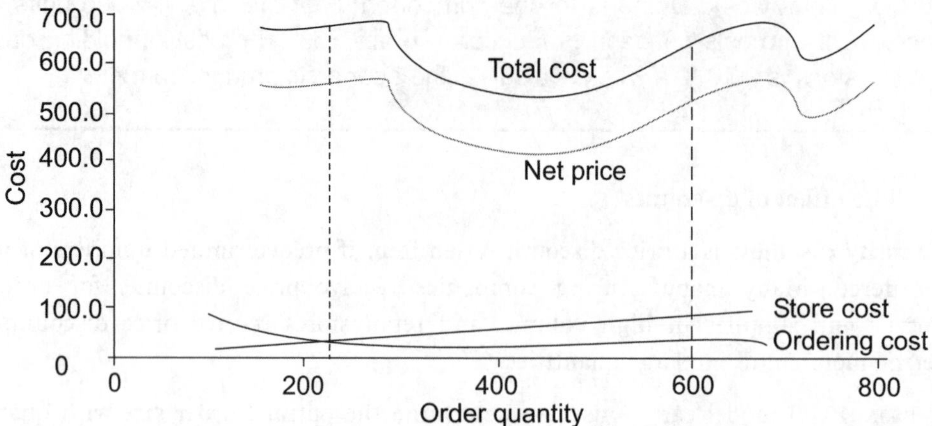

Figure 9.7: Optimal order quantity

To decide mathematically whether it would be worthwhile taking a discount and ordering larger quantities, it is necessary to minimise the total of the following.

(a) Total material costs
(b) Ordering costs
(c) Stock holding costs

The total cost will be minimised:

(a) at the pre-discount EOQ level, so that a discount is not worthwhile; or
(b) at the minimum order size necessary to earn the discount.

If, as in the case above, there is more than one trigger level for discounts of increasing size, each trigger order size must be evaluated to find the one that gives the lowest total cost.

EXAMPLE: BULK DISCOUNTS

The annual demand for an item of stock is 45 units. The item costs £200 a unit to purchase, the holding cost for one unit for one year is 15% of the unit cost and ordering costs are £300 an order.

The supplier offers a 3% discount for orders of 60 units or more, and a discount of 5% for orders of 90 units or more. What is the cost-minimising order size?

SOLUTION

(a) The EOQ ignoring discounts is

$$\sqrt{\frac{2 \times 300 \times 45}{15\% \text{ of } 200}}$$

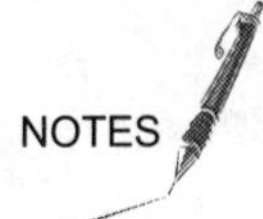

	£
Purchases (no discount) 45 × £200	9,000
Holding costs 15 units × £30	450
Ordering costs 1.5 orders × £300	450
Total annual costs	9,900

(b) With a discount of 3% and an order quantity of 60 units, costs are as follows.

	£
Purchases £9,000 × 97%	8,730
Holding costs 30 units × 15% of 97% of £200	873
Ordering costs 0.75 orders × £300	225
Total annual costs	9,828

(c) With a discount of 5% and an order quantity of 90 units, costs are as follows.

	£
Purchases £9,000 × 95%	8,550.0
Holding costs 45 units × 15% of 95% of £200	1,282.5
Ordering costs 0.5 orders × £300	150.0
Total annual costs	9,982.5

The cheapest option is to order 60 units at a time

(d) Note that the value of Ch varied according to the size of the discount, because Ch was a percentage of the purchase cost. This means that total holding costs are reduced because of a discount. This could easily happen if, for example, most of Ch was the cost of insurance, based on the cost of stock held.

Activity 5 **(10 minutes)**

A company uses an item of stock as follows.

Purchase price:	£96 per unit
Annual demand:	4,000 units
Ordering cost:	£300
Annual holding cost:	10% of purchase price
Economic order quantity:	500 units

Should the company order 1,000 units at a time in order to secure an 8% discount?

3.6 Sensitivity analysis

If there are doubts about the accuracy of the estimated ordering costs and holding costs, or there is uncertainty about the volume of demand, sensitivity analysis may be used to measure the effect on annual costs of selecting an EOQ based on inaccurate figures. We simply compare the actual costs with the costs which would have been incurred, had the correct EOQ been used.

NOTES

EXAMPLE: SENSITIVITY ANALYSIS

Montelimar Ltd estimated that it would use 100 tons of Catcomine during the last financial year. The annual holding costs of Catcomine are £5 a ton. The cost of placing one order should be £10. Using the basic EOQ formula, Montelimar Ltd calculated that the economic order size was 20 tons and established a policy of ordering this quantity every time stocks were exhausted. At the end of the year the company found it had actually used 120 tons of Catcomine and that the actual cost of placing each order was £14. The managing director wishes to know the net financial effect of the bad forecasting.

SOLUTION

The actual costs incurred were as follows.

					£
Holding costs	$\frac{ChQ}{2}$	=	$\frac{5 \times 20}{2}$	=	50
Ordering costs	$\frac{CoD}{Q}$	=	$\frac{14 \times 120}{20}$	=	84
					134

The economic order quantity should have been

$$\sqrt{\frac{2 \times 14 \times 120}{5}} = 25.92 \text{ tons}$$

The total costs would then have been as follows.

			£
Holding costs =	$\frac{5 \times 25.92}{2}$	=	64.80
Ordering costs =	$\frac{14 \times 120}{25.92}$	=	64.81
			129.61

The company therefore incurred costs £4.39 higher than necessary. Thus the total costs are insensitive to modest forecasting errors.

4 MATERIALS REQUIREMENTS PLANNING (MRP)

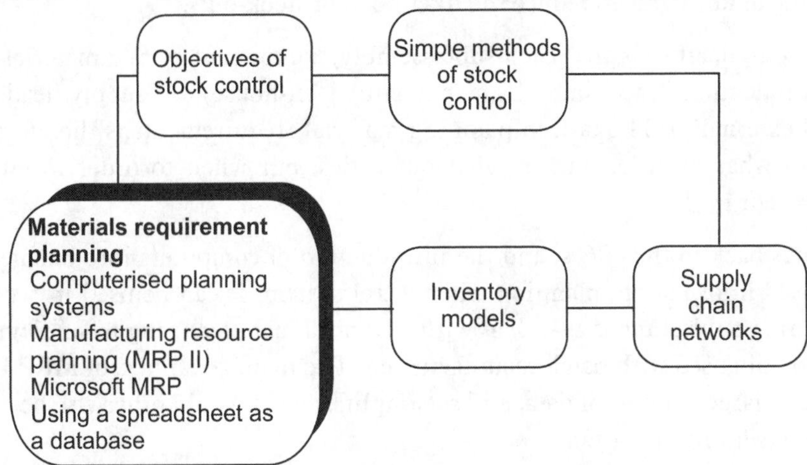

4.1 Computerised planning systems

Within traditional manufacturing systems, the planning process has been improved enormously by computerisation.

Definition

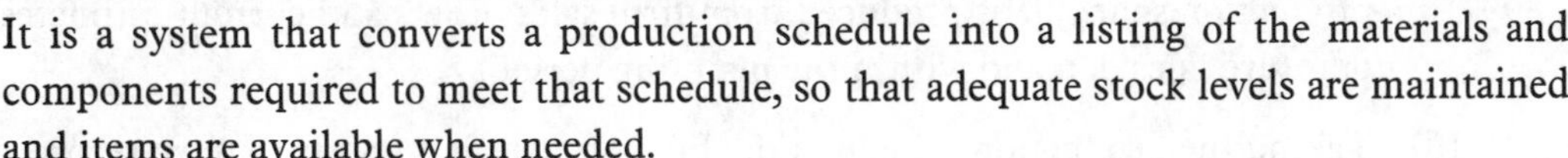

Materials requirement planning, or *MRP I*, is a computerised system for planning the requirements for raw materials and components, sub-assemblies and finished items.

It is a system that converts a production schedule into a listing of the materials and components required to meet that schedule, so that adequate stock levels are maintained and items are available when needed.

EXAMPLE: BENEFITS OF MRP

The potential benefits of MRP I can perhaps be understood with a simple example. Suppose that a company manufactures product X, which consists of two units of sub-assembly A and one unit of sub-assembly B. The company makes the sub-assemblies. One unit of sub-assembly A needs six units of component C and three units of component D, and one sub-unit of sub-assembly B needs four units of component D and five units of component E.

In a traditional materials procurement system, new orders are generated for finished goods, sub-assemblies, components or raw materials when the stock level for the item falls to a re-order level. A new batch is then ordered. In the example above, the production of a new batch of product X could result in new production orders for sub-assembly A or B, and these in turn could generate new orders for any of the components, depending on stock levels.

Where a manufacturing process uses many sub-assemblies, components and raw materials items, it could be difficult to keep check on materials requirements and the re-

ordering process, and there would be a risk of stock-outs of key items, or possibly overstocking of key items to reduce the likelihood of stock-outs.

A further complication is that each sub-assembly, component or raw material item has its own production lead time (if manufactured in-house) or supply lead time (if purchased externally). The task in planning materials requirements is therefore not just a matter of what to order and in what quantities, but when to order to ensure that deliveries occur in time.

MRP I dates back to the 1960s, and the introduction of computers into business. It is a computerised information, planning and control system. It can be used in a traditional manufacturing environment as well as with advanced manufacturing technologies, but is most commonly used with batch manufacturing. The main advantage of MRP I is that it can process a large amount of data, and so simplifies what would otherwise be a complex and time-consuming operation.

The elements of an MRP I system are as follows.

(a) The system has access to **inventory records**, for all items of stock (finished goods, sub-assemblies, components, raw materials) and so is aware of current stock levels. For each inventory item, there are also records for the production lead time or purchase lead time.

(b) The system has access to a **bill of materials** for each item of production. A bill of materials is simply a detailed list of the sub-assemblies, components and raw materials, including the quantities of each, needed to make the item.

(c) The system also has access to a **master production schedule**. This is a production schedule, detailing the quantities of each item that need to be produced, and the time by which completed output is required. The master production schedule is produced from firm sales orders and current estimates of future sales demand within the planning period.

(d) Taking the production schedule, the bills of materials and inventory records, the system computes what quantities of materials are required, and by when. In the case of items purchased externally, the system will report when the **purchase orders** must be placed. Where items are produced in-house, the system will provide a schedule for the commencement of production for each item.

(e) The system can produce **works orders** and **materials plans** and automatic **purchase orders** for use by the purchasing department.

(f) As information about sales orders changes, the production schedule can be altered quickly, and a new **materials procurement programme** prepared automatically.

The aims of MRP I are to:

(a) Minimise stock levels by avoiding over-stocking and earlier-than-necessary materials requisitions

(b) Avoid the costs of rush orders

(c) Reduce the risk of stock outs and resulting disruptions to the flow of production.

MRP I is therefore concerned with maximising efficiency in the timing of orders for raw materials or parts that are placed with external suppliers and efficient scheduling of the manufacturing and assembly of the end product.

A simple summary of the Material Requirements Planning (MRP) process steps is as follows.

1. The orders and forecast for each time period, usually one day, for each end item are subtracted from the stock on hand plus any scheduled receipts to give the day to day projected available balance.
2. If the projected available balance falls below zero, or the safety stock if there is one, the MRP program will suggest rescheduling an existing order. If there are no orders to re-schedule, MRP will create a planned order to correct the projected available balance.
3. The planned order quantity is set to either just enough to restore the projected available balance (lot for lot), a fixed quantity multiple (lot size) or can be a number of more complex calculations involving looking periods ahead, minimums, maximums, multiples and so on.
4. All planned orders offset by the lead time either create purchase orders or, for manufactured parts, are exploded into the component parts using the part's bill of material.
5. Planned orders at one level are exploded into projected gross requirements at the next level down in the bill of material.
6. The above steps are repeated for all components. The demand for components is generally called projected gross requirements which is a combination of orders and forecast.

4.2 Manufacturing resource planning (MRP II)

Manufacturing resource planning (MRP II) evolved out of MRP I in the 1970s.

Definition

Manufacturing resource planning (MRP II) is an expansion of material requirements planning (MRP I) to give a broader approach than MRPI to the planning and scheduling of resources, embracing areas such as finance, logistics, engineering and marketing.

MRP II plans production jobs and also calculates resource needs such as labour and machine hours.

The difference between MRP II and MRP I is principally that MRP II extends the computer system beyond manufacturing operations, and provides a common database for all functions in the organisation, such as sales and marketing, finance and distribution and transportation (logistics). It attempts to integrate materials requirement planning, factory capacity planning, shop floor control, production design, management accounting, purchasing and even marketing into a single complete (and computerised) control system.

Without an MRP II system, each separate function within the company would need its own stand-alone database, even though some of the information they use is common to each. For example:

EXAMPLE: MRP II

The production engineering department needs information about bills of materials. If it makes a change to a product specification, the bill of materials for the product must be changed. In the absence of an MRP II system, the same changes would have to be made to the databases of both the production department and the production engineering department. There would also be the risk of one database being updated but not the other.

The finance department uses information from a production budget and bills of materials to produce budgets and reports on product costs and product profitability. When a bill of materials is changed, the accounts department needs to know so that product costs can be re-calculated. When the production schedule is amended, the accounts department needs to know in order to prepare revised production cost estimates. Without an MRP II system, any changes to the production schedule would have to be fed into the production database and the accounting database separately.

MRP II therefore offers the advantages of a common database – easier updating and a common set of data for all departments to use.

MRP I and MRP II systems have their critics, particularly from advocates of just-in-time production and lean production. A problem the MRP approach is that it creates a model of what currently happens in the manufacturing plant, not what perhaps ought to happen. It builds in bad habits and waste. It allows for long lead times, bottlenecks in production, large batch sizes. Management will not be motivated to achieve improvements and eliminate waste when poor productivity and poor quality are built into the MRPII planning system.

4.3 Microsoft MRP

Microsoft MRP is a database used for the planning of material requirements in a manufacturing process, based on inventory, open purchase orders, multiple bills of material and multiple types of forecast plan. It is developed in the Microsoft Access database environment and is fairly straightforward to use.

NOTES

The following diagram gives an overview of the system:

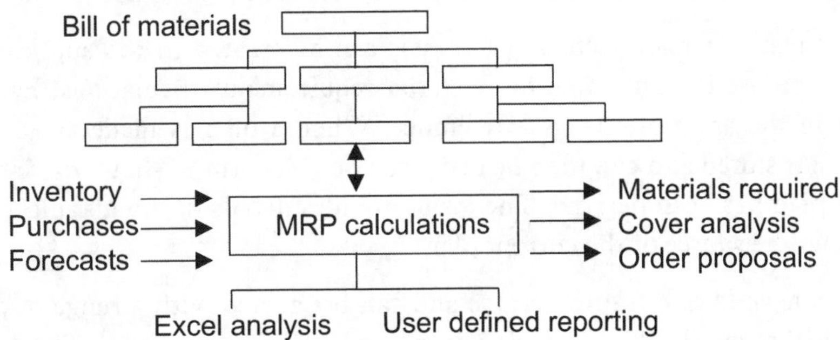

Figure 9.8: Microsoft MRP

The system is based on tables with each table holding information about a particular object of the system. The tables might include the following

(a) The **Spare Parts** table where each record would contain data for a single spare part. There would be fields in each record for descriptions, units of measure, location etc.

(b) The **Suppliers** table where a record would contain data for a single supplier and the fields within the record for name, address, telephone number etc.

(c) The **Warehouse** table.

(d) The **Locations** table.

The information in each of the tables is developed into a system by creating relationships between the tables. For example:

(a) which suppliers supply which part
(b) which spares are stored in which location, and
(c) which locations are in which warehouses.

The user interacts with the system by means of forms such as the one shown below.

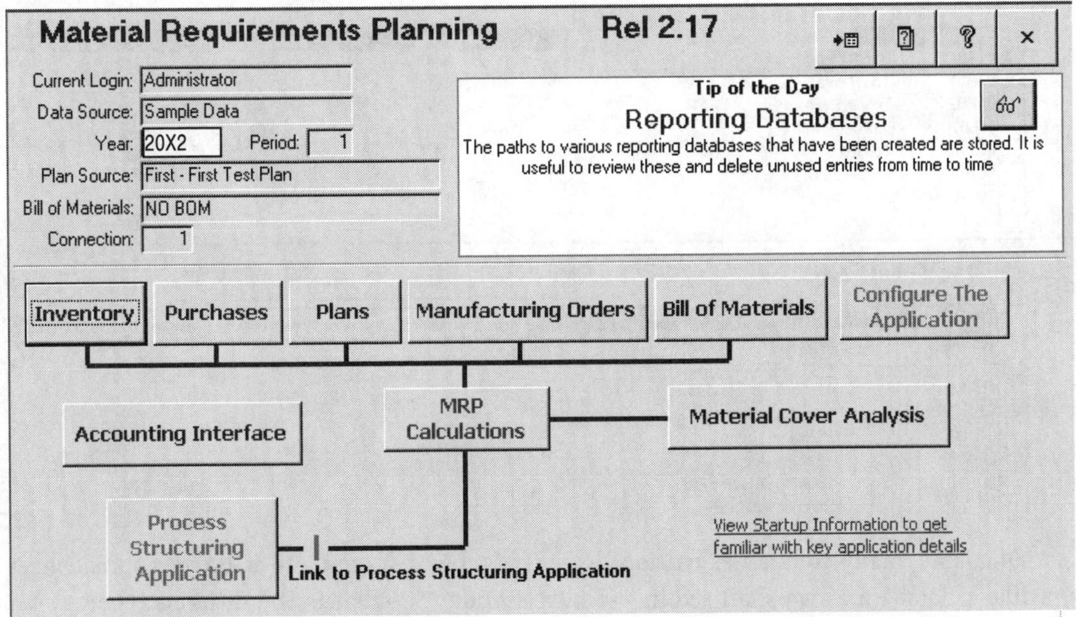

Menus and toolbars allow access to the functions of the application, including the forms and reports. The system includes queries for selective retrieval of information.

Multiple plans or manufacturing forecasts can be created in the application. Only one plan can be used at any time for material requirement calculations. Each plan that is created in the application has a reference. When a plan is made the current plan, its reference is stored and can then be displayed on this form to show where the data for the current plan has been derived. The form provides details of the manufacturing forecasts and shows the source of the current plan.

All plans have twelve future periods and can be created with a range of period lengths, although the length of each period in a single plan is the same. The form shows the manufacturing requirement forecast for all finished products and semi-finished products.

Each line of the tabular display shows the forecast for a single finished or semi-finished product over the next twelve periods of the plan. For each period the starting date of the period is shown, showing the lengths of plan periods at a glance.

Other forms shown below are used to calculate the material requirements for the current plan over the periods that the plan runs, the items in stock and the suppliers of the goods.

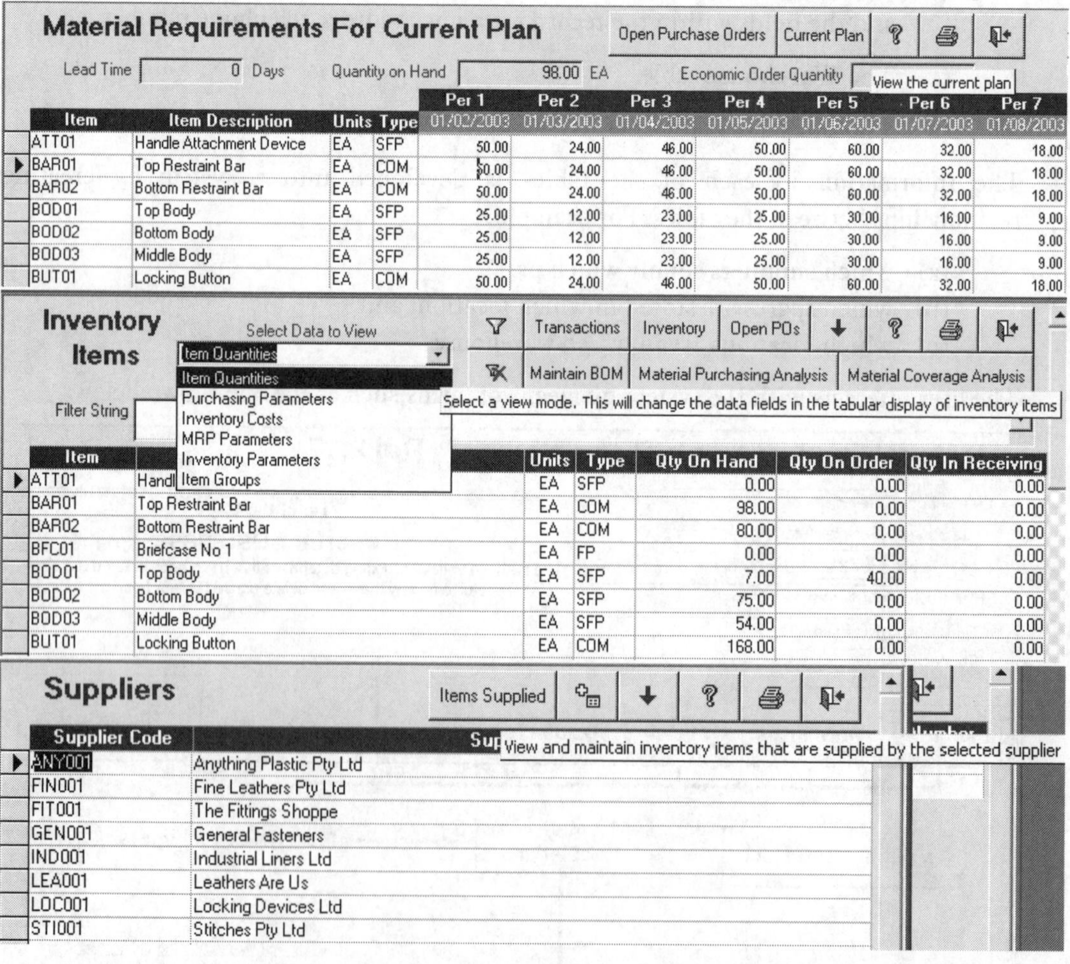

Material Requirements For Current Plan

Open Purchase Orders | Current Plan

Lead Time 0 Days   Quantity on Hand 98.00 EA   Economic Order Quantity   View the current plan

Item	Item Description	Units	Type	Per 1 01/02/2003	Per 2 01/03/2003	Per 3 01/04/2003	Per 4 01/05/2003	Per 5 01/06/2003	Per 6 01/07/2003	Per 7 01/08/2003
ATT01	Handle Attachment Device	EA	SFP	50.00	24.00	46.00	50.00	60.00	32.00	18.00
BAR01	Top Restraint Bar	EA	COM	50.00	24.00	46.00	50.00	60.00	32.00	18.00
BAR02	Bottom Restraint Bar	EA	COM	50.00	24.00	46.00	50.00	60.00	32.00	18.00
BOD01	Top Body	EA	SFP	25.00	12.00	23.00	25.00	30.00	16.00	9.00
BOD02	Bottom Body	EA	SFP	25.00	12.00	23.00	25.00	30.00	16.00	9.00
BOD03	Middle Body	EA	SFP	25.00	12.00	23.00	25.00	30.00	16.00	9.00
BUT01	Locking Button	EA	COM	50.00	24.00	46.00	50.00	60.00	32.00	18.00

Inventory Items

Select Data to View: Item Quantities (Item Quantities, Purchasing Parameters, Inventory Costs, MRP Parameters, Inventory Parameters, Item Groups)

Filter String

Transactions | Inventory | Open POs | Maintain BOM | Material Purchasing Analysis | Material Coverage Analysis

Select a view mode. This will change the data fields in the tabular display of inventory items

Item		Units	Type	Qty On Hand	Qty On Order	Qty In Receiving
ATT01	Handl	EA	SFP	0.00	0.00	0.00
BAR01	Top Restraint Bar	EA	COM	98.00	0.00	0.00
BAR02	Bottom Restraint Bar	EA	COM	80.00	0.00	0.00
BFC01	Briefcase No 1	EA	FP	0.00	0.00	0.00
BOD01	Top Body	EA	SFP	7.00	40.00	0.00
BOD02	Bottom Body	EA	SFP	75.00	0.00	0.00
BOD03	Middle Body	EA	SFP	54.00	0.00	0.00
BUT01	Locking Button	EA	COM	168.00	0.00	0.00

Suppliers

Items Supplied

View and maintain inventory items that are supplied by the selected supplier

Supplier Code	Sup
ANY001	Anything Plastic Pty Ltd
FIN001	Fine Leathers Pty Ltd
FIT001	The Fittings Shoppe
GEN001	General Fasteners
IND001	Industrial Liners Ltd
LEA001	Leathers Are Us
LOC001	Locking Devices Ltd
STI001	Stitches Pty Ltd

Of course, many companies will not have this type of system and will use a spreadsheet like a database as we shall see in the next section. So what is the difference between a spreadsheet and a database?

Spreadsheets are designed more for flexibility in manipulation and presentation of information. Generally, mathematical manipulation of data is more easily achieved in a spreadsheet.

Databases are designed to store greater volumes of data, and they enable data required for different purposes to be stored in a single location. Databases can manipulate data using Queries, which are particularly useful when dealing with large data volumes. In very simple terms, a spreadsheet is the electronic equivalent of a piece of graph paper, while a database could be likened to a filing cabinet.

4.4 Using a spreadsheet as a database

Spreadsheet packages are **not true databases,** but they often have database-like facilities for manipulating tables of data, if only to a limited extent compared with a true database.

A database is a **collection of data** which is integrated and organised so as to provide a **single comprehensive system.** The data is governed by rules which define its structure and determine how it can be accessed.

The **purpose** of a database is to provide **convenient access** to common data for a **wide variety** of **users** and **user needs.** The point of storing all the data in a single place is to avoid the problems that arise when several similar versions of the same data exist, so that it is not clear which is the **definite version,** and also to avoid the need to have to input the same data more than once.

For instance, both the sales administration and the marketing departments of an organisation may need **customer name and address details.** If these two departments operated **separate** systems they will **both** need to input details of any change of address. If they **share a common database** for this information, it **only needs to be input once.**

Sorting facilities

In the illustration that follows, data has been sorted by highlighting columns A to C and then clicking on **Data** and then **Sort**. It has been sorted into **ascending** product name order and **descending** order of number of parts used in that product. Then the data has been copied into columns E to G where it can be **re-sorted** according to part number and product name.

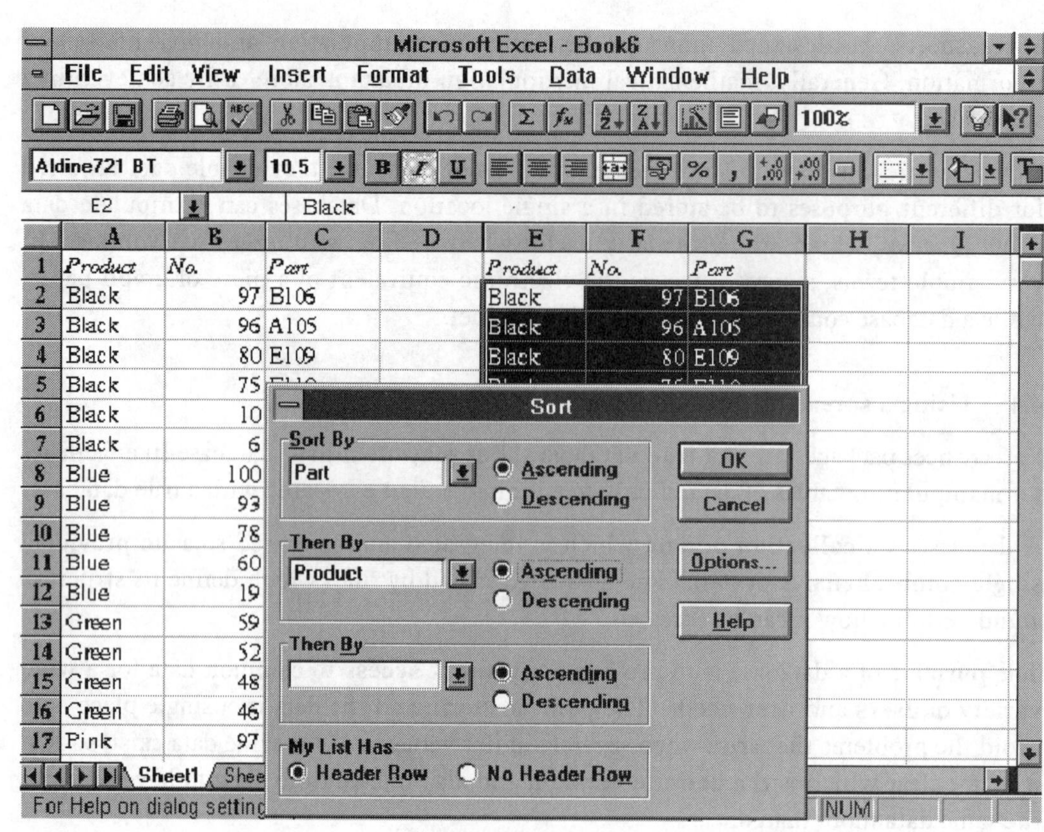

EXAMPLE: SPREADSHEETS AND DATABASES

Here is a spreadsheet used for **stock control**.

	A	B	C	D	E	F	G	H	I
1	*Component*	*Product*	*Quantity*	*In stock*	*Re-order level*	*Free stock*	*Reorder quantity*	*On order*	*Supplier*
2	A001	A	1	371	160	211	400	-	P750
3	A002	B	5	33	40	-	100	100	P036
4	A003	A	5	206	60	146	150	-	P888
5	A004	D	3	176	90	86	225	-	P036
6	A005	E	9	172	120	52	300	-	P750
7	A006	C	7	328	150	178	375	-	P684
8	A007	C	2	13	10	3	25	-	P227
9	A008	C	6	253	60	193	150	-	P036
10	A009	E	9	284	90	194	225	-	P888
11	A010	B	3	435	100	335	250	-	P720
12	A011	B	2	295	110	185	275	-	P036
13	A012	A	3	40	190	-	475	475	P036
14	A013	A	7	23	120	-	300	300	P227
15	A014	C	4	296	110	186	275	-	P750
16	A015	D	7	432	40	392	100	-	P684
17	A016	D	4	416	100	316	250	-	P141
18	A017	A	3	463	150	313	375	-	P888

If you scrutinise this table you may notice that there are certain common items. For instance both components A001 and A003 are used to make Product A. Both components A001 and A005 are bought from supplier P750.

Wouldn't it be handy if we could **manipulate** this data in some way, say, to get a full list of all components used to make product A, or a list of all components supplied by supplier P750? Of course, we **can** do this, almost at the click of a button.

In Excel you simply click in the **Data** menu and choose the option **Filter ... Auto filter.** A downward pointing arrow now appears beside each heading, and if you click on one of the arrows a list of each different item in the corresponding column drops down.

	A	B	C	D	E	F	G	H	I
1	Component	Product	Quantity	In stock	Re-order level	Free stock	Reorder quantity	On order	Supplier
2	A001	A	1	371	160	211	400	-	
3	A002	B	5	33	40	-	100	100	
4	A003	A	5	206	60	146	150	-	
5	A004	D	3	176	90	86	225	-	
6	A005	E	9	172	120	52	300	-	
7	A006	C	7	328	150	178	375	-	
8	A007	C	2	13	10	3	25	-	
9	A008	C	6	253	60	193	150	-	P036
10	A009	E	9	284	90	194	225	-	P888
11	A010	B	3	435	100	335	250	-	P720
12	A011	B	2	295	110	185	275	-	P036
13	A012	A	3	40	190	-	475	475	P036
14	A013	A	7	23	120	-	300	300	P227
15	A014	C	4	296	110	186	275	-	P750
16	A015	D	7	432	40	392	100	-	P684
17	A016	D	4	416	100	316	250	-	P141
18	A017	A	3	463	150	313	375	-	P888

Supplier drop-down list: (All), (Top 10...), (Custom...), P036, P141, P227, P684, P720, P750, P888

Sheet1 / Sheet2 / Sheet3

In this illustration the user has clicked on the arrow in the Supplier column and is about to select Supplier 750. This is what happens.

	A	B	C	D	E	F	G	H	I
1	Component	Product	Quantity	In stock	Re-order level	Free stock	Reorder quantity	On order	Supplier
2	A001	A	1	371	160	211	400	-	P750
6	A005	E	9	172	120	52	300	-	P750
15	A014	C	4	296	110	186	275	-	P750

Sheet1 / Sheet2 / Sheet3

This shows that supplier P750 supplies components A001, A005 and A014, that there is nothing on order from this supplier at present, that this supplier is important for products A, E and C only, and so on.

If the original data were restored (by clicking on the Supplier arrow and choosing All) and then we clicked on the arrow in the **Product** column we would be able to see at a glance all the components used for product A and all the suppliers for those components, whether any components were on order at present (possibly meaning delays in the availability of the next batch of Product A) and so on.

Activity 6 **(20 minutes)**

Construct the spreadsheet shown on the previous page. You may have to use the on-line help facility (press the F1 key) if you are unsure of the formulae used.

Use the **Data ... Filters** option to answer the following questions.

(a) What components does supplier P888 supply?
(b) What components are used in product E?
(c) Which suppliers are due to deliver fresh supplies?

We can go back to the example that we used earlier for calculating the EOQ and the EBQ and show how we could use the system efficiently. The estimated sales figure in the sheet below (Sheet 1) is linked to Sheet 2 as shown on the formula bar so that any changes on Sheet 2 will automatically reflect on the ordering of the components and reworking the EOQ.

Sheet 1

Sales = =Sheet2!F7

	A	B	C
1		First Qty	175
2		Qty Inc	25
3		Sales	3600
4		Order Cost	3.5
5		Store Cost	0.4
6		Production Rate	18000
7			
8		Unit Price	0.15
9		Discount Qty 1	250
10		Discount % 1	2.0
11		Discount Qty 2	700
12		Discount % 2	3.0

On Sheet 2 below any changes in expected sales of Product A, B or C or any changes in the arrangement of components for the products input by the user, or by another area of the system spreadsheet, will reflect on the sheet containing the component details - in our example it is Component 1. The figure computed in F7 will automatically update Sheet 1 and change the ordering structure for this component.

Sheet 2

F7 = =SUM(F3:F5)

	A	B	C	D	E	F	G	H	I	J
1					Number of each component used in each product:					
2			Product	Expected Sales	**Component 1**	Sales 1	**Component 2**	Sales 2	**Component 3**	Sales 3
3			**Product A**	1400	2	2800	1	1400	0	0
4			**Product B**	1200	0	0	3	3600	4	4800
5			**Product C**	800	1	800	2	1600	0	0
6						----------		----------		----------
7				Total Sales:		3600		6600		4800

There could be many sheets for each process - each linked to the others so that any changes will reflect throughout the whole process. The spreadsheet for material requirements of the process would be linked to the cash flow and accounting system, as well as with the sales.

5 SUPPLY CHAIN NETWORKS

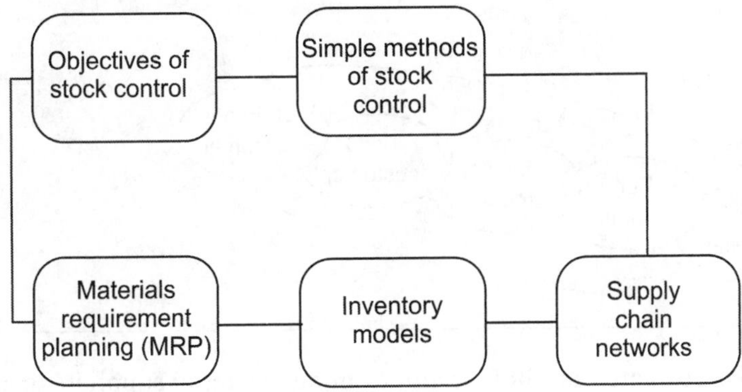

Definitions

> A **supply chain network** is an interconnecting group of organisations which relate to each other through linkages between the different processes and activities involved in producing products/services to the ultimate consumer.

Increasingly, organisations are recognising the need for and benefits of establishing **close links** with companies in the supply chain. Historically, businesses in the supply chain have operated relatively **independently** of one another to create value for an ultimate customer. **Independence was maintained** through holding buffer stocks, managing capacity and lead-times. There was very little control over other channel members, and no wider perspective on the system as a whole.

Market and competitive demands are now, however, **compressing lead times** and businesses are reducing inventories and excess capacity. Linkages between businesses in the supply chain must therefore become much tighter. This new condition is shown in the '**Integrated supply chain**' model (the second model in the following diagram).

Traditional and integrated supply chain models

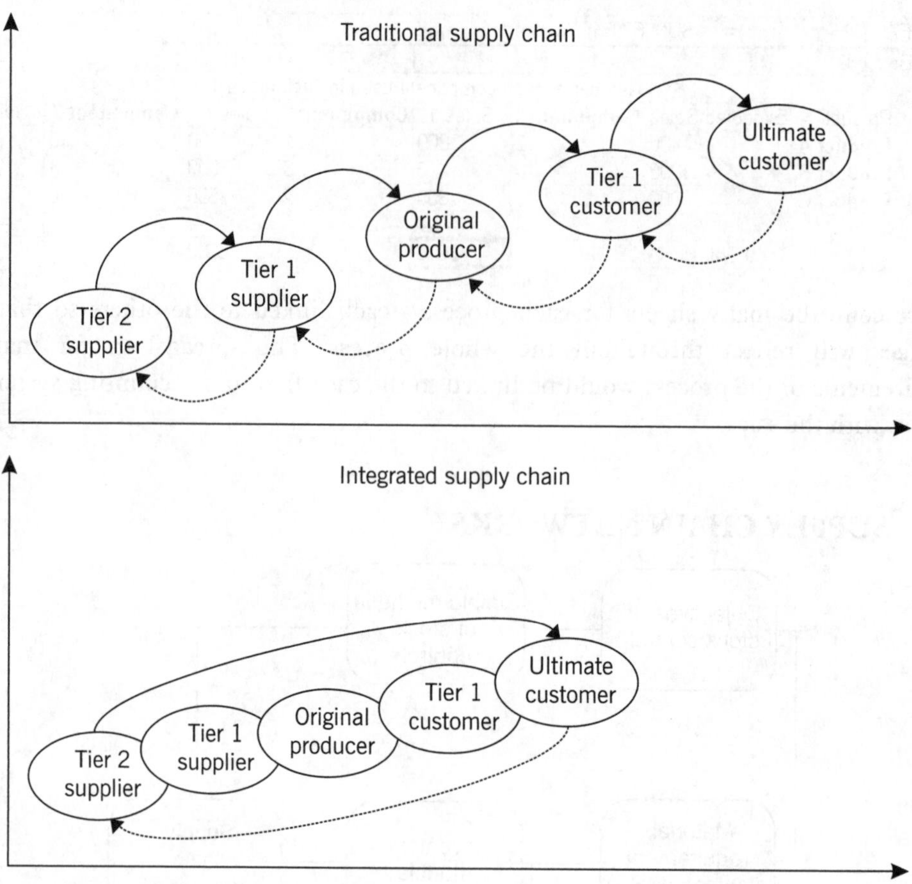

The aim is to co-ordinate the whole chain, from raw material suppliers to end customers. The chain should be considered as a **network** rather than a **pipeline** – a network of vendors support a network of customers, with third parties such as transport businesses helping to link the companies. In marketing channels, organisations have to manage the trade-off between the desire to remain **independent and autonomous,** and the need to be **interdependent and co-operative.**

Definitions

Independence: each channel member operates in isolation and is not affected by others, so maintaining a greater degree of control.

Interdependence: each channel member can affect the performance of others in the channel.

If the supplier 'knows' what its customers want, it does not necessarily have to guess, or wait until the customer places an order. It will be able to better plan its own delivery systems. The potential for using the **Internet** to allow customers and suppliers to acquire up-to-date information about forecasted needs and delivery schedules is a recent development, but one which is being used by an increasing number of companies. Some supply chain relationships are strengthened and communication facilitated through the use of **extranets** (intranets accessible to authorised outsiders).

5.2 Implications for supply chain management

Supply chain management involves optimising the activities of companies working together to produce goods and services. The trend towards closer links with suppliers and the development of supply chain networks has implications for supply chain management.

(a) **Reduction in customers served**. For the sake of focus, companies might concentrate resources on customers of high potential value.

(b) **Price and stock co-ordination**. Businesses co-ordinate their price and stock policies to avoid problems and bottlenecks caused by short-term surges in demand, such as promotions.

(c) **Linked computer systems**. Closer links may be facilitated through the use of Electronic Data Interchange (EDI), for example to allow paperless communication, billing and payment and through the use of a computer extranet.

(d) **Early supplier involvement** in product development and component design.

(e) **Logistics design**. Hewlett-Packard restructured its distribution system by enabling certain product components to be added at the distribution warehouse rather than at the central factory. For example user-manuals which are specific to the French market would be added at the French distribution centre.

(f) **Joint problem-solving**.

(g) **Supplier representative on site**.

The business case for supply chain management is the **benefit** to **all** the **participants** in terms of the performance objectives of speed, dependability and cost.

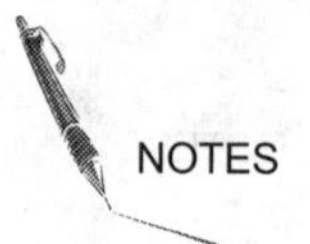

Chapter roundup

- Inventory control aims to minimise the costs of holding stocks whilst also ensuring that stocks are available when required.
- Simple methods of inventory control include demand re-order timing, perpetual inventory and periodic review
- Pareto analysis is a simple attention-directing technique highlighting the fact that the real value in anything may be concentrated in just a few areas.
- JIT is an approach to planning and control based on the idea that goods should be produced only when they are needed.
- The EOQ model sets out the relationship between demand, ordering costs and holding costs. The EOQ formula is

  $$Q=\sqrt{\frac{2CoD}{Ch}}$$

- The EOQ model has to be modified for batch production to take account of the production rate. The EBQ formula is

  $$Q=\sqrt{\frac{2CoD}{Ch(1-D/R)}}$$

- Where discounts are available it is necessary to compare the annual costs of buying the EOQ without discounts and the annual costs of buying quantities that earn discounts.
- There are various systems for improving operations management. Materials requirements planning (MRP I) is a computerised system for planning and ordering materials based on a master production schedule, bills of materials and stock level records.
- Materials requirements planning (MRP II) is an extension of MRP I, that integrates the manufacturing, materials requirements planning, engineering, finance and possibly marketing databases into a single planning control system database.

Quick quiz

1. State the objective of stock control.
2. Explain the demand reorder timing method of inventory control.
3. What is perpetual inventory?
4. What are the assumptions of the EOQ model?
5. Why is an amended EOQ formula (sometimes called the EBQ formula) necessary?
6. At what order quantity might costs be minimised when bulk discounts are available?
7. When is sensitivity analysis useful?

Answers to quick quiz

1 The objective of stock control is to maintain stock levels so that the total of the following costs is minimised.

- Holding costs
- Ordering costs
- Stock out costs

2 The demand reorder timing method of inventory control involves calculating a level of stock (reorder level) which will let management know that it is time to order more stock. If stock outs are to be avoided, a prudent reorder level is calculated as follows.

Reorder level = maximum delivery period × maximum usage

Management should ensure that occasional checks are performed to check that stock has not fallen to the reorder level.

The reorder quantity is the amount of stock that should be ordered when stock reaches the reorder level. The reorder quantity is the optimum stock level to be ordered when new stock is required.

3 A perpetual inventory involves knowing stock levels of all items at all times. A record is kept of all items showing receipts, issues and balances of stock.

4 The assumptions of the EOQ model are as follows.

(a) Demand is certain, constant and continuous over time.

(b) Supplier lead time is constant and certain or else there is instantaneous resupply.

(c) Customers' orders should be held while fresh stocks are awaited.

(d) No stock outs are permitted.

(e) All prices are constant and certain and there are no bulk purchase discounts.

(f) The cost of holding stock is proportional to the quantity of stock held.

5 An amended EOQ formula is sometimes necessary when resupply is gradual instead of instantaneous.

6 Costs might be minimised at:

(a) The pre-discount for EOQ level, so that a discount is not worthwhile; or

(b) The minimum order size necessary to earn the discount

7 Sensitivity analysis may be useful if there are doubts about the accuracy of the estimated ordering costs and holding costs or if there is uncertainty about the volume of demand.

NOTES

Answers to activities

1 (a)

	£
Rent £(8,000/40,000) (W1)	0.20
Delivery £(24,000/480,000) (W2)	0.05
Purchasing £((45,400 + 31,400)/480,000)	0.16
Stores £((75,600 + 34,800)/480,000)	0.23
Insurance £(4,800/40,000)	0.12
	0.76

Workings

1 Only enough space for 40,000 items needs to be rented, and only 40,000 items need to be insured.

2 Delivery and other charges are for a whole year's stock. 12 × 40,000 = 480,000.

(b) Many of the costs listed in Paragraphs 1.2 and 1.3 may also be relevant, particularly the cost of tying up £(2.50 + 0.76) × 40,000 = £130,400 of capital per month in stocks (interest paid or not earned, other more profitable uses of the money and so on), and the cost of any wastage of stock in storage. You should not have included production costs like materials handling, or wastage in the course of manufacturing.

Note that a more detailed analysis of all the figures given would also be useful. Part of these costs may not be connected with stock acquisition and holding.

2 Re-order level = 13 weeks × 4,000 kg
= 52,000 kg

Re-order quantity = 60,000 – (52,000 – 10,000) (W)
= 18,000 kg

Working

The firm will place an order when stocks reach 52,000 kg. It will use at least 5 weeks × 2,000 kg before the new delivery arrives and will therefore have up to (52,000 –10,000) kg left at this time. It can only hold 60,000 kg so the order must not take stock levels above this. In brief:

Re-order quantity = maximum stock – (re-order level – minimum usage in delivery period)

3 Co = £170
D = 600,000
Ch = £30 × 15% = £4.50

$$\text{EOQ} = \sqrt{\frac{2 \times 170 \times 600{,}000}{4.5}} = 6{,}733 \text{ units}$$

4 $$Q = \sqrt{\frac{2 \times 50 \times 2{,}000}{0.001(1 - 2{,}000/4{,}000)}}$$

= 20,000 units (giving a stock cycle of 10 weeks)

BPP LEARNING MEDIA

5 The total annual cost at the economic order quantity of 500 units is as follows.

	£
Purchases 4,000 × £96	384,000
Ordering costs £300 × (4,000/500)	2,400
Holding costs £96 × 10% × (500/2)	2,400
	388,800

The total annual cost at an order quantity of 1,000 units would be as follows.

	£
Purchases £384,000 × 92%	353,280
Ordering costs £300 × (4,000/1,000)	1,200
Holding costs £96 × 92% × 10% × (1,000/2)	4,416
	358,896

The company should order the item 1,000 units at a time, saving £(388,800 - 358,896) = £29,904 a year.

6 Make sure you do this using the spreadsheet facilities rather than just by looking through the table. You would have to use the spreadsheet facilities if you had 2,000 stock components to search through!

(a) A003, A009 and A017
(b) A005 and A009
(c) P036 and p227

Chapter 10 :

PROJECT MANAGEMENT TOOLS AND TECHNIQUES

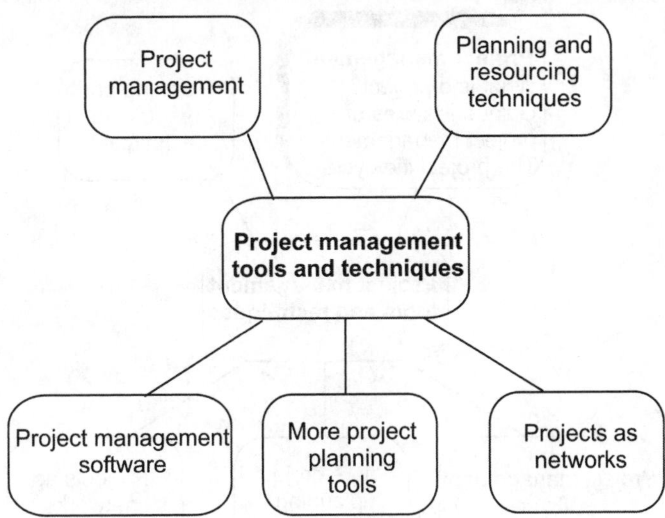

Introduction

We start this chapter by studying some of the management tools and techniques available to help the project management process. These tools and techniques are important so it is desirable that you understand and are able to apply the techniques covered.

Network analysis is a way of mapping out the activities in a project and showing the interrelationships. Timing is often crucial and we will see how to find the critical path, which is a sequence of those activities which, were any of them to run late, would mean that the whole project would be delayed. Activities may take more or less time than anticipated and so we will look at PERT, a method of dealing with such uncertainties. We will also look at Gantt charts, which can be used to estimate the amount or resources required for a project.

As with many tasks, project management activities are now usually carried out using computers. Specialist project management software packages are available but it is possible to perform all of the techniques using a spreadsheet package.

Your objectives

After completing this chapter you should:

(a) Understand the operational processes and techniques associated with project management

(b) Be able to plan a project

(c) Understand how to draw up a work breakdown structure

(d) Understand how to use some project planning tools eg, Gantt charts, network diagrams and resource histograms

(e) Be able to identify the critical path

(f) Be able to set up a basic project plan using either a spreadsheet or project management software

1 PROJECT MANAGEMENT

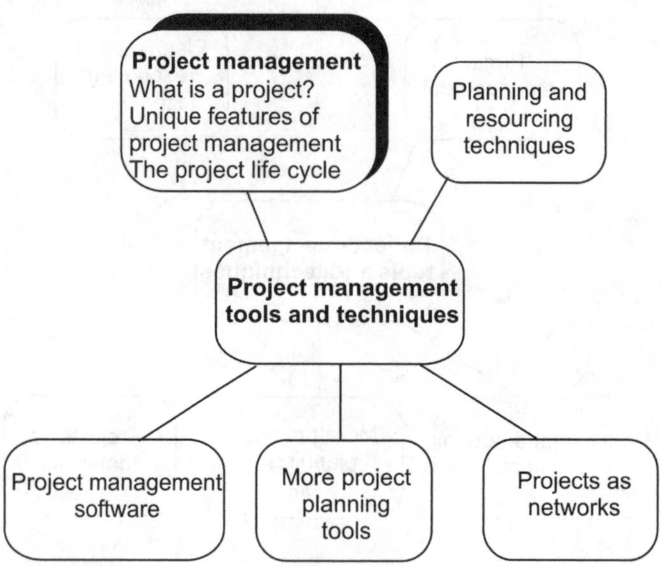

1.1 What is a project?

Definition

A **project** is 'an undertaking that has a beginning and an end and is carried out to meet established goals within cost, schedule and quality objectives' (Haynes, *Project Management*). Spinner (*Elements of Project Management*) defines a project as having the following characteristics.

(a) 'There is a specific start and end point.'

(b) 'There is a well-defined objective.'

(c) 'The project endeavour is to a degree unique and not repetitious.'

(d) 'The project usually contains costs and time schedules to produce a specified product or result.'

(e) 'A project cuts across many organisational and functional lines.'

Here are some examples of projects (as categorised by Dennis Lock).

(a) **Building and construction**. The construction of the Channel Tunnel was a project, which ended when the tunnel opened for normal service.

(b) In **manufacturing**, a project can be a feature of **job production**. For example, the manufacture of an oil rig, normally to precise specifications, involves co-

ordinating a large number of separate activities which will cease when the rig is finished.

(c) In **management**, a project can include the development of a new computer system, and mounting a major trade exhibition.

(d) **Research and development** is a tricky area.

(i) On the one hand, some research projects, such as the international project for mapping the human genome, have definite objectives but it is not always possible to keep them to a strict timetable, especially if new ground is to be broken.

(ii) Some research activities are open-ended however, and some projects will be suggested by the results of other pieces of research.

According to Dennis Lock, all projects involve the 'projection of ideas and activities into new endeavours. No project can ever be exactly the same as anything which has gone before.' The steps and tasks leading to completion can never be described accurately in advance. Therefore, according to Lock, 'the job of project management is to foresee as many dangers as possible, and to plan, organise and control activities so that they are avoided.'

1.2 Unique features of project management

Project managemen*t* is directed at an end. It thus has a limited objective within a limited time span.

As a result there are some special management problems.

(a) **Teambuilding**. The work is carried out by a team of people who may be assembled for just one project but who must be able to communicate effectively and immediately with each other.

(b) There can be many novel **expected problems**, each one of which should be resolved by careful design and planning prior to commencement of work.

(c) There can be many novel **unexpected problems**, particularly with a project working at the limits of existing and new technologies. There should be mechanisms within the project to enable these problems to be resolved during the time span of the project without detriment to the objective, the cost or the time span.

(d) **Delayed benefit**. There is normally no benefit until the work is finished. This can cause a strain on the eventual recipient who is faced with increasing expenditure for no immediate benefit, and who feels deprived until the benefit is achieved, even though it is often a major improvement.

(e) Contributions made by **specialists** are of differing importance at each stage. Assembling a team is made difficult by the tendency of specialists to regard their contribution as more important than other people's and not understand the inter-relationship of specialities in the context of the project.

(f) If the project involves several **parties with different interests** in the outcome, there might be disputes between them.

Why do projects go wrong? From all the above examples we can make the following deductions.

(a) Estimating the project duration can be difficult when it involves new technology or existing technology at its limits.

(b) Costs are often wildly underestimated by optimistic designers, particularly with new technology.

(c) Client specifications that are vague or continually changing make it impossible to adhere to the planned duration and cost.

(d) Project management teams often fail to exercise control under changing circumstances.

(e) When a project goes wrong in terms of time and money, the project management team and various contractors make optimistic comments and the client is committed politically to its completion, it becomes difficult to cancel as nobody dares make the decision.

There are, however, numerous instances of projects that have been completed on time, within budget and performing to specification. Typical examples can be found in the world of commercial property development when experienced teams can be assembled and the project is subject to the strict control of market forces. One example is the construction of a terminus for Channel Tunnel trains at London's Waterloo station: the building was complete some time before the commencement of Channel Tunnel passenger services.

The objectives of project management

The objectives, broadly speaking, of project management arise out of the deficiencies listed above.

(a) **Quality**. The end result should conform to the proper specification. In other words, the result should achieve what the project was supposed to do.

(b) **Budget**. The project should be completed without exceeding authorised expenditure.

(c) **Timescale**. The progress of the project must follow the planned process, so that the result is ready for use at the agreed date. As time is money, proper time management can help contain costs.

1.3 The project life cycle

It is possible to identify all the stages of a typical project, whether it is a construction project or system design project. The **project life cycle** has the following stages.

(a) Conceiving and defining the project

(b) Planning the project – this involves three stages, once the basic project objective and the underlying activities have been agreed.

(i) Break the project down into **manageable units**. This process establishes a **work breakdown structure**.

(ii) For each unit, **resources** needed must be estimated, broken down into materials, money and time.

(iii) The varying time and resource requirements of each **sub-unit** are then estimated, and co-ordinated into a planning framework to schedule and group the activities in the most appropriate way. **Gantt charts** and **network analysis** may be used here. **Costing** is also part of the project planning stage.

(c) Carrying out the plan (**project implementation**) and **control** – Project control charts use budget and schedule plans to report cumulative time and cost so that variances can be calculated.

(d) **Completing** and **evaluating** the project

Remember that, in all stages of the project, the most important guiding factors are quality (of design and conformance), cost and time.

2 PLANNING AND RESOURCING TECHNIQUES

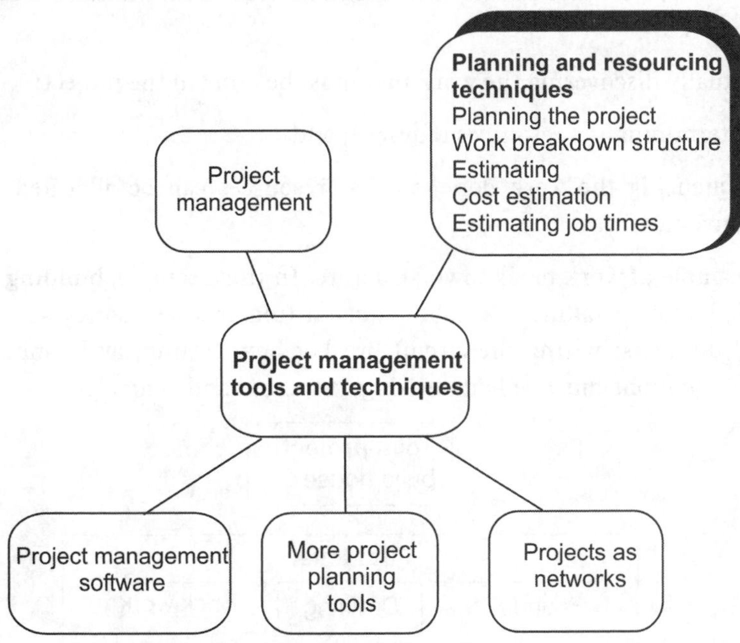

2.1 Planning the project

Different people suggest various ways of planning a project. We are going to use the following steps to explain the process:

(a) **Analyse the project.** The project is broken down into its constituent tasks or activities. The way in which these activities relate to each other is examined eg, which activities cannot be undertaken until some previous activity or activities are complete?

(b) **Estimate the time and costs of each activity.** The amount of time that each activity will take is estimated, and where appropriate the associated costs are estimated.

(c) **Draw the network.** The sequence of activities is shown in a diagrammatic form called the 'network diagram'.

(d) **Locate the critical path.** This is the chain of events that determines how long the overall project will take. Any delay to an activity on the critical path will delay the project as a whole; delays to other activities may not affect the overall timetable for completion. That is the distinction between critical and non-critical activities.

(e) **Schedule the project.** Determine the chain of events that leads to the most efficient and cost effective schedule.

(f) **Monitor and control the progress of the project.** This implies careful attention to the schedule and any other progress charts that have been drawn up so that we can monitor actual progress in the light of planned achievement.

(g) **Revise the plan.** The plan may need to be modified to take account of problems that occur during the progress of the project.

2.2 Work breakdown structure

Breaking down a project into phases or stages (*work breakdown structure*) is often the best way of:

(a) actually discovering the work that must be done in the project;

(b) determining the resources required; and

(c) sequencing the work done, so that resources can be allocated in the most convenient way.

Here is an example of work breakdown structure. In this example, building a house can be sub-divided into installing the cable runs; fitting the accessories such as sockets, switches and dimmers; wiring the circuit breaker box; testing; and connecting to the mains. The foundations must be laid out, dug, inspected and concreted.

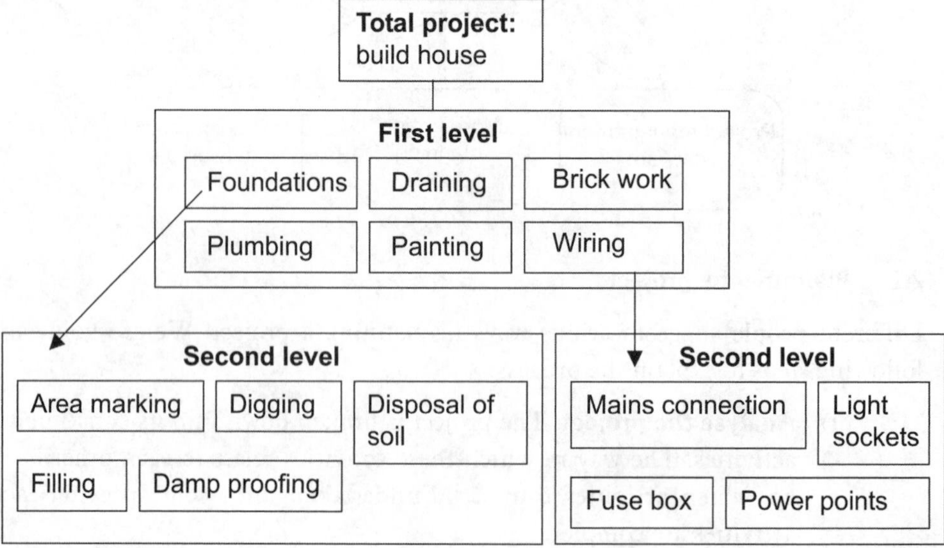

Figure 10.1: Example work breakdown structure

The process of work breakdown continues until the smallest possible sub-unit is reached. Digging the foundations for example would be analysed so that number of labour hours needed, and hence the cost, could be determined.

Activity 1 **(20 minutes)**

Draw up a work breakdown structure for the recruitment of a new person to fill a vacant post.

2.3 Estimating

Dennis Lock writes that 'an accurate estimate of project costs provides a proper basis for management control.'

Some industries use different classifications to denote the accuracy of estimates.

(a) **Ball-park estimates** are made before a project starts. These are very rough indeed and might be accurate to within 25%.

(b) **Comparative estimates** are made if the project under consideration has some similarities with previous ones. Accuracy will depend, of course, on how similar the project is to the projects it is compared with. Lock suggests that it is possible to be accurate to within 15%.

(c) **Feasibility estimates** (probably accurate to within 10%) arise from preliminary aspects of the design. Building companies use feasibility estimates.

(d) **Definitive estimates** (accurate to within 5%) are only made when *all* the design work has been done.

Any estimate must be accompanied by a proviso detailing its expected accuracy. However, project estimation inevitably involves fallible guesswork. It is unreasonable to expect exact accuracy, but the project manager should be able to keep within estimates, particularly for projects:

(a) where there is no 'margin of safety'
(b) with tight profit margins.

Activity 2 **(10 minutes)**

Springfield Builders has agreed to do some building work at Gowley House, a stately home in Hertfordshire. Springfield Builders are charging the owners of Gowley House the sum of £100,000. They estimate that the job will cost them £80,000, plus an estimated profit of £20,000. What would be the effect on profit of cost estimating errors of:

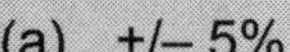

(a) +/– 5%
(b) +/– 10%
(c) +/– 20%

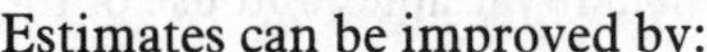

Estimates can be improved by:

(a) Learning from past mistakes

(b) Obtaining sufficient design information

(c) Ensuring as detailed a specification as possible from the customer, and

(d) Properly analysing the job into its constituent units, especially where labour costs are concerned.

2.4 Cost estimation

The work breakdown structure (WBS) can be used in devising estimates.

From the WBS (and the families of items) it is possible to compile a complete list of every item that is going to attract expenditure. Checklists can be used to ensure that all factors (technical, legal, planning) can be taken into account. (Checklists can also include factors such as incidental processes, eg paint spraying.)

Costs should be analysed into these component parts.

(a) Direct costs of a project include labour, raw materials and sub-components.

(b) Project overhead costs include heating, lighting and so forth, and can be fixed and/or variable.

In some projects, a large element of the work might be fixed costs. For example, a building company is unlikely to buy a brand new crane for every house it builds. For systems design work, a company may have developed a set of unique design tools for modelling work. The cost of such items might be spread over individual projects according to some measure. For example, an element of a crane's depreciation charge might be charged to a project.

Estimation forms can be designed to be based on the work breakdown structure, so that by each work unit number, there are columns for labour, materials and so forth.

Materials require two types of estimate.

(a) **Total materials cost**. Design engineers should prepare provisional lists of materials required for each task. The purchasing department should provide some idea of the costs.

(b) **Lead times for receipt**. Failure to receive materials on time can result in unexpected delay.

Estimating problems arise out of the following.

(a) **Contingencies**. Projects can be delayed because of design errors, production mistakes, material and component failures. An allowance is sometimes built in. This contingency allowance can be estimated by reviewing problems in previous projects.

(b) **Additional work** can be included in the contract price on a 'provisional basis'.

(c) **Escalation** (increases in prices) will increase costs over the contract's life. This might also be built into the contract.

2.5 Estimating job times

In many projects, labour costs can be one of the most significant variables and use of the labour resource is critical to keeping within budget.

Many activities in the project depend on each other. In other words, job B may need to be done before job C. For example, the foundations of a house are *always* laid before the roof is constructed.

The project manager may have to cope with constraints on the supply of labour. For example, a computer project manager may have to compete with other project managers for the availability of certain skilled staff.

The project manager needs to schedule the activities in the most efficient way, given:

(a) the dependency of some activities on others; and
(b) the fact that some resources will not be available at the ideal time.

The project manager will have been given a broad-brush time estimation. For this you need:

(a) the duration of each sub-unit;
(b) the earliest time work in a particular unit must be started; and
(c) the latest time it must be started.

Some use a mathematical model to estimate the time of a particular activity for project planning purposes. A formula based on the *normal distribution* can be used.

t_o = the most optimistic duration (shortest time)
t_m = the most likely duration
t_p = the most pessimistic duration (longest time)

The estimated time, $t_e = \dfrac{t_o + 4t_m + t_p}{6}$

Not every case will be suitable for modelling in this way. Many would dispute that this type of approach can be used, as the normal distribution is not appropriate.

3 PROJECTS AS NETWORKS

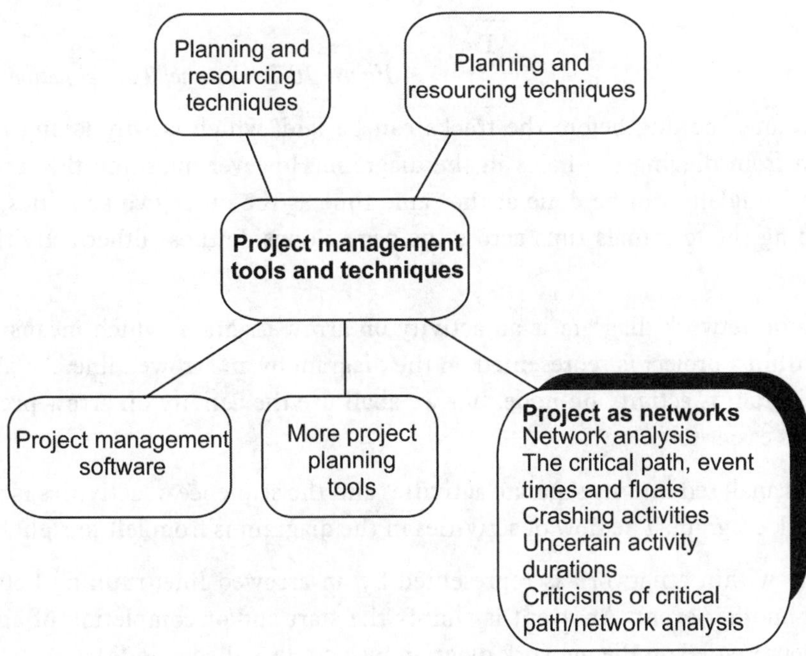

3.1 Network analysis

Network analysis is a technique for planning and controlling large projects, such as construction work, research and development projects or the computerisation of

business systems. Network analysis helps managers to plan when to start various tasks, to allocate resources so that the tasks can be carried out within schedule, to monitor actual progress and to find out when control action is needed to prevent a delay in completion of the project. The events and activities making up the whole project are represented in the form of a diagram or chart. Network analysis is sometimes called critical path analysis (CPA) or critical path method (CPM).

Definition

Network analysis is basically concerned with the deployment of available resources for the completion of a complex task.

Drawing a network diagram: the activity on arrow presentation

Here is an example of a network for building the Channel Tunnel, with the whole project simplified to just three activities.

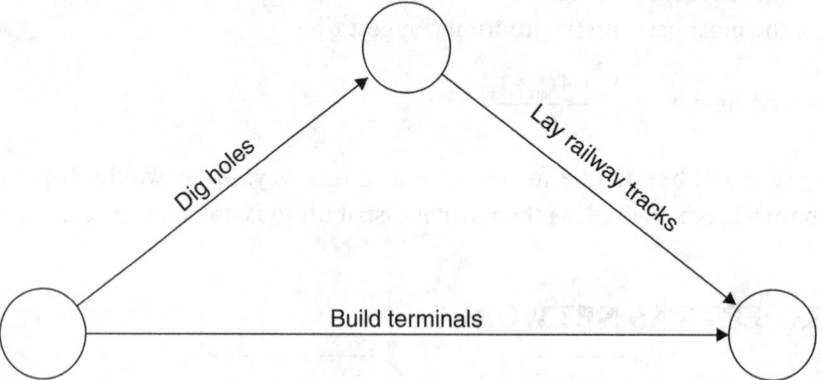

Figure 10.2: Channel Tunnel network diagram

The holes must be dug before the tracks can be laid, which is why laying the tracks follows on from digging the holes in the diagram. However, building the terminals in France and England can be done at the same time as the other two activities, which is why building the terminals runs across the page alongside those other activities in the diagram.

This form of network diagram is an activity on arrow diagram, which means that each activity within a project is represented on the diagram by an arrowed line. An alternative form of diagram is activity on node, but we shall use the activity on arrow presentation because it is easier to follow.

A project is analysed into its separate activities and the sequence of activities is presented in a network diagram. The flow of activities in the diagram is from left to right.

An activity within a network is represented by an arrowed line, running between one event and another event. An event is simply the start and/or completion of an activity, which is represented on the network diagram by a circle (called a **node**).

Let us suppose that in a certain project there are two activities A and B, and activity B cannot be started until activity A is completed. Activity A might be building the walls of a house, and activity B might be putting the roof on. This would be represented as follows.

Event Activity Event Activity Event

(1) —— A —— (2) —— B —— (3)

The rule is that an activity cannot start until all activities leading into the event at its start have been completed.

Events are usually numbered, just to identify them. In this example, event 1 is the start of Activity A, event 3 is the completion of Activity B, and event 2 is both the completion of A and the start of B.

Let us now suppose that another project includes three activities, C, D and E. Neither activity D nor E can start until C is completed, but D and E could be done simultaneously if required. This would be represented as follows.

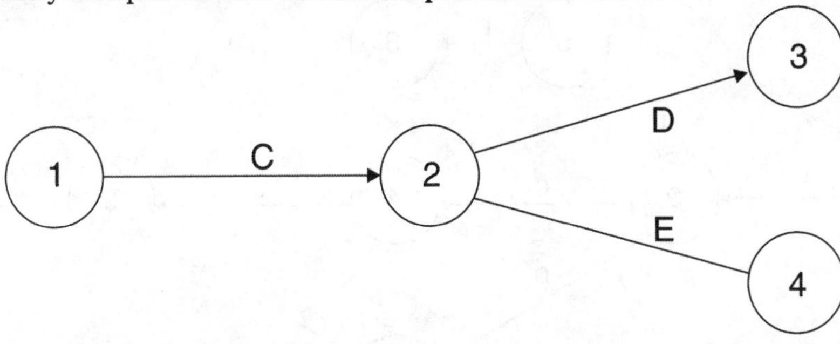

In this diagram, event 2 represents the point when C is completed and also the point when D and E can start, so the diagram clearly shows that D and E must follow C.

A third possibility is that an activity cannot start until two or more activities have been completed. If H cannot start until F and G are both complete, then we would represent the situation like this.

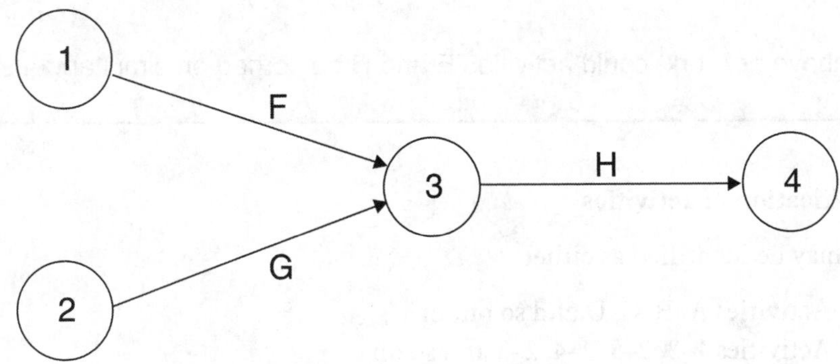

Figure 10.3: Network diagrams

EXAMPLE: NETWORK DIAGRAMS

Draw the network for the following project to build a factory.

Activity		*Preceding activity*
A:	lay foundations	–
B:	build walls	A
C:	lay drains	A
D:	install electricity cables	A
E:	fit window frames	B
F:	fit door frames	B
G:	fit windows	E

Activity		*Preceding activity*
H:	fit doors	F
I:	plaster inside walls	G,H
J:	lay floor	C
K:	fit power outlets	D
L:	install machines	I, J, K

SOLUTION

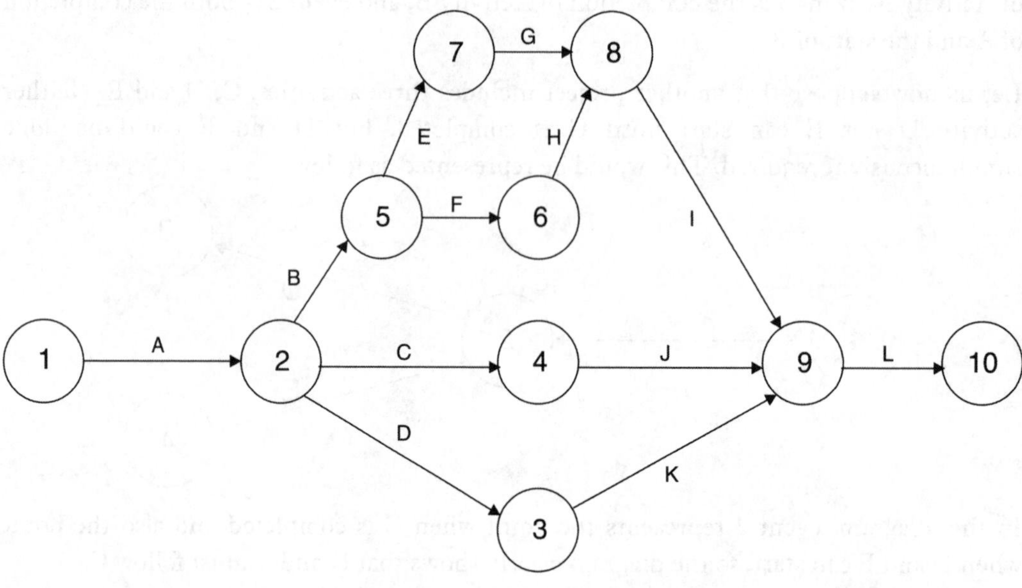

Activity 3 **(5 minutes)**

In the above network, could activities E and H be carried on simultaneously?

The identification of activities

Activities may be identified as either:

(a) Activities A, B, C, D and so on; or
(b) Activities 1–2, 2–5, 2–4, 2–3 and so on.

Dummy activities

It is a convention in network analysis that two activities are not drawn between the same events. The convention makes diagrams clearer.

To avoid having two activities running between the same events, we use a dummy activity. A dummy activity takes no time and no resources to complete.

Definition

> A **dummy activity** is used in network analysis when two activities could start at the same time and finish at the same time too. It is represented by a broken arrowed line.

For example, suppose that the sequence of activities in a project to install a computer system is as follows.

Activity		*Preceding Activity*
A:	install computer	–
B:	write programs	A
C:	hire trained staff	A
D:	test system	B, C

In theory, we could draw the network as follows.

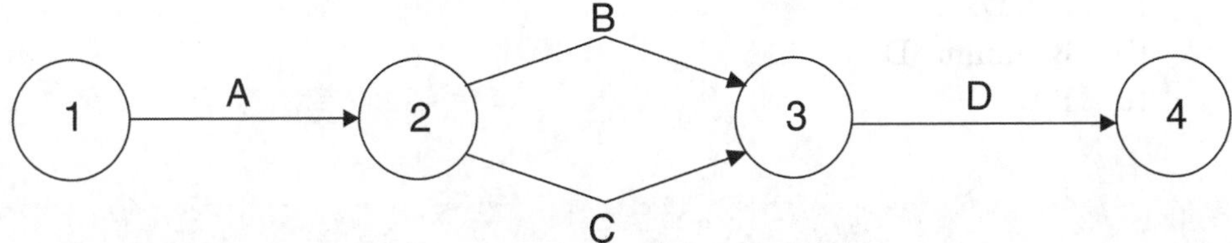

By convention, this would be incorrect. Two separate activities must not start and end with the same events. The correct representation is shown below.

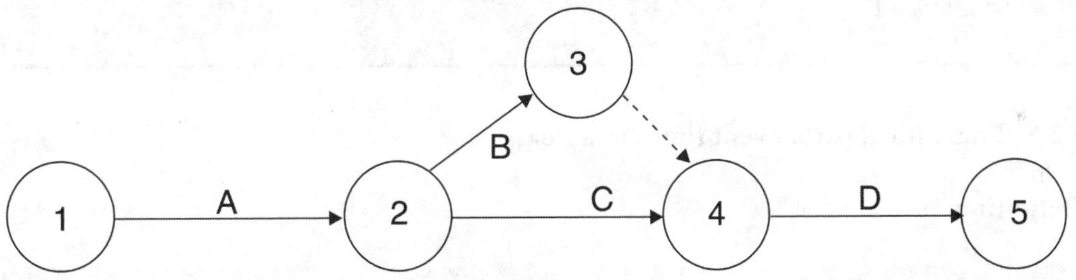

Sometimes it is necessary to use a dummy activity not just to comply with the convention, but to preserve the basic logic of the network.

Consider the following example of a project to install a new office telephone system.

Activity		*Preceding Activity*
A:	buy equipment	–
B:	allocate extension numbers	–
C:	install switchboard	A
D:	install wiring	B, C
E:	print office directory	B

The project is finished when both D and E are complete.

The problem arises because D can only start when both B and C have been finished, whereas E is only required to follow B. The only way to draw the network is to use a dummy activity.

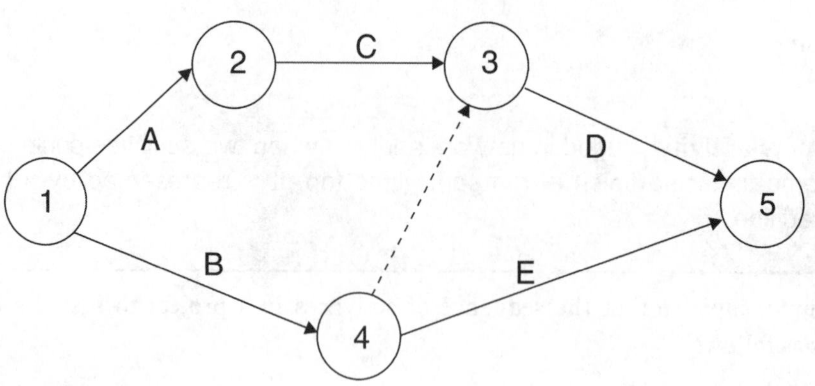

Paths through the network

Any network can be analysed into a number of different paths or routes. A path is simply a sequence of activities from the start to the end of the network. In the example above, there are just three paths.

(a) A C D;
(b) B Dummy D;
(c) B E.

Activity 4 **(5 minutes)**

List the paths through the network in the earlier example to build a factory with activities A – L.

3.2 The critical path, event times and floats

Definition

The **critical path** is the path through the network with the greatest total duration

The time needed to complete each individual activity in a project must be estimated. This time is shown on the network above or below the line representing the activity. The duration of the whole project will be fixed by the time taken to complete the path through the network with the greatest total duration. This path is called the *critical path* and activities on it are known as *critical activities*. A network can have more than one critical path, if several paths tie for the greatest duration.

Activities on the critical path must be started and completed on time, otherwise the total project time will be extended. The method of finding the critical path is illustrated in the example below.

EXAMPLE: THE CRITICAL PATH

The following activities comprise a project to renovate a block of flats.

Activity	*Preceding Activity*	*Duration (weeks)*
A: replace windows in lounges	–	5
B: rewire	–	4
C: replaster walls of lounges	A	2
D: fit lights in lounges	B	1
E: decorate bedrooms	B	5
F: install plumbing	B	5
G: decorate lounges	C,D	4
H: decorate kitchens	F	3
I: decorate bathrooms	F	2

(a) What are the paths through the network?
(b) What is the critical path and what is its duration?

SOLUTION

The first step in the solution is to draw the network diagram, with the time for each activity shown.

A network should have just one start node and one completion node, and in the diagram below, this is achieved by introducing a dummy activity after activity I. Dummy activities always have zero duration.

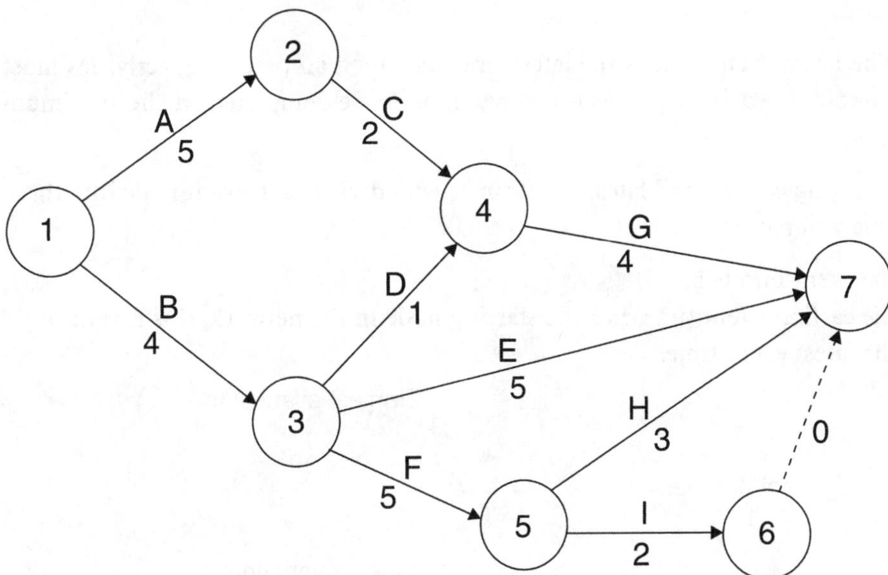

We could list the paths through the network and their durations as follows.

Path	*Duration (weeks)*	
A C G	(5 + 2 + 4)	11
B D G	(4 + 1 + 4)	9
B E	(4 + 5)	9
B F H	(4 + 5+ 3)	12
B F I Dummy	(4 + 5 + 2 + 0)	11

The critical path is the longest path, BFH, with a duration of twelve weeks. This is the minimum time needed to complete the project. Note that a network may have more than one critical path, if two or more paths have equal highest durations.

Activity 5 **(10 minutes)**

The following activities comprise a project to agree a price for some land to be bought for development.

Activity		*Preceded by*	*Duration Days*
P:	get survey done	–	4
Q:	draw up plans	–	7
R:	estimate cost of building work	Q	2
S:	get tenders for site preparation work	P	9
T:	negotiate price	R, S	3

Within how many days could the whole project be completed?

Listing paths through the network in this way is easy for small networks, but it becomes tedious for bigger and more complex networks.

Earliest event times and latest event times

Another way to find the critical path is to include earliest times and latest times for each event, showing them on the network diagram.

(a) The earliest event time is the earliest time that any subsequent activities can start.

(b) The latest event time is the latest time by which all preceding activities must be completed if the project as a whole is to be completed in the minimum time.

One way of showing earliest and latest event times is to divide each event node into three sections. These will record:

(a) the event number;
(b) the earliest event time. For the starting node in the network, this is time 0;
(c) the latest event time.

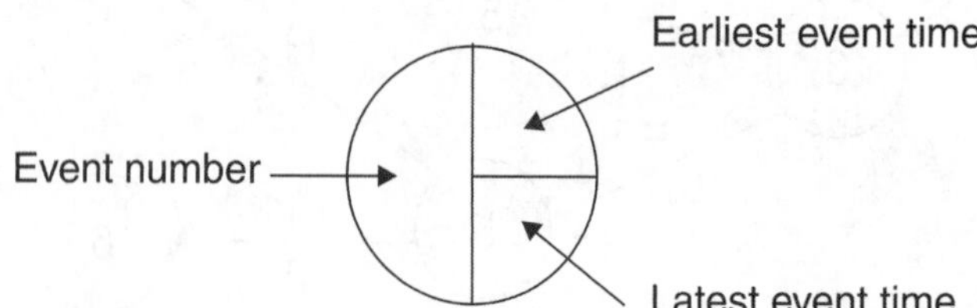

Earliest event times

The next step is to calculate the earliest event times. Always start at event 1 with its earliest starting time of 0. We will continue the previous example to show how times are calculated.

Work from left to right through the diagram calculating the earliest time that the next activity following the event can start. For example, the earliest event time at event 2 is the earliest time activity C can start. This is week 0 + 5 = 5. Similarly, the earliest event time at event 3 is the earliest time D, E and F can start, which is week 0 + 4 = 4, and the

earliest time at event 5 is the earliest time activities H and I can start, which is 4 + 5 = week 9.

A slight problem occurs where more than one activity ends at the same node. For example, event 4 is the completion node for activities C and D. Activity G cannot start until both C and D are complete, therefore the earliest event time at event 4 is the higher of:

(a) Earliest event time, event 2 + duration of C = 5 + 2 = 7 weeks;
(b) Earliest event time, event 3 + duration of D = 4 + 1 = 5 weeks.

The earliest event time at event 4 is seven weeks.

Similarly, the earliest event time at event 7 is the highest of:

Earliest event time, event 3 + duration of E	=	4 + 5 = 9
Earliest event time, event 4 + duration of G	=	7 + 4 = 11
Earliest event time, event 5 + duration of H	=	9 + 3 = 12
Earliest event time, event 6 + duration of dummy activity	=	11 + 0 = 11

The highest value is twelve weeks. This also means that the minimum completion time for the entire project is twelve weeks.

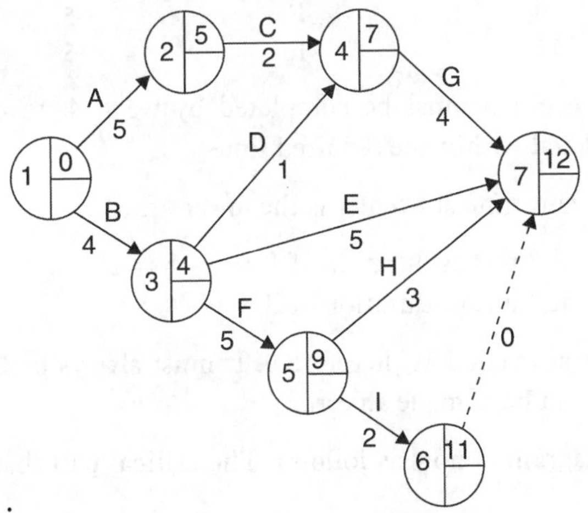

Activity 6 **(5 minutes)**

If activity C had taken four weeks, which earliest event times would have been affected, and what would they have changed to?

Latest event times

The next step is to calculate the latest event times. These are the latest times at which each event can occur if the project as a whole is to be completed in the shortest possible time, twelve weeks. The latest event time at the final event must be the same as the earliest event time, which in this example is twelve weeks.

Work from right to left through the diagram calculating the latest time at which each activity can start, if it is to be completed by the latest event time of the event at its end.

The latest event time for:

(a) Event 4 is 12 – 4 = week 8;
(b) Event 6 is 12 – 0 = week 12;
(c) Event 2 is 8 – 2 = week 6.

Event 5 might cause difficulties as two activities, H and I lead back to it.

(a) Activity H must be completed by week 12, and so must start at week 9.
(b) Activity I must also be completed by week 12, and so must start at week 10.

The latest event time at node 5 is the earlier of week 9 or week 10, that is, week 9. All activities leading up to node 5, which in this case is just F, must be completed by week 9 so that both H and I can be completed by week 12.

The latest event time at event 3 is calculated in the same way. It is the earliest time which enables all subsequent activities to be completed within the required time. Thus, at event 3, we have the following.

Subsequent event	*Latest time of that event (a)*	*Intermediate activity*	*Duration of the activity (b)*	*Required event time at event 3 (a) – (b)*
4	8	D	1	7
5	9	F	5	4
7	12	E	5	7

All activities before event 3 must be completed by week 4, to enable all subsequent activities to be completed within the required time.

Similarly, the latest event time at event 1 is the lower of:

Latest event time, event 2 minus duration of A = 6 – 5 = 1
Latest event time, event 3 minus duration of B = 4 – 4 = 0

The latest event time at event 1 is therefore 0. It must always be 0. If your calculations give any other value, you have made an error.

The final network diagram is now as follows. The critical path has been indicated by a double line.

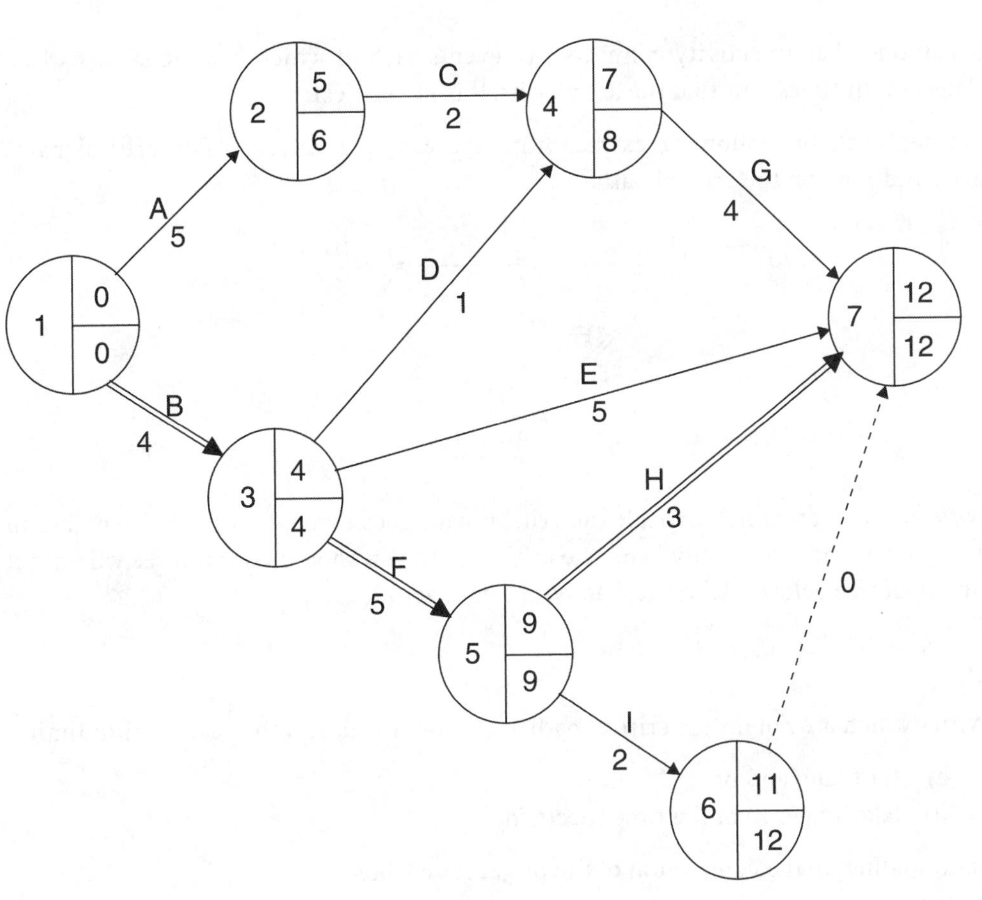

Finding the critical path

Critical activities are those activities which must be started on time, otherwise the total project time will be increased. It follows that each event on the critical path must have the same earliest and latest times. The critical path for the above network is therefore B F H (events 1,3,5,7). An event with the same earliest and latest times is called a **critical event.**

Activity 7 **(10 minutes)**

The following activities comprise a project to make a film.

Activity	*Preceded by*	*Duration* Weeks
J: negotiate distribution	–	6
K: arrange publicity	J	5
L: write screenplay	–	3
M: hire cast and crew	L	5
N: shoot and edit	M, Q	4
P: design sets	L	2
Q: build sets	P	1

What are the earliest and latest event times of the event at the end of activity P?

You may find that an activity connects two events each of which has the same earliest and latest event times, but that the activity itself is not critical.

For example, in the following extract from the example entitled 'The critical path', events 3 and 7 are on the critical path.

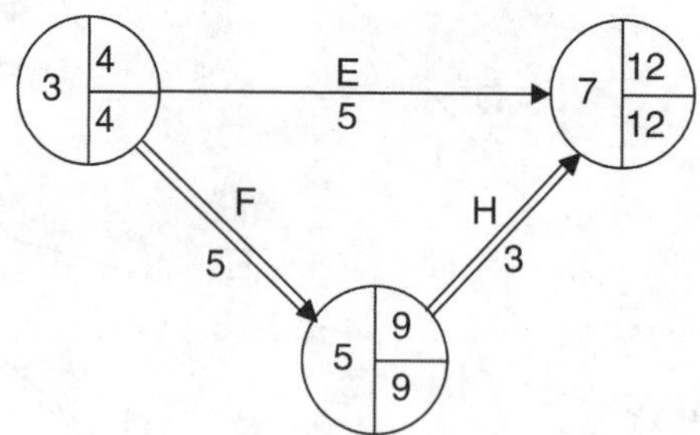

Activity E, however, is not critical: the critical path goes through event 5. If you are in doubt as to whether an activity is on the critical path you should check to see whether it has any float (see below). All critical activities have zero float.

Float

Activities which are not on the critical path are non–critical, and they can, within limits:

(a) start late; and/or
(b) take longer than the time specified,

without holding up the completion of the project as a whole.

The float for any activity is the amount of time by which its duration could be extended up to the point where it would become critical. This is the same as the amount of time by which its duration could be extended without affecting the total project time.

The effect on the time available for preceding and subsequent activities is ignored. The total float for an activity is therefore equal to its latest finishing time minus its earliest starting time minus its duration.

For example, look at activity C in the above example to renovate a block of flats. This must be completed by week 8 if the total project time is not to be extended. It cannot be started until week 5 at the earliest, but as it only takes two weeks there is one spare week available. The float for activity C is (8 – 5 – 2) = 1 week.

Activity 8 **(5 minutes)**

What are the floats for activities D and G in the above example?

3.3 Crashing activities

With some projects, it may be possible, at extra expense, to cut the overall project time by assigning extra labour or equipment to various activities.

The critical path is the 'bottleneck route'. Only by finding ways to shorten jobs along the critical path can the overall project time be reduced.

(a) The time required to perform **non-critical jobs** is **irrelevant** in terms of affecting the total project time.

(b) This means that the costly practice of '**crashing**' non-critical jobs to complete them more quickly is an unnecessary waste of expense; yet it can all happen too easily in practice.

(c) However, if some means is found to reduce the time required to complete activities along the critical path, not only would the **total project time be shortened,** but also the **critical path itself might shift** and some **previously non-critical jobs** may now **become critical.**

Network analysis can be used to calculate by how much time the **minimum completion time for a project can be shortened.** It is then possible to assess whether the cost of shortening activity durations is worth the extra benefits, whatever these might be.

EXAMPLE: CRASH TIMES

Digitalis Limited is planning the annual shutdown of its furnace for maintenance purposes. The shutdown has six phases and the estimated normal times and costs are as follows.

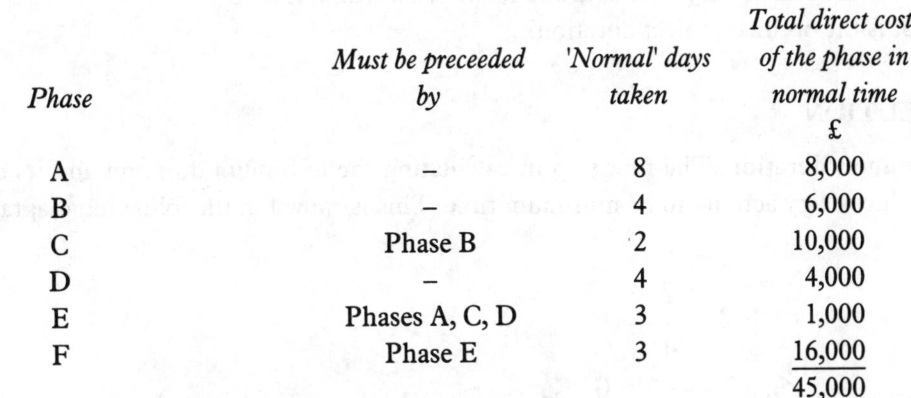

Phase	*Must be preceeded by*	*'Normal' days taken*	*Total direct costs of the phase in normal time*
			£
A	–	8	8,000
B	–	4	6,000
C	Phase B	2	10,000
D	–	4	4,000
E	Phases A, C, D	3	1,000
F	Phase E	3	16,000
			45,000

The network might look like this (some variations in the layout are possible).

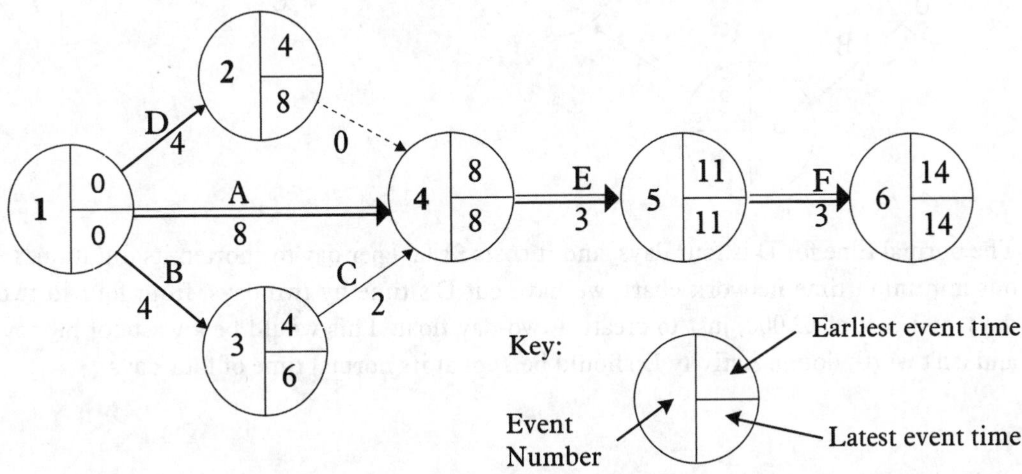

Note. A dummy activity has been introduced since A and D can both start at time 0, and E cannot start until both A and D are completed.

Suppose that the chief engineer has suggested that the total time could be reduced by putting more resources into each phase of the project. This would increase the direct costs of the maintenance programme, but in respect of each day saved in the total project time, there would be some elimination of lost business, which occurs whenever the furnace is shut down. This loss of business has been estimated by the sales manager to be £5,000 per day, measured in contribution terms.

Crash times and costs are as follows.

Phase	*'Normal' days taken*	*Minimum days required in 'crash' programme*	*Extra direct costs, per day saved*
			£
A	8	4	3,000
B	4	3	1,000
C	2	1	4,000
D	4	2	1,000
E	3	2	2,000
F	3	1	6,000

What is the minimum project duration, and what would it cost?
What is the optimal project duration?

SOLUTION

Minimum duration. The first step in calculating the minimum duration and its cost is to reduce every activity to its minimum time. This is shown in the following diagram.

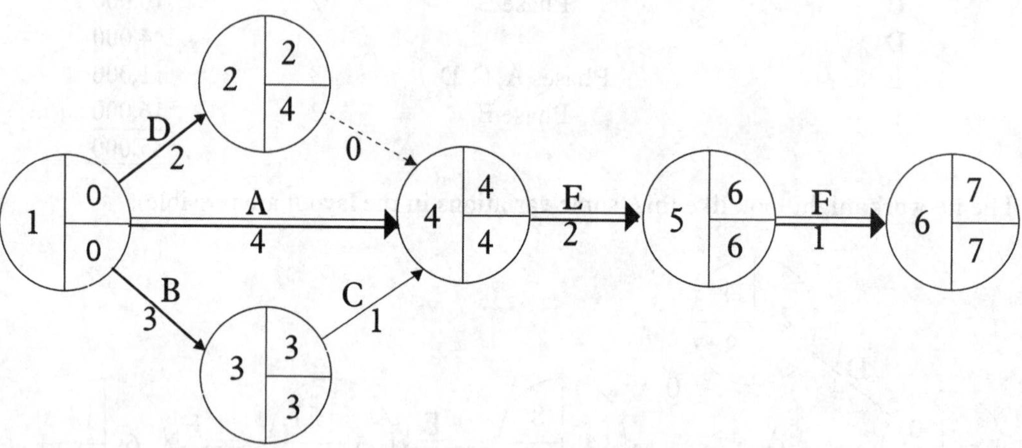

The normal time for D is four days, and it costs £1,000 per day to shorten its duration. In our minimum time network chart, we have cut D's time by two days, from four to two days, at a cost of £2,000, just to create a two-day float. This would be a waste of money, and isn't worth doing. Activity D should be kept at its normal time of four days.

BPP LEARNING MEDIA

The costs of the minimum time shutdown would be as follows.

Activity	*Duration* Days		*Basic cost*	*Extra cost of crashing the duration*	*Total cost*
			£	£	£
A	4	(minimum)	8,000	12,000	20,000
B	3	(minimum)	6,000	1,000	7,000
C	1	(minimum)	10,000	4,000	14,000
D	4	(normal)	4,000	-	4,000
E	2	(minimum)	1,000	2,000	3,000
F	1	(minimum)	16,000	12,000	28,000
			45,000	31,000	76,000

It is important to remember that when project times are crashed, float should be eliminated as much as possible in order to save the additional costs of unnecessarily crashing non-critical activities. (The benefits would be nil, therefore the costs of crashing such non-critical activities cannot be justified.)

The optimal shutdown time

The minimum project duration in the example shown above is seven days, compared to a 'normal' time of fourteen days. The benefits from shortening the total project time may be measured in terms of the extra £5,000 per day in contribution that would be earned if the furnace were open and working.

So how much would it cost to reduce the shutdown time, and would the extra cost be justified by these benefits of £5,000 per day saved?

There are two approaches to deciding what the optimal time should be.

(a) To consider, day by day, whether it is worth reducing the project time any further.

(b) To calculate the minimum project time first, and then to consider whether any increase in time above the minimum would save more in costs than the benefits from keeping the time reduced.

In the solution which follows, method (b) is used.

Seven days can be saved by crashing the project duration from fourteen to seven days, and this would result in an additional contribution of (£5,000 per day) £35,000. The extra costs of reducing the shutdown to seven days are £31,000, and so shutting down for seven days rather than fourteen days would improve contribution and profits by £4,000.

But is seven days the optimal shut down period? Would it be better to shut down for 8, 9, 10, 11, 12 or 13 days instead?

We can now work up from a minimum time of seven days, one day at a time, and work out the cost savings and benefits forgone, by increasing the shutdown period.

(a) **Eight-day shutdown**. Starting from the minimum shutdown time of seven days, an eight-day shutdown would mean that we could do one of the following.

			Savings
			£
(i)	Add 1 day to A and add 1 day to B	(3,000 + 1,000)	4,000
(ii)	Add 1 day to A and add 1 day to C	(3,000 + 4,000)	7,000
(iii)	Add 1 day to E		2,000
(iv)	Add 1 day to F		6,000

It would be best to save one day on A (increasing its duration to five days) and also save one day on C, increasing its duration to the 'normal' two days. Cost savings would be £7,000, which exceed the contribution earned from keeping the project time reduced to seven days (£5,000). An eight-day shutdown would therefore improve profits by £2,000 over a seven-day shutdown.

(b) **Nine-day shutdown**. Activity C is now at its normal time, and so the options for a nine-day shutdown instead of an eight-day shutdown are as follows.

		Savings
		£
(i)	Add 1 day to A and add 1 day to B	4,000
(ii)	Add 1 day to E	2,000
(iii)	Add 1 day to F	6,000

It is worth adding to the time to complete F, saving £6,000, because this exceeds the contribution of £5,000 per day from the shorter shutdown.

A nine-day shutdown is therefore more profitable than an eight-day shutdown, by £1,000. Activity F would now be two days long.

(c) **10-day shutdown**. For exactly the same reason, a ten-day shutdown would be more profitable than a nine-day shutdown by £1,000. Activity F would now have its normal duration of three days.

(d) **11-day shutdown**. Referring back to the table in (b), you should be able to see that making the shutdown any longer than ten days would reduce contribution and profit, because the savings from adding a day to A and B would be less than the contribution forgone of £5,000 per day.

We have now reached our optimal solution, which is a 10-day shutdown.

Activity	*Duration*		*Cost*	
	Days		£	£
A	5	(8,000 + 9,000)	17,000	
B	3	(6,000 + 1,000)	7,000	
C	2		10,000	
D	4		4,000	
E	2	(1,000 + 2,000)	3,000	
F	3		16,000	
			57,000	

Total duration of shutdown: ten days	
Saving in time, compared with normal time shutdown: four days	
Contribution saved, at £5,000 per day	20,000
Net cost of shutdown, compared with normal time shutdown	37,000

This shows a net saving of £8,000 on the direct costs of a normal time shutdown, which were £45,000.

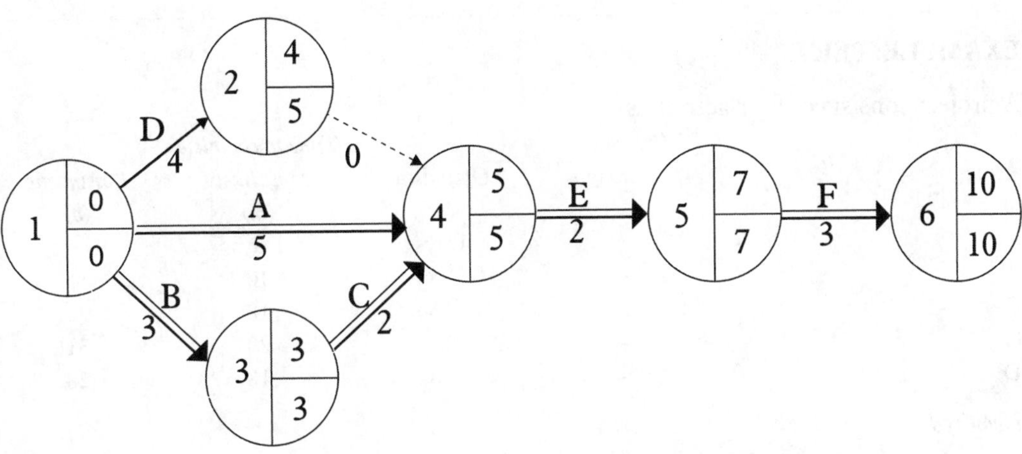

The project time would be ten days, and only activity D would have float (of one day).

3.4 Uncertain activity durations

Network problems may be complicated by uncertainty in the durations of individual activities. For example, building works can easily be delayed by bad weather.

Definition

> **PERT (project evaluation and review technique)** is a form of network analysis which takes account of uncertainty.

Using PERT, optimistic, most likely and pessimistic estimates of durations are made for each activity in the project. These estimates are converted into a mean duration and a variance, using the following formulae.

(a) Mean $\mu = \dfrac{a + 4m + b}{6}$

where a = optimistic estimate of activity duration
m = most likely estimate of activity duration
b = pessimistic estimate of activity duration

(b) Variance $\sigma^2 = \dfrac{1}{36}(b-a)^2$

The standard deviation, σ, is $\dfrac{1}{6}(b-a)$.

Once the mean duration and the standard deviation of durations have been calculated for each activity, we can find the critical path using the mean activity durations.

NOTES

EXAMPLE: PERT

A project consists of four activities.

Activity	*Preceding activity*	*Time to complete* Optimistic (a) Days	Most likely (m) Days	Pessimistic (b) Days
A	–	5	10	15
B	A	16	18	26
C	–	15	20	31
D	–	8	18	28

Required

Analyse the project using PERT.

SOLUTION

The mean duration for each activity is calculated by the formula $\frac{a+4m+b}{6}$

Activity	*a + 4m + b*	*Divided by 6* Days
A	5 + 40 + 15 = 60	10
B	16 + 72 + 26 = 114	19
C	15 + 80 + 31 = 126	21
D	8 + 72 + 28 = 108	18

The standard deviation of durations for each activity is calculated by the formula $\frac{b-a}{6}$

Activity	*b − a*	*Divided by six* Days
A	15 – 5 = 10	1.67
B	26 – 16 = 10	1.67
C	31 – 15 = 16	2.67
D	28 – 8 = 20	3.33

The network can be drawn using the mean durations.

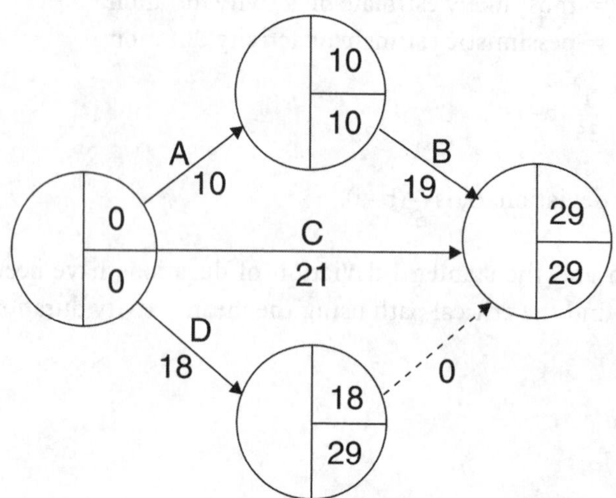

We add the *variances* of the uncertain activities in a path. We can do this provided the activity durations are independent.

Variance of activity A's time = 1.67^2	2.78
Variance of activity B's time = 1.67^2	2.78
Combined variance of path AB	5.56

The standard deviation of the durations of path AB is $\sqrt{5.56}$ = 2.36 days.

3.5 Criticisms of critical path/network analysis

The critical path method is an invaluable aid to planning and scheduling but it does have certain drawbacks.

(a) It is not always possible to devise an effective WBS for a project.

(b) It assumes an essentially linear and sequential relationship between activities: in other words it assumes that once Activity A is finished, Activity B proceeds, and that Activity B has no impact on Activity A. Consequently, it is not very good at coping with the possibility of *feedback* or iteration (in other words, the result of an activity later in the sequence may be relevant to an earlier activity). The inter-relationship between activities may be more complex than the simple linear relationship. This might apply to open-ended research projects where the results of later activities can suggest refinements to additional activities.

(c) There are inevitable problems in estimation. Where the project is completely new, the planning process may be conducted in conditions of relative ignorance.

(d) A problem in using network analysis or variant as a costing technique is that costs are based only on labour hours, and all the problems relating to absorption of indirect overheads apply. Labour hours may only be a small proportion of the money involved in the project.

(e) Although network analysis plans the use of resources of labour and finance, it does not appear to develop plans for contingencies, other than crashing time. This is not so much a criticism of network analysis in itself, as an indication that the project manager must take other considerations into account: planning involves more than scheduling. For example, the manager might have a contingency source of computer support to avoid computer breakdown.

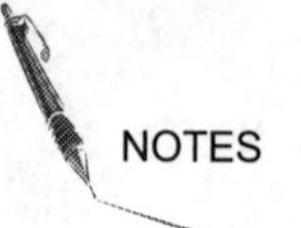

4 MORE PROJECT PLANNING TOOLS

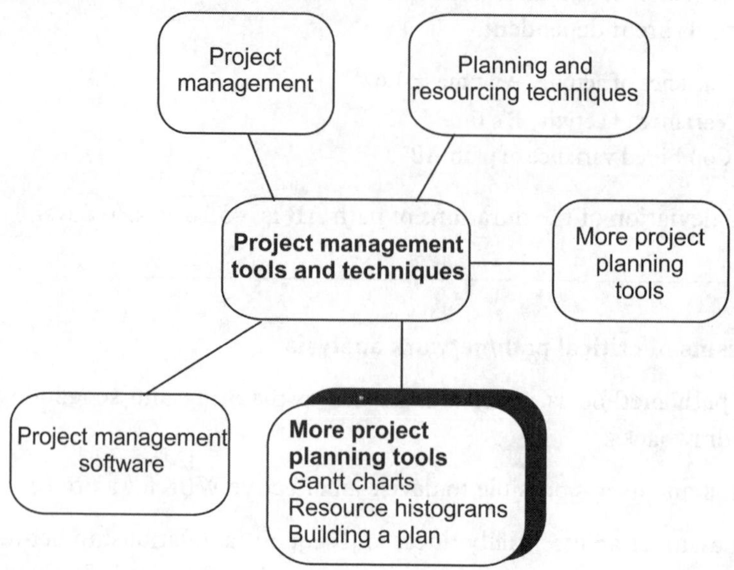

4.1 Gantt charts

A simple plan for a project is based on a **bar line chart**. This is sometimes called a **Gantt chart**. It is a horizontal bar chart used to plan the **time scale** for a project and to estimate the amount of **resources** required. Two lines are usually used to show the time allocated for each task, and the actual time taken.

A simple Gantt chart, illustrating some of the activities involved in a network server installation project follows.

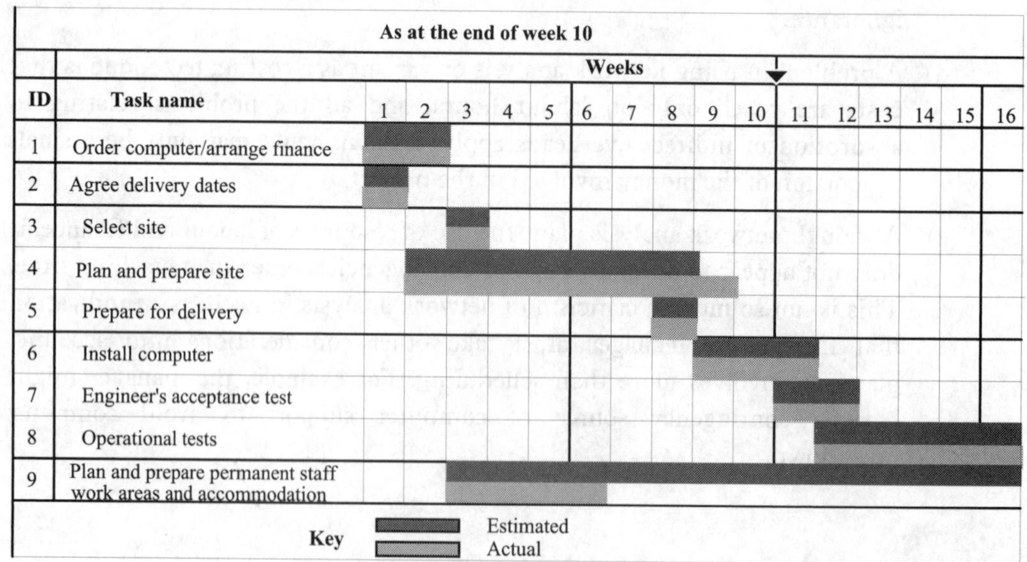

Figure 10.4: Gantt chart

This type of chart has the advantage of being very easy to understand. It can also be used as a progress control chart with the lower section of each bar being completed as that activity is undertaken.

The chart shows that at the end of the tenth week Activity 9 is running behind schedule. More resources may have to be allocated to this activity if the staff accommodation is to be ready in time for the changeover to the new system.

NOTES

Activity 4 had not been completed on time, and this has resulted in some disruption to the computer installation (Activity 6), which may mean further delays in the commencement of Activities 7 and 8.

A Gantt chart does not show the interrelationship between the various activities in the project as clearly as a **network diagram**. A combination of Gantt charts and network analysis will often be used for project planning and resource allocation.

EXAMPLE: GANTT CHARTS

Flotto Limited is about to undertake a project about which the following data is available.

Activity	*Must be preceded by activity*	*Duration* Days	*Men required for the job*
A	–	3	6
B	–	5	3
C	B	2	4
D	A	1	4
E	A	6	5
F	D	3	6
G	C,E	3	3

There is a labour force of nine men available, and each man is paid a fixed wage regardless of whether or not he is actively working on any day. Every man is capable of working on any of the seven activities. If extra labour is required during any day, men can be hired on a daily basis at the rate of £120 per day. If the project is to finish in the minimum time what extra payments must be made for hired labour?

SOLUTION

Draw the network to establish the duration of the project and the critical path. Then draw a Gantt chart, using the critical path as a basis, assuming that jobs start at the earliest possible time. Float times on chains of activities should be shown by a dotted line.

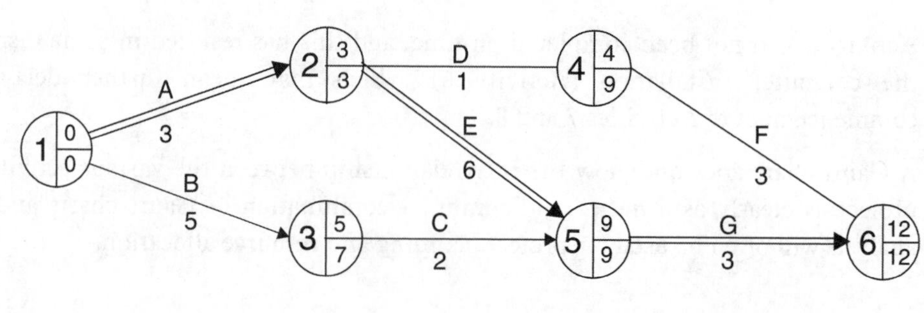

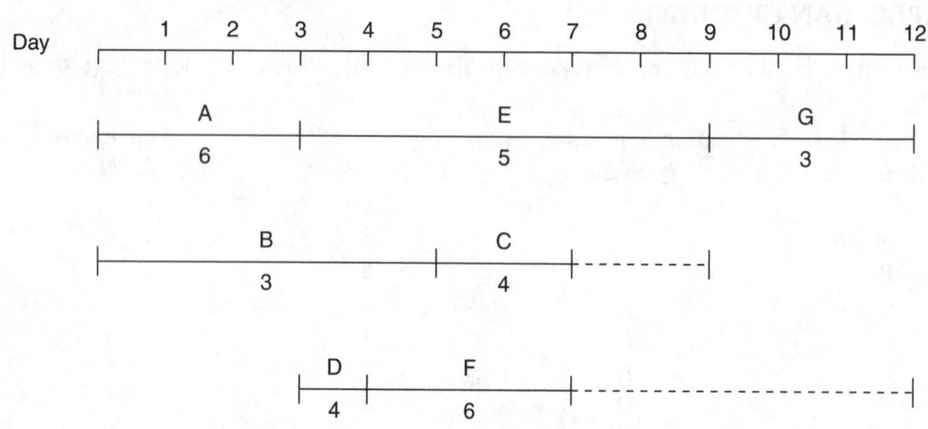

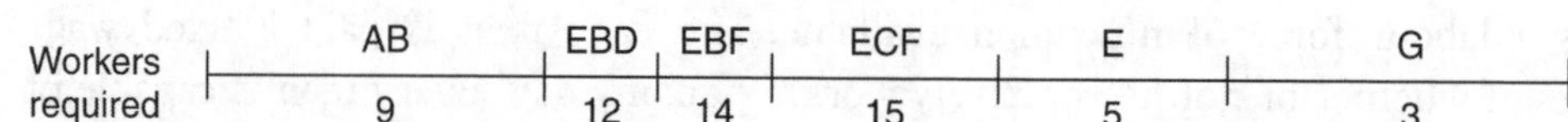

It can be seen that if all activities start at their earliest times, as many as fifteen men will be required on any one day (days 6–7) whereas on other days there would be idle capacity (days 7–12). The problem can be reduced, or removed, by using up float time on non-critical activities. Suppose we deferred the start of activities D and F until the latest possible day. This would be the end of day 8/start of day 9 – leaving four days to complete the activities by the end of day 12. The Gantt chart would be redrawn as follows.

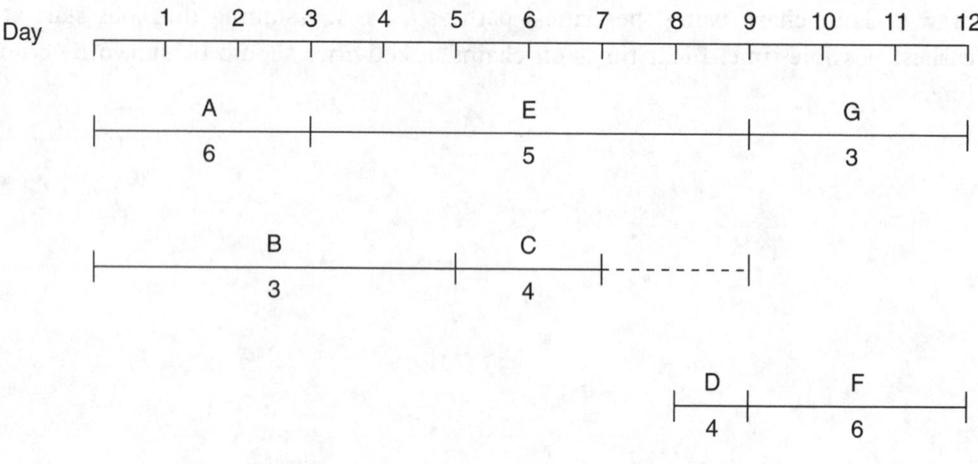

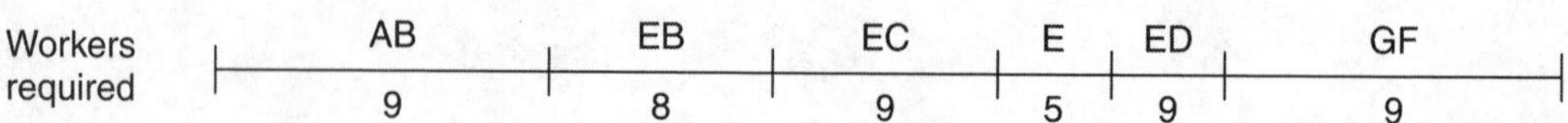

The project can be completed in the minimum time without hiring any additional labour.

Activity 9 **(40 minutes)**

Thurnon plc are to initiate a project to study the feasibility of a new product. The end result of the feasibility project will be a report recommending the action to be taken for the new product. The activities to be carried out to complete the feasibility project are given below.

Activity	*Description*	*Immediate predecessors*	*Expected time Weeks*	*Number of staff required*
A:	preliminary design	–	5	3
B:	market research	–	3	2
C:	obtain engineering quotes	A	2	2
D:	construct prototype	A	5	5
E:	prepare marketing material	A	3	3
F:	costing	C	2	2
G:	product testing	D	4	5
H:	pilot survey	B, E	6	4
I:	pricing estimates	H	2	1
J:	final report	F, G, I	6	2

(a) Draw a network for the scheme of activities set out above. Determine the critical path and the shortest duration of the project.

(b) Assuming the project starts at time zero and that each activity commences at the earliest start date, construct a chart showing the number of staff required at any one time for this project.

4.2 Resource histograms

Definition

A **resource histogram** shows a view of project data in which resource requirements, usage, and availability are shown against a time scale.

It is simply a stacked bar chart showing the number and mix of staff over the duration of the project. It is used to plan and control the human resource requirements of the project.

If we know how many project staff are required to perform each activity in a project, and also what skills are required, this information can be added to a Gantt chart and used to create the resource histogram

A simple resource histogram showing programmer time required on a software development program is shown below.

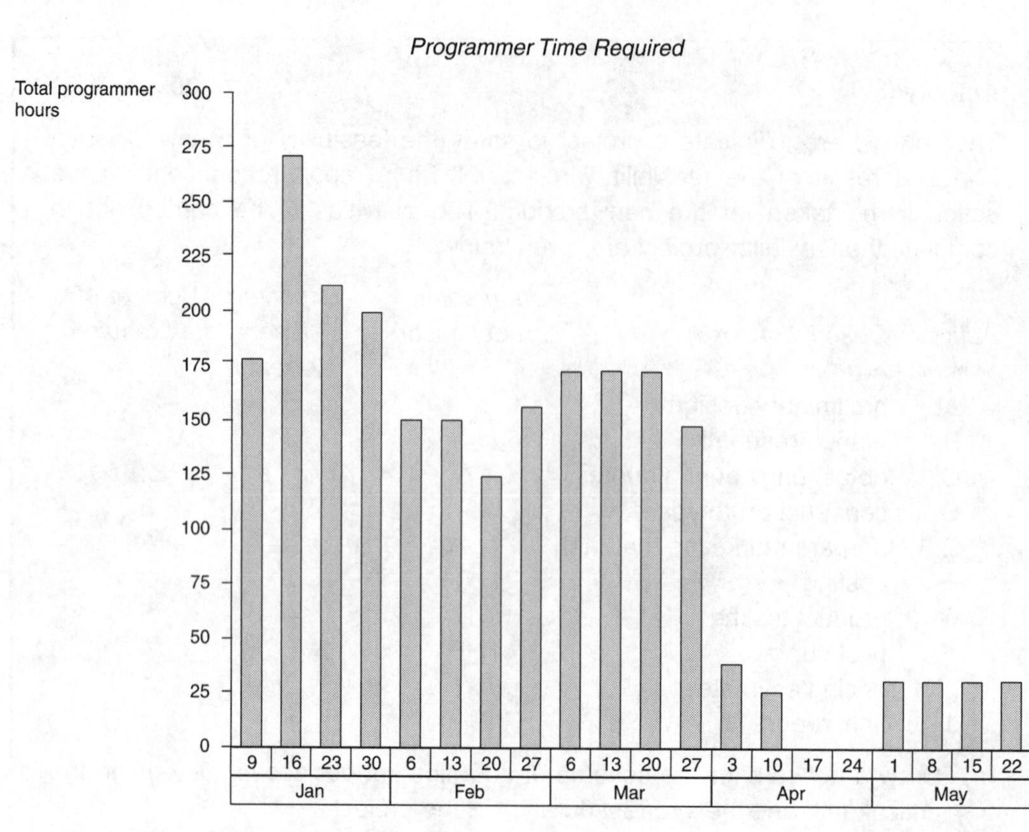

Figure 10.5: Resource histogram

For a simple project such as this, the resource histogram seems to show very little. For a more complex project, however, this is a useful manpower-planning tool. A project manager might use a resource histogram to help with decisions as to when to schedule non-critical activities.

In organisations undertaking a series of projects, each with their own complex resource requirements, the project histograms may be consolidated into one for the whole organisation. This will allow decisions to be taken about recruitment, retraining and redundancy.

4.3 Building a plan

You are to initiate a project to study the feasibility of building a new supermarket. The end result of the feasibility project will be a report recommending the action to be taken for the new store. The activities to be carried out to complete the feasibility project are given below.

Activity	Description	Immediate predecessors	Expected time (wks)	Staff required
A	Preliminary design		5	3
B	Materials research		3	2
C	Obtain material quotes	A	2	2
D	Draw up plans	A	5	5
E	Marketing research	A	3	3
F	Costing	C	2	2
G	Get planning permission	D	4	5
H	Design and research fittings and finishes	B, E	6	4
I	Pricing estimates	H	2	1
J	Final report	F, G, I	6	2

The first step is to draw the network and identify its critical path thus:

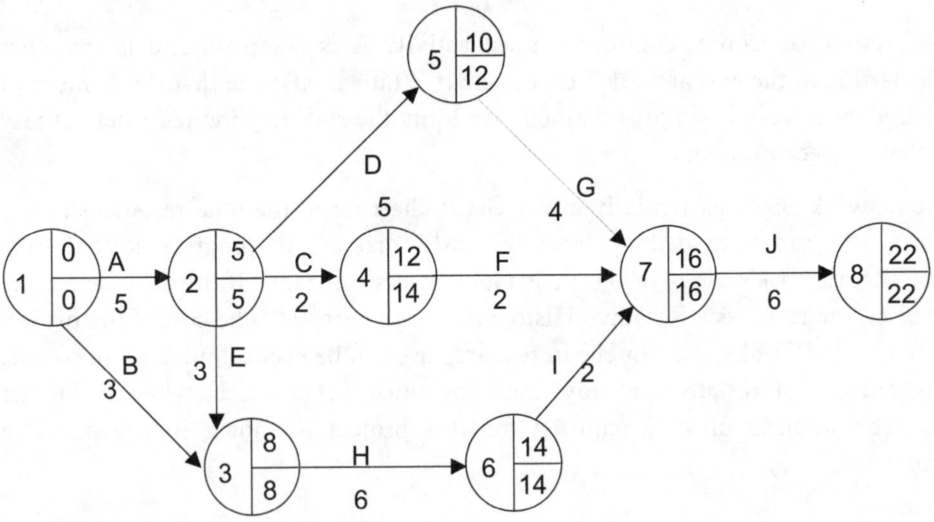

The numbers are the expected durations in weeks.

- The critical path is A, E, H, I, J.
- Total expected duration = 5 + 3 + 6 + 2 + 6 = 22 weeks

The Gantt chart is constructed with reference to the earliest start times for each activity, the duration of each activity and the number of staff required for each activity thus:

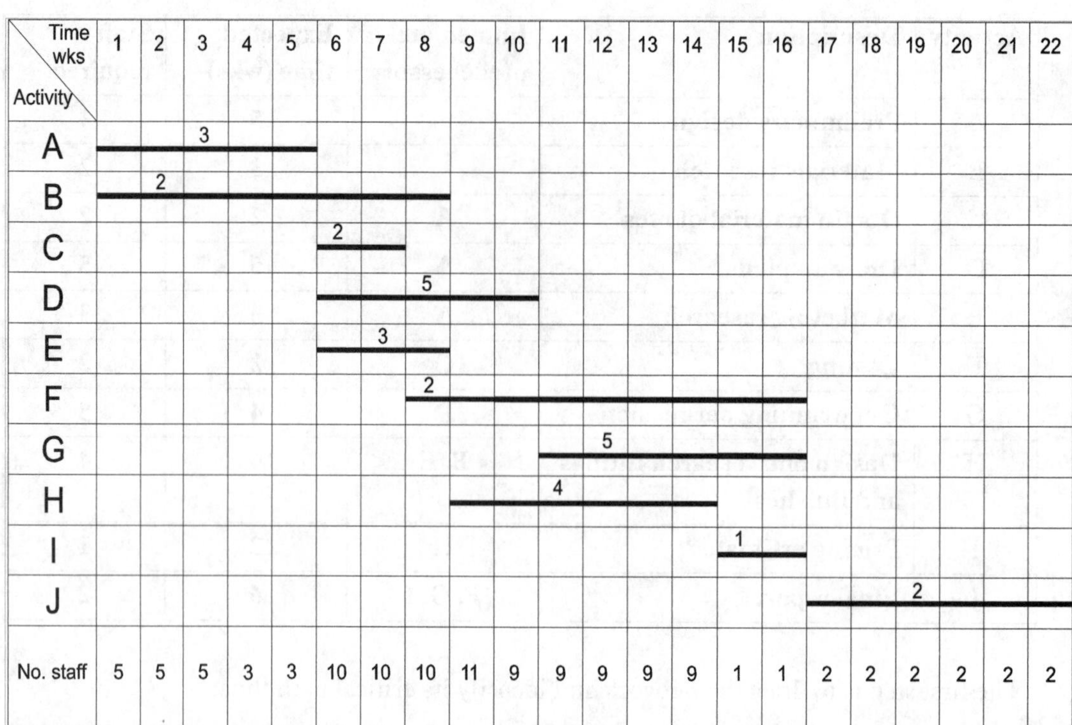

Note that activity C cannot commence until activity A is complete and is therefore drawn as starting at the end of week 5 on the chart. You will also see that the number of staff required each week is simply obtained by adding the staff requirements per activity for the relevant week number.

From the network chart, particularly in the Gantt chart form, the total resources in use at any one time can be added up from the tasks that are in progress at that time (assuming that the task's use of resources is more or less constant). If this is done for the whole project, the result is a Resource Histogram for the project. The cost of the project is likely to be less if peaks and troughs in resource use can be evened out, and, of course, the estimated use of resources at any one time must never exceed what is in fact available. The number of staff required for this project is shown in the resource histogram below.

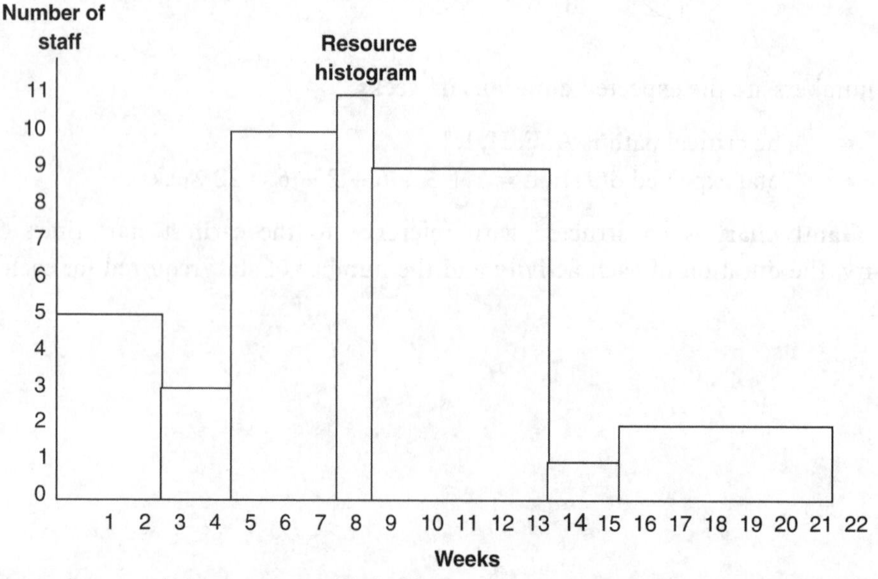

The Gantt chart and histogram will indicate the resource requirements needed to complete the project successfully.

5 PROJECT MANAGEMENT SOFTWARE

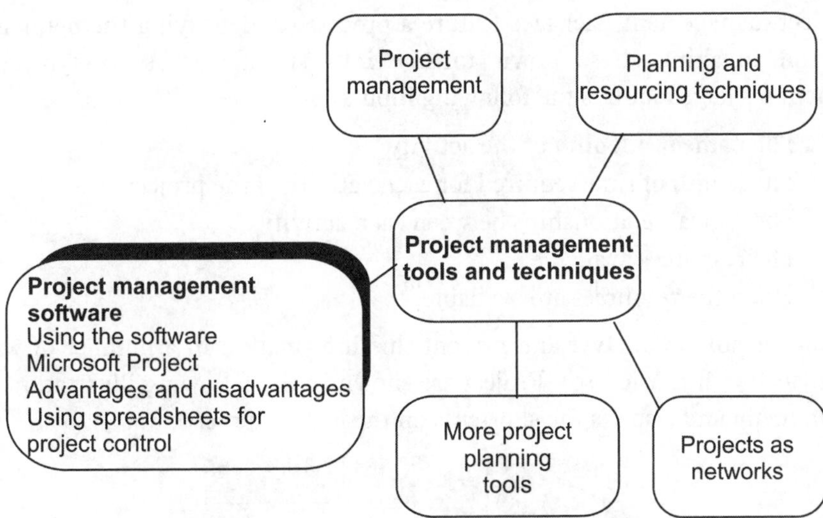

5.1 Using the software

Project management techniques are ideal candidates for computerisation. Project management software packages have been available for a number of years. Microsoft Project and Micro Planner X-Pert are two popular packages.

Software might be used for a number of purposes.

(a) **Planning**

Network diagrams (showing the critical path) and Gantt charts (showing resource use) can be produced automatically once the relevant data is entered. Packages also allow a sort of 'what if?' analysis for initial planning, trying out different levels of resources, changing deadlines and so on to find the best combination.

(b) **Estimating**

As a project progresses, actual data will become known and can be entered into the package and collected for future reference. Since many projects involve basically similar tasks (interviewing users and so on), actual data from one project can be used to provide more accurate estimates for the next project. The software also facilitates and encourages the use of more sophisticated estimation techniques than managers might be prepared to use if working manually.

(c) **Monitoring**

Actual data can also be entered and used to facilitate monitoring of progress and automatically updating the plan for the critical path and the use of resources as circumstances dictate.

(d) **Reporting**

Software packages allow standard and tailored progress reports to be produced, printed out and circulated to participants and senior managers at any time usually at the touch of a button. This helps with co-ordination of activities and project review.

5.2 Microsoft Project

Most project management packages feature a process of identifying the main steps in a project, and breaking these down further into specific tasks. A typical project management package requires the following inputs.

- The name or identity of the activity
- The length of time required for each activity of the project.
- The logical relationships between each activity.
- The resources available.
- When the resources are available.

The package is able to analyse and present this information in a number of ways. The views available within Microsoft Project are shown in the following illustration – on the drop down menu and also via the shortcuts on the left of the screen.

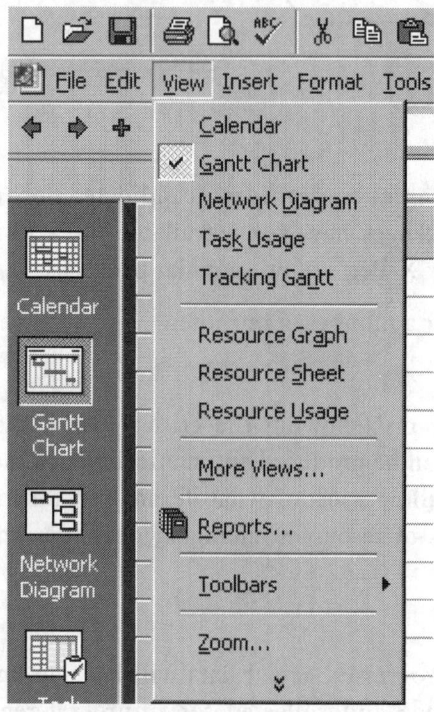

When you have defined project goals and thought out the major phases of your project, you can begin creating your plan. We are going to use the same example that we used in Section 4.1 to illustrate the main parts of the software.

The links on the left describe common project management activities. Click one to see more detailed information, including procedures and project management practices.

Project management is a complex process, and not all of these activities may apply to your situation. So there is a map that can serve as a general guide or it can provide details about setting up, managing, and completing your project. You can access this Project Map by clicking the Map button anywhere in Help.

First, enter and organise the list of tasks to be completed, along with each task's duration. By entering durations for tasks rather than desired start or finish dates, you allow the software to create a schedule for you.

You do this on the default sheet, which is the Gantt chart. As you will notice from the screen dump below, we convert the duration into days. In a standard week, the package assumes a five-day or 40-hour week. This can be changed to a 24-hour day or night shift.

	Task Name	Duration
1	Preliminary design	25 days
2	Materials research	15 days
3	Obtain material quote	10 days
4	Draw up plans	25 days
5	Marketing research	15 days
6	Costing	10 days
7	Get planning permission	20 days
8	Design fittings and finishes	30 days
9	Pricing estimates	10 days
10	Final report	30 days

After you have entered task durations, you can set the task dependencies and constraints. You can even create task dependencies between tasks in different projects.

To do this, position the cursor over the task you are dealing with and click on Project in the toolbar and then Task Information. Click on Predecessors and enter the ID of the task – in our example before obtaining the material quote, the preliminary design must be completed.

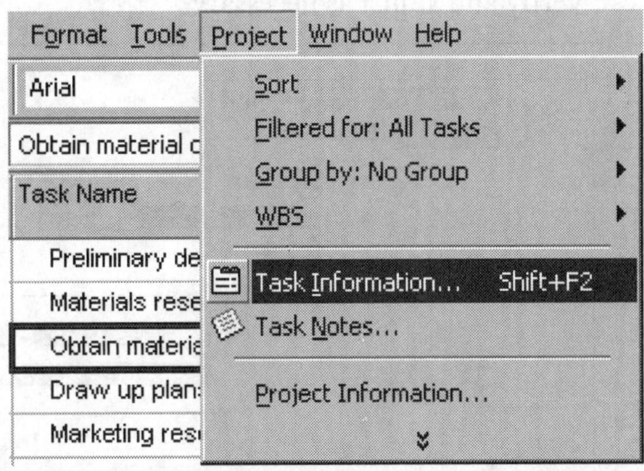

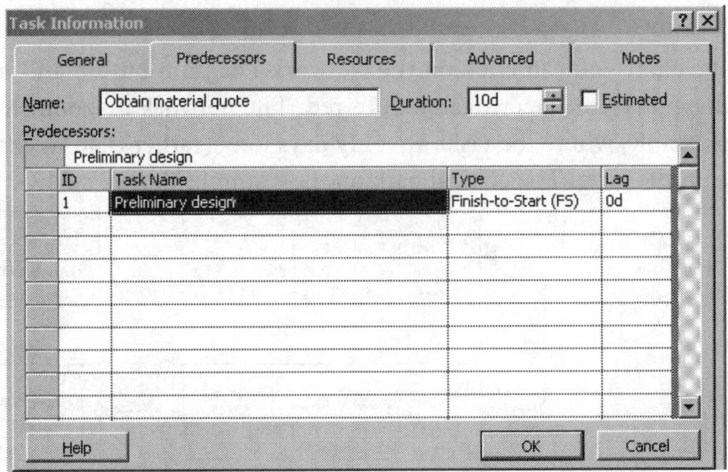

By clicking on Resources (next to Predecessors), you can then assign people, equipment, and materials to the task. You can add people's names to the project and how much of their time will be spent on the task as a percentage.

The assignment units percentage is based on the working time available as set in the resource calendar. If the resource calendar indicates that the resource is available for eight

hours on Monday, then 100% on a task scheduled for Monday means eight hours of work on the task. If the resource calendar indicates that the resource is available for four hours on Tuesday, however, then 100% on a task scheduled for Tuesday means four hours of work on the task.

If you want to allocate three people eg designers, full-time to a task then adjust the time to 300% and then reduce the duration back to the previous amount – because the software will adjust the number of days allowed (triple it) and you may not want to do this.

To assign a material resource to a task, type the quantity of material to be used. The unit of measurement label (tons, boxes, yards, and so on) that you used to define the material resource appears in the Units field, and the default is 1.

When you have added the resource you can then go to the *Resource Sheet*, which gives the name of the resource – work or material – and you can enter details such as standard rate and overtime of pay for each group.

The *Resource Usage* sheet shows the resource name and hours allocated to each part of the project. If there is an exclamation mark in red it indicates that the resource has been over-allocated so an adjustment needs to be made.

With this information the software creates a schedule with details of the resources allocated, which you can verify and adjust as necessary.

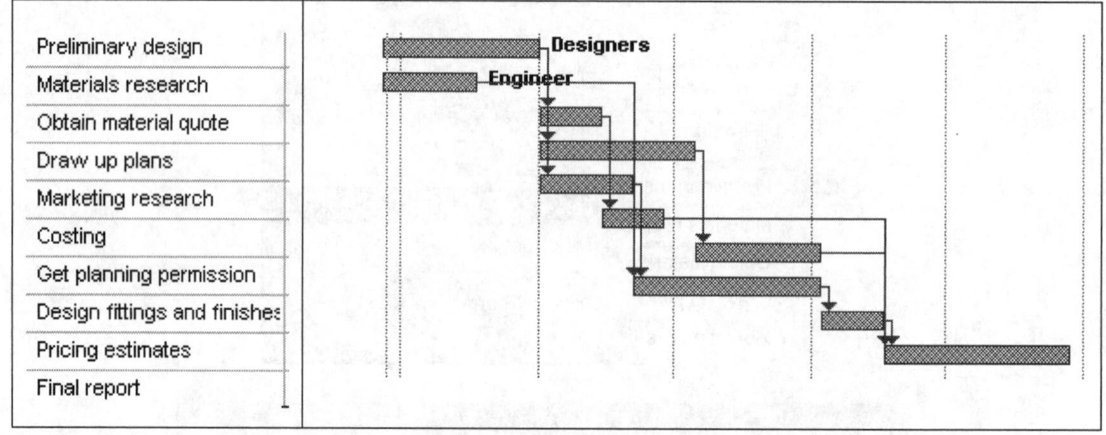

From the Gantt chart you can click on the Network Diagram button and it will display the network diagram with the critical path in red. The network diagram shown below is of a different example, where the tasks are only days long (rather than weeks) so it makes it easier to see on the page. The critical path on the example shown is AEG.

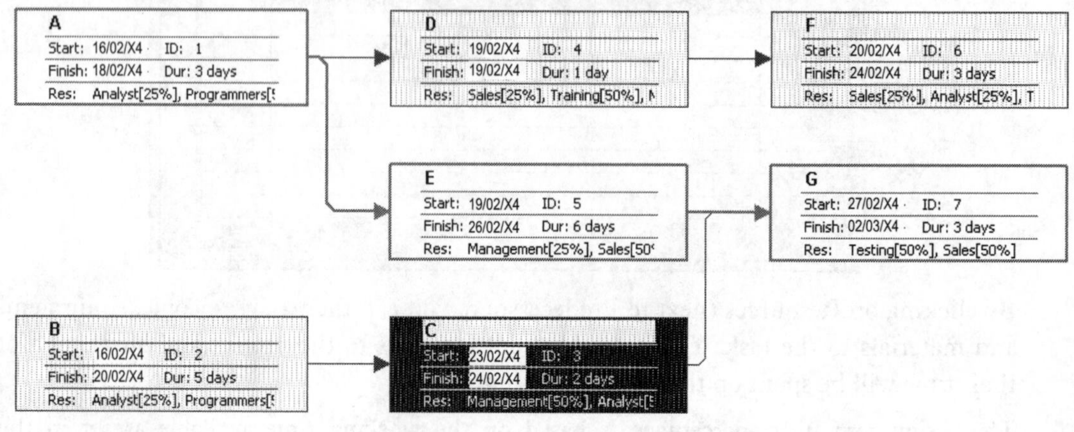

You can break down a task into sub-tasks. Click on the cell under the one where you want your new subtask to be and then click on Insert and then New Task. Name the task and fill in the time allocated to it. Click on the task bar and drag it to the right so it is indented. It has the effect of changing the main task into a folder, which you can collapse or expand to suit as you are working on different parts of the project plan. You will also notice the time allocated to the main task changes as you enter the sub-tasks. You can then fill in any dependencies and resources used as before on the task information sheet.

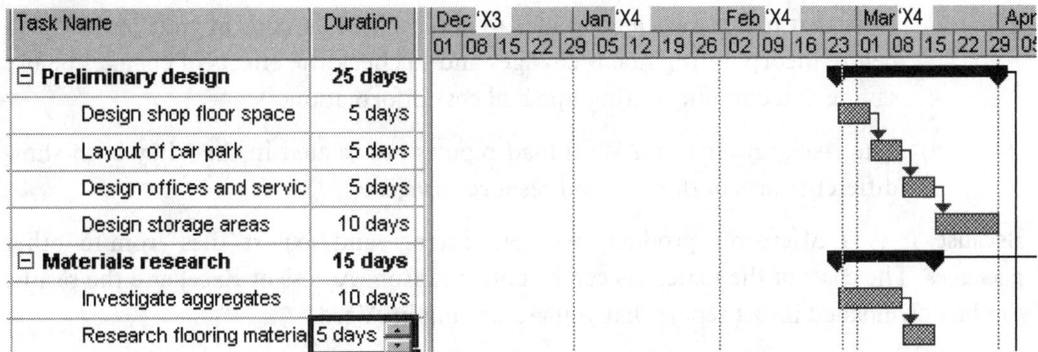

There are many other facilities that you can explore:

You can unlink tasks or split them if you want to add more resources or double up on staff instead of staggering the task.

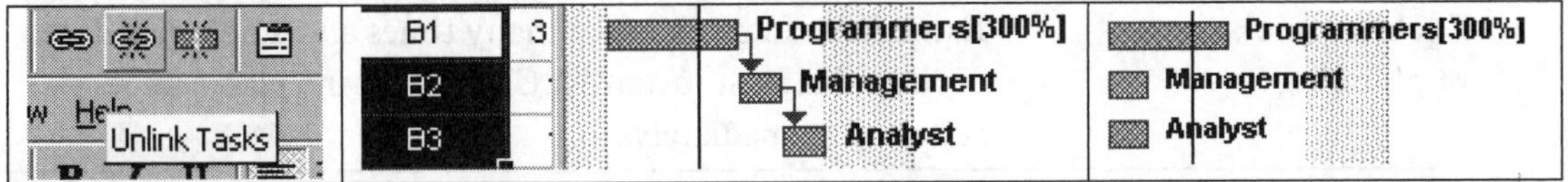

You can add supporting information about tasks by typing notes, attaching files, or creating hyperlinks to related information in your project file or in other locations.

Once your plan gets under way, you can monitor its progress, allocate resources to it and make any amendments deemed necessary.

As you would expect, there are many reporting facilities.

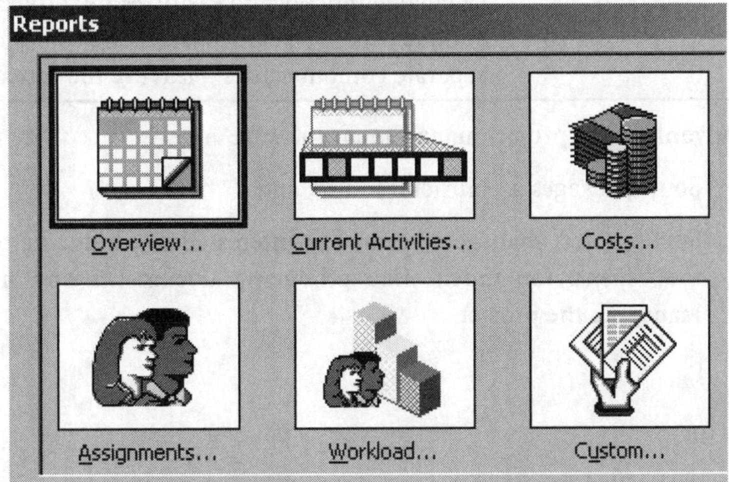

(a) The **Overview** gives a project summary with top-level tasks, critical tasks and milestones.

(b) The report on **Current Activities** shows tasks that have not started, tasks that are in progress and tasks starting soon. It highlights what should have started and slipping tasks.

(c) The **Costs** report shows the project budget and highlights overbudget tasks and resources. To keep costs within budget, you will want to review cost variances that occur over time so you can make adjustments where needed. Note that it is always a good idea to make a backup copy of your project plan before incorporating major changes and to check the effects of changes before saving and communicating updated cost information.

(d) The **Assignments** and **Workload** reports are related in that they both show different parts of the task and resource usage.

Because it is a Microsoft product, you can import and export files from/to other packages. The costs of the materials can be obtained from Access or Excel and the results can be downloaded into a report that you are writing in Word.

5.3 Advantages and disadvantages

The **advantages** of using project management software are summarised in the following table.

Advantage	Comment
Enables quick re-planning	Estimates can be changed many times and a new schedule produced almost instantly. Changes to the plan can be reflected immediately.
Document quality	Well-presented plans give a professional impression and are easier to understand.
Encourages constant progress tracking	The project manager is able to compare actual progress against planned progress and investigate problem areas promptly.
What if? analysis	Software enables the effect of various scenarios to be calculated quickly and easily. Many project managers conduct this type of analysis using copies of the plan in separate computer files – leaving the actual plan untouched.

Two **disadvantages** of project management software are:

(a) Some packages are difficult to use; and

(b) Some project managers become so interested in producing perfect plans that they spend too much time producing documents and not enough time managing the project.

5.4 Using spreadsheets for project control

Not everyone will have access to project management software but most will be familiar with spreadsheets.

Spreadsheets have most of the facilities of a specialised package but not so nicely put together and requiring input of some very unpleasant looking formulae. It is very common for a project budget to be constructed on a spreadsheet. It makes variance analysis and financial control much easier.

Spreadsheet packages also have a calendar (of sorts) so you can enter start and finish dates or start dates and the number of days required to complete so the scheduling can be activated.

Dates and times are numbers – the way that a time or date is displayed on a worksheet depends on the number format applied to the cell. When you type a date or time that Excel recognises, the cell's format changes from the General number format to a built-in date or time format. By default, dates and times are right-aligned in a cell. If Excel cannot recognize the date or time format, the date or time is entered as text, which is left-aligned in the cell.

The 12-hour or 24-hour clock – to type a time based on the 12-hour clock, type a space followed by **AM** or **PM** (or **A** or **P**) after the time. Otherwise, Excel bases the time on the 24-hour clock. For example, if you type **3:00** instead of **3:00 PM,** the time is stored as **3:00 AM.**

Calculating with dates and times – times and dates can be added, subtracted, and included in other calculations. To use a date or time in a formula, enter the date or time as text enclosed in quotation marks. For example, the following formula would display a difference of 216:

="5/12/2004"-"3/5/2004"

They have the facility of linking many sheets together so we could have sheets dealing with ordering stock, sheets with lists of available resources, lists of cost prices, availability and lead times of the many items needed to produce stock etc.

For years spreadsheets have been used to design and prototype scheduling systems and are now being used to develop serious production scheduling applications.

We looked at a basic stock control model in the last chapter and we can use the same example to illustrate how the spreadsheet can be used to control a production-scheduling project. In this example, the strategy (which is only one of many possibilities) is to take the product with the minimum stock and make enough of that product to bring it up to the Max Cover – the optimal level (but not compensating for sales during the period that they are being made). How the schedule works will be best explained using a screen dump from the Excel worksheet.

Starting from the top left, the production days/year, the start date, max cover and min. quantity to make are all added by the user at the beginning of the project/production run. The Max Cover in days shows that with 48 units of stock of Product B you can keep customers of Product B happy for fourteen days [(1,200 units produced per annum ÷ 350 production days) × 48 units]. The Min quantity is the lowest amount that would be considered to manufacture in one run.

NOTES

Sheet 3

I12 = =MAX(ROUND(I11+((A12=I$10)*D12)-(E12*F$5/ProdnDays),0),0)

	A	B	C	D	E	F	G	H	I	J
1					Product	Sales	Prodn rate	Total days	Max Cover	Initial
2	Prodn days/year		350			(year)	units/day	assembly	units	Stock
3	Start date		14-Mar		**Product A**	1400	9	155.6	56	30
4	Max cover (days)		14		**Product B**	1200	12	100.0	48	35
5	Min qty to make		5		**Product C**	800	10	80.0	32	10
6										
7								335.6		
8										
9	**Production run:**		Max	Qty to			Projected stock			Min.
10	Product	Stock	Cover	make	Days	Start	Product A	Product B	Product C	Stock
11							30	35	10	10
12	Product C	10	32	22	2.2	14-Mar	21	27	27	21
13	Product A	21	56	35	3.9	16-Mar	40	14	18	14
14	Product B	14	48	34	2.8	20-Mar	29	38	12	12
15	Product C	12	32	20	2.0	22-Mar	21	31	27	21
16	Product A	21	56	35	3.9	24-Mar	40	18	18	18
17	Product B	18	48	30	2.5	28-Mar	30	39	12	12
18	Product C	12	32	20	2.0	31-Mar	22	32	27	22

Continuing on to the headings – the Products are the same ones that we used in the EOQ and stock control examples. The estimated sales are automatically inserted into this sheet from Sheet 2 in this example. If you remember, we link the two with a formula =Sheet2!D3 – this gets the contents of D3 and puts them into it – in this case the expected sales figure for Product A.

Sheet 2

		Number of each component used in each product:					
Product	Expected Sales	**Component 1**	Sales 1	**Component 2**	Sales 2	**Component 3**	Sales 3
Product A	1400	2	2800	1	1400	0	0
Product B	1200	0	0	3	3600	4	4800
Product C	800	1	800	2	1600	0	0
	Total Sales:		3600		6600		4800

The production rate can be altered and any amendments will affect the production rate throughout the predicted production run. The total assembly days is derived from the estimated sales per year divided by the production rate per day. The Max cover in units is linked to the max cover in days. The amount is derived by taking the max cover and multiplying it by the estimated sales in a year and then dividing by the number of production days a year (in this case 350). The initial projected stock is entered by the user and is linked to the production run. It triggers the process, which begins by comparing the initial stock and selecting the product with the minimum stock – in this case 10 of Product C – to start the production.

This brings us to the strategy ie, to take the product with the minimum stock and make enough of that product to bring it up to the Max Cover. We can see that the max cover for C is 32 and therefore 22 need to be manufactured. At a production rate of 10 a day this will take 2.2 days. During this period the estimated sales of all of the products will be calculated and will be subtracted from the projected stock holding. The cycle repeats automatically.

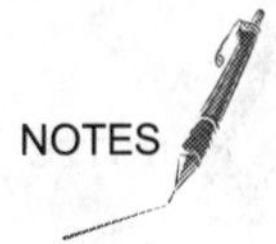

Chapter roundup

- The objectives of project management are to ensure that the end product conforms with customer specification and is produced on time and within budget.
- The project life cycle can be broken down into the stages of project definition, planning, implementation, completion and review.
- Relatively small estimating errors can dent profits significantly.
- Work breakdown structure (WBS) is the analysis of work into tasks. This can be used to estimate costs (by defining the resources needed for each task), and to schedule activities by determining which activities depend on which.
- A network represents a project by breaking it down into activities and showing their interdependence.
- Activities are represented by arrows, which are drawn between nodes which represent events. Dummy activities may be needed. Any sequence of activities from the start to the end of a network is a path through the network.
- The path with the greatest duration is the critical path. Any delay on this path will delay the project as a whole.
- The earliest event time for an event is the earliest time that activities starting at that event can start. The latest event time is the latest time by which all activities leading into that event must be completed if the whole project is to be completed in the minimum time.
- For events on the critical path, the earliest and latest event times are the same. Activities on the critical path have zero float: an activity's float is the latest event time of the event at its end minus the earliest event time of the event at its start minus its duration.
- If activity durations are uncertain, the PERT formulae can be used to estimate mean durations and variances of durations. The variances of the durations of activities on the critical path can then be added, and the probability that the duration of the critical path will exceed any given value can be computed.
- Gantt charts can be used to estimate the amount of resources required a project.
- Project management techniques are ideal candidates for computerisation using project management software.

Quick quiz

1. What are the distinctive problems of project management?
2. What is involved in project definition?
3. What four different types of estimate can be given?
4. What is Work Breakdown Structure?

NOTES

5 When is a dummy activity necessary in a network?

6 What is the critical path?

7 What is an activity's float?

8 What are the formulae used in PERT to estimate the mean and the standard deviation of an activity's duration?

9 Where we have a chain of activities with uncertain durations, can we add the standard deviations of their durations?

10 What is the purpose of a Gantt chart?

11 What is a Resource Histogram?

Answers to quick quiz

1 The special management problems include the team – they must be able to communicate effectively and immediately with each other working on a variety of projects. There will always be the expected and unexpected novel problems to sort out as well as coping with any contributions by outside parties eg, specialists who may think their contribution is more important. The delayed benefits associated with some projects may also cause strain on the eventual recipient who might put pressure on the project leader when times become tough.

2 Defining the project is an iterative process. In other words, there will be several stages, with each definition being more detailed and refined than before. The project might be defined in a contract, in a product specification or in a customer's specification.

3 The four types of estimate are Ball-park estimates, Comparative estimates, Feasibility estimates and Definitive estimates.

4 Work Breakdown Structure (WBS) is the process of breaking down the project into manageable tasks.

5 A dummy activity is used in network analysis when two activities could start at the same time and finish at the same time too. It is represented by a broken arrowheaded line.

6 The critical path is the path through the network with the greatest total duration.

7 An activity's float is the amount of time by which its duration could be extended up to the point where it would be critical. This is the same as the amount of time by which its duration could be extended without affecting the total project time. The effect on the time available for preceding and subsequent activities is ignored. The total float for an activity is therefore equal to its latest finishing time minus its earliest starting time minus its duration.

8 Mean, $\mu = \dfrac{a + 4m + b}{6}$

Standard deviation, $\sigma = \dfrac{1}{6}(b - a)$

9 No, we can add the variances of the uncertain durations in order to calculate the variance of their deviation, and if we then take the square root of the variance, we obtain the standard deviation of the uncertain duration of the chain of activities.

10 A Gantt chart displays the time relationships between tasks in a project. It is a horizontal bar chart used to estimate the amount and timing of resources required.

11 A Resource Histogram is a bar chart showing the labour requirements of a project.

Answers to activities

1

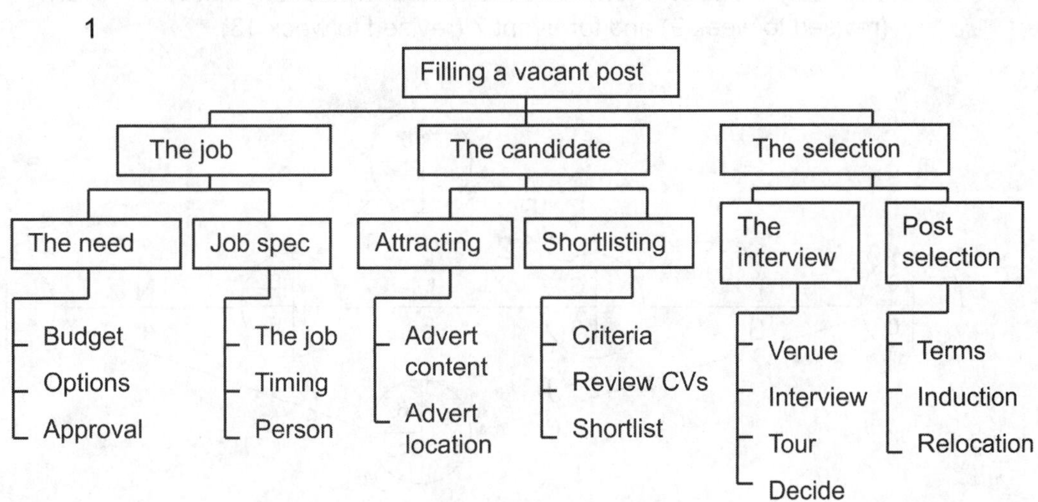

2 (a) An error of +/– 5% would mean that the profit would be increased or reduced by £4,000 (ie 5% × £80,000) in other words 20%.

(b) A 10% error would increase or reduce profits by £8,000 which is 40% of the profit.

(c) A 20% error would increase or decrease profits by £16,000 or 80% of profit.

3 Yes, E and H could be carried on simultaneously. Indeed, that might be the most sensible thing to do. If E took five days and F only took one day, H could be started while E was still in progress.

4 There are four paths, as follows.

A B E G I L
A B F H I L
A C J L
A D K L

5

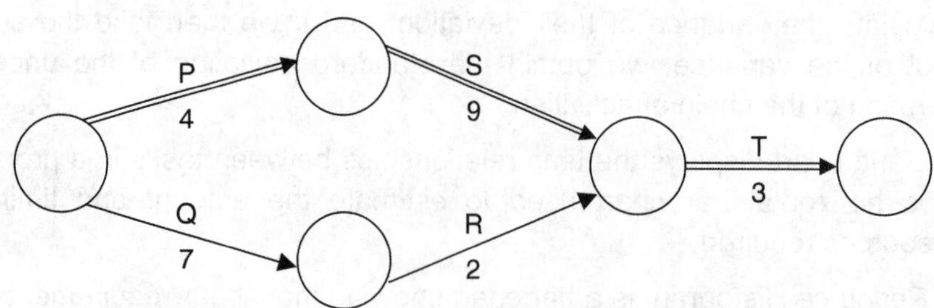

The paths are PST (4 + 9 + 3 = 16 days) and QRT (7 + 2 + 3 = 12 days). The minimum overall duration is 16 days. The critical path is PST.

6 The only earliest event times affected would be those for event 4 (revised to week 9) and for event 7 (revised to week 13).

7

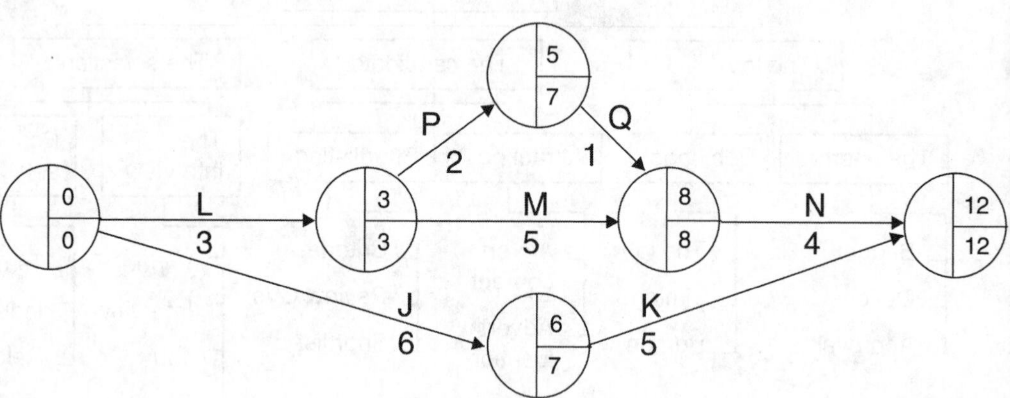

8 Float for activity D = 8 – 4 – 1 = 3 weeks.

Float for activity G = 12 – 7 – 4 = 1 week.

NOTES

9 (a)

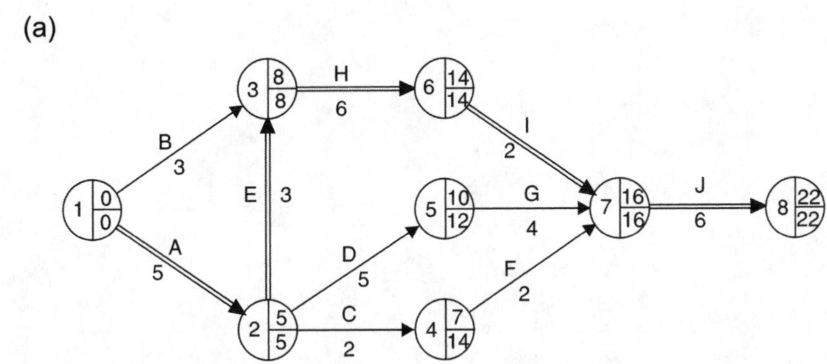

The critical path is AEHIJ, and the minimum total duration is 22 weeks.

(b) To construct a Gantt chart we need to list all possible paths through the network.

A E H I J
A D G J
A C F J
B H I J

Then using the critical path as the basis, we can construct the Gantt chart as follows.

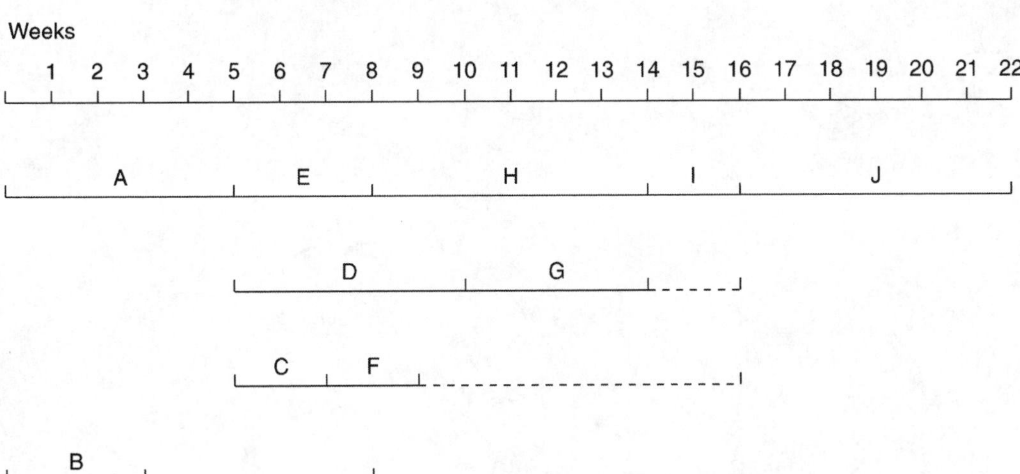

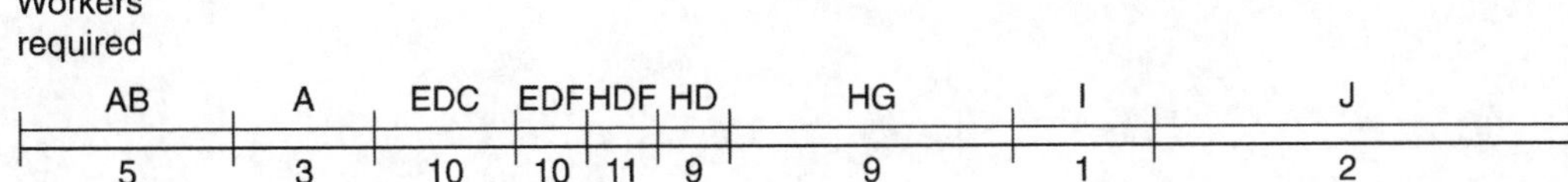

BPP LEARNING MEDIA

Chapter 11 : INVESTMENT APPRAISAL

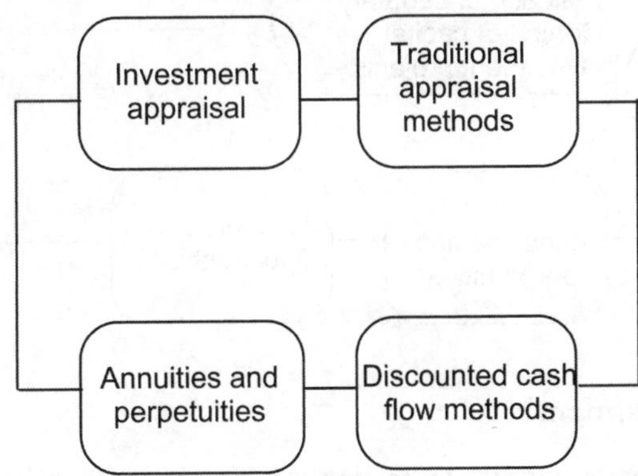

Introduction

Financial analysis is used to estimate the profitability of a potential investment. It includes two types of information: (1) financial parameters and (2) cost and revenue data. The financial parameters include information on depreciation, inflation, income tax rates, your organisation's discount rate, and the timing of the Initial Investment and Annual Operating Costs. The cost and revenue data include both Initial Investment Costs and Annual Operating Costs.

Initially we will be looking at Payback and the Accounting Rate of Return. These are the two methods of Capital Investment Appraisal, which can conveniently be grouped together as the 'Traditional Methods'. Essentially, the Payback Period method tells you how long it would take to recover an investment from the returns attributable to that investment. We will then move on to look at Discounted Cash Flow (DCF) methods.

The principles underlying the investment appraisal techniques that use the DCF method: Net Present Value (NPV) and Internal Rate of Return (IRR) are cash flow (as opposed to profit), and the time value of money. Whichever of these methods of appraisal is used, a method of discounting the projected cash flows of the project is used to ascertain its present value.

Your objectives

After completing this chapter you should:

(a) Appreciate the importance of investment decisions

(b) Be able to discuss the advantages and disadvantages of the accounting rate of return (ARR) for appraising capital investment projects

(c) Understand how to find the payback method

(d) Understand the concept of discounting

(e) Be able to calculate the net present value (NPV) method

(f) Understand the internal rate of return (IRR) method

(g) Be able to explain annuities and perpetuities

(h) Understand compounding and discounting

1 INVESTMENT APPRAISAL

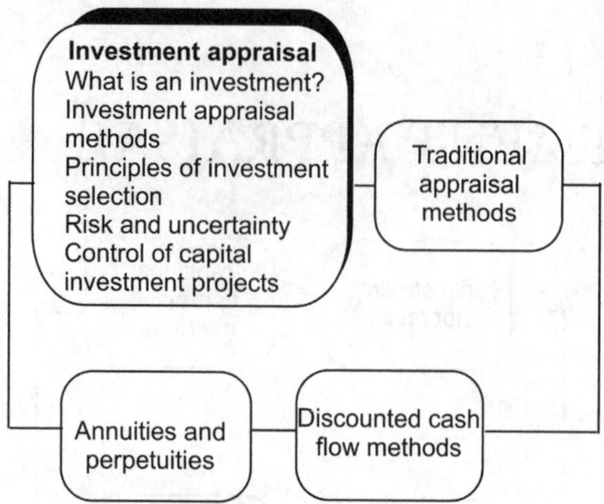

1.1 What is an investment?

An investment requires expenditure on something today that is expected to provide a benefit in the future. It involves the sacrifice of current consumption opportunities in order to obtain the benefit of future consumption possibilities. The purpose of investment appraisal is to evaluate whether or not the current sacrifice is worthwhile.

Investment decisions are extremely important because they are invariably concerned with the future survival, prosperity and growth of the organisation. The organisation's primary objective of maximisation of shareholder wealth is a basic assumption that continues to hold true. Investments must be made both to maintain shareholder wealth and to increase it. To meet the shareholder wealth maximisation objective it is crucial that those managing the organisation make the best decisions that are based on the best information available and use the most appropriate appraisal techniques.

At the corporate level investment relates to the amount that shareholders are willing to invest in the equity of a company in the expectation of future cash flows in the form of dividends and enhancement of share price. The level of future dividends and share price enhancement are in turn dependent to what extent the company is able to optimise returns on 'real' investment (investment in companies, plant, machinery, working capital) in new products, projects, new business, and so on. Investment may appear within fixed (non-current) assets in the balance sheet, for example, land buildings, plant, machinery, etc. It may also appear in the profit and loss account in terms of public relations, staff training, or research and development.

The commitment of funds to capital projects gives rise to a management decision problem, the solution of which, if incorrectly arrived at, may seriously impair company profitability and growth.

Capital investment decisions have certain characteristics that are not always present in other management decisions, and as a result, special techniques are required to ensure that only the best information is available to the decision maker.

These characteristics are:

(a) A significant outlay of cash
(b) Long-term involvement with greater risks and uncertainty because forecasts of the future are less reliable
(c) Irreversibility of some projects due to the specialised nature of, for example, plant which having been bought with a specific project in mind may have little or no scrap value
(d) A significant time lag between commitment of resources and the receipt of benefits
(e) Management's ability is often stretched with some projects demanding an awareness of all relevant diverse factors
(f) Limited resources requiring priorities on capital expenditure, and
(g) Project completion time requiring adequate continuous control information as costs can be exceeded by a significant amount.

In order to handle investment decisions, organisations have to make an assessment of the size of the outflows and inflows of funds, the lifespan of the investment, the degree of risk attached and the cost of obtaining funds.

The main stages in the capital budgeting cycle can be summarised as follows.

1 **Forecasting** investment needs
2 **Identifying** project(s) to meet needs
3 **Appraising** the alternatives
4 **Selecting** the best alternatives
5 **Investing** in the chosen project(s)
6 **Monitoring** project(s)

Looking at investment appraisal involves us in stages 3 and 4 of this cycle.

We can classify capital expenditure projects into four broad categories:

1 **Maintenance** – replacing old or obsolete assets, for example
2 **Profitability** – quality, productivity or location improvement, for example
3 **Expansion** – new products, markets and so on
4 **Indirect** – social and welfare facilities

Even the projects that are unlikely to generate profits should be subjected to investment appraisal. This should help to identify the best way of achieving the project's aims. So investment appraisal may help to find the cheapest way to provide a new staff restaurant, even though such a project may be unlikely to earn profits for the company.

1.2 Investment appraisal methods

When considering any capital investment project there are six factors which to be examined.

(a) The initial cost of the project
(b) The phasing of the expenditure
(c) The estimated life of the investment
(d) The amount and timing of the resulting cash flow
(e) The effect, if any, on the rest of the undertaking
(f) The working capital required.

One of the most important steps in the capital budgeting cycle is working out if the benefits of investing large capital sums outweigh the costs of these investments. The range of methods that business organisations use can be classified into those that ignore the time value of money and the ones that account for it. We will call these Traditional methods and Discounted cash flow (DCF) methods.

Traditional methods – (that ignore the time value of money) include:

(a) The **accounting rate of return** (ARR) for appraising capital investment projects is based on profits and the costs of investment, taking no account of cash flows or the time value of money; and

(b) The **payback method** for appraising capital investment projects is based on cash flows, but also ignores the time value of money.

Discounted cash flow (DCF) methods – (that account for the time value of money) include:

(a) Net Present Value (NPV) – this is one of the two most widely used investment decision criteria that are based on cash flow and the time value of money

(b) Internal Rate of Return (IRR) – this is the other of the two most widely used investment decision criteria that are based on cash flow and the time value of money

(c) Discounted Payback – this is also based on cash flow and the time value of money

We will look at each of these methods in more detail in the following sections.

1.3 Principles of investment selection

'£1 received today is worth more than £1 received in a year's time is an expression of what is meant by the 'time value of money'. There are two reasons for this.

1 The money could have been alternatively invested in, say, risk-free Government gilt-edged securities that would yield the amount invested plus interest in one year's time. In fact the actual rate of interest that an investor in a project would expect will be higher than the Government rate, to include a risk premium, because neither companies nor individuals are risk-free borrowers. Generally, the higher the risk of the investment, the higher the return the investor will expect from it.

2 Purchasing power will have been lost over a year due to inflation.

The principles underlying the investment appraisal techniques that use the DCF method: NPV, IRR, and discounted payback, are **cash flow** (as opposed to profit), and the **time value of money**.

Additional factors impacting on investment criteria calculations:

(a) The effect of inflation on the cost of capital
(b) Whether additional working capital is required for the project
(c) The length of the project
(d) Taxation, and
(e) Risk and uncertainty.

1.4 Risk and uncertainty

There may be a number of risks associated with each of the variables included in a capital investment appraisal decision:

(a) Estimates of initial costs,
(b) Uncertainty about the timing and values of future cash revenues and costs,
(c) The length of project, and
(d) Variations in the discount rate.

Actual outcomes usually differ considerably from expected outcomes. In terms of capital investment, the greater the timescale of the project the more time there is for more things to go wrong and the larger the investment, the greater may be the impact.

As a final step in evaluation of the investment in a project it is prudent to carry out some sort of sensitivity analysis. Sensitivity analysis may be used to assess the risk associated with a capital investment project. A project may seem viable, but it is useful to calculate the degree to which changes to the factors used in the appraisal exercise could occur before we would change our decision whether or not to invest in the project.

The same technique of sensitivity analysis may be used as an early warning system before a project begins to show a loss.

However, there are limitations to the use of sensitivity analysis:

(a) Two or more factors may change simultaneously, and

(b) There may be an absence of clear rules governing acceptance or rejection of projects, which require the subjective judgement of management.

1.5 Control of capital investment projects

Once a project has been appraised, and a sensitivity analysis carried out and the approval given at the relevant level in the organisation, project controls must be established and then post project completion audits carried out. The controls cover three main areas.

(a) **Capital spend** – note the number of subjective areas where things can go wrong.

(b) **Project timing** – delays appear to be 'routine' in many major projects as evidenced almost daily in the financial press.

(c) **Benefits** – evidenced almost as frequently in the financial press, this is another area where things may not turn out as planned.

To establish the appropriate levels of control, the appointment of a good project manager with the appropriate level of responsibility and authority, together with regular project reviews, are absolute essentials to ensure that projects run to plan.

Capital investment decisions are made on the basis of estimates – estimates of expenditure, estimates of income, estimates of timing, and so on. But how accurate are these estimates?

Investment projects must be kept under continual review. As part of this review, a detailed study of what actually did happen will periodically be carried out.

Perhaps one year after the start of a capital investment, the organisation should ask a number of questions such as:

- What was the *actual* expenditure?
- On what dates was the expenditure *actually* made?
- Are estimates of future expenditure (amounts and dates) still valid?
- What was the *actual* income?
- On what dates was the income *actually* received?
- Are estimates of future income (amounts and dates) still valid?
- Have the promised non-financial benefits *actually* materialised?

For large investments, it may be appropriate to repeat this detailed analysis at a later point in time.

It could be argued that, once an organisation has made a capital expenditure decision, it is committed – it often can't reverse that decision. This may be so, but it can learn from experience. All organisations make some mistakes, but the well-managed, learning organisation tries not to repeat them.

2 TRADITIONAL APPRAISAL METHODS

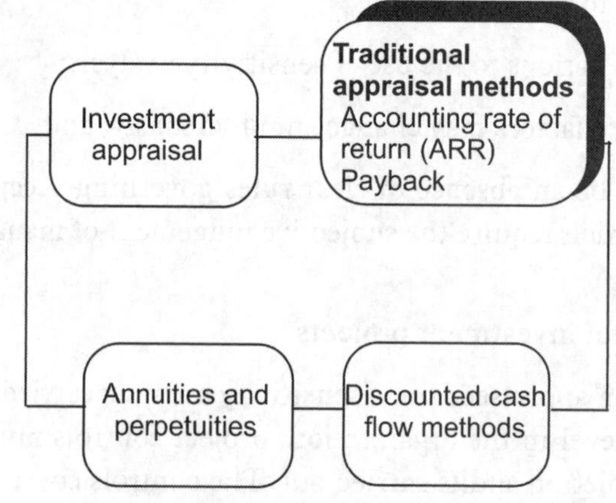

2.1 Accounting rate of return (ARR)

The accounting rate of return expresses the profits arising from a project as a percentage of the initial capital cost. However, the definition of profits and capital cost are different depending on which textbook you use. For instance, the profits may be taken to include depreciation, or they may not. It is a useful indicator of whether an investment is likely to offer a good margin or profit, and it can be compared with the company's overall return on capital employed to indicate if profitability might increase. Any project undertaken must achieve an acceptable rate of return. This is usually set at either the company's average cost of capital, or the cost of financing the individual project. The formula for its calculation is:

ARR = (Average annual revenue / Initial capital costs) × 100%

EXAMPLE: ACCOUNTING RATE OF RETURN

A project to replace an item of machinery is being appraised. The machine will cost £240, 000 and is expected to generate total revenues of £45, 000 over the project's five year life. What is the ARR for this project?

$$ARR = \frac{(£45,000/5)}{£240,000} \times 100$$

$$= \frac{£9,000}{£240,000} \times 100\%$$

$$= 3.75\%$$

Advantages and disadvantages of ARR

The chief advantage with ARR method is that it is a simple method, which is readily understood and may be used as an initial screening test. It can provide an 'overview' of a new project but it lacks the sophistication of other methods.

There is a link with some accounting measures that are commonly used. The Average Rate of Return (ARR) is similar to the Return on Capital Employed (ROCE) in its construction; this may make the ARR easier for business planners to understand. The ARR is expressed in percentage terms and this, again, may make it easier for managers to use.

There are several criticisms of ARR, which raise questions about its practical application.

(a) Ignores the time value of money.

(b) Disregards the timing of the profits: the profit average will remain the same whether profits are higher in earlier years or *vice versa*.

(c) No definitive signal is given by the ARR to help managers decide whether or not to invest. This lack of a guide for decision-making means that investment decisions remain subjective.

2.2 Payback

Definitions

> **Payback period** is the number of years it takes the cash inflows from a capital investment project to equal the cash outflows.
>
> The **payback period method** tells you how long it would take to recover an investment from the returns attributable to that investment.

An organisation may have a target payback period, above which projects are rejected.

The usual way that organisations decide between two or more competing projects is to accept the project that has the shortest payback period. Payback is often used as an initial screening method.

Payback period = Initial payment / Annual cash inflow

So, if £4 million is invested with the aim of earning £500, 000 per year (net cash earnings), the payback period is calculated thus:

P = £4,000,000 / £500,000 = 8 years

NOTES

This all looks fairly easy! But what if the project has more uneven cash inflows? Then we need to work out the payback period on the cumulative cash flow over the duration of the project as a whole.

EXAMPLE: PAYBACK PERIOD WITH UNEVEN CASH FLOWS

The following project has an initial investment in year 0 of £4,000 with uneven cashflows over a six-year period. By calculating the cumulative cash flow for the project each year we can find the payback period.

Year	*Cash flow (£000)*	*Cumulative cash flow (£000)*
0	(4,000)	(4,000)
1	750	(3,250)
2	750	(2,500)
3	900	(1,600)
4	1,000	(600)
5	600	0
6	400	400

The payback period is precisely five years.

The shorter the payback period, the better the investment, under the payback method. We can appreciate the problems of this method when we consider appraising several projects alongside each other.

Year	*Project*					
	1	2	3	4	5	6
0	(50)	(100)	(80)	(100)	(100)	(100)
1	5	50	40	40	30	5
2	10	30	20	30	30	10
3	15	20	20	20	40	85
4	20	40	20	10	10	10
5		20	20	5	20	20
6		10	20	10	40	30
Payback period (Yrs)	4	3	3	4	3	3

You can see that the payback period for four of the projects (2, 3, 5 and 6) is three years. In this case, then, the four projects are of equal merit. But, here we must face the real problem posed by payback: the time value of income flows.

Put simply, this issue relates to the sacrifice made as a result of having to wait to receive the funds. In economic terms, this is known as the opportunity cost. More on this point follows later.

So, because there is a time value constraint here, the four projects cannot be viewed as equivalent. Project 2 is better than 3 because the revenues flow quicker in years one and two. Project 2 is also better than Projects 5 and 6, because of the earlier flows and because the post-payback revenues are concentrated in the earlier part of that period.

Advantages and disadvantages of payback period

First, it is popular because of its simplicity. Payback is useful in the appraisal of risky investment opportunities Research over the years has shown that UK firms favour it and perhaps this is understandable given how easy it is to calculate.

Second, in a business environment of rapid technological change, new plant and machinery may need to be replaced sooner than in the past, so a quick payback on investment is essential. This method (unlike ARR) does make some recognition of the time value of money – although it is quite coarse.

Third, the investment climate, in the UK in particular, demands that investors are rewarded with fast returns. Many profitable opportunities for long-term investment are overlooked because they involve a longer wait for revenues to flow.

There are several arguments against Payback.

(a) It lacks objectivity. Who decides the length of optimal payback time? No one does – it is decided by pitting one investment opportunity against another.

(b) It fails to recognise receipts or expenditure after the payback point.

(c) It fails to recognise the pattern of receipts during the Payback period.

(d) It takes no account of the effect on business profitability; its sole concern is cash flow.

Income expected after the payback point has been reached is not recognised by the Payback technique. Any such income could be substantial and long-term, or could be minimal and short-term. However, this method will not distinguish because the income is expected after the payback point. Equally, any expenditure made after the payback point is reached will be ignored. So potentially substantial dismantling costs or shutdown costs expected at the end of an investment's useful life would be ignored purely because they are made after the payback point has been reached.

The pattern of receipts expected during the payback period is ignored by the Payback Period technique. There may be two projects, each promising a Payback Period of 3.00 years. One promises a large return in year 1, with smaller returns in years 2 and 3. The other promises a small return in years 1 and 2, with a larger return in year 3. Clearly, the pattern of returns with the first investment is more desirable, but this will not be recognised by the Payback Period technique, which only considers the *total* returns during the Payback period.

It is probably best to regard Payback as one of the first methods you use to assess competing projects. It could be used as an initial screening tool, but it is inappropriate as a basis for sophisticated investment decisions.

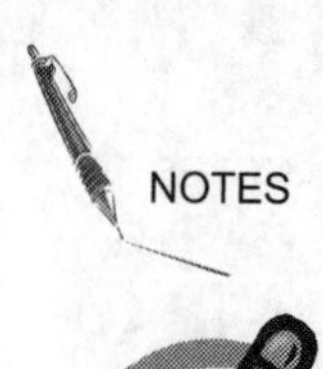

Activity 1 **(10 minutes)**

A project requires a capital outlay of £900,000 and earns the following cash inflows over the following seven years.

Year	1	2	3	4	5	6	7
Inflows (£'000)	200	250	300	450	400	200	150

(a) In what year does payback occur?
(b) Calculate the ARR.

3 DISCOUNTED CASH FLOW (DCF) METHODS

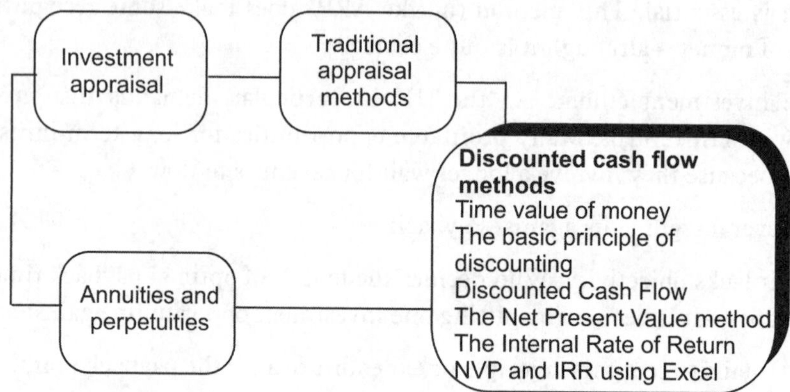

3.1 Time value of money

Neither the Accounting Rate of Return nor the Payback method takes into account the time value of money. Even disregarding inflation, £1 today is not worth the same as £1 at a future date.

The concept of the time value of money suggests that, in investment terms, money has a value depending on the exact date on which it is received or paid. It is easiest to explain this concept by reference to an illustration.

Suppose that I had a contract under which I had to pay you precisely £100 in exactly one year's time. Suppose that it is convenient for both of us if I settled this debt today (ie exactly one year early). How much should I pay you?

Clearly, I would not pay you £100 today, because I am settling the debt one year early and I will lose the investment value of that £100 for the year. Also, you would gain an investment opportunity, since you would have the £100 one year early. If you could invest the money to earn 10% p.a. interest, you would have £110.00 at the end of the year (ie the date on which I am due to make the payment according to the contract). Remember that the contract provided for you to receive £100 at the end of the year – not £110.

So, I would pay an amount less than £100 to settle the debt today, recognising the investment opportunity to you and the loss of investment opportunity to me. But exactly how much should I pay to settle the debt today?

The answer is that I would pay £90.91 to settle the debt today. You would then invest that amount of £90.91. You would earn £9.09 in interest (ie 10% of £90.91) and will have £100.00 in one year's time – £90.91 from me and £9.09 from the one-year investment.

In investment terms, assuming that the best interest rate that you could receive is 10% pa, you would not care whether I paid you £90.91 today or £100 in exactly one year's time, since both amounts would have the same value to you. Note that, in making this statement, we have ignored risk and tax.

Definition

> The term **'present value'** simply means the amount of money which must be invested now for n years at an interest rate of r%, to earn a particular future sum of money at the time it will be due

3.2 The basic principle of discounting

To understand the calculations involved in discounting, it is useful to look at compounding first.

The basic principle of **compounding** is that if we invest £X now for n years at r% interest per annum, we should obtain £X $(1 + r)^n$ in n years' time.

Thus if we invest £10,000 now for four years at 10% interest per annum, we will have a total investment worth £10,000 × 1.10^4 = £14,641 at the end of four years (that is, at Year 4 if it is now Year 0).

Definition

> The basic principle of **discounting** is that if we wish to have £V in n years' time, we need to invest a certain sum *now* (year 0) at an interest rate of r% in order to obtain the required sum of money in the future (year n).

For example, if we wish to have £14,641 in four years' time, how much money would we need to invest now at 10% interest per annum? This is the reverse of compounding.

Using our corresponding formula, $S = X(1 + r)^n$

Where X = the original sum invested

r = 10%

n = 4

S = £14,641

$$£14,641 = X(1 + 0.1)^4$$

$$£14,641 = X \times 1.4641$$

$$\therefore X = \frac{£14,641}{1.4641} = £10,000$$

£10,000 now, with the capacity to earn a return of 10% per annum, is the equivalent in value of £14,641 after four years. We can therefore say that **£10,000 is the present value (PV) of £14,641 at Year 4, at an interest rate of 10%.**

The formula for discounting

FORMULA TO LEARN

The **discounting formula** is

$$X = S \times \frac{1}{(1+r)^n}$$

where S is the sum to be received after n time periods
X is the present value (PV) of that sum
r is the rate of return, expressed as a proportion
n is the number of time periods (usually years).

The rate r is sometimes called a cost of capital.

Note that this equation is just a rearrangement of the compounding formula.

EXAMPLE: DISCOUNTING

(a) Calculate the present value of £60,000 at Year 6, if a return of 15% per annum is obtainable.

(b) Calculate the present value of £100,000 at Year 5, if a return of 6% per annum is obtainable.

(c) How much would a person need to invest now at 12% to earn £4,000 at year 2 and £4,000 at Year 3?

SOLUTION

The discounting formula, $X = S \times \frac{1}{(1+r)^n}$ is required.

(a) S = £60,000
n = 6
r = 0.15

$$PV = 60{,}000 \times \frac{1}{1.15^6}$$
$$= 60{,}000 \times 0.432$$
$$= £25{,}920$$

(b) S = £100,000
n = 5
r = 0.06

$$PV = 100,000 \times \frac{1}{1.06^5}$$
$$= 100,000 \times 0.747$$
$$= £74,700$$

(c) S = £4,000
n = 2 or 3
r = 0.12

$$PV = (4,000 \times \frac{1}{1.12^2}) + (4,000 \times \frac{1}{1.12^3})$$
$$= 4,000 \times (0.797 + 0.712)$$
$$= £6,036$$

This calculation can be checked as follows.

	£
Year 0	6,036.00
Interest for the first year (12%)	724.32
	6,760.32
Interest for the second year (12%)	811.24
	7,571.56
Less withdrawal	(4,000.00)
	3,571.56
Interest for the third year (12%)	428.59
	4,000.15
Less withdrawal	(4,000.00)
Rounding error	0.15

Activity 2 **(10 minutes)**

Work out the present value at 7% interest of £16,000 at Year 12.

3.3 Discounted Cash Flow (DCF)

Discounted cash flow (DCF) involves the application of discounting arithmetic to the estimated future cash flows (receipts and expenditures) from a project in order to decide whether the project is expected to earn a satisfactory rate of return.

DCF makes use of the Present Value concept, the idea that money you have now should be valued more than an identical amount you would receive in the future. Why? The money you have now could (in principle) be invested now and gain return or interest, between now and the future time. Money you will not have until some future time cannot be used now. Therefore, the future money's value is discounted in financial evaluation, to reflect its lesser value. What that future money is worth today is called its 'Present Value,' and what it will be worth when it finally arrives in the future is called its 'Future Value'. Just how much present value should be discounted from future value is determined by two things: the amount of time between now and future payment and an interest rate.

There are two methods of using DCF techniques.

- The net present value (NPV) method
- The internal rate of return (IRR) method

3.4 The Net Present Value (NPV) method

Definition

The **net present value (NPV) method** works out the present values of all items of income and expenditure related to an investment at a given rate of return, and then works out a net total. If it is positive, the investment is considered to be acceptable. If it is negative, the investment is considered to be unacceptable.

Net Present Value (NPV) over a given period of time equals the sum of the Discounted Cash Flows and requires a firm's Discount Rate for calculation. A project is profitable if its NPV is greater than zero. If multiple projects are under consideration, the one with the most positive NPV is the most profitable.

NPV is a very useful indicator because it is a direct measure of the project's profitability in money terms and therefore most directly relates to the company's interest in higher cash flows. It does, however, depend significantly on the value of the Discount Rate.

EXAMPLE: THE NET PRESENT VALUE OF A PROJECT

Dog Ltd is considering whether to spend £5,000 on an item of equipment. The 'cash profits', the excess of income over cash expenditure, from the project would be £3,000 in the first year and £4,000 in the second year.

The company will not invest in any project unless it offers a return in excess of 15% per annum.

Task

Assess whether the investment is worthwhile, or 'viable'.

SOLUTION

In this example, an outlay of £5,000 now promises a return of £3,000 **during** the first year and £4,000 **during** the second year. It is a convention in DCF, however, that cash flows spread over a year are assumed to occur **at the end of the year,** so that the cash flows of the project are as follows.

	£
Year 0 (now)	(5,000)
Year 1 (at the end of the year)	3,000
Year 2 (at the end of the year)	4,000

The NPV method takes the following approach.

(a) The project offers £3,000 at year 1 and £4,000 at year 2, for an outlay of £5,000 now.

(b) The company might invest elsewhere to earn a return of 15% per annum.

(c) If the company did invest at exactly 15% per annum, how much would it need to invest now, at 15%, to earn £3,000 at the end of year 1 plus £4,000 at the end of year 2?

(d) Is it cheaper to invest £5,000 in the project, or to invest elsewhere at 15%, in order to obtain these future cash flows?

If the company did invest elsewhere at 15% per annum, the amount required to earn £3,000 in year 1 and £4,000 in year 2 would be as follows.

Year	*Cash flow* £	*Discount factor* 15%	*Present value* £
1	3,000	$\frac{1}{1.15} = 0.870$	2,610
2	4,000	$\frac{1}{(1.15)^2} = 0.756$	3,024
			5,634

The choice is to invest £5,000 in the project, or £5,634 elsewhere at 15%, in order to obtain these future cash flows. We can therefore reach the following conclusion.

- It is cheaper to invest in the project, by £634.
- The project offers a return of over 15% per annum.

The net present value is the difference between the present value of cash inflows from the project (£5,634) and the present value of future cash outflows (in this example, £5,000 $\times 1/1.15^0$ = £5,000).

An NPV statement could be drawn up as follows.

Year	*Cash flow* £	*Discount factor* 15%	*Present value* £
0	(5,000)	1.000	(5,000)
1	3,000	$\frac{1}{1.15} = 0.870$	2,610
2	4,000	$\frac{1}{(1.15)^2} = 0.756$	3,024
		Net present value	+634

The project has a positive net present value, so it is acceptable.

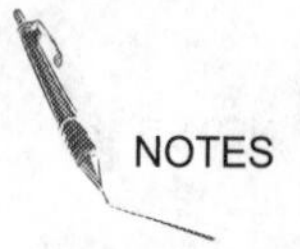

NOTES

Activity 3 **(20 minutes)**

A company is wondering whether to spend £18,000 on an item of equipment, in order to obtain cash profits as follows.

Year	£
1	6,000
2	8,000
3	5,000
4	1,000

The company requires a return of 10% per annum.

Required

Use the NPV method to assess whether the project is viable.

Discount tables

Assuming that money earns, say, 10% per annum:

(a) the PV (present value) of £1 at year 1 is $£1 \times \frac{1}{1.10} = £1 \times 0.909$

(b) similarly, the PV of £1 at year 2 is $£1 \times \frac{1}{(1.10)^2} = £1 \times 0.826$

(c) the PV of £1 at year 3 is $£1 \times \frac{1}{(1.10)^3} = £1 \times 0.751$

Discount tables show the value of $1/(1 + r)^n$ for different values of r and n. The 10% discount factors of 0.909, 0.826 and 0.751 will be shown in the discount tables that you are using for 10%. (Discount tables are at the end of this book.)

Project comparison

The NPV method can also be used to compare two or more investment options. For example, suppose that Daisy Ltd can choose between the investment outlined in Question 2 above *or* a second investment, which also costs £28,000 but which would earn £6,500 in the first year, £7,500 in the second, £8,500 in the third, £9,500 in the fourth and £10,500 in the fifth. Which one should Daisy Ltd choose?

The decision rule is to choose the option with the highest NPV. We therefore need to calculate the NPV of the second option.

Year	*Cash flow*	*Discount factor*	*Present value*
	£	11%	£
0	(28,000)	1.000	(28,000)
1	6,500	0.901	5,857
2	7,500	0.812	6,090
3	8,500	0.731	6,214
4	9,500	0.659	6,261
5	10,500	0.593	6,227
			NPV = 2,649

Daisy Ltd should therefore invest in the second option since it has the higher NPV.

Expected values and discounting

Future cash flows cannot be predicted with complete accuracy. To take account of this uncertainty an expected net present value can be calculated which is a weighted average net present value based on the probabilities of different sets of circumstances occurring. Let us have a look at an example.

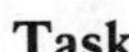

EXAMPLE: EXPECTED NET PRESENT VALUE

An organisation with a cost of capital of 5% is contemplating investing £340,000 in a project which has a 25% chance of being a big success and producing cash inflows of £210,000 after one and two years. There is, however, a 75% chance of the project not being quite so successful, in which case the cash inflows will be £162,000 after one year and £174,000 after two years.

Task

Calculate an NPV and hence advise the organisation.

SOLUTION

	Discount	*Success*		*Failure*	
Year	*factor*	*Cash flow*	*PV*	*Cash flow*	*PV*
	5%	£'000	£'000	£'000	£'000
0	1.000	(340)	(340.00)	(340)	(340.000)
1	0.952	210	199.92	162	154.224
2	0.907	210	190.47	174	157.818
			50.39		(27.958)

NPV = (25% × 50.39) + (75% × –27.958) = –8.371

The NPV is – £8,371 and hence the organisation should not invest in the project.

Limitations of using the NPV method

There are a number of problems associated with using the NPV method in practice.

(a) **The future discount factors** (or interest rates) which are used in calculating NPVs can only be **estimated** and are not known with certainty. Discount rates that are estimated for time periods far into the future are therefore less likely to be accurate, thereby leading to less accurate NPV values.

(b) Similarly, NPV calculations make use of estimated **future cash flows**. As with future discount factors, cash flows which are estimated for cash flows several years into the future cannot really be predicted with any real certainty.

(c) When using the NPV method it is common to assume that all cash flows occur **at the end of the year**. However, this assumption is also likely to give rise to less accurate NPV values.

There are a number of computer programs available these days which enable a range of NPVs to be calculated for a number of different circumstances (best-case and worst-case situations and so on). Such programs allow some of the limitations mentioned above to be alleviated.

3.5 The internal rate of return (IRR) method

The internal rate of return (IRR) method of evaluating investments is an alternative to the NPV method. The NPV method of discounted cash flow determines whether an investment earns a positive or a negative NPV when discounted at a given rate of interest. If the NPV is zero (that is, the present values of costs and benefits are equal) the return from the project would be exactly the rate used for discounting.

Definition

The **IRR method of discounted cash flow** is a method which determines the rate of interest (the internal rate of return) at which the NPV is 0. The internal rate of return is therefore the rate of return on an investment.

The IRR method will indicate that a **project is viable if the IRR exceeds the minimum acceptable rate of return**. Thus if the company expects a minimum return of, say, 15%, a project would be viable if its IRR is more than 15%.

EXAMPLE: THE IRR METHOD OVER ONE YEAR

If £500 is invested today and generates £600 in one year's time, the internal rate of return (r) can be calculated as follows.

$$\text{PV of cost} = \text{PV of benefits}$$

$$500 = \frac{600}{(1+r)}$$

$$500\,(1 + r) = 600$$

$$1 + r = \frac{600}{500} = 1.2$$

$$r = 0.2 = 20\%$$

The arithmetic for calculating the IRR is more complicated for investments and cash flows extending over a period of time longer than one year. A technique known as the **interpolation method** can be used to calculate an approximate IRR.

EXAMPLE: INTERPOLATION

A project costing £800 in year 0 is expected to earn £400 in Year 1, £300 in Year 2 and £200 in Year 3.

Task

Calculate the internal rate of return.

SOLUTION

The IRR is calculated by first of all finding the NPV at each of two interest rates. Ideally, one interest rate should give a small positive NPV and the other a small negative NPV. The IRR would then be somewhere between these two interest rates: above the rate where the NPV is positive, but below the rate where the NPV is negative.

A very rough guideline for estimating at what interest rate the NPV might be close to zero, is to take

$$\frac{2}{3} \times \left(\frac{\text{profit}}{\text{cost of the project}} \right)$$

In our example, the total profit over three years is £(400 + 300 + 200 – 800) = £100. An approximate IRR is therefore calculated as:

$$\tfrac{2}{3} \times \frac{100}{800} = 0.08 \text{ approx.}$$

A starting point is to try 8%.

(a) Try 8%

Year	*Cash flow*	*Discount factor*	*Present value*
	£	8%	£
0	(800)	1.000	(800.0)
1	400	0.926	370.4
2	300	0.857	257.1
3	200	0.794	158.8
		NPV	(13.7)

The NPV is negative, therefore the project fails to earn 8% and the IRR must be less than 8%.

(b) Try 6%

Year	*Cash flow*	*Discount factor*	*Present value*
	£	6%	£
0	(800)	1.000	(800.0)
1	400	0.943	377.2
2	300	0.890	267.0
3	200	0.840	168.0
		NPV	12.2

The NPV is positive, therefore the project earns more than 6% and less than 8%.

The **IRR is now calculated by interpolation**. The result will not be exact, but it will be a close approximation. Interpolation assumes that the NPV falls in a straight line from +12.2 at 6% to –13.7 at 8%.

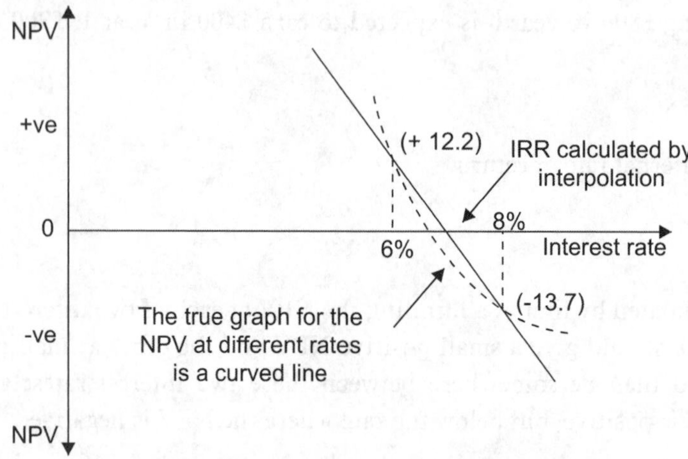

Figure 11.1: Graph to show IRR calculation by interpolation

FORMULA TO LEARN

The IRR, where the NPV is zero, can be calculated as follows.

IRR = $a\% + [\frac{A}{A-B} \times (b-a)]\%$ where

a is one interest rate
b is the other interest rate
A is the NPV at rate a
B is the NPV at rate b

(c) Thus, in our example, IRR = $6\% + \left[\frac{12.2}{(12.2+13.7)} \times (8-6)\right]\%$

= 6% + 0.942%

= 6.942% approx

(d) The answer is only an **approximation** because the NPV falls in a slightly curved line and not a straight line between +12.2 and –13.7.

Provided that NPVs close to zero are used, the linear assumption used in the interpolation method is nevertheless fairly accurate.

(e) Note that the formula will still work if A and B are both positive, or both negative, and even if a and b are a long way from the true IRR, but the results will be less accurate.

Activity 4 **(10 minutes)**

The net present value of an investment at 15% is £50,000 and at 20% is £10,000. The internal rate of return of this investment (to the nearest whole number) is:

A 16%
B 17%
C 18%
D 19%

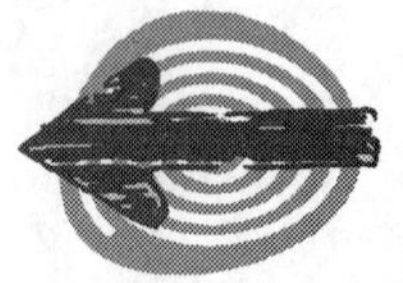

The IRR of a project can be estimated by plotting NPVs and their corresponding discount rates accurately on a graph. When all of the points are joined together, the approximate IRR value can be read off the graph at the point at which the line plotted crosses the x-axis.

3.6 NPV and IRR using Excel

The NPV and IRR functions are best explained through a worked example.

EXAMPLE: NPV AND IRR ON A SPREADSHEET

An organisation is considering undertaking a project, the financial details of which are shown below.

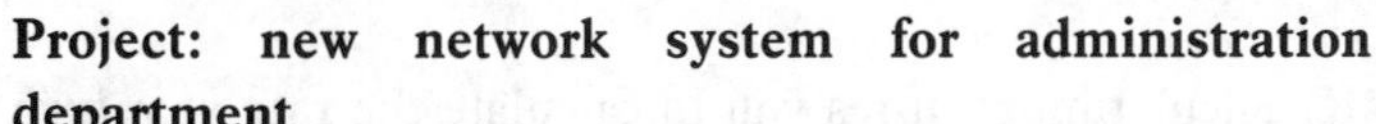
Project: new network system for administration department

Development and hardware purchase costs (all incurred now)		£150,000
Operating costs of new system (cash outflows per annum)	£55,000	
Annual savings from new system (cash inflow)	£115,000	
Annual net savings (net cash inflows)		£60,000
Expected system life	4 years	
Required return on investment	15% pa	

An **NPV calculation** for this project could be performed in Microsoft Excel as follows.

	A	B	C
1	**NPV calculation**		
2			£
3	Costs incurred now		(150,000)
4	Benefits in year 1	60,000	
5	Benefits in year 2	60,000	
6	Benefits in year 3	60,000	
7	Benefits in year 4	60,000	
8	Discounted value		171,299
9	**Net present value**		21,299
10			
11	**Variables**		
12			
13	Discount rate	15%	

The underlying formula are shown below, together with the 'function wizard' entries used (click on the *fx* symbol in the toolbar, or select Insert, Function, to start the function wizard – NPV and IRR are **Financial** functions).

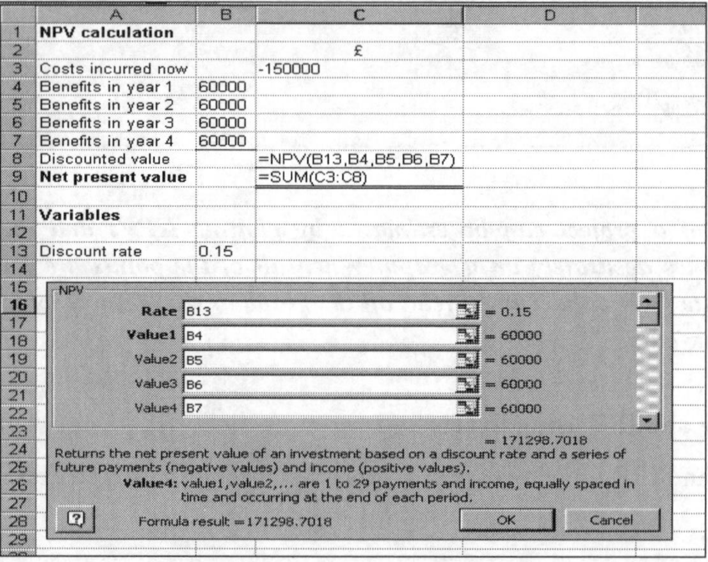

	A	B	C	D
1	**NPV calculation**			
2			£	
3	Costs incurred now		-150000	
4	Benefits in year 1	60000		
5	Benefits in year 2	60000		
6	Benefits in year 3	60000		
7	Benefits in year 4	60000		
8	Discounted value		=NPV(B13,B4,B5,B6,B7)	
9	**Net present value**		=SUM(C3:C8)	
10				
11	**Variables**			
12				
13	Discount rate	0.15		

In this example, the present value of the expected **benefits** of the project **exceed** the present value of its **costs**, all discounted at 15% pa, and so the project is financially **justifiable** because it would be expected to earn a yield greater than the minimum target return of 15%. Payback of the development costs and hardware costs of £150,000 would occur after 2½ years.

An internal rate of return (**IRR**) calculation requires you to calculate the **rate of return** on a project or investment and then **compare** this rate of return with the **cost of capital.**

If a project earns a higher rate of return than the cost of capital, it will have a positive NPV and should therefore go ahead (from a financial point of view).

If the rate of return is lower than the cost of capital, the NPV will be negative – the project is not financially worthwhile.

If a project earns a return that is exactly equal to the cost of capital, the NPV will be 0, meaning the project will break-even financially.

In our example the IRR is 22%, easily exceeding the cost of capital of 15%. The IRR calculation may be set up using the function wizard (click on the *fx* symbol in the toolbar, or select **Insert**, **Function**, to start the function wizard – NPV and IRR are **Financial** functions).

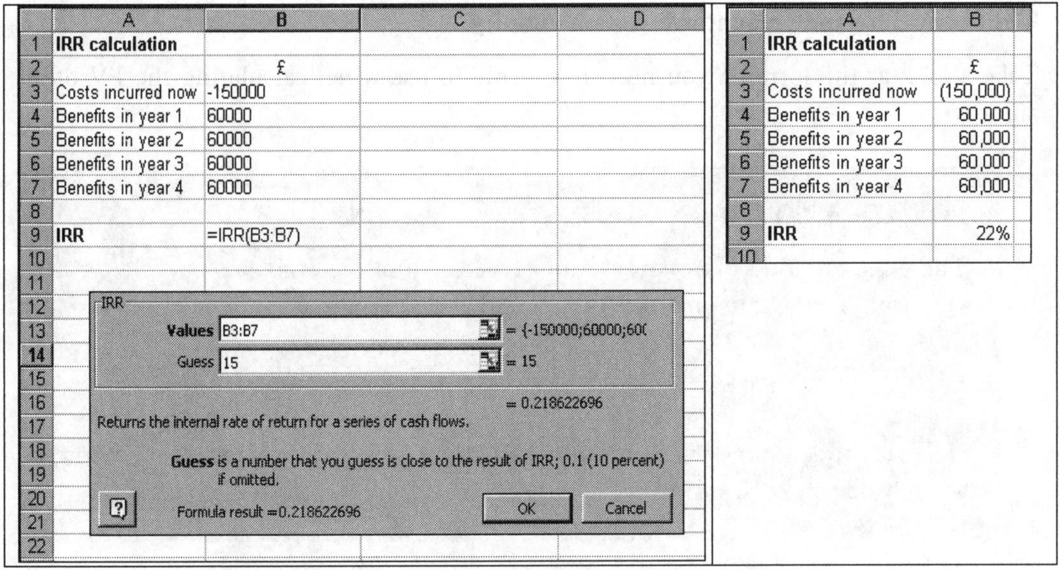

	A	B	C	D
1	**IRR calculation**			
2		£		
3	Costs incurred now	-150000		
4	Benefits in year 1	60000		
5	Benefits in year 2	60000		
6	Benefits in year 3	60000		
7	Benefits in year 4	60000		
8				
9	**IRR**	=IRR(B3:B7)		

	A	B
1	**IRR calculation**	
2		£
3	Costs incurred now	(150,000)
4	Benefits in year 1	60,000
5	Benefits in year 2	60,000
6	Benefits in year 3	60,000
7	Benefits in year 4	60,000
8		
9	**IRR**	22%

4 ANNUITIES AND PERPETUITIES

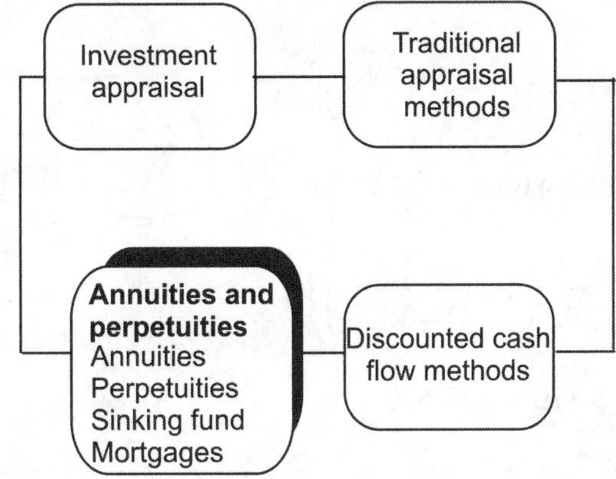

4.1 Annuities

Definition

An **annuity** is a constant sum of money received or paid each year for a given number of years.

Many individuals nowadays may invest in **annuities** that can be purchased either through a single payment or a number of payments. For example, individuals planning for their retirement might make regular payments into a pension fund over a number of years. Over the years, the pension fund should (hopefully) grow and the final value of the fund can be used to buy an annuity.

An **annuity** might run until the recipient's death, or it might run for a guaranteed term of n years.

The formula for the present value of an annuity

Take a look at the formula you need to be able to use when calculating the PV of an annuity.

FORMULA TO LEARN

The **present value of an annuity** of *£1* per annum receivable or payable for n years commencing in one year, discounted at r% per annum:

$$PV = \frac{1}{r}\left(1 - \frac{1}{(1+r)^n}\right)$$

Note that it is the PV of an annuity of *£1* and so you need to multiply it by the actual value of the annuity.

EXAMPLE: THE ANNUITY FORMULA

What is the present value of £4,000 per annum for years 1 to 4, at a discount rate of 10% per annum?

SOLUTION

Using the annuity formula with r = 0.1 and n = 4.

$$PV = 4{,}000 \times \left(\frac{1}{0.1}\left(1 - \frac{1}{(1+0.1)^4}\right)\right)$$

$$= 4{,}000 \times 3.170 = £12{,}680$$

Calculating a required annuity

If PV of £1 $= \frac{1}{r}\left(1 - \frac{1}{(1+r)^n}\right)$, then PV of £a $= a\left(\frac{1}{r}\left(1 - \frac{1}{(1+r)^n}\right)\right)$

$$\therefore a = \frac{\text{PV of £a}}{\left(\frac{1}{r}\left(1 - \frac{1}{(1+r)^n}\right)\right)}$$

This enables us to calculate the annuity required to yield a given rate of return (r) on a given investment (P).

EXAMPLE: REQUIRED ANNUITY

The present value of a ten-year annuity receivable which begins in one year's time at 7% per annum compound is £3,000. What is the annual amount of the annuity?

NOTES 

SOLUTION

$$\text{PV of } \pounds a = \pounds 3{,}000$$

$$r = 0.07$$

$$t = 10$$

$$a = \frac{3{,}000}{\left(\frac{1}{0.07}\left(1 - \frac{1}{(1.07)^{10}}\right)\right)}$$

$$= \frac{\pounds 3{,}000}{7.024} = 427.11$$

Activity 5 **(20 minutes)**

(a) It is important to practise using the annuity factor formula. Calculate annuity factors in the following cases.

(i) n = 4, r = 10%
(ii) n = 3, r = 9.5%
(iii) For 20 years at a rate of 25%

(b) What is the present value of £4,000 per annum for four years, **Years 2 to 5**, at a discount rate of 10% per annum? Use the annuity formula.

Activity 6 **(10 minutes)**

In the formula:

$$PV = \frac{1}{r}\left(1 - \frac{1}{(1+r)^n}\right)$$

$$r = 0.04$$

$$n = 10$$

what is the PV?

A 6.41
B 7.32
C 8.11
D 9.22

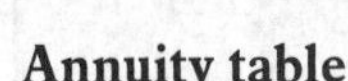

Annuity tables

To calculate the present value of a constant annual cash flow, or annuity, we can multiply the annual cash flows by the sum of the discount factors for the relevant years. These total factors are known as **cumulative present value factors** or **annuity factors**.

As with 'present value factors of £1 in year n', there are tables for annuity factors. (For example, the cumulative present value factor of £1 per annum for five years at 11% per annum is in the column for 11% and the Year 5 row, and is 3.696.)

The use of annuity tables to calculate a required annuity

Just as the formula can be used to calculate an annuity, so too can the tables. Since the present value of an annuity is PV = a × annuity factor from the tables, we have

FORMULA TO LEARN

$$\textbf{Annuity } (a) = \frac{\text{Present value of an annuity}}{\text{Annuity factor}}$$

EXAMPLE: ANNUITY TABLES

A bank grants a loan of £3,000 at 7% per annum. The borrower is to repay the loan in ten annual instalments. How much must she pay each year?

SOLUTION

Since the bank pays out the loan money *now*, the present value (PV) of the loan is £3,000. The annual repayment on the loan can be thought of as an annuity. We can therefore use the annuity formula

$$\text{Annuity} = \frac{\text{PV}}{\text{annuity factor}}$$

in order to calculate the loan repayments. The annuity factor is found by looking in the cumulative present value tables under n = 10 and r = 7%. The corresponding factor = 7.024.

$$\text{Therefore, annuity} = \frac{£3{,}000}{7.024}$$

$$= £427.11$$

The loan repayments are therefore £427.11 per annum.

4.2 Perpetuities

Definitions

A **perpetuity** is an annuity which lasts for ever, instead of stopping after n years.

The **present value of a perpetuity** is PV = a/r where r is the cost of capital as a proportion.

FORMULA TO LEARN

The present value of £1 per annum, payable or receivable in perpetuity, commencing in one year, discounted at r% per annum

$$PV = \frac{1}{r}$$

EXAMPLE: A PERPETUITY

How much should be invested *now* (to the nearest £) to receive £35,000 per annum in perpetuity if the annual rate of interest is 9%?

SOLUTION

$$PV = \frac{a}{r}$$

where a = £35,000

r = 9%

$$\therefore PV = \frac{£35,000}{0.09}$$

$$= £388,889$$

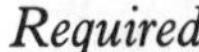

EXAMPLE: A PERPETUITY IN INVESTMENT APPRAISAL

Mostly Ltd is considering a project which would cost £50,000 now and yield £9,000 per annum every year in perpetuity, starting a year from now. The cost of capital is 15%.

Required

Assess whether the project is viable.

SOLUTION

Year	*Cash flow*	*Discount factor*	*Present value*
	£	15%	£
0	(50,000)	1.0	(50,000)
$1 - \infty$	9,000	1/0.15	60,000
		NPV	10,000

The project is viable because it has a positive net present value when discounted at 15%.

The timing of cash flows

Note that both annuity tables and the formulae assume that the first payment or receipt is a year from now. Always check assessment questions for when the first payment falls.

BPP LEARNING MEDIA

NOTES

For example, if there are five equal payments starting now, and the interest rate is 8%, we should use a factor of 1 (for today's payment) + 3.312 (for the other four payments) = 4.312.

Activity 7 **(15 minutes)**

Hilarious Jokes Ltd has arranged a fifteen year lease, at an annual rent of £9,000. The first rental payment is to be paid immediately, and the others are to be paid at the end of each year.

What is the present value of the lease at 9%?

A £79,074 B £72,549 C £81,549 D £70,074

Activity 8 **(10 minutes)**

How much should be invested now (to the nearest £) to receive £20,000 per annum in perpetuity if the annual rate of interest is 20%?

A £4,000
B £24,000
C £93,500
D £100,000

4.3 Sinking funds

A sinking fund is an investment into which equal annual instalments (an **annuity**) are paid in order to earn interest, so that by the end of a given period, the investment is large enough to pay off a known commitment at that time (**final value**).

EXAMPLE: A SINKING FUND (1)

Jamie wants to buy a Porsche 911. This will cost him £45,000 in two years' time. He has decided to set aside an equal amount each quarter until he has the amount he needs. Assuming he can earn interest in his building society account at 5% pa how much does he need to set aside each year? Assume the first amount is set aside one period from now.

(a) Calculate the amounts using the annuity formula.
(b) Calculate the amounts using annuity tables.

SOLUTION

If Jamie needs £45,000 in two years' time, the present value that he needs is:

$$PV = \frac{£45,000}{(1+0.05)^2}$$

$$= £40,816$$

(a) **Using the annuity formula**

The annuity factor = $\frac{1}{r}\left(1-\frac{1}{(1+r)^n}\right)$

where r = 0.05
n = 2

Annuity factor $= \frac{1}{0.05}\left(1-\frac{1}{(1+0.05)^2}\right)$

= 1.8594

The amount to save each quarter is an annuity. We can therefore use the formula

Annuity $= \frac{\text{PV}}{\text{Annuity factor}}$

$= \frac{£40{,}816}{1.8594}$

= £21,951

Therefore Jamie must set aside £21,951 per annum.

(b) **Using annuity tables**

When n = 2 and r = 5%, the annuity factor (from cumulative present value tables) is 1.859.

Annuity $= \frac{\text{PV}}{\text{Annuity factor}}$

$= \frac{£40{,}816}{1.859}$

= £21,956

The difference of £5 (£21,956 – £21,951) is due to rounding.

EXAMPLE: A SINKING FUND (2)

At this point it is worth considering the value of the fund that would have built up if we had saved £21,956 pa for two years at an interest rate of 5%, with the first payment at the end of Year 1.

BPP LEARNING MEDIA

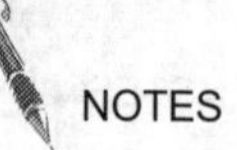

SOLUTION

The situation we are looking at here can be shown on the following time line.

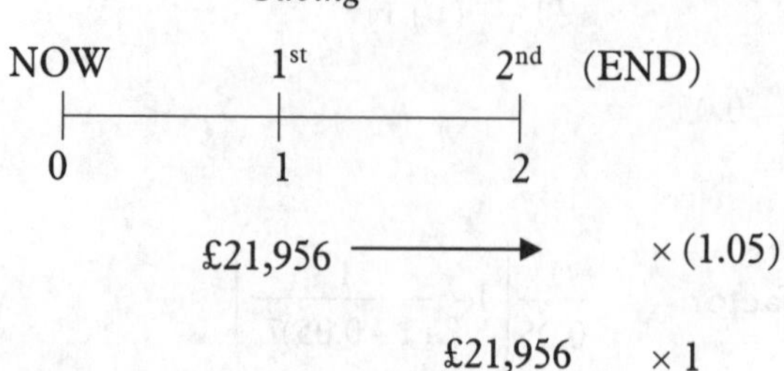

The value of the fund at the end of Year 2 is

21,956 + 21,956(1.05)

This is a geometric progression with

A = £21,956

R = 1.05

n = 2

$$\text{If} \quad S = \frac{A(R^n - 1)}{R - 1}$$

$$= \frac{21{,}956(1.05^2 - 1)}{1.05 - 1}$$

= £45,000 (to the nearest £100)

Therefore, if we were to save £21,956 for two years at 5% per annum we would achieve a final value of £45,000. Can you see how compounding and discounting really are the reverse of each other? In our first example, we calculated that Jamie needed to save £21,956 pa for two years at a cost of capital of 5%. In the second example, we demonstrated that using the equation for the sum of a geometric progression, saving £21,956 pa for two years would result in a sinking fund of £45,000.

Work through these two examples again if you are not totally clear: it is vitally important that you understand how compounding and discounting are linked.

4.4 Mortgages

When an individual takes out a mortgage, the present value of the mortgage is the amount of the loan taken out. Most mortgages will be taken out at a given rate of interest for a fixed term.

$$\textbf{Annuity} = \frac{\text{Present value of annuity (original vaue of mortgage)}}{\text{Annuity factor (from formula or tables)}}$$

The annuity is the regular repayment value.

Look at the following example.

EXAMPLE: MORTGAGES

Tim has taken out a £30,000 mortgage over 25 years. Interest is to be charged at 12%. Calculate the monthly repayment.

SOLUTION

Present value of mortgage = £30,000

Annuity factor $= \frac{1}{0.12}\left(1 - \frac{1}{(1+0.12)^{25}}\right)$

= 7.843

Annuity (annual repayments) $= \frac{\text{PV}}{\text{annuity factor}}$

$= \frac{£30{,}000}{7.843}$

= £3,825

Monthly repayment = £3,825 ÷ 12 = £318.75

Sinking funds are an example of **saving** while mortgages are an example of **borrowing**.

Borrowing versus saving

The chief advantage of borrowing money via a loan or mortgage is that the asset the money is used to purchase can be owned now (and therefore be put to use to earn money) rather than waiting. On the other hand, borrowing money takes some control away from the business's managers and makes a business venture more risky. Because an obligation is owed to the lender the managers may have less freedom to do what they like with their assets. If the business is not successful the debt will still be owed, and if the lender demands that it is repaid immediately the business might collapse.

The advantages of saving up are that no interest has to be paid and the business does not have to surrender any control to a third party. The savings will earn interest. However the money will not be available for other, potentially more profitable, uses. Also, the business cannot be sure in advance that it will be able to generate the cash needed over the timescale envisaged.

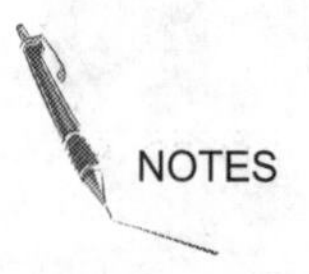

NOTES

Chapter roundup

- Discounting is the reverse of compounding. The discounting formula is $X = S \times 1/(1+r)^n$.
- The concept of present value can be thought of in two ways.
  - It is the value today of an amount to be received some time in the future.
  - It is the amount which would have to be invested today to produce a given amount at some future date.
- The discounting formula is $X = S \times \frac{1}{(1+r)^n}$ which is a rearrangement of the compounding formula.
- Discounted cash flow techniques can be used to evaluate capital expenditure projects. There are two methods: the NPV method and the IRR.
- The NPV method works out the present values of all items of income and expenditure related to an investment at a given rate of return, and then works out a net total. Only if it is positive, is the investment considered to be acceptable.
- The IRR method determines the rate of interest (the IRR) at which the NPV is 0. Interpolation, using the following formula, is often necessary. The project is viable if the IRR exceeds the minimum acceptable return.
- $IRR = a\% + \left[\frac{A}{A-B} \times (b-a)\right]\%$
- An annuity is a constant sum of money each year for a given number of years. The present value of an annuity can be calculated using the following formula, or by using annuity factors found in annuity tables.

$$PV = \frac{1}{r}\left(1 - \frac{1}{(1+r)^t}\right)$$

- $\text{Annuity} = \frac{\text{PV of annuity}}{\text{Annuity factor}}$
- A perpetuity is an annuity which lasts forever, instead of stopping after n years. The present value of a perpetuity = a/r.
- Compounding and discounting are directly linked to each other. Make sure that you understand clearly the relationship between them.

Quick quiz

1 What does the term present value mean?

2 The discounting formula is $X = S \times \frac{1}{(1+r)^n}$

where

S =
X =
r =
n =

} Choose the correct descriptions from the list below.

(a) the rate of return (as a proportion)
(b) the sum to be received after n time periods
(c) the PV of that sum
(d) the number of time periods

3 What are the two usual methods of capital expenditure appraisal using DCF techniques?

4 What is the formula used to calculate the IRR and what do the symbols used represent?

5 An annuity is a sum of money received every year.

TRUE ☐

FALSE ☐

6 What is a perpetuity?

7 What is the formula for the present value of a perpetuity?

8 If Fred were to save £7,000 per annum, and we used the formula for the sum of a geometric progression to calculate the value of the fund that would have built up over ten years at an interest rate of 20%, what is the value of A to be used in the formula if:

(a) the first payment is now
(b) the first payment is in one year's time

9 What is the main advantage of borrowing as opposed to saving?

Answers to quick quiz

1 The amount of money which must be invested now for n years at an interest rate of r% to give a future sum of money at the time it will be due.

2 S = (b)

X = (c)

r = (a)

n = (d)

3 The net present value (NPV) method

The Internal rate of return (IRR) method

4 $IRR = a\% + \left[\frac{A}{A - B} \times (b - a)\right]\%$

where a = one interest rate
b = another interest rate
A = the NPV at rate a
B = the NPV at rate b

5 False. It is a **constant** sum of money **received** or **paid** each year for a **given number** of years.

6 An annuity which lasts forever.

7 PV = a/r

8 (a) A = £7,000 × 1.2
(b) A = £7,000

9 The money is available **now** to buy the required asset as opposed to at the end of the savings period.

Answers to activities

1 Payback occurs during Year 4. £450 000 revenues are generated in Year 4. Because £150 000 remained to be paid off at the start of Year 4, the payback period is 3 years + 150/450 = $^1/_3$ of a year.

Payback = 3 $^1/_3$ years = 3 years and 4 months

Accounting Rate of Return

$$ARR = \frac{\text{Average annual profits}}{\text{Initial capital costs}} \times 100\%$$

$$= \frac{£278{,}571}{£900{,}000} \times 100\%$$

= 30.95 %

2 PV = £7,104

Working

Using the discounting formula, $X = S \times \frac{1}{(1+r)^n}$

where S = £16,000

n = 12

r = 0.07

X = PV

$$PV = £16{,}000 \times \frac{1}{1.07^{12}} = £7{,}104$$

3

Year	*Cash flow*	*Discount factor*	*Present value*
	£	10%	£
0	(18,000)	1.00	(18,000)
		0	
1	6,000	$\frac{1}{1.10} = 0.909$	5,454
2	8,000	$\frac{1}{1.10^2} = 0.826$	6,608
3	5,000	$\frac{1}{1.10^3} = 0.751$	3,755
4	1,000	$\frac{1}{1.10^4} = 0.683$	683
		Net present value	(1,500)

The NPV is negative. We can therefore draw the following conclusions.

(a) It is cheaper to invest elsewhere at 10% than to invest in the project.

(b) The project would earn a return of less than 10%.

(c) The project is not viable (since the PV of the costs is greater than the PV of the benefits).

4

$$\text{IRR} = a\% + \left[\frac{A}{A-B} \times (b-a)\right]\%$$

Where a = one interest rate = 15%
b = other interest rate = 20%
A = NPV at rate a = £50,000
B = NPV at rate b = –£10,000

$$\text{IRR} = 15\% + \left[\frac{£50{,}000}{£50{,}000-(-10{,}000)} \times (20-15)\right]\%$$

= 15% + 4.17%
= 19.17%
= 19%

The correct answer is therefore D.

5

(a) (i) $\frac{1}{0.1}\left(1-\frac{1}{(1+0.1)^4}\right) = 3.170$

(ii) $\frac{1}{0.095}\left(1-\frac{1}{(1+0.095)^3}\right) = 2.509$

(iii) $\frac{1}{0.25}\left(1-\frac{1}{(1+0.25)^{20}}\right) = 3.954$

(b) The formula will give the value of £4,000 at 10% per annum, not as a year 0 present value, but as a value at the year preceding the first annuity cash flow, that is, at Year (2 – 1) = Year 1. We must therefore discount our solution in Section 4.5 further, from a Year 1 to a Year 0 value.

$$PV = £12{,}680 \times \frac{1}{1.10} = £11{,}527.27$$

6

$$PV = \frac{1}{0.04}\left(1 - \frac{1}{(1+0.04)^{10}}\right)$$

$$= 8.11$$

The correct answer is therefore C.

7 The correct way to answer this question is to use the cumulative present value tables for r = 9% and n = 14 because the first payment is to be paid immediately (and not in one year's time). A common trap in a question like this would be to look up r = 9% and n = 15 in the tables. If you did this, get out of the habit now, before you sit your exam!

From the cumulative present value tables, when r = 9% and n = 14, the annuity factor is 7.786.

The first payment is made now, and so has a PV of £9,000 (£9,000 × 1.00). Payments 2-15 have a PV of £9,000 × 7.786 = £70,074.

∴ The total PV = £9,000 (1st payment) + £70,074 (Payments 2-15)
= £79,074.

The correct answer is A.

(Alternatively, the annuity factor can be increased by 1 to take account of the fact that the first payment is *now*.

∴ annuity factor = 7.786 + 1 = 8.786

∴ PV = annuity × annuity factor
= £9,000 × 8.786 = £79,074)

8

$$PV = \frac{a}{r}$$

where a = annuity = £20,000
r = cost of capital as a proportion = 0.2

$$PV = \frac{£20{,}000}{0.2}$$

$$= £100{,}000$$

The correct answer is therefore D.

Appendix

Edexcel Guidelines for the BTEC Higher Nationals in Business

This book is designed to be of value to anyone who is studying Business Decision Making, whether as a subject in its own right or as a module forming part of any business-related degree or diploma.

However, it provides complete coverage of the topics listed in the Edexcel Guidelines for Optional Unit 6, Business Decision Making, of the BTEC Higher Nationals (revised 2010). We include the Edexcel Guidelines here for your reference, mapped to the topics covered in this book.

EDEXCEL GUIDELINES FOR OPTIONAL UNIT 6: BUSINESS DECISION MAKING

QCF Level 5

Aim

The aim of this unit is to give learners the opportunity to develop techniques for data gathering and storage, and an understanding of the tools available to create and present useful information, in order to make business decisions.

Unit abstract

In business, good decision making requires the effective use of information. This unit gives learners the opportunity to examine a variety of sources and develop techniques for four aspects of information: data gathering, data storage, and the tools available to create useful information and present it.

ICT is used in business for much of this work and an appreciation and use of appropriate ICT software is central to completion of this unit. Specifically, learners will use spreadsheets and other software for data analysis and the preparation of information. The use of spreadsheets to manipulate numbers, and understanding how to apply the results, are seen as more important than the mathematical derivation of formulae used.

Learners will also gain an appreciation of information systems currently used at all levels in an organisation as aids to decision making.

Learning outcomes

On successful completion of this unit a learner will:

1 Be able to use a variety of sources **for the collection of data**, both primary and secondary

2 Understand a range of **techniques to analyse data** effectively for business purposes

3 Be able to produce **information in appropriate formats** for decision making in an organisational context

4 Be able to use **software-generated information** to make decisions in an organisation

	Content	Covered in chapter(s)
1	**Sources for the collection of data**	
	Primary sources: survey methodology, questionnaire design, sample frame, sampling methods, sample error	1
	Secondary sources: Internet research, government and other published data, by-product data	1
2	**Techniques to analyse data**	
	Representative values: mean, median, mode, calculation from raw data and frequency distributions; using the results to draw valid conclusions	2
	Measures of dispersion: standard deviation for small and large samples; typical uses (statistical process eg control, buffer stock levels)	3
	Calculation: use of quartiles, percentiles, correlation coefficient	3, 4
3	**Information in appropriate formats**	
	Creation and interpretation of graphs using spreadsheets: line, pie, bar charts and histograms	6
	Scatter (XY) graphs and linear trend lines: extrapolation for forecasting – (reliability)	5
	Use of presentation software and techniques and report writing	6, 7
4	**Software-generated information**	
	Management information systems: computers and information processing tools for operational, tactical and strategic levels of the organisation	8
	Project management: networking and critical path analysis, Gantt and PERT charts	10
	Financial tools: net present value; discounted cash flow, internal rates of return (IRR function)	11

Learning outcomes **On successful completion of the unit a learner will:**	**Assessment criteria for pass** **The learner can:**
LO.1 Be able to use a variety of **sources for the collection of data**, both primary and secondary	1.1 Create a plan for the collection of primary and secondary data for a given business problem 1.2 Present the survey methodology and sampling frame used 1.3 Design a questionnaire for a given business problem
LO.2 Understand a **range of techniques to analyse data** effectively for business purposes	2.1 Create information for decision making by summarising data using representative values 2.2 Analyse the results to draw valid and useful conclusions in a business context 2.3 Analyse data using measures of dispersion to inform a given business scenario 2.4 Explain how quartiles, percentiles, and the correlation coefficient used to draw useful conclusions in a business context
LO.3 Be able to produce **information in appropriate formats** for decision making in an organisational context	3.1 Produce graphics using spreadsheets and draw valid conclusions based on the information derived 3.2 Create trend lines in spreadsheet graphs to assist in forecasting for specified business information 3.3 Prepare a business presentation using suitable software and techniques to disseminate information effectively 3.4 Produce a formal business report
LO.4 Use **software generate information** to make decisions at operational, tactical and strategic levels in an organisation	4.1 Use appropriate information processing tools 4.2 Prepare a project plan for an activity and determine the critical path 4.3 Use financial tools for decision making

Mathematical Tables

MATHEMATICAL TABLES

PRESENT VALUE TABLE

Present value of 1, ie $(1+r)^{-n}$

where r = discount rate

n = number of periods until payment

Periods (n)	Discount rates (r) 1%	2%	3%	4%	5%	6%	7%	8%	9%	10%
1	0.990	0.980	0.971	0.962	0.952	0.943	0.935	0.926	0.917	0.909
2	0.980	0.961	0.943	0.925	0.907	0.890	0.873	0.857	0.842	0.826
3	0.971	0.942	0.915	0.889	0.864	0.840	0.816	0.794	0.772	0.751
4	0.961	0.924	0.888	0.855	0.823	0.792	0.763	0.735	0.708	0.683
5	0.951	0.906	0.863	0.822	0.784	0.747	0.713	0.681	0.650	0.621
6	0.942	0.888	0.837	0.790	0.746	0.705	0.666	0.630	0.596	0.564
7	0.933	0.871	0.813	0.760	0.711	0.665	0.623	0.583	0.547	0.513
8	0.923	0.853	0.789	0.731	0.677	0.627	0.582	0.540	0.502	0.467
9	0.914	0.837	0.766	0.703	0.645	0.592	0.544	0.500	0.460	0.424
10	0.905	0.820	0.744	0.676	0.614	0.558	0.508	0.463	0.422	0.386
11	0.896	0.804	0.722	0.650	0.585	0.527	0.475	0.429	0.388	0.350
12	0.887	0.788	0.701	0.625	0.557	0.497	0.444	0.397	0.356	0.319
13	0.879	0.773	0.681	0.601	0.530	0.469	0.415	0.368	0.326	0.290
14	0.870	0.758	0.661	0.577	0.505	0.442	0.388	0.340	0.299	0.263
15	0.861	0.743	0.642	0.555	0.481	0.417	0.362	0.315	0.275	0.239

(n)	11%	12%	13%	14%	15%	16%	17%	18%	19%	20%
1	0.901	0.893	0.885	0.877	0.870	0.862	0.855	0.847	0.840	0.833
2	0.812	0.797	0.783	0.769	0.756	0.743	0.731	0.718	0.706	0.694
3	0.731	0.712	0.693	0.675	0.658	0.641	0.624	0.609	0.593	0.579
4	0.659	0.636	0.613	0.592	0.572	0.552	0.534	0.516	0.499	0.482
5	0.593	0.567	0.543	0.519	0.497	0.476	0.456	0.437	0.419	0.402
6	0.535	0.507	0.480	0.456	0.432	0.410	0.390	0.370	0.352	0.335
7	0.482	0.452	0.425	0.400	0.376	0.354	0.333	0.314	0.296	0.279
8	0.434	0.404	0.376	0.351	0.327	0.305	0.285	0.266	0.249	0.233
9	0.391	0.361	0.333	0.308	0.284	0.263	0.243	0.225	0.209	0.194
10	0.352	0.322	0.295	0.270	0.247	0.227	0.208	0.191	0.176	0.162
11	0.317	0.287	0.261	0.237	0.215	0.195	0.178	0.162	0.148	0.135
12	0.286	0.257	0.231	0.208	0.187	0.168	0.152	0.137	0.124	0.112
13	0.258	0.229	0.204	0.182	0.163	0.145	0.130	0.116	0.104	0.093
14	0.232	0.205	0.181	0.160	0.141	0.125	0.111	0.099	0.088	0.078
15	0.209	0.183	0.160	0.140	0.123	0.108	0.095	0.084	0.074	0.065

ANNUITY TABLE

Present value of an annuity of 1, ie $\frac{1-(1+r)^{-n}}{r}$

where r = discount rate

n = number of periods

Periods	Discount rates (r)									
(n)	**1%**	**2%**	**3%**	**4%**	**5%**	**6%**	**7%**	**8%**	**9%**	**10%**
1	0.990	0.980	0.971	0.962	0.952	0.943	0.935	0.926	0.917	0.909
2	1.970	1.942	1.913	1.886	1.859	1.833	1.808	1.783	1.759	1.736
3	2.941	2.884	2.829	2.775	2.723	2.673	2.624	2.577	2.531	2.487
4	3.902	3.808	3.717	3.630	3.546	3.465	3.387	3.312	3.240	3.170
5	4.853	4.713	4.580	4.452	4.329	4.212	4.100	3.993	3.890	3.791
6	5.795	5.601	5.417	5.242	5.076	4.917	4.767	4.623	4.486	4.355
7	6.728	6.472	6.230	6.002	5.786	5.582	5.389	5.206	5.033	4.868
8	7.652	7.325	7.020	6.733	6.463	6.210	5.971	5.747	5.535	5.335
9	8.566	8.162	7.786	7.435	7.108	6.802	6.515	6.247	5.995	5.759
10	9.471	8.983	8.530	8.111	7.722	7.360	7.024	6.710	6.418	6.145
11	10.37	9.787	9.253	8.760	8.306	7.887	7.499	7.139	6.805	6.495
12	11.26	10.58	9.954	9.385	8.863	8.384	7.943	7.536	7.161	6.814
13	12.13	11.35	10.63	9.986	9.394	8.853	8.358	7.904	7.487	7.103
14	13.00	12.11	11.30	10.56	9.899	9.295	8.745	8.244	7.786	7.367
15	13.87	12.85	11.94	11.12	10.38	9.712	9.108	8.559	8.061	7.606
	11%	**12%**	**13%**	**14%**	**15%**	**16%**	**17%**	**18%**	**19%**	**20%**
1	0.901	0.893	0.885	0.877	0.870	0.862	0.855	0.847	0.840	0.833
2	1.713	1.690	1.668	1.647	1.626	1.605	1.585	1.566	1.547	1.528
3	2.444	2.402	2.361	2.322	2.283	2.246	2.210	2.174	2.140	2.106
4	3.102	3.037	2.974	2.914	2.855	2.798	2.743	2.690	2.639	2.589
5	3.696	3.605	3.517	3.433	3.352	3.274	3.199	3.127	3.058	2.991
6	4.231	4.111	3.998	3.889	3.784	3.685	3.589	3.498	3.410	3.326
7	4.712	4.564	4.423	4.288	4.160	4.039	3.922	3.812	3.706	3.605
8	5.146	4.968	4.799	4.639	4.487	4.344	4.207	4.078	3.954	3.837
9	5.537	5.328	5.132	4.946	4.772	4.607	4.451	4.303	4.163	4.031
10	5.889	5.650	5.426	5.216	5.019	4.833	4.659	4.494	4.339	4.192
11	6.207	5.938	5.687	5.453	5.234	5.029	4.836	4.656	4.486	4.327
12	6.492	6.194	5.918	5.660	5.421	5.197	4.988	4.793	4.611	4.439
13	6.750	6.424	6.122	5.842	5.583	5.342	5.118	4.910	4.715	4.533
14	6.982	6.628	6.302	6.002	5.724	5.468	5.229	5.008	4.802	4.611
15	7.191	6.811	6.462	6.142	5.847	5.575	5.324	5.092	4.876	4.675

Glossary

Acceptance sampling 'The middle of the road' approach between no inspection and 100% inspection.

Additive model A model for time series analysis which assumes that the components of the series are independent of each other, an increasing trend not affecting the seasonal variations, for example.

Annuity A constant sum of money received or paid each year for a given number of years.

Arithmetic mean Calculated from the sum of values of items divided by the number of items. The arithmetic mean of a variable x is shown as $\overline{x}$ ('x bar').

Attribute Something an object either has or doesn't have.

Bar chart A method of presenting data in which quantities are shown in the form of bars on a chart, the length of the bars being proportional to the quantities.

Base weighted index See Laspeyre indices.

Buffer stock Safety stocks held in case of unexpectedly high demand. Buffer stocks should only be required from time to time during the lead time between ordering fresh quantities of an item and their delivery. If there is excessive demand, or a delay in delivery, the buffer stocks might be used.

Census A survey in which all of the population is examined.

Coefficient of correlation Measures the degree of correlation between two variables.

Coefficient of determination The square of the correlation coefficient, r^2. This measures the proportion of the total variation in the value of one variable that can be explained by variations in the value of the other variable.

Coefficient of variation Compares the dispersion of two distributions.

Combination A set of items, selected from a larger collection of items, regardless of the order in which they are selected.

Continuous stocktaking A number of items are counted and checked daily or at frequent intervals and compared with the bin cards. Each item is checked at least once a year and any discrepancies are investigated and corrected immediately.

Correlation Variables are said to be correlated when the value of one variable is related to the value of another.

Critical path In network analysis, the longest sequence of consecutive activities through the network.

Cube root The value which, when multiplied by itself twice, equals the original number.

Cumulative frequency distribution Can be used to show the total number of times that a value above or below a certain amount occurs.

Data A scientific term for facts, figures, information and measurements.

Data mining The analysis of large pools of data to unearth unsuspected or unknown relationships, patterns and associations that can be used to guide decision-making and predict future behaviour.

Data warehouse A database, containing data from various operational systems and reporting and query tools.

Database A collection of structured data with minimum duplication, which is common to all users of the system but is independent of programs that use the data.

Decision support system Combines data and analytical models or data analysis tools to support semi-structured or unstructured decision-making.

Deseasonalisation The process of removing seasonal variations from data to leave figures indicating the trend.

Discounting The basic principle that if we wish to have £V in n years' time, we need to invest a certain sum *now* (year 0) at an interest rate of r% in order to obtain the required sum of money in the future (year n).

Dual price The amount by which the value of total contribution will go up (or down) if one unit more (or less) of a scarce resource is made available.

Dummy activity Used in network analysis when two activities could start at the same time and finish at the same time too. It is represented by a broken arrowed line.

Economic order quantity (EOQ) The order quantity for an item of stock which will minimise costs.

Equation An expression of the relationship between variables.

Executive support system A decision-making tool which pools data from internal and external sources and makes information available to managers in an easy-to-use form.

Expert systems Computer programs that allow users to benefit from expert knowledge, information and advice.

Extranet An intranet that is authorised to external users.

Extrapolation The simple (linear or non-linear prolongation into the future of historical relations.

Feasible area The area on a graph of a linear programming problem within which all the inequalities are satisfied.

Fractions A way of showing parts of a whole.

Frequency The number of times each value occurs.

Frequency distribution (or **frequency table**) Records the number of times each value occurs.

Gantt charts A line diagram, with lines representing both time and activities. It can be used to estimate the amount of resources required for a project. Where activities are in a continuous 'chain' of one able to follow immediately after the other, these can be drawn as a continuous line on the chart.

Geometric progression A sequence of numbers in which there is a common or constant ratio between adjacent terms.

Gradient A linear equation has a gradient which is $(y_2 - y_1) / (x_2 - x_1)$ where (x_1, y_1) and (x_2, y_2) are two points on the straight line.

Groupware Software that provides functions for the use of collaborative work groups.

Histogram A data presentation method for (usually) grouped data of a continuous variable. Visually similar to a bar chart but frequencies are represented by areas covered by the bar rather than by their height.

Historigram A graph of a time series.

Identity matrix (I) A square matrix which behaves like the number 1 in multiplication.

Index A measure, over time, of the average changes in the values (prices or quantities) of a group of items. An index comprises a series of index numbers.

Index relative (or **relative**) The name given to an index number which measures the change in a single distinct commodity.

Integer A whole number, either positive or negative.

Intercept The point at which a straight line crosses the y axis.

Inter-quartile range The difference between the values of the upper and lower quartiles, hence showing the range of values of the middle half of the population.

Knowledge Information in people's mind.

Knowledge management The process of collecting, storing and using knowledge held within an organisation.

Intranet An internal network used to share information.

IRR method of discounted cash flow A method which determines the rate of interest (the internal rate of return) at which the NPV is 0. The internal rate of return is therefore the rate of return on an investment.

Laspeyre indices Indices that use weights from the base period and are therefore sometimes called base weighted indices.

Lead time The time which elapses between the beginning and end of something, in this case between the placing of an order for stock and its eventual delivery. Thus, a supply lead time of two months means that it will take two months from the time an order is placed until the time it is delivered.

Linear equation An equation of the form $y = a + bx$.

Linear programming A technique for solving problems of profit maximisation (or cost minimisation) and resource allocation. The word 'programming' is simply used to denote a series of events. The various aspects of the problem are expressed as linear equations.

Linear regression analysis (least squares method) A technique for estimating the equation of a line of best fit.

Logarithm The power to which 10 must be raised to equal a given number.

Management Information Systems This text gives you several definitions. For example, CIMA's **Computing Technology** defines an MIS as converting data from internal and external sources into information, and communicating that information in an appropriate form to managers at all levels. This enables them to make timely and effective decisions for planning, directing and controlling the activities for which they are responsible.

Manufacturing resource planning (MRP II) An expansion of material requirements planning (MRPI) to give a broader approach than MRPI to the planning and scheduling of resources, embracing areas such as finance, logistics, engineering and marketing.

Materials requirement planning (MRP I) A computerised system for planning the requirements for raw materials and components, sub-assemblies and finished items.

Matrix (plural **matrices**) An array or table of numbers or variables.

Mean deviation A measure of the average amount by which the values in a distribution differ from the arithmetic mean.

Median The value of the middle member of a distribution once all of the items have been arranged in order of magnitude.

Mode An average which indicates the most frequently occurring value.

Moving averages Consecutive averages of the results of a fixed number of periods.

Multiplicative model A model for time series analysis which expresses each actual figure as a proportion of the trend.

Negative correlation Low values of one variable are associated with high values of the other, and high values of one variable with low values of the other.

Net present value (NPV) method Works out the present values of all items of income and expenditure related to an investment at a given rate of return, and then works out a net total. If it is positive, the investment is considered to be acceptable. If it is negative, the investment is considered to be unacceptable.

Network analysis A technique basically concerned with the deployment of available resources for the completion of a complex task.

Non-linear equations Equations in which one variable varies with the nth power of another, where $n > 1$.

Null matrix A matrix in which every element is 0.

Objective function The mathematical expression of the aim of a linear programming exercise.

Office Automation Systems Computer systems designed to increase the productivity of data and information workers.

Ogive Used to show the cumulative number of items with a value less than or equal to, or alternatively greater than or equal to, a certain amount.

Order quantity The number of units of an item in one order. A fixed size is usually estimated for the order quantity.

Payback period The number of years it takes the cash inflows from a capital investment project to equal the cash outflows.

Paasche indices Use current time period weights; in other words the weights are changed every time period.

Pearsonian correlation coefficient See coefficient of correlation.

Percentage Indicates the relative size or proportion of an item.

Perpetual inventory This method of stock control involves knowing stock levels of all items at all times. A record is kept of all items showing receipts, issues and balances of stock.

Perpetuity An annuity which lasts forever.

Pie chart Shows pictorially the relative sizes of the component elements of a total.

Pivot table An interactive table that summarises and analyses data from lists and tables.

P^{th} Percentile Where a data set is arranged in ascending (or descending) order, the pth percentile is a number such that p% of the observations of the data set fall below and (100-p)% of the observations fall above it.

Positive correlation Low values of one variable are associated with low values of the other, and high values of one variable are associated with high values of the other.

Present value The amount of money which must be invested now for n years at an interest rate of r%, to earn a particular future sum of money at the time it will be due.

Present value of a perpetuity $PV = a/r$ where r is the cost of capital as a proportion.

Price index Measures the change in the money value of a group of items over time.

Primary data Data collected especially for the purpose of whatever survey is being conducted.

Product moment correlation coefficient See coefficient of correlation.

Project 'An undertaking that has a beginning and an end and is carried out to meet established goals within cost, schedule and quality objectives' (Haynes, *Project Management*).

Project evaluation and review technique (PERT) A form of network analysis that takes account of uncertainty.

Proportional model See multiplicative model.

Quadratic equations A type of non-linear equation in which one variable varies with the square (or second power) of the other variable.

Quantiles A collective term for quartiles, deciles and percentiles, and any other similar dividing points for analysing a frequency distribution.

Quantity index (also called a **volume index**) Measures the change in the non-monetary values of a group of items over time.

Random sample A sample selected in such a way that every item in the population has an equal chance of being included.

Range The difference between the highest observation and the lowest observation.

Raw data Primary data which have not been processed at all, but are still just (for example) a list of numbers.

Reciprocal The reciprocal of a number is 1 divided by that number.

Reorder level The balance of units remaining in stock, at which an order for more units will be placed.

Resource histogram A stacked bar chart which shows a view of project data in which resource requirements, usage, and availability are shown against a timescale.

Residual The difference between the actual results and the results which would have been predicted (for a past period for which we already have data) by the trend line adjusted for the average seasonal variation.

Sampling Selecting a sample of items from a population.

Sampling frame A numbered list of all the items in the population.

Scattergraph method Involves plotting pairs of data for two related variables on a graph to produce a scattergraph, and then to use judgement to draw what seems to be a line of best fit through the data.

Seasonal variations Short-term fluctuations in recorded values, due to different circumstances which affect results at different times of the year, on different days of the week and so on.

Secondary data Data which have already been collected elsewhere, for some other purpose, but which can be used or adapted for the survey being conducted.

Semi-logarithmic graph This has a normal horizontal axis against which time is plotted but, on the vertical axis, equal intervals represent equal proportional changes in the variable. For example, the distance on the axis between $y = 10$ and $y = 30$ is the same as the distance between $y = 30$ and $y = 90$ (both represent a three-fold increase).

Sensitivity analysis Involves changing significant variables in order to determine the effect of these changes on the planned outcome.

Shadow price See dual price.

Simplex technique A linear programming technique which tests a number of feasible solutions to a problem until the optimal solution is found. The technique is a repetitive step-by-step process and therefore an ideal computer application. If the manual process is used, however, this is done in the form of a tableau (or 'table' or 'matrix') of figures.

Simultaneous equations Two or more equations which are satisfied by the same variable values.

Skewness The asymmetry of a frequency distribution curve.

Slack variable The amount of a constraining resource or item that is unused.

Spearman's rank correlation coefficient Measures the correlation between the order or rank of two variables.

Spreadsheet An electronic piece of paper divided into rows and columns. It provides an automated way of performing calculations.

Square root A value which, when multiplied by itself, equals the original number.

Standard deviation Square root of the variance.

Stock-outs These arise when there is a requirement for an item of stock, but the stores or warehouse is temporarily out of stock.

Table A matrix of data in rows and columns, with the rows and columns having titles.

Time series A series of figures or values recorded over time.

Trend The underlying long-term movement over time in the values of the data recorded.

Unit matrix See identity matrix.

Variable Something which can be measured. Variables may be classified as discrete (can only take a finite or countable number of values within a given range) or continuous (may take on any value).

Variance Average of the squared mean deviation for each value in a distribution.

Vector A table of numbers or variables which has just one row or column.

Word processing software Enables you to use a computer to create a document, store it electronically, display it on-screen, modify it by entering commands and characters from the keyboard, and print it using a printer.

Z chart A form of time series chart.

Index

NOTES

NOTES

NOTES

NOTES

NOTES

NOTES

NOTES

NOTES

NOTES

NOTES

Review Form – Business Essentials – Business Decision Making (07/10)

BPP Learning Media always appreciates feedback from the students who use our books. We would be very grateful if you would take the time to complete this feedback form, and return it to the address below.

Name: ______________________________ **Address:** ______________________________

____

____

How have you used this Course Book?
(Tick one box only)

☐ Home study (book only)

☐ On a course: college ______________________

☐ Other ______________________

Why did you decide to purchase this Course Book? *(Tick one box only)*

☐ Have used BPP Learning Media Texts in the past

☐ Recommendation by friend/colleague

☐ Recommendation by a lecturer at college

☐ Saw advertising

☐ Other ______________________

During the past six months do you recall seeing/receiving any of the following?
(Tick as many boxes as are relevant)

☐ Our advertisement

☐ Our brochure with a letter through the post

Your ratings, comments and suggestions would be appreciated on the following areas

		Very useful	*Useful*	*Not useful*
Introductory pages		☐	☐	☐
Topic coverage		☐	☐	☐
Summary diagrams		☐	☐	☐
Chapter roundups		☐	☐	☐
Quick quizzes		☐	☐	☐
Activities		☐	☐	☐
Discussion points		☐	☐	☐
	Excellent	*Good*	*Adequate*	*Poor*
Overall opinion of this Course Book	☐	☐	☐	☐

Do you intend to continue using BPP Learning Media Business Essentials Course Books? ☐ Yes ☐ No

Please note any further comments and suggestions/errors on the reverse of this page.

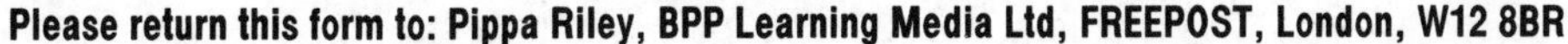

Please return this form to: Pippa Riley, BPP Learning Media Ltd, FREEPOST, London, W12 8BR

Review Form (continued)

Please note any further comments and suggestions/errors below

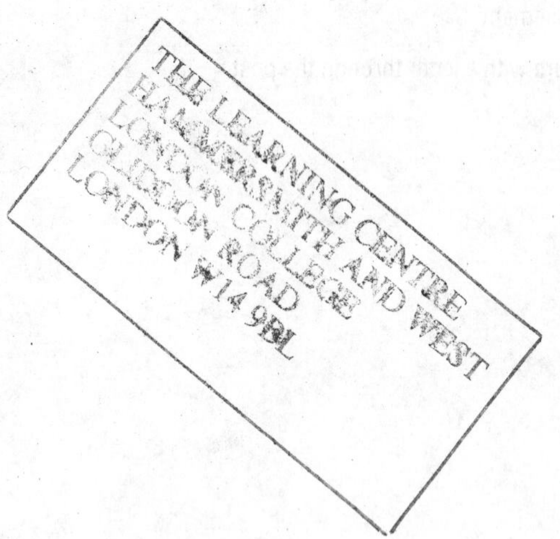